OPERATIONAL THEORIES OF PERSONALITY

Operational Theories
of Personality

Edited by

ARTHUR BURTON

BRUNNER/MAZEL, *Publishers*   New York

For VICKI ANN BURTON

CONTENTS

v

CONTRIBUTORS

HEINZ L. ANSBACHER, Ph.D.
  Professor of Psychology, University of Vermont; Editor, Journal of Individual Psychology.

ARTHUR BURTON, Ph.D.
  Psychotherapist, Sacramento, California; Formerly Professor of Psychology, California State University, Sacramento.

HILDE BRUCH, M.D.
  Professor of Psychiatry, Baylor University, Houston, Texas.

RUDOLF EKSTEIN, Ph.D.
  Director of Research, Childhood Psychosis Project, Reiss-Davis Clinic; Training Analyst, Los Angeles Psychoanalytic Society and Institute, and Southern California Psychoanalytic Society and Institute; Clinical Professor, University of California at Los Angeles.

ALBERT ELLIS, Ph.D.
  Executive Director, Institute for Advanced Study in Rational Psychotherapy, New York, N.Y.

JAMES HILLMAN, Ph.D.
  Jungian Psychoanalyst; Faculty, C. G. Jung Institute, Zurich, Switzerland; Visiting Professor, Yale University.

ALEXANDER LOWEN, M.D.
  Executive Director, Institute for Bioenergetic Analysis, New York, N. Y.

DONALD T. LUNDE, M.D.
    Associate Professor of Psychiatry, Stanford University School of Medicine, Palo Alto, California.

JOHN N. MARQUIS, Ph.D.
    Staff Psychologist, Veterans Administration Hospital, Palo Alto, California.

CARL R. ROGERS, Ph.D.
    Resident Fellow, Center for the Study of Persons, La Jolla, California.

HELM STIERLIN, M.D., Ph.D.
    Acting Chief, Family Studies Section, Adult Psychiatry Branch, National Institute for Mental Health; Member, Baltimore-District of Columbia Psychoanalytic Institute.

JOHN K. WOOD, Ph.D.
    Resident Fellow, Institute for the Study of Persons, La Jolla, California.

Preface

My experience with theories of personality has been a varied one: as a student taking courses in them, as a long-time instructor teaching them, and as a psychotherapist who daily applies a theory of personality to patients. In all of these capacities, I have in the past been less than fully satisfied with personality theories.

Textbooks on theories of personality are almost uniformly written by people with weighted academic interests, so that even the best have an abstract, arid, and uninviting tone to them. They put students and professionals off. Yet, a course in theories of personality can be one of the most exciting on campus, and is certainly one of the key necessities in a variety of curricula. It is a paradox that those who daily work with personality change, and know a great deal about it, do not write books on theories of personality. The motivation for this book was precisely to change such paradox.

Almost all of the major theories of personality are products of helping ministrations to clients and patients. This is surprising, for the empirical models should have more to say. But, in my opinion, trait, physique, factor analytic, and similar approaches to personality have not given us the breakthrough we expected of them. We are still dependent upon Freud's "way" for the basic constructs which allow us to hypothecate man's inner life. And the fact that psychoanalysis and psychotherapy are now dominant values in our society is a validation of a kind of the theories behind their operations.

This book, then, attempts a number of things which have never been done before: (1) It limits the theories of personality discussed to those which have growth operations (and operatives) connected with them. (2) It demands of each theory that its associated technique be spelled out by a case

ix

history example, and in this way sets limits on the pedantic. (3) And finally, it seeks out the theory founder himself (if he is still alive) or a major apostle, to depict the theory in question. Thus Freudian theory is described by a man who knew and studied with both Freuds; Jungian theory by an associate of C. G. Jung at the Jung Institute in Zurich; Adlerian theory by a friend of Adler and editor of the definitive Adlerian journal in the United States; and so it goes. All of this, I hope, will make theories of personality more stimulating in a way which can interest and excite students and professionals on all levels.

Here are found the theories of personality ranging from Freud to Jung to Adler to Sullivan to Reich to Jackson to Rogers to Laing to Skinner to Allport and to others. But one thing this book does not do is to select or rate one theory over another. It is alas too early for a paradigm to have emerged from the study of personality and we must for now be content with multiple theories.

The student can decide on the basis of this material which approach best fits his inclinations and knowledge, or he can select from all of them to become an eclectic. The professional, on the other hand, will find in this book a more specific spelling out of what he has already been doing. It is at any rate certain that a technique which has no manifest theory connected with it is doomed to the limbo. Techniques come and go but major theories provide the necessary creative tension for research and investigation and open new vistas. This is our need today.

I want to thank my eleven colleagues who participated in this venture. It was, I am told, a labor of love for all.

ARTHUR BURTON

Sacramento, California
February, 1974

1

The Nature of Personality Theory

by ARTHUR BURTON

ON PERSONALITY

It always comes as something of a surprise that most theories of personality arise from the healing of personalities. Reflection leads to the insight that only when a personality is in difficulty does it stand forth and require definition. Personality theory is thus in a sense a tool of anxiety. Normative people who go about their integrated business do little reflecting upon a self/ego. But should that self/ego begin to fractionate or lose identity, then the core of the person becomes obsessed and anxious, and a special scientist called psychotherapist may have to be called upon to correct the damage. Inevitably, as they must, such scientists begin to speculate on the structure of man's personality. The fact of the cure, and its accompanying theory, are inextricably bound, so that over the years theories of personality and theories of psychopathology have had a high degree of concordance.

Now the state of psychic healing is such, in part because of its youth and process complexity, that it is no shining model of empirical science. There are still a great many investigators who do not accept Sigmund Freud as a scientist, let alone C. G. Jung. Yet it is precisely on this clinical or applied area of science that we are largely dependent for our theories as to what personality is. The concept of the ego is a product of Freud, and that of the self, the original work of C. G. Jung. And it must also be said that other pathways to the theory of personality—say, body structure or psychometric approaches—have been a vast disappointment. In earlier days supreme hope was held as well for factor analysis as a way to personality for it had the precision and objectivity of mathematics. But factor analysis always fell short in that in the final aspect of its operations it had to fall back upon linguistic or clinically based terms to give the mathematical products meaning. Other empirical approaches to personality similarly suffered in that the summation of traits never seemed to match up with the dynamic person himself or with his motivational systems. And the body or physique approaches of Spranger, Kretschmer, and Sheldon, as I have said above, provided interesting correlations between mood, emotion and body type but no lasting or useful paradigm for a healing or descriptive science of personality.

Clinical science at least, it can be said, delved deeply into the psyche, made correlations of problem behavior with the human condition overall, and lived or died by the adequacy of the theory it derived from its helping ministrations—and the patient's response to it. Psychotherapy as a flourishing social entity validates the usefulness of its personality theories.

Now there are some who say that no theory of personality is required. Sullivan felt that a thoroughgoing description of the interpersonal transaction itself sufficed for any necessary understanding of the person—even though he himself posited a self—and the behavioral modifiers seem similarly indifferent to theories of personality. Still others—say, Gordon Allport—after years of study of self-theory, question whether a self/ego has any superior usefulness. It can thus be seen that the entire field of personality theory still remains a wide open one with resistance on many sides.

My thesis is that not only are there theories of personality, but that they are vitally necessary to the understanding of man in relationship to his world. It is not incidental that every university in the land gives a course on theories of personality. If we deny the validity of thought on the nature of personality, we deny the inner or intrapsychic life which, as we know today, has a structure, and a considerable influence on the consciousness of man.

The empiricist forgets that when he leaves his laboratory he goes home to reverie, dream, and imagination, that is, to theory of a kind. The energy of the inner life channels itself into fantasies, wishes, dreams, and even body organs. Without a theory of personality, we have no way of making sense of the intrapsychic life of man. In the paragraphs which follow, then, a case is made for the need for a personality construct and for the theories which approximate the parameters of personality.

Growth and Deficit

It is a truism that every organism grows and declines. This is the biological process which contains as well the major events of birth and death. On such a biological level the measurement of growth and deficit is fairly straightforward, is helpfully attained by instrumentation, and has a fairly well-defined scientific methodology. On the psychological level no such comfortable mensuration is available. The best approximation can be, let us say, seriatim intelligence quotients over certain developmental and deficit periods of time, but these are far short of the objectivity of measurement of, say, a kidney function. And the further we stray from the biological, to the cognitive and the emotive, the more and more unreliable, and even invalid, the measurement grows.

A construct is needed by which an up or down change in emotional, motivational, or other psychological status can be noted. An individual also needs from time to time to assess where he stands in regard to his own feelings, motives, and emotions. As we know, there is an enormous discrepancy between a job well done, an achievement, and the feelings of satisfaction gained from it. Neurotic patients almost invariably are better than average work-performers, but they are just as often as not miserable with their success, which, if the truth be told, they usually convert to a failure experience. A personality construct such as a self/ego permits an observer, or the individual himself, to evaluate his growth, his change, or his decline in an area of subjective functioning largely untouched by positivistic science. It is ironic that it has taken 50 years of research on personality to win a grudging acceptance of the simple personality dimensions of *introversion* and *extroversion,* facts which every person who introspects and extrospects is aware of. The self/ego of an infant is quite different from that of a child, and again different from an adolescent. In later maturity, it makes a difference whether one is describing a 25-year-old woman, a menopausal woman, or a senile one of 80. We are justified in claiming that something is behaviorally different with aging and maturity, and we label this, for convenience, *personality* and proceed to theorize about it the best way we can. The constructs of personality are the language by which changes in the psychology and behavior of the person are designated, and then discriminated and measured.

Personality as Symbol

Formal language names are insufficient to describe people, which is perhaps why ghetto argot does so much better in characterizing people. Descriptions in anger are more efficient than those in calm. Adjectives and pronouns also fall way short of describing the quality of existence of a personality. If one investigates the deepest fantasies of people, and particularly those in relationship to self-reference, then one finds that language, and even pictures, are very poor representations of what one is. In many instances words conceal more than they reveal. If on the other hand one asks people to pick their favorite animal, as we do in certain psychological tests, they then come closer to a true self-description than the reply to, "Well, what are you like?" or, "Which of these adjectives describes you best?"

A person finds his deepest description in a symbol, which is perhaps why symbology (and astrology) are now so popular, particularly with college youth. The symbol not only describes an individual's being, his ontology, but moves him as well in the energetic direction of the elaboration of that symbol. Totemism which is less complex than Jung's mandalas is a case in point. We find our symbol from our world, and it becomes the "secret" sign of ourselves, our symbolic personality. The same occurs in collective movements, as the cross for Christianity and the Star of David for Judaism. It can be strong, weak, heroic, loving, sensual, and a variety of other things. But it represents our true inner self, as compared with what we present to the social world, the persona, and the movement of psychic energy is to and from this symbol.

If such a personality symbol becomes severely distorted, or irrevocably lost, schizophrenia may supervene. This is so because the organism has no internal basis upon which to order itself. It may then overrespond by the creation of a plethora of symbolizations, which is precisely what schizophrenic cognition is all about. Patients in psychotherapy invariably come to the ancient geometrical form called mandala. The mandala may be tertiary or quaternary in design, and one sees it best if the patient paints or sculpts as a part of his treatment. The Jungians have had most to say about symbols and mandalas and their relationship to archetypal processes (1). The evolving formation of a mandala becomes the governing symbol and reveals the growing concept of self/ego as the core of the individual in his search for wholeness and fulfillment.

Without a theory of personality, symbolic constructs such as these would be unavailable, and the metaphoric understanding of the inner part of the individual would return to the Middle Ages where life had no molecular or fantasy richness. I do not concur with Allport that the science of behavior can do as well without a self-theory, or that the interactional quotient of Sullivan is sufficient to account for the ontology of the person. Molar behavior falls short of defining the molecular inner life; but a self/ego hypostatizes the highest level of self-function and the transcendence necessary beyond it.

The Unconscious

It is beyond speculation, or even adherence to any particular scientific school, that human existence is a parameter which runs from consciousness to unconsciousness. The history of psychology has been the over-exaggeration of now one and then the other. Wundt and Freud need some common meeting place. The clinical phenomena of repression, parapraxes, multiple personality, complexes, fugues, dreams, hysteria, and similar others demonstrate that a life of a kind exists below the level of immediate awareness or recall. It can also easily be demonstrated by the use of the hypnotic trance.

If no conception of a personality were possible, how is one to understand the fact that impulses of which the individual is totally unaware drive him in one or other direction, sometimes with a viciousness and at times to his death. It is not only necessary to infer that consciousness has levels—the associations experiment proves that—but that a repressing or dissociating agent is needed as well for his survival. The entire question of legal and moral responsibility in society defers to this question of consciousness.

A self/ego construct helps in the understanding of how certain conflicting situations in human beings force them to forget, dissociate, and to act without knowledge of performance. Such a construct makes feasible the postulating of defense mechanisms which permit the individual to compromise the pull of the instincts and carry the burden of civilization conveniently if not at times unhappily. Without it violence and affect in the person must be interpreted on the reflexive instinct level of lower-order species and denied the evolvement and complexity of the human brain. All behavioristic or nonego psychologies suffer from the simplicity which follows a tight natural science model, but is indeed not found sufficient with homo sapiens.

Change

A century of the study of behavior through what we call psychology validates one single universal finding if it does no other. This finding is that existence is a dynamic flux and is static only when caught in cross-section. Even the body, which shows a tremendous corrective stability and homeostasis, is a dynamic field in which organs compete, flourish, and diminish in their energetic field. The lessons of gestalt psychology extend beyond perception to the structure of the organism itself.

Now, only a theory of personality can account for *change* as the regular order of things. Biology assumes a firmament and regularity which exclude exceptions as rarities or mutations. But such absolute regularity is itself the unusual phenomenon, and we have been over-impressed with the reported invariability of Lorenz's ducklings and not sufficiently impressed with the variability of Pavlov's dogs. Science lives by regularity and tends to hide exceptions. The common-sense of everyday life is the expectancy and realization of change, and ultimate prediction becomes boredom even in science.

Fixation, the root of neurosis, is the inability of the patient to change his behavior. He clings to the vestiges of infantile trauma, to ancient attitudes and beliefs, to old rearings and developmental practices, to family mythologies, to limited body orifices, etc., and is unable to accommodate to the principle of change. He finds in a historical development both security and insecurity, is subsequently unable to have either, and is seduced by the concept of "adjustment." The older he gets, the more he tends to find security in his past. Psychotherapy then becomes that process by which the past is forced to relinquish its hold on the present, and change and becoming are made more a part of the scheme of things. Why people become fixated in this way, and how they finally adopt change rather than adjustment, is a matter of interpretation by a theory of personality. Without such theory we could not understand the gain in the fixation which is the basis of the neurosis itself.

Organization of Experience

All neurophysiological theories see the organism as bombarded by multiple sensory impulses which require organization into a controlled cognition, motivation, and emotion of a socially useful sort. The socialized individual is the product of a long chain of precursor events before he becomes an interpersonal being. And it always comes as something of a shock to meet low-grade idiots, or individuals with incomplete nervous systems, who are incapable of attaining such developmental integration and mastery.

The key to life is experiencing. The experiential transformation is from systemic energy to interpersonal encounter; the schizoid individual deprives himself of the last radical in the equation by accepting fantasy instead. But experiences have in some way to be converted into satisfaction/dissatisfaction and meaning, for no one can go through life on a simply sensual basis. The experiential feedback is what permits the individual to continue his experiencing, to change it, or to withdraw from it. Put another way, an internal executive is required to sort out, channel, repress, and stimulate function. The significant question is how from among millions of sub $S \rightarrow R$ reactions the individual discriminates those which further his social development and survival. Until the formulation of a self/ego concept there was no proper way to describe this internalized administrative function which copes with the sensory and perceptual world and gives it meaning. That such a function does exist in the personality is easily seen in those psychopathological states in which the ability to discriminate and organize experience becomes lost or displaced. Psychotherapy, furthermore, is demonstrably instrumental in recovering such functions.

Whether one calls it an ego or something else is immaterial. What is important is that the individual is conceived of as a personality, as a living, holistic entity, with goals, purposes, needs, and meanings and that he everlastingly seeks to actualize something within him in relationship to himself and other people. This organizational principle we call personality, and it serves to unify many levels of experience and give it a social structure. Personality is thus self-organization.

Morality

Love and guilt are the great motivators and inhibitors of men. Moral and ethical questions are inherently bound up in family and personal development, in becoming a person, and even psychotherapy which strives to be scientifically objective is not free of values. It is a fact that patients struggle every day with feelings of guilt which to others seem entirely ludicrous. But the personal guilt is usually as strong as steel as a deterrent. Freud made a case for what he called the superego. In so doing he was simply reflecting the phenomena of the moral structure into which the individual grows, and as he saw it manifested in his patients. Hysteria is a conflict between passion and morality, between the Judeo-Christian ethic of purity/cleanliness and the pull of instinctual needs, and it is resolved in neurosis by denying the passion and exaggerating the morality.

The inhibition of the direct expression of Eros and aggression, which is the phenomenon of guilt, is supremely homo sapiens. It is part and parcel of every civilization, and is behind today's social rebellion of youth, women, Blacks, and others. Ultimate freedom is release from guilt, obligation, and moral responsibility. There must thus be a balance between drives and impulsions and their socialized inhibitors. Of course, the inhibitions become internalized or introjected very early, and are then carried as a kind of invisible taboo. It is extremely difficult, for example, for this writer to understand, in terms of his background, how another writer could fabricate a biography of Howard Hughes, or of anyone else for that matter. Or how psychopaths, with great abandon, float "hot paper" with money they haven't earned. But I realize that the psychopath would look quizzically at my moral development and find it just as strange.

A theory of personality permits the positing of a moral structure in the person and attempts to account for its varied influence on behavior. Morality places the person squarely in his history and relates him to the social institutions which surround him. It helps explain murder, suicide, incest, cannibalism, and all of the remaining defections from the human code of behavior. The superego, in relationship to id and ego, Freud's structural theory of personality, as Rudolf Ekstein writes about in this book, helps us to understand man as opposed to his civilization—the differences between a Hitler and a Saint Francis, both produced by culture. Spiritual, artistic, and religious forces have no meaning if not backed by a theory of personality.

Values

The function of values in existence is more and more receiving center stage in our century. Positivistic science opposes values as subjective phenomena and as not within its purview. Values have been tarred with the same brush as have the soul, original sin, absolution, and similar concepts of Judeo-Christianity. But more recent humanistic research indicates that man is a valuing person and that he builds a character and life-style around his values. The neurotic or psychotic patient is by definition one who has no grounding in a set of values, or is confused in them.

The problem then becomes which set of values best facilitates the development of the person. Invariably, the child finds his values in the family structure, and then makes subsequent adult adaptations to them. But in this century it is becoming a confused thing, since there is a general revolt from middle-class family values, and parents themselves are no longer certain of what their values are or should be. The increase in depression and suicide, in both the young and the aged, as a modern manifestation, is the reaction to the loss of the values by which people formerly lived and guided themselves. The heroic figures of the past—Prometheus, Apollo, Sisyphus—no longer serve as archetypes and so every man becomes lost in his own grounding. The acquisition of wealth, formerly an important concern, is now generally diminished as a value, and seems to bring smaller returns in fulfillment. While we buy more books and read less, and the world of McLuhan's hot media is the greatest influence on us, people do at any rate spend more time at learning tasks, and they are in classrooms in goodly numbers.

A theory of personality helps explain how values become central to existence, how they become ordered into a structure or philosophy of life, and what takes place when one becomes de-valued or loses his values. No person lives as a biological being alone, and culture is itself a value which makes still other values possible. The self/ego seeks out those values by which the personality can come to terms with itself, and with its phenomenological world. From this come homo religioso, homo natura, homo scientifica, and the many other styles of life open to man. By so doing the self/ego provides a central purpose for being, and a clustering of the various parts of the organism into an identified whole, which we then call personality. Values can then become as much a motivating force, through the process of functional autonomy, as is instinct itself. And it is not rare for life itself to be given up for such value-structures. We call the one who yields it heroic.

Motivation or Intentionality

The motives of men are more complex than any biological theory of drives can account for. We had the opportunity once of studying a confined group of men who had killed either their mothers, their fathers, or in one instance both father and mother. We were expected to describe the motives for the violation of this extraordinarily tabooed behavior. How were we to begin to answer such a question? Since all had been found sane, it was a question of normative motives, but of an extraordinary kind.

The point here is that one can begin to understand such events by studying the personality of the murderer. By this we mean how he came to be as he is, what his major drive/needs are, how he meets them, and what his superego structure is like. It must be obvious that a man who murders his mother and is not insane at the time expresses himself in a most unique way. He kills a part of himself and a part of society by his act, and he destroys the one who not only thrust him into this world but first nurtured him as well. The inference is that he protested being "thrown into the world," or that the nurturing milk was "sour." All of us want to kill our mothers but, with exceedingly rare exceptions, no one ever does. Is mother perhaps the love object we can never have, and is she therefore doomed? Such a murderer does not take upon himself the self-inflicted blindness of Sophocles' Oedipus, but he accepts still another kind with which he is familiar: a life sentence.

This is not a treatise on murderers but simply a demonstration of the wide range of the motives of men. The higher one goes in the evolution of the species, the greater is the possibility of individual differences in motivation. While science has most effectively demonstrated such individual differences, as an institutional discipline scientists seek a biological singleness of motive. With a developed cortex and mid-brain come a heightened capacity for emotion, a qualitative appreciation of one's environment, and a reaching for difference and uniqueness.

A theory of personality permits us to describe the normative as well as the outlandish motives of men. We once saw in treatment an adolescent girl who had burned both arms with cigarettes. She said that she enjoyed doing it. There are also men who live out entire lives without a peak experience, and women who have never been orgastic. The primitiveness and boredom of their personalities are complete, often without their being aware of it. These are matters of the mind's intentionality, of the organism's drive in certain directions, and make most descriptive and predictive sense in terms of a theory of personality.

The Actor and Acted Upon

If one meets with a patient and his family in regular sessions with the intent to alter something in the family or member structure, then one becomes impressed with the enormity of the transactions which take place between related people. The flow of energy from one to the other, the need for homeostasis, and the real and pseudo affection and aggression are the apogee and nadir of human relationships. They carry a message quality which can be deadly or transcending.

The "personality" of each family member has been formed by the other "personalities" present, by a family dialogue, and by the family itself as a collective. Some, like Dr. Stierlin, claim that even second and third generations have to be included in family therapy for the most effective reorganization of individual structure. In such treatment situations one can "watch" the disintegration of a personality, and can see as well its reformation or regrowth under therapeutic auspices. All of the building blocks of personality are represented in the family structure and it is possible to demonstrate how dominance-submission, extroversion-introversion, risk-taking-non-risk-taking, and a hundred other personality traits and tendencies, are facilitated or retarded by the real or incorporated family. The family experience, backed by the constitutional, results in a unique and variable individual. By calling the developmental process personality, we personify it in the sense that it is person-centered, utilitarian, and interpersonal. There is even the possibility that eventually we will talk of a family "personality" as distinct from that of its members. A theory of personality gives scientific meaning to the family transaction.

ON THEORY

Now that we have attempted to demonstrate the need and value of a theory of personality for behavioral and social science, it is incumbent upon us to outline the nature of theory itself, and how the propositions and postulates of theory enhance our phenomenal understanding of personality. While scientific theories differ over wide parameters, sometimes even being in exact contradiction, it is the elaboration and competition of theories which make possible the paradigm by which a clinical method is derived. Coming, then, first to the structure and function of theory, their essential quality may perhaps best be described by using the categorization which follows.

Theory as Cognition

While theory construction occupies a special and often sacrosanct place in the schema of positivistic science, it is actually an everyday phenomenon when stripped of its formal and logical properties. We are all theory building animals. The process of thought is one of induction and deduction, based upon hypotheses, propositions, and inferences which are then subjected to validation procedures against our sensory world. Their recognition as formal theories is obtruded because they occur so rapidly, are often outside the range of acute awareness, and because they are so numerous. We hardly dignify them by the title *theory*. But it must be clear that any formal theory at the fulcrum of the behavioral sciences—say, homeostasis theory or, perhaps, humanistic theory—is identical in logical structure and purpose with those of our thought processes. It may in addition be that the function of a theory, the purpose it serves, may have analogues between the needs of the inner person and those of his "outer" science.

It is necessary for a person to discriminate from the mass of data which impinges on him, just as a science has to bring order into the overwhelming number of its observations. Theories are ways of sorting such data as related to special purposes and needs. Many great discoveries—say, sulfanilimide—were made years before a theory made their application possible. Obversely, some theories are put immediately into practice—say, Newton's—and then wait years for theoretical confirmation or disaffirmation. Much in the mentation of individuals lies fallow as hypothesis and theory until by proper timing it can be actualized or discarded. In the case of paranoia, we know the syllogism goes awry—the deductions from the premise and the special urgency of the mentation lead to an incorrect validation of a theory and to incorrect action. We as people often bet our lives on such theories, just as scientists bet their reputations on their own theories.

Theory as Tension

Theories build tensions which require resolution. Kuhn (2) describes the tension which accompanied the discovery of oxygen, the formulation of the heliocentric view of the world, and of Einstein's relativity. Theory initiates a dialogue—sometimes a violent one—in which evidence is marshalled to give a theory a commanding position, to establish the paradigm, or to replace it with still another and better theory. In this process, a major new theory lodges as a thorn in the side of established theorists, for there is indigenous resistance to it, and no theory fits perfectly the data which supports it. As tension producers, theories both liberate the imagination and bind it. But this seems the disorderly way by which Wissenschaft has operated since the dawn of history. There is a dynamic reciprocal facilitation and inhibition of theory which maintains a certain constancy of knowledge and does not allow serious anarchy to enter its domain, for otherwise no practice or application could ever get off the ground and the populace would suffer. The rise and fall of theory-tension is in a sense the index of the creative health of civilizations, and the historical record of man verifies this. Tyrants and demagogues reduce theory-tension by eliminating theory and thus provide for their own entropy. Absolutistic philosophies, even if well intentioned, tend to do the same.

Theory as Counter-Nihilism

The natural state of the psyche is the embracing of nihilism. Nothing counts. The rise of depression as an accompaniment of civilization—now at highest levels—is an indication that the wolf of nihilism has ever to be kept from the door. Denial thus seems a natural state to man, whereas positivism comes with greater difficulty.

Theories arise to combat the Intellectual Nothingness which is the bio-

logical way, and in which the cortex has little or nothing to do psychologically. Beauty, truth, justice, art, religion and others all arise to combat such
biological aridity and give meaning and purpose to the evolvement of the
brain. In this work theories range far and wide, and theory-making is therefore a part of fantasy as well as reality. All theory-makers are more or less
socially engaged people, and involved in filling space with truth and meaning.
For where a theory exists Nothingness cannot be, and scientists above all
cannot stand a void. Theory must lead to the facilitation of man by leading
away from his biological emptiness.

Theory as Temporality

With the coming of Heidegger, we have a better understanding of the relationship of ontology to temporality. Placing things in time—past, present,
future—is a relevant part of theory-making. The field of psychotherapy is
now being torn by differences in when the crucial experiences of man take
place. But more than this, a theory places a set of observations in a proper
locus of time in relation to nature and history. Time on the psychological
level is not the universal constant mathematicians employ. And even history
has peculiar temporal relationships which are certainly not linear but often
turn back upon themselves. Selecting the critical period in human or cultural
development is no gratuitous act; even on the molecular or atomic level time
is a fundamental parameter. When to seek is as important as where to seek.
Why great breakthroughs occur through a certain socially-designated man,
or to a number of men simultaneously, at a specific time is still an unanswerable question, but it certainly has something to do with a social or survival
necessity. Alan Watts believes, in this sense, that a change in genetic structure
will save us from the irradiation effects of the atomic bomb.

Thus it is that theories proliferate at certain times in civilizations and not
at others, locate those intervals pressing to survival and growth, and then
proceed to define temporality more precisely as it relates to being, as Heidegger has done. Older investigators have different and perhaps less socially
useful theories than younger men, as creativity studies show, but at any rate
theory is always a matter of temporality, in the sense that the theory
organizes and makes time useful and meaningful as well.

Theory as Clarification

Scientific observations of natural or behavioral phenomena regularly offer
themselves with major discrepancies. That is, in the absence of total knowledge of a phenomenon, or of the genesis and development of an event, cross-

sectional observations are taken which lack a certain depth and clarity. It is then necessary to infer the basis for these discrepancies, the probable error, and correct for them. Interestingly enough, no amount of additional data may resolve the difference. Thus the relativity theory of Einstein accounted for certain high-speed phenomena which Newtonian physics had applied across the board, and was to this extent discrepant. In animal psychology the atypical behavior of rats in certain experimental situations was resolved by labeling them "neurotic," or perhaps "maze dull" or "maze bright"; but there is a gap between rats and men which in learning experiments is not so easily bridged.

A theory pulls together observed and discrepant data and gives them a "best fit." It validates some discrepant findings, discards others, and ignores still others. And it does this by fitting all of the observations to a meaningful, albeit provisional, imaginative structure. A theory works like a gestalt figure-ground illusion in that now it brings the figure forth, and then again the ground. How one sees it depends on the context and the readiness with which one sees. A theory is a schema upon which measurement hangs its hat, and leads the way for still additional measurement. *Repression* as the theory of the neurosis served as the ground from which a number of revolutionary movements to gain freedom originated. The Victorian outlook on manners and the self-containment of past decades have now become expressionism at any cost. But while we all believe that more people are now mentally healthier because they "express" themselves, this has yet to be proven. In the scientific process, and in other processes as well, there must be a clarificant which precipitates the gestalt from against the background. In the search for knowledge, theory-making serves this purpose.

Theory as Prediction

The older textbooks concerned with the philosophy of science singled out theory as the *gran via* to prediction. If a new theory could predict a set of future circumstances, then that theory was a valid and "good" theory. Such theoretical prediction is no less desirable today, but a theory does not rise or fall on its predictive value alone. As we have said earlier, theories have tensional, catalyzing, and collating value which go to the bedrock of the whole question of Wissenschaft. They are integral with the fact *qua* fact, and the historical process which validates a theory as "truth" at the moment. The distinction between a fact and a theory has always been overdrawn.

Still, a theory which does not "show the way," which does not offer a better precision of application, or a new application, is certainly limited.

The goal of science is not only increased knowledge but a more efficient technology as well. In medical science the number of "diseases without known causes" grows steadily less, and the diseased become ever more comfortable. Very few men die today of tuberculosis or pneumonia, which were certainly the great killers of the past. But "prediction" is also a value, and what to predict a choice. The ancient gnostic concept of an alchemy which would be the basic metaphysical formula of life has never been found. It has its modern incarnation in C. G. Jung, but even he did not find the psychological touchstone he sought. Western science seeks prediction in its own right, for its elegance, and has mathematics as the model. Scientists often love the beauty of a discovery as much as the discovery itself. But there is today an evident surfeit with the predictions and products of science, and a desire to return to a less predictive and harmonious past. Man feels that it is necessary to maintain some of the mysteries of life, for a perfectly predictable world would perhaps not be worth living in.

It therefore becomes necessary to use scientific theory as prediction where values of civilization enhance such prediction. To some this would sound like a moral intrusion into science; but no one believes any longer that science, or the scientist, operates in a value-free world, or that prediction is a royal road to the fulfilled life.

A theory can lead to a consequence or away from it. It can also go in several directions simultaneously. But its important function is that it leads researchers in the direction of new vistas, and the marshalling of evidence already known but not collated into meaning. A number of people had seen X-ray clouds on plates before Roentgen did, but he labeled it and gave it meaning and usefulness. The unconscious was not discovered by Freud, but he put it in the service of those repressed. Very few theories lead to straight-line breakthrough discoveries in the neat predictive descriptions of textbooks.

Theory as "Showing"

Following the idea of Wittgenstein, theories do not need to demonstrate anything. They have their own phenomenological aspect of numinosity. By this we mean that the fact that a *theory is a theory* and is considered seriously (sometimes hostilely) by scientists, providing the tensional function outlined above, makes the theory already worthwhile. Every theory has therefore "showing" or disclosing properties, which even without their propositions or postulates change something, and this is true even if they are quickly discarded. The phlogiston theory, and schizophrenia as organic brain disease, are both "showing" theories and useful by their "presence," even if sadly incorrect. That they now have only heuristic value does not detract from their numinous properties and their worth. Such theories are also precursors of later evolvements which formal science cannot yet formally countenance.

Theory as "Silence"

In the behavioral and social sciences words are overabundant and are frequently used to conceal as well as reveal. This is particularly true in psychotherapy where the amount catharted is deemed correlated with the cure. But nature maintains its own silence and words are often the panic of men. Healing takes place in silence, and when to be silent is seldom considered formally in psychiatric training.

There are two aspects of *theory as silence*. Where no theory exists, or is possible, then perhaps the silence is the necessity of the moment. But a theory can also lead to a "silence" where a phenomenon requires the social incubation necessary to its application. Theories, like language, cover and conceal as well as open and point; but this may be precisely the function of a specific theory. Openness and disclosure in nature are not the fetish we in the 20th century have made of them. The "silence" of a theory is the salient theory-property, in that society is not yet ready for the disclosure. In psychotherapy silence is as important as the interpretation and no psychotherapy can be effective without silence. The point is that silence is an important aspect of the theory of a specific curative approach. The theory is there but its quietude is the necessity for all of its elements to form a gestalt.

More conventionally, theories are evaluated by their *extensiveness, parsimony, internal consistency, empirical validity, usefulness,* and *testable aspects* (3). A theory which has these capabilities is usually considered worthwhile.

Extensiveness is that quality of a theory which permits it to embrace the largest number of observations. There have been theories, such as that of Copernicus, which take the entire cosmos into their reckoning, and still others which purport to interpret why a rat turns left rather than right in a maze. It is not, however, only the global phenomena involved that interest us but how wide a theory can range. The rat's choice point may offer a paradigm of all human learning, and the heliocentric theory on the other hand embrace only certain tidal actions. "Large" theories, because they apply to more people and more phenomena, are, according to our values, more important than those highly circumscribed.

A theory which is *parsimonious* is one which involves the smallest number of propositions, assumptions and inferences, and has therefore a certain elegance about it. Parsimony is generally admired in science which is the principle of Occam's razor. Mathematics is a model of parsimony since several pages of equations, for example, can serve as a doctoral dissertation. This would never be allowed in the social sciences regardless of its merit. Freud's collected works vastly outnumber Einstein's, but their creative value to science (and society) is certainly equal. And Freud was known for the parsimony of his prose! Perhaps because of the redundancy and prolixity of the scholastics and religious, positivistic science reacted by mandate that a statement or proposition must be made as concise as possible. Is this perhaps why logic is today so heavily mathematical?

A theory must have *empirical referents*. That is, it must bind observational data and help valuate or give them meaning. A theory without a factual nexus approaches the fantasy theories of schizophrenia—theories which never come to social relevance. Autism is theory without a referent. But it is possible for a theory to be posited without such empirical coordinates and to govern for centuries. Because theories represent the frontiers of knowledge, they may have to wait for new measurement or conceptual ways of assessing their adequacy.

On the other hand, many empirical methodologies have no visible or rational theory behind them, but are still in constant use. Even on a bio-chemical level there is, for example, no adequate theory as to exactly how tranquilizers work. Yet they are the most widely prescribed drugs. Thus theory and technique are parts of a unity that can still be independent of each other for long periods of time. Man is, however, best facilitated by their conjunction.

Both a theory and a methodology must be *internally consistent*. That is, they must not negate themselves by their autonomies. Theories often seem to be paradoxes but still change one's way of seeing the world. They are in this sense courageous and daring. But since they receive so much direct attack from the outside, they must more than ever be internally consistent. The consistency lies not only in the phenomena theorized about, but its formal logic, its linguistic statement, and its relevance to neighboring theories. This is well illustrated by Freudian theory where the subject is the motives of man, the logic is based upon man who has fallen into dis-ease, its linguistic statement is neurosis as repression, and the neighboring theories are those of Kraepelin and Janet, as well as the revisionists, Jung, Adler, and others.

Eventually a theory must be *tested* and it must be found *useful*. But many theories are only partly useful, and some never receive full testing. They are gradually replaced by still other theories which better "fit" the social circumstances which gave rise to the theory, or they are taken over and elaborated into still other theories. The theory of homeostasis has been an important one in the behavioral sciences and it is a carryover from certain physiological theories (Cannon). But this theory which states that man needs and seeks neutrality—a minimal energetic charge—is disputed by, for example, some of the findings of family structures where dynamics rather than statics are the rule. Neurotics also reveal that not quiescence but a certain existential tension is required in them for a life tone. Homeostasis as a complete theory is only perfectly justified by death. Entropy also corrupts homeostasis by setting limits to its own possible nature.

There is also a theory of "no-theory." Because it is so difficult to formulate adequate theories, and to validate them, many investigators are satisfied with merely a certain set of operations they can define. This is particularly true in the clinical aspects of a science. Healing or "bedside" application becomes the *tour de force* and theories are often considered distractions. From this it becomes easy to deride theory, and even claim that none is involved. "No-theory" is therefore most probably eclectic theory, and draws many theories together but with minimal conscious awareness. The great significance of Freud as a healer was that he was never content just to heal. Healing was for him a means of empirically checking the validity of theories or concepts about man he had formulated, and, as far as we know, he never boasted about what a great healer he was. Sullivan, on the other hand, who prided himself on a "no-theory" of personality, also prided himself on his healing abilities, but despite this came up with the important interpersonal theory.

Theories can be major or minor. A theory may have a complex structure, with sub-theories and multiple propositions and postulates, or the theory can be stated simply in one sentence. On the broader scale, theories approach attitudes and shape whole legions of scientists as well as the public at large. Two such major theories which are counterposed in the behavioral and social sciences are *humanistic* theory and *behaviorism*. The first places man at the center of things, whereas the second stresses his place in the natural world and his learning opportunities. One sets him upon the throne of the species, but the other attempts to place him naturally in its evolutionary order. Humanistic theory then goes on to employ concepts of value, hope, ideals, soul, and the like; but behaviorism is content with conditioning, reinforcement, generalization, and similar Pavlovian concepts.

Psychotherapy, that is, the revaluation of psychic problems, can be either humanistic or behavioristic. Both approaches are seemingly effective, and both have a tremendous following of patients. Both theories have over the ages had declines and resurgences, and been validated and invalidated by major social upheavals. They both represent the dialogue of inner and outer, of subjective and objective, but at any rate no resolution of the humanism-behaviorism dialogue is at yet possible. Humanism, which denies religion the exclusive possession of man's soul, is on the rise, after Auschwitz, but the seeming decline of Christian morality, individuality, and brotherhood propels Skinner to the thesis that man needs proper shaping and reinforcement schedules by behavioristic principles rather than ideals.

Personality, which is life itself, will probably never have a total theory. This is perhaps in the nature of things. But we will come eventually to understand enough of personality to avoid man's destruction from his own impulses and to bring him a greater fulfillment. Whether one likes it or not—approves it or not—the theories of Sigmund Freud have changed the behavior of an entire civilization. Something similar will some day occur with a new theory, and will open the vistas now closed in the understanding of man's inner life and his utilization of it. Positivistic science has failed us in this regard, and promises never to succeed in this quest without a theoretical revision.

REFERENCES

1. JUNG, C. G. *Man and His Symbols*. New York: Doubleday, 1964.
2. KUHN, T. S. *The Structure of Scientific Revolutions* (2nd ed.). Chicago: University of Chicago Press, 1973.
3. HALL, C. S. & LINDZEY, G. *Theories of Personality* (2nd ed.). New York: John Wiley, 1970.

Sigmund Freud

2

Psychoanalytic Theory:
Sigmund Freud

by RUDOLF EKSTEIN

FREUD'S DEFINITION OF PSYCHOANALYSIS

The particular psychotherapeutic procedure which Freud practices and describes as *"psycho-analysis"* is an outgrowth of what was known as the "cathartic" method and was discussed by him in collaboration with Joseph Breuer in their *Studies on Hysteria* . . . (1).

The task which the psychoanalytic method seeks to perform may be formulated in different ways, which are, however, in their sense equivalent. It may, for instance, be stated thus: the task of treatment is to remove the amnesias. When all gaps in memory have been filled in, all the enigmatic products of mental life elucidated, the continuance and even a renewal of the morbid condition are made impossible. Or the formula may be expressed in this fashion: all repressions must be undone. The mental condition is then the same as one in which all amnesias have been removed. Another formulation reaches further: the task consists in making the unconscious accessible to consciousness, which is done by overcoming the resistances. But it must be remembered that an ideal condition such as this is not present even in the normal, and further that it is only rarely possible to carry the treatment to a point approaching it. Just as health and sickness are not different from each other in a sense but are only separated by a quantitative line of demarcation which can be determined in practice, so the aim of the treatment will never be anything else but the practical recovery of the patient, the restoration of his ability to lead an active life and of his capacity for enjoyment. In a treatment which is incomplete or in which success is not perfect, one may at any rate achieve a considerable improvement in the general mental condition, while the symptoms (though now of smaller importance to the patient) may continue to exist without stamping him a sick man (2).

THEORY

Basic Metapsychological Concepts

Every theory rests on basic assumptions which need no further explanation and are taken for granted. Freud suggested that the instinct theory could be considered "our mythology," a basic assumption on which the system rests. But changes in theory make us question what ought to be considered as basic and what ought to be considered as derived. In the earlier days we stressed as basic assumptions: the concept of the unconscious, childhood sexuality, childhood amnesia, the forces of repression, the notion that each dream has meaning and that each symptom represents unconscious forces in conflict. A philosophical clarification of these basic assumptions will instantly show that we speak here about different levels of theory, and that we do not clearly differentiate between theory, fact of observation, etc.

Later on, Freud made an attempt to establish basic assumptions through his discussion of the so-called metapsychological principles. They were to be the basis of the system. He never completed the attempt, and discussion throughout the history of psychoanalysis indicates that the evaluation as to what is basic frequently disguises technical and theoretical preferences. A classical paper by Rapaport and Gill (3) on *The Points of View and Assumptions of Metapsychology* suggests that current theory is best understood through the following basic assumptions:

1. The *dynamic point of view* suggests that psychoanalytic explanations concerning any psychological phenomenon are to contain the psychological forces involved in this phenomenon. In other words, the phenomenon can be explained as an interplay between psychological forces which have to be understood in terms of their direction and their magnitude and the nature of their interplay.

2. The *economic point of view* requires that every psychological phenomenon has to be understood in terms of the psychological energy involved. This introduces a quantitative factor concerning the "amount of energy" and recent discussions indicate that more and more difficulties are seen when psychological energy is compared with physical energy. The problem of creating ways of measuring clinical data has occupied psychoanalytic researchers. See, for example, the most recent contribution by Wallerstein and Sampson (4) on issues in research in the psychoanalytic process. These psychological energies, containing propositions concerning drive forces, are related to the law of conservation, to a law of entropy, to transformations.

3. The *structural point of view* defines structures as configurations of a slow rate of change, within which and between which and by means of which mental processes take place. These structures are hierarchically ordered, and describe hierarchical orders of ego functions, etc.

4. The *genetic point of view* implies that one can trace back every psychic structure through another which preceded it and out of which it developed. Freud considered psychoanalysis a genetic psychology: all psychological phenomena must be understood in terms of their psychological origin and development. The earlier forms of psychological phenomena, even though superseded by later ones, remain potentially active and can be revived.

5. The *adaptive point of view* requires that psychological states also have to be described and studied in terms of their adaptedness. Man is seen as someone who adapts to his society, his reality, as well as adapting his reality to himself. In other words, adaptation relationships are mutual: the human being adapts to the world and vice versa.

The basic notion of psychoanalysis as a technique also changed. Freud spoke earlier about psychoanalysis as having the therapeutic goal *to make the unconscious conscious.* This was related to the topographic model before the introduction of the structural model and the adaptive point of view. Later he spoke about the goal of analysis in terms of *where id was, there shall ego be,* and he referred indeed to the necessity of developing the technique in a way not only to make the unconscious conscious but to strengthen the ego organization in such a way that it must not defend itself against the past via repression, is able to endure and restore continuity between the past and the present, to use this continuity towards adaptation, that is, the capacity for new problem solutions. While the early therapeutic attempts of psychoanalysis were past-oriented—the reliving of the infantile neurosis in the transference neurosis—more current techniques have added to this. Psychoanalysts have not, as it is sometimes thought, given up the genetic point of view, or the method of reconstruction, or the rediscovery of the childhood neurosis in the transference neurosis, but the process of working through is intended to bring about a strengthening of the new forces, an increase in the synthetic function, the capacity for adaptation. Today, psychoanalytic technique is not only past-oriented but sees an interplay between the past, the current reality situation, the plans for the future and the tasks for tomorrow. This is reflected in the vicissitudes of the transference, that unique replica of the past which, however, during the course of the analysis through the analysis of the transference, permits the patient to see the analyst not merely as a repetition of the past but also as a realistic therapeutic ally, a concept that is similar to the notion of working alliance developed by Greenson (5).

I believe that one can justify a therapeutic method only through the willingness to constantly expose this method to the light of day, to make data available to others and to rely on clinical testing and verification. Freud stated: "Gentlemen—as you know, we have never prided ourselves on the completeness and finality of our knowledge and capacity. We are just as ready now as we were earlier to meet the imperfections of our understanding, to learn new things and to alter our methods in any way that can improve them" (6).

Theory of Personality

Ever since Gordon W. Allport's classic volume on *Personality* (7), we have become wary of trying to define this frayed concept. Sometimes we think of its origin, persona, as did Jung, and are reminded of the mask the actor of antiquity used to cover his face, and through which he speaks the role he plays but hides what he really is. Whether we think of personality as the mask which hides the real self, or whether we think of it as that which is characteristic of any given individual, all agree that we are referring to consistent and persisting patterns which give continuity in the history of the individual and which usually are thought to develop out of earlier characteristic patterns. Personality traits then are those aspects of the individual characterized by a slow rate of change.

In Freudian psychology, these enduring patterns, which are usually referred to through the concept of personality in other systems of psychology, have been described through concepts such as character, or even more frequently, as in the work of Freud, through the "structure of the mind," the "model of the mind." Freud speaks in the *New Introductory Lectures on Psychoanalysis* (8) about "the dissection of the psychical personality," in which characteristic features of the person, symptoms, for example, or character traits, are seen as derived from the repressed, from representatives of an earlier struggle before the ego took its dominant position. The "psychical apparatus," the underlying structure of what might otherwise be called personality, itself is seen as having developed its complexity out of earlier, primitive forms.

Psychoanalytic notions concerning the development of personality stress indeed physiological, social and psychological aspects.

Physiological Aspects

All propositions concerning maturation essentially follow physiological considerations. They refer to the inborn function of the small baby and suggest that the original embryonic development is carried forth after birth as *Anlage,* as disposition which permits the unfolding of psychosexual and psychosocial development. Psychoanalytic propositions concerning the oral phase, the anal, and the phallic one, are essentially references to certain physiological changes which take place after birth and which change the system of drives.

Social Aspects

All these psychoanalytic propositions which describe the outcome of exchanges between the organism of the baby on the one hand and the environment, social and personal ones on the other, are propositions concerning development and have to be understood as the social and psychological aspects which are to be taken into account as we follow the changes from essential nondifferentiation at birth to the kind of differentiation that exists at the time when character, personality, a stable psychic organization are established. Freud's *Three Essays on Sexuality* (9), Erikson's discussion of the eight phases in psychosocial development (10), or Spitz's study on *The First Year of Life* (11), are classics on Freudian psychogenesis, the epigenetic ground plan of personality development.

We then see operating inner and outer organizers of the mind which lead toward personality development. The inner organizers are to a large extent physiological in nature, developed from the drive systems, while the outer organizers refer to the influence of the mother on the child, the emotional tie which leads to the experience of self and non-self. These outer organizers, the impact of reality, of changing reality, the parents and the total family, the school, society at large, are in constant interchange with the facts of maturation. Maturation and development, as they meet in internal conflict and in continuous attempts at adaptation, are the factors which either lead to psychic health or to psychological illness, to symptom formation.

Psychological Aspects

For the psychoanalytic observer there are not merely features to be *measured* but features to be *understood* in terms of having become the result of internal struggle. Beyond the overt facade they represent a latent picture. Therefore, psychoanalysis considers personality traits not merely in terms of constituting a behavior pattern, but in terms of deeper, inner meaning. The personality features of a person permit us then to reconstruct the "psychic apparatus" which gave rise to these features. The "dissection" of the psychical personality has led to more and more refined studies, such as the assessments of development as described by Anna Freud in *Normality and Pathology in Childhood* (12) in which she establishes methods of studying developmental lines which permit us to assess the child in terms of the tasks that he has mastered or the psychic disturbances he has acquired. These personality assessment studies allow contributions to education and psychotherapy of a much more refined order than was true in the days Freud contributed the *Three Essays on Sexuality* (13). But the limit of these studies has been well described by Anna Freud: "For the analyst's inquiring mind, it is a second, vital objection that fact finding about assessment is at an end when the analytic method is not used. We need to be absolutely certain of the classification of a given case before taking the choice of therapeutic element away from the patient and into our own hands, i.e., before limiting the chances of therapy to one single factor. As our skill in assessment stands today, however, such accuracy of diagnostic judgment seems to me an ideal to be realized not in our present state of knowledge but in the distant future" (14).

How then are we to use this blueprint for personality theory to picture how a person becomes "sick," develops problems that require treatment?

Variety of Concepts

The notion as to what "causes" emotional or mental illness has changed during the development of psychoanalysis. The idea of "cause of illness" itself deserves some consideration at this point. The original notion of causality, the beginning of scientific considerations in terms of cause and effect, actually has its roots in theology, the notion of the *prima causa,* the origin of life and the world through an act of God. Scientific explanations held on to the *prima causa* and offered explanations in terms of an original cause, the one and only cause. Such search of the one cause, has been extremely productive and many scientific answers were made possible through that way of thinking. And, indeed, determinism is but a way of thinking. The meta-psychological or theological underpinning of determinism has not only led us frequently into oversimplifications concerning the one and only cause that has to be known in order to control the effect, but has also made us repeat over and over again the notion that the idea of human freedom is incompatible with a deterministic psychology. This second misunderstanding, which I have discussed elsewhere (15), has probably induced Skinner (16) recently to tie up his notions on reinforcement theories with the belief that human freedom and dignity were outdated notions, perhaps opposing techniques which aim at the possibility of our survival.

Psychological determinism, however, is a way of thinking actually unrelated to the issue of human freedom versus oppressive forms of social life. The one special form of determinism which looks for the one and single cause is another oversimplification with which we must dispense.

The original attempt of Freud was to establish one single cause for the hysterical symptom. He saw the cause for a while in the small child's experience of early seduction through a parent of the opposite sex. This concrete search for the specific cause of a difficulty, very typical, of course, in the life of every patient as he develops a personal myth, an autobiography which is to explain how he came to be what he is, led to psychotherapeutic assumptions which could not withstand methods of verification. The original *Topographic Model* of the mind (Figure 1), which led to the technical rule that the psychotherapist must make the unconscious conscious, is perhaps derived from notions concerning the one existing cause for the symptom. As pointed out earlier, a good many of the psychotherapeutic schools frequently fall back on this one-cause notion which is to determine their choice of psychotherapeutic technique.

An old Greek myth explodes the myth of "one cause being responsible" for emotional or mental illness. Suppose Oedipus Rex after having blinded himself, wandering through the countryside with a deep melancholic depression, could have found an ancient psychotherapist to help him. Would this psychotherapist have determined that Oedipus suffered from an oedipus complex, having struggled with the impulse to murder his father and to sleep with his mother? The seer as well as the Oracle of Delphi had made him conscious of these unconscious impulses which he could not prevent

THE TOPOGRAPHIC MODEL OF THE PSYCHIC APPARATUS (1900)

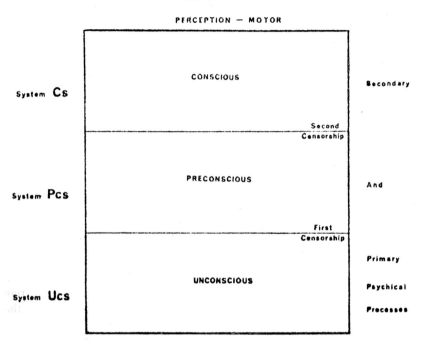

THE STRUCTURAL (FUNCTIONAL) MODEL OF THE PSYCHIC APPARATUS (1923)

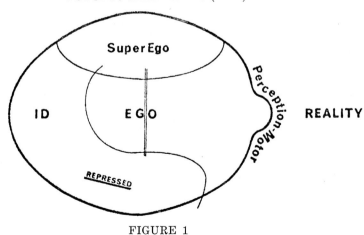

FIGURE 1

himself from carrying out. The therapist would now be confronted with the question as to why the generic conflict had to be acted out, could not be stopped, and had to lead to disaster and to eternal, unresolvable guilt. He would delve into the childhood history of Oedipus and he might find that Oedipus had to cope earlier with rejecting, anxious parents, who had sent him out into the wilderness. His feet were pierced, and the young boy, growing up elsewhere, had to cope with a symptom that might have made the psychotherapist believe the swollen foot, organ inferiority, was the cause of the child's illness. He might also have chosen the particular relationships the child had to father and mother, the relationship that existed between Jocasta and Laius, etc. He might have delved into the history of this boy and might have found that his school experience, learning, becoming an adult, as was so beautifully illustrated in the myth describing the experience of Oedipus with the Sphinx and her famous riddle, are to be made responsible for later developments.

But, actually, as he and the patient would have put pieces together in order to restore the continuity of life, and to replace the neurotic myth of Oedipus through a more realistic appraisal of inner and outer experiences, not one cause would then have been seen as having determined the pathogenic outcome, but a series of causes. Some of them would have represented the endless repetition of the same social climate or family climate. The incidents of his life which would have been dominant in his memory, the outstanding points which make up the personal myth, would have been condensed representations of a series of traumata which became effective and neurosis-producing. They occurred during circumstances of maturation where the trauma which might otherwise have been growth-producing had to lead to a pathogenic development. Oedipus then during this treatment would have replaced the early meanings he had attached to the events of his life and his personality characteristics with new and better meanings which would have replaced the early alibi through insight, better self-awareness, a knowledge of his limits, the strengthening of his capacity to perceive, to judge, to feel and to act.

But such a psychotherapeutic attitude would have presupposed in the therapist a deeper knowledge of what was constant in Oedipus, what was characteristic for his personality, and what the meaning of each personality trait was that had sent him out into the world, at first against his will and later with his will, repeating as he now had to do actively what had happened to him passively, such as having now identified with the aggressor and becoming the aggressor himself. This psychotherapist would have put more and more emphasis not on the external trauma but on the internal conditions, and he would have to describe both the internal conflict as well as the internal battlefield of that conflict.

He would have done well if he could have used a tripartite model of inner human organization such as Freud's Structural Model (Figure 1) (17). He would have demonstrated the conflict between the id forces, the love of Oedipus for, as well as his yearning for, his mother, and the forces of the conscience, the superego, early internalized prohibitions, delay functions. This conflict is carried out on the battleground of the ego, which is unable to delay, is unable to judge correctly, and is driven by this internal battle towards symptom formation, towards murderous and incestuous acting out, towards deep, self-destructive impulses as well as into depressions. Actually, there was once used in Greek antiquity a model of personality, a beautiful metaphor by Plato, which seems analogous to the tripartite model. He compared human personality to driver, chariot, and two horses. The driver represents reason and the horses represent love and hate. If reason can hold the horses together so that they go in the same direction, the human being can function in a goal-directed manner and get to the desired destination. If the horses pull in different directions and cannot be controlled by the driver, he will flounder and will be dragged to his destruction. In our own language the driver refers to the ego, while the horses refer to id and superego.

Psychoanalytic personality theory, however, has become more complicated. As was pointed out earlier, much of what will make the concept of self, this inner feeling of identity, is derived from earlier identifications, earlier relations to other human beings, and goes back to a time when an intensive struggle took place within the human being by means of which a differentiation between self and non-self was carried out, the capacity for internal representations of self and objects. That psychotherapist of antiquity would then have found himself confronted with the task of using Oedipus' capacity for seeing the therapist as an object, his struggle towards and away from the object, his capacity to maintain self under pressure in order to assess the very disturbances in object-relations which gave rise to the development of his pathogenic character.

The point is, of course, to stress that Oedipus Rex did not have an oedipus complex but turned out to be an Oedipus. An unconscious conflict which is phase-specific and must be resolved during the growing-up period, became more than an unconscious determinant for later character traits. It became the compelling force which made the symptom into a reality. The psychotherapeutic problems with people who act out their conflicts, who cannot simply represent them through symptoms or fantasies, are witness to the endless technical problems we have if we want to extend psychoanalytic insight and psychoanalytic understanding to therapeutic techniques which are to be applied to delinquents and criminals, and all these characters who are impulse-ridden and who suffer from the compulsion to repeat rather than from symptoms.

Freudian psychoanalysis, concerned in the beginning with symptom neurosis, subsequently turned its interests to these stable, slowly changing patterns of personality which are called character difficulties, deeply ingrained patterns which affect the whole being, rather than producing, for example, comparatively simple and isolated hysterical symptoms. Recently, we have become more and more interested in character difficulties which are so far-reaching that they have been frequently described as ego deficits, serious borderline and psychotic disturbances which require modifications both in treatment technique as well as in certain basic theoretical assumptions. Object-relations theory and ego psychology have been greatly enriched by these clinical experiences, the treatment of certain personality patterns which are beyond the reach of earlier techniques.

Fortunately, the psychoanalytic theory of personality has remained an open system. The search for causes has always remained attached to the search for cures. Determinism as a principle has never remained on the level of the more primitive notions of cause and effect, a fact that has been well expressed by Waelder in his classic paper on *The Principle of Multiple Function* (18). It is this principle of multiple function, of overdetermination, which is characteristic for psychoanalytic therapy.

Concerning the Theory of Psychoanalytic Technique

As has been indicated earlier, psychoanalytic psychotherapy today represents a much wider field of application than classical psychoanalytic technique. It is practiced not only by psychoanalysts but by psychiatrists trained in dynamic psychiatry, by psychologists and social workers. The patients treated by psychoanalytic methods of psychotherapy represent not only the types of patients who may benefit from classic psychoanalytic procedures, but many of them may also suffer from emotional and mental disorders which require a much wider spectrum of psychotherapeutic intervention than is represented through the original method to which Freud gave the name "psychoanalysis." We are now not only treating adults but children and adolescents as well; and psychoanalytic principles have been utilized not only in individual treatment but in forms of group treatment, casework, marital counseling, child guidance, family therapy, etc. In order to allow for a clarity of notions, we will want to go back to the original model of psychoanalysis itself from which were derived many of the techniques mentioned above. To avoid misunderstanding I would like to suggest that the word *model* is used in differing contexts. We may think of the model as we think of the beautiful young women who model clothes, a sort of idealization of the average. We may think of the model as a small replica, like the miniature model train which is operated on a tiny track. And we may finally think of the model as a kind of simplification by means of which to make clear a way of thinking and a way of operating. Psychoanalysis proper, of course, is frequently experienced by people in the field as a kind of over-idealized method, the queen of all the methods which ought to remain pure and only in emergency mix with lesser mortals. Freud spoke of psychoanalysis as the gold which perhaps will have to be mixed with the copper of suggestion and other less valuable ingredients. I want to use the concept of model not in terms of idealization, or in terms of status, or even in terms of a small replica. The early model of psychoanalysis is used in order to convey a method of reasoning, a way of thinking. This will not only permit didactic simplicity but it will also maintain a genetic point of view and will allow us to outline a history in the development of psychoanalytic technique.

The theory of psychoanalytic technique is a direct consequence of its theory of personality, its concept of the psychic apparatus. Psychoanalytic theories, actually all psychotherapeutic theories, assumptions concerning the development of personality organization, respectively personality disorganizations, can really be considered as hidden descriptions of the therapeutic technique under consideration. In an earlier work I tried to make this point (19). In order to bring a current view of psychoanalytic technique, I have chosen to utilize a picture of the psychic apparatus which is to represent a synthesis between two of the basic models Freud had used as he discussed the nature of the psychic apparatus.

In earlier sections reference was made to the Topographic Model, perhaps representing the first phase of psychoanalytic technique around the turn of the century, which was slowly superseded by the second phase in which the Structural Model was used, introduced by Freud in 1923 (Figure 1) (20).

If the reader could take the picture, the graphic illustration of the Topographic Model which is represented in two-dimensional space and roll it into a cylinder, he would find a three-dimensional model which reminds one of a layer cake: the lowest layer representing the system of the unconscious, the middle layer representing the system of the preconscious, and the top layer representing the system of consciousness.

If he were to take Freud's picture of the Structural or Tripartite Model of the mind and use it in order to cover the top of the cylinder, he would see on top of that cylinder the outlines of ego, superego and id, while the bottom of the cylinder would represent an area without differentiation, representing the undifferentiated aspects of the human mind, characteristic for the beginning of psychic life. While there would be no overt differentiation on that lowest level, we assume latent dispositions towards differentiation. As psychic life grows, structure would emerge out of the undifferentiated archaic structure, would grow and develop slowly towards that organization of the mind which is represented by the top of the cylinder. Each time, if we were to cut that cylinder in a horizontal way, we would get a picture of the mind with less differentiated functions, that is, in relation to ego, superego and id representations.

We now have a three-dimensional model of the mind (Figure 2) which allows us to discuss many functional and structural aspects of psychic organization important for our current considerations, and which allows us to create a synthesis of the topographic and the structural model.

This three-dimensional model of the mind permits a discussion of genetic aspects, of dynamic and economic aspects, of the aspects of the drive system, as well as those of adaptation. This model permits a discussion of the relationship between different intrapsychic agencies, as well as of the relationship between psychic agencies, particularly the ego and reality itself, outside that cylinder, and conceived as a dynamic, ever-changing reality rather than as a static representation.

As is true for every and any spatial representation of the psychic apparatus, we will soon push towards inconsistencies within the model, and must be careful lest the spatial model is assumed to be a concrete illustration of the mind rather than an auxiliary device for the purpose of thinking through a variety of therapeutic problems.

Freud himself warned of the use of spatial models which, if taken too seriously, would lead us into difficulties.

This new model is merely an attempt to allow for a psychological language which will not give up the advantages of either of the models Freud has utilized. The model allows us to speak about hierarchic organizations of superego, ego and id, and thus permits us to "locate" within that model the very difficulties that the patient presents via his symptomatology or more widespread disturbances and/or deficits. As we move up and down the cylinder, we are able to utilize the concept of regression, the patient's return to earlier

SYNTHESIS Of TOPOGRAPHIC
& STRUCTURAL MODEL
Of The Psychic Apparatus (1968)

BY R. EKSTEIN, PH.D.

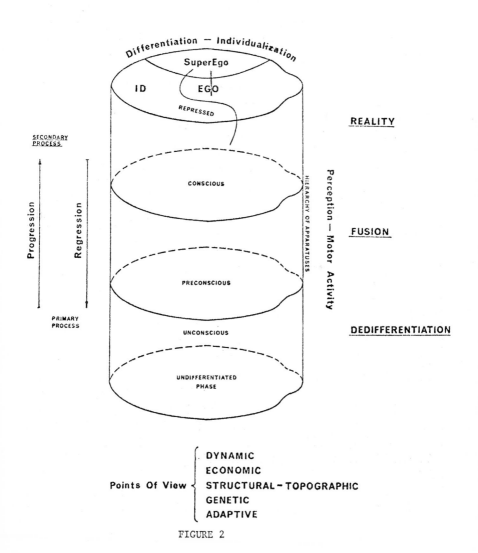

FIGURE 2

phases of mental functioning, and we are able to include these types of regression which are typical for the development of the transference neurosis in psychoanalysis and do not necessarily include regressions of equal magnitude in every area of psychic functioning. We may find ego and superego regressions while the ego remains intact. We may sometimes deal with severe ego regressions and these disturbances which lead to borderline and psychotic conditions. This three-dimensional model permits a profile of the illness, as it were, and better predictions concerning psychotherapeutic outcome as well as recommendations concerning modifications in technique.

In the next graphic illustration (Figure 3) we will find use of this model which is shown at the beginning and at the end of the therapeutic process.

Through this illustration we seem to assume, for the moment, a kind of mechanical process in which the psychic apparatus is put through the therapeutic process, at the end of which we find the psychic apparatus changed.

The symptomatology which is indicated in the beginning stage through shaded areas has disappeared in the end stage. At the risk of creating misunderstandings which might make the reader believe that in the end the patient will emerge lily-white from the process while he has started it full of black spots, a movement from guilt to innocence, so to speak, from the symptomatology of sin to the mental health of paradise, we will nevertheless proceed with these mechanical and spatial analogies. Let us make it even a little cruder. Let us assume that we put some dirty linen into a washing machine so that it goes through the correct wash cycle which is indicated for the special kind of dirt, and the material which is put into the washing machine will come out clean.

Obviously, the "diagnosis" as to the kind of spots on the material, as to the nature of the material itself, will decide what kind of wash cycles to be used, what degree of heat of water is to be used, etc. A correct understanding of the material and of the agents of change is necessary in order to bring the cleaning of the garment to a successful conclusion.

Now, the garment which we are using is not really a psychic apparatus, a mechanical instrument. Rather our notions of the psychic apparatus are short-cut representations describing a suffering human being, the illness and the health that he brings to us which have to be taken into consideration as he starts treatment with us in order to go through a *process of treatment,* the *therapeutic cycle* which is to lead to recovery and health.

The decision for treatment, the nature of the treatment, depend then not only on the symptomatology, the shaded area, the complaints that the patient brings and the signs that the diagnosing therapist records, but also on the rest of his total personality, his social reality, his external support system

A GRAPHIC MODEL
OF THE ANALYTIC PROCESS

BY R. EKSTEIN, PH.D.

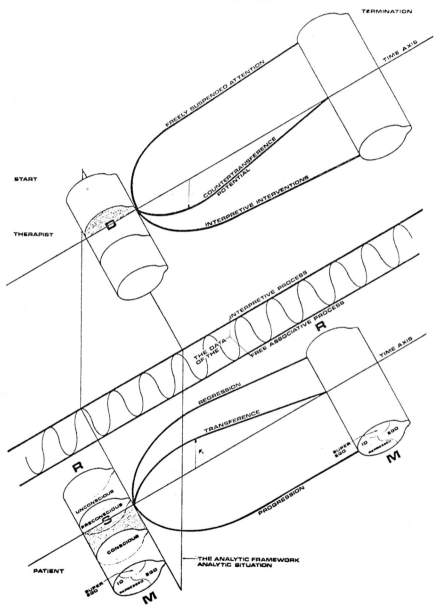

FIGURE 3

(family, friends, job, job opportunities, total social situation) which all become part of the total social diagnosis. We must assess his illness as well as these factors which come into play during the psychotherapeutic process and which create the motivational force and the commitment to treatment. For example, people with very similar symptomatology but with other factors being different, may represent completely different problems for the therapist, different pictures of the combinations between illness and health, and of such a kind that we may have in one case good recovery and in another case an interminable analytic process, or an interrupted treatment caught in a dead-end street.

Our blueprint of the psychic apparatus permits us to measure what are the available forces for recovery. It allows us to go beyond a mere quantitative concept of "ego strength" and to describe the qualities of the ego, its capacity for regression and progression, the nature of regressions and progressions which may be in the service of recovery or deepening pathology, and permits us to describe the adaptive and defensive apparatuses as available. The same holds true for our evaluation of superego conflicts, some of them pernicious and related to a hateful, revengeful, everlasting persecutor, or carried by a loving superego, or, as is so often true, by an essentially corrupt superego.

The picture of the psychic apparatus at the beginning of treatment not only includes symptomatology but also describes certain aspects of personality assessment, not necessarily manifest symptoms or traits, but as yet invisible components of maturational dispositions or lack of capacity for regression in the service of the ego's drive towards a fruitful and happy life.

Freud's suggestion that mental health is best described in terms of the capacity to love and to work, needs, of course, further elaboration, since there are many stages and states of the capacity for work and the capacity for love. Work is usually seen in terms of progression and maturation but it is true that creative work will have regressive elements in it and not only progressive ones. Love is frequently but incompletely described in terms of certain regressive tendencies, but it is also true that mature love must include progressive ones as well. A good many impoverished personalities may then benefit from psychoanalytic help not only in terms of being freed from crippling symptoms but being enabled now to progress and regress in terms of adaptation, in terms of self-realization.

The picture of the psychic apparatus which we have been using is merely a spatial picture of the mind, a quasi-mechanical equivalent of what we are really after. It will be possible as the discussion proceeds to put life into that picture, and to put the man back, put the person back into the psychic apparatus. In olden days it was suggested that everybody has a soul. May I paraphrase that and suggest that there is a person in the psychic apparatus. Conceptualization sometimes turns human meaning into psychic mechanics. The psychoanalyst faces similar dangers as does the Watsonian behaviorist who equates human psychic life with behavior.

What then are the facts of the beginning phase of psychoanalysis? First of all, there is the "psychic apparatus" which is to be moved into the process, into the psychotherapeutic machine, so to speak, like the dirty clothing which is to be put into the washing machine, exposed to the washing cycle. The psychoanalytic cycle which leads towards the end of the process when there is recovery or cure, will be described in the next section concerned with the process of psychoanalysis. But we are still occupied with another aspect of psychoanalytic technique best described by that part of the graphic illustration on the left side of our model of psychoanalytic technique which refers to the beginning situation, a special structural arrangement which makes the psychoanalytic cycle possible.

The beginning situation has been described as the *analytic contract* by Karl Menninger (21), an assumption by patient and analyst of certain obligations which are different in nature for the patient and for the therapist. This structural arrangement marks the beginning of the classical psychoanalytic procedure. This is well known and does not need much elaboration. The patient is to come for his psychoanalytic sessions four or five times per week. He will usually use the couch while the analyst will sit behind him. He will speak freely about whatever comes to mind, will try to withhold nothing, and will try to overcome all conscious resistances caused by the feeling that he does not want the analyst to know, that he is ashamed, that he feels guilty, or that he sounds silly and unintelligent, etc. He will try to overcome self-condemnation, vanity, the wish to be as rational as possible, and he will learn to follow the *basic rule,* actually a kind of unique basic privilege, and thus will try to say what comes to mind. This technique, the method of *free association,* difficult to learn, describes the key activity of the patient.

The analyst, on the other hand, will listen carefully, will try to abstain from criticism, from advice giving, from moral condemnation, from guidance, from decision making, from suggestion, etc., and will try to remain on a level of interpretive work. His main task is *interpretation,* that is, to make conscious the meaning of the material which the patient brings to him, and he sees his main activity as the analysis of transference and of resistance, concepts to be elaborated on later.

The regular hour, the continuity of the treatment, the different tasks of patient and analyst, describe well what is called the analytic situation.

We see here a special use of time, a special use of different activities on the part of the patient and analyst, and a special use of theory of personality organization which leads to psychoanalytic technique and defines the analytical situation.

The pact between psychoanalyst and patient includes certain arrangements about fee, about vacations, about interruptions, and also includes the usual assumption that the analyst will see only the patient, will not communicate with other relatives when he deals with adults or with older adolescents, and will try to maintain an analytic situation which permits reflection, a certain isolation from decision making, and by means of which he initiates the analytic process.

It is quite clear that this particular beginning situation, the analytic situation to be maintained throughout the treatment, will have most powerful consequences for the process and for the material which will emerge. In an old paper concerning the structural aspects of psychotherapy (22), I have tried to pinpoint the structural features that will be decisive for the nature of the process. It is exactly this analytical situation which sets up a kind of structure by means of which the curative process can take place. Recently, Stone (23) examined the nature of this psychoanalytic situation which is usually defined and set forth in the beginning of treatment and which has to be maintained.

Freud once compared the classical psychoanalytic procedure to the game of chess, and he suggested that the beginning chess situation, the definition of the field on which the game takes place, the definition of the pieces which are to move in certain ways, will define the process and the outcome of the game. It is quite clear in this example that two people who play a different kind of game will develop a different kind of process, and possibly also a different outcome. In the paper mentioned above it is suggested how we might differentiate between different schools of psychotherapy in terms of the rules and regulations that are set up in the beginning and which then allow for different processes to develop. But that is not to say that Freud's simile, recently overused in best sellers, namely that psychoanalysis therefore *is* a game, will help to understand all aspects of its process. Sometimes it is a play. Sometimes it is a play within a play. Sometimes it seems to be a monologue or develops into a dialogue, but it does always refer to inner processes, and we do not describe its nature well if we remain with the external rules and regulations and the gambits which describe forms of resistances and usually do describe the struggle about the maintenance of that very beginning situation, the analytical situation.

The diagram to illustrate psychoanalytic technique (Figure 3), its standard procedure, the basic model, shows on the upper left side as well as the right side, two cylindrical forms which refer to the analyst at the beginning and the end of the analytical process.

At this moment, considering only the initial situation, the analyst, too, brings himself to the situation, his person, and with tongue in cheek we might say that he brings to the process his psychic apparatus.

We assume that he does not bring his symptoms to the process, hoping that he is well trained and well analyzed, and that he is able to keep out of the process to a large extent those aspects of his personality which would not allow him to function well as an analyst, as a helper for suffering people. His task is best described in Anna Freud's classical formula (24) that he must maintain equidistance from all parts of the psychic organization, from ego, superego and id. He is impartial, makes no suggestions, recommendations, does not give orders, prohibitions or moral precepts, but tries to understand the meaning of the material, and he will rely on his most important tool, the interpretive act. The shaded area refers to his diagnostic impression of the patient. He has a certain picture of the patient, a beginning picture, a theoretical model of the patient as to what the patient is up against and what his symptoms mean. We hope, of course, that this shaded area will not turn into a shady area, that is, that he does not know what he is talking about, nor that he has a completely misleading model of the patient. But, in any case, regardless of how excellent he will be, the first model of the patient will be tentative. The analyst will be required later on to change his picture just as he gets deeper and deeper insight into the process. It was once said by Anna Freud that a true diagnosis about a patient can only be made after the treatment. We might suggest, however, that he, the analyst, can make a *working diagnosis,* one which permits him to put the patient into the process and to begin the process. This working diagnosis will also require an assessment from him of himself as the helper as to whether he is capable of helping this particular patient and to assess himself as the helper. The first assessment will be the beginning equivalent of certain aspects of countertransference which will occupy us later. And thus the process begins.

The Psychoanalytic Process

This section deals with that aspect of psychoanalysis which can be de-described in behavioral terms, in terms of what can be seen and what can be heard. If we turn once more to our graphic model of the psychoanalytic process, we will find but two lines parallel to the *time line* which refer to the empirical data of psychoanalysis. They signify the empirical material around which we have constructed a model of the treatment process by means of which the mechanisms of the treatment, the activities of the patient and of the psychoanalyst are to be elaborated. A variety of treatment features have been described earlier: the regular fifty minute hour, four to five sessions per week, the reclining position of the patient on the couch, the position of the analyst behind that couch, and the fact that there is a minimum of the ordinary social interchange between them. The coming and going of the patient, while, of course, important, is somewhat under-emphasized at this moment, as is perhaps the special way that the analyst greets the patient, calls time at the end of the session, decides on a billing system, etc. Telephone contacts are usually kept to the bare minimum of changing or setting appointments, or emergency situations, and the main emphasis is on the process that takes place while the patient free associates on the couch and the doctor listens and interprets. We have then two empirical lines to consider pictured on our graphic model: the line which refers to the process of free association and the line which refers to the process of interpretation. The interpretive process and the free associative process, both indicated through curved lines which somehow run parallel, actually refer to that which can be seen and heard, and stand for the actual data which one would have to consider if one would, for example, use taped interviews or otherwise recorded interviews for research study. The question, of course, as to what is behind that process, what is explaining these lines which refer to data, is to occupy us in a later section.

At this point we wish to describe what usually happens. Considering presently one of the more ordinary cases which is most suitable for the analytical process, let us describe what possibly might happen and illustrate the surface nature of these data. In the beginning the patient is most likely to use the analytic hour in order to give an explicit description of his sufferings, his symptoms, trying to explain how he came to be the way he is. He will speak with much hesitation, and will not give the impression of true freedom during the associative process. It will be comparatively rare that he will have the subjective feelings of having mastered the art of free association, and very frequently his free associations will be interrupted by silence, by hesitancy, by obsessive ruminations, by endless repetition and by other forms of anxious avoidance. In the beginning he will use a scheme trying to seek the cause of his difficulties, not within but outside of him. His confessional, and much of the beginning is a sort of confessional under the auspices of guilt and shame, will frequently be tied up with attempts at alibi, such as describing an endless series of traumatization in the past and in the present.

During that beginning phase the analyst most likely will not be very active. He will occasionally reflect on the material, he may ask pertinent questions to understand the reality situation which the patient is describing, and he will occasionally make remarks about the difficulty the patient has during the beginning phase. He will react to the patient's expressions of anxiety concerning the nature of treatment, the possibility of outcome, the severity of his symptoms, the nature of his illness, and the fear that he may not have chosen the right kind of treatment, that his analyst does not understand him, and the like.

He will usually remain on the surface and he will not use the beginning weeks—and I refer to what would be more common practice among classically oriented analysts—to interpret deep content, deeper meanings. He will be cautious about the use of dreams and fantasy material, knowing that much of his effectiveness as an interpreter does not depend so much on his seeing clearly what the material may have meant at any given moment, but on his estimate as to when the patient is ready to use interpretive interventions. He will use clarification of content, occasionally confrontation, inquiry, and carefully selected interpretations until a new situation develops.

This new situation develops when the associative process finds subject matter which is neither in the past nor in the outside reality, but seems to slowly include usually very careful and only indirect thoughts and fantasies about the analyst and the analytical situation. The analyst will become included in the analytic material, and the thoughts and remarks about him are brought forward usually under a great deal of anxiety, expressions of anger and unexpected feelings, and also occasionally within an eroticized vein, a background of sexual fantasy, which will go hand in hand with phases of silence, embarrassment again, and overt expressions of anxiety. This inclusion of the analyst in the free associative process will never cease but will reach different forms, and will lead these free associations more and more into the consulting room. The patient will express, in and through his fantasies and thoughts, more and more notions of dependency on the analyst, need for the analyst, and a struggle with and against the analyst.

The analyst's interpretations will tie up these feelings and thoughts about him both with experiences and reality and with experiences in the past. The interpretive comments of the psychoanalyst will become wider and frequently less specific as he deems the patient ready to see his life and to understand the material against a broader background of experience.

While much of the early one or two phases of analysis seem to be oriented towards cause and towards the need for the analyst, we find that in the latter phases of the analysis the material slowly changes from concern for the cause of the illness to concern for the cause of the cure. Material becomes desperate expression of questions as to whether the patient can ever change, whether analytic technique will help him, and whether the insights gathered are applicable towards the future. He will now bring in more and more material about his inner world, and some phases will be dominated by dream analysis, by consideration of fantasy, reactions to other people which are inappropriate, and he will reveal the most inner thoughts and feelings.

In a successful analysis the end phase will tie up the future with the past and with the reality situation. Concern with the past will be replaced by concern with the present and the future, but in all these considerations thoughts about the analyst will have an important place.

As the analysis grows and moves towards the end, the interpretive activities of the analyst will become more risky. The analyst will be more free and caution will give way to interpretations which will indicate not only a creative grasp of the total situation, but which will also be related to the patient's growing capacity to make use of these interpretations and to respond to them in more adaptive terms.

Towards the end of the analysis, one will find in the patient's free association more and more material which indicates that he himself is playing with the idea of ending, and if the end is announced, we will find that he may frequently reproduce his symptoms, seemingly become sicker again as far as the material is concerned. Actually, however, he will now deal with issues of separating from the analyst, questions as to whether he has reached a goal, questions as to whether he could be without the analyst, a kind of dress rehearsal of mourning, as he gives up the analyst and the analytical process, and also a dress rehearsal for the future when he tries to see how he can do without. The analyst's remarks will be an attempt to link up new insight into illness with the new solutions that the patient seems to have worked out, and to react to the patient's feelings about impending loss, and to assess with him the meaning of separation and a new beginning. Shakespeare's "What is past is prologue" will characterize the material of both the free associating patient and the interpreting analyst (25).

The general nature of the free associative process has been well summed up by Lewin (26). He likens the free associative process to the three rings of the old Ballantine beer advertisement. One ring refers to material about current reality; the second ring refers to material about past reality; and the third ring refers to material about the relationship to the psychoanalyst. These three rings are overlapping and share one common sector.

Sometimes the material seems to be clearly in an area where there is no overlapping. But even then any material about current reality may refer to the relationship to the analyst and to past experience. Any material about the past also involves the relationship to the analyst and current reality. And, of course, any reality about the material concerning the analyst also has its reference in the past as well as in current reality. The interpretive process depends very much on the capacity of the analyst to sense what is dominant in the material and to relate one Ballantine ring to the other, or to the other two, as needed. One can think of the free associative material as well as the interpretive material in terms of four overlapping rings. The fourth ring would be material about the future, about solution of problems, about adaptation.

One simple example may suffice. Suppose the patient speaks about the relationship to his boss, its specific nature. This may well have to do with genetic material about his father, may have to do with his displaced feelings about the analyst, and may also hide the problem of future-directed adaptation. The analyst will try to link all four fields together in order to restore continuity between past, present and future.

Mechanisms of Psychotherapeutic Change

The reader is referred once more to the diagram of the psychoanalytic process. In the middle of the diagram are two lines connected through a wavy line. The bottom line refers to the material which the patient brings and which is characterized through the concept of *free associative process*: not only the words he speaks, the thoughts he expresses, but all the observable behavior such as the way he enters the consulting room, the way he is observed earlier in the waiting room, his style of going to the couch. This includes the movements he will make on the couch, his breathing technique, his way of dressing, the expression of his feelings, his anger or his love as it can be observed by the analyst. Primarily, of course, we are concerned with his very words, his verbal expressions of thoughts and feelings, of despair, hope, and confusion as well as his thoughts of solutions, and all the kinds of remarks which inform us about his life situation, the analytical situation, his reflections on the past and anticipations of the future. He has learned to use the method of free association to the degree that this method can be acquired. He is sometimes confronted with hesitancy, anxiety; confronts the analyst with silence, with obsessive ruminations or hysterical emoting, etc. All these are observable data.

The top line refers to those things the analyst says during the process of therapy—the *interpretive process*. Primarily, he will interpret, that is, try to see the meaning of the material of the patient, particularly the meaning of which the patient is not aware. Not all the analyst's remarks will be classical interpretations. He will use confrontation, sometimes mere description, repetition, non-directive remarks without giving orders, without offering direction, without conscious implications as to what is right or wrong, etc. Part of his interventions consists of certain behavior, such as how he opens the door, how he guides the patient to the couch, how he finishes the hour, what kind of milieu he confronts the patient with, and the like. All the behavior of the analyst will be important to us, as it may be observable by the patient or observable by us.

But the main accent of the study of the *psychoanalytic process* rests with the verbal behavior of the patient and the analyst, and the wavy line between the top and the bottom line in Figure 3 indicates that the synthesis of the free associative process and the interpretive process reveals the nature of the psychotherapeutic process. We might picture for a moment all the data of a psychoanalytic treatment in terms of what one might hear if one were to listen to a tape which reproduces a psychoanalytic hour. In the teaching of psychoanalysis, and also in most research studies, greatest emphasis has been placed on verbal data. We assume words to be decisive, to explain change or lack of change. They become less decisive in other forms of psychoanalytic psychotherapy which are modified derivatives of the classic psychoanalytic method. Non-verbal communications will be particularly important in work with children and with severely disturbed patients where situations arise in which the verbal cues exchanged are not always decisive.

That which constitutes our empirical data is illustrated through these two lines in the middle of the diagram. The graphs above and below these two lines connected with the wavy line are not descriptions of data but are meant to be the rationale of the underlying process explaining the happenings underneath the surface of the observable data.

The lower part of the diagram illustrates what goes on in the patient as he moves from the beginning of psychoanalysis towards its ending.

We are limiting the features of change, the *modus operandi* of psychoanalytic treatment, to three curves through which the patient, his "psychic apparatus," moves. First we will use a mechanistic model and will replace it later, when a case illustration is offered, through a more humanistic one.

The curve of interest is the middle curve, named "T," meaning *transference*.

As we observe the material the patient brings to the hour, being encouraged as he is to use the basic rule, that is to say, whatever comes to his mind, we find that after hours of complaints, remarks about his life in general, the material takes on a form which indicates that the psychoanalyst becomes more and more the focal point of the patient's fantasies, interest, anxieties, worries. The thoughts and the feelings that the patient starts to express about the analyst take on forms which could not be understood even if one were to take into account the normal kinds of responses a patient has vis-à-vis any doctor. Perhaps they can be likened to the responses of a patient who is tied to his physician because of very serious illness, and experiences himself as being completely helpless and at the mercy, good or bad, of the physician. Under such circumstances a dependency pattern develops which Freud recognized to be the replica, the second edition, of an earlier state of mind. Freud's classical paper *The Dynamics of Transference* (27) does not represent his first remarks on the nature of transference. He dealt with that phenomenon in his famous "Dora" case (28) and, of course, discussed its implications in many other papers, and finally near the end of his life in *Analysis Terminable and Interminable* (29). In this paper he describes the mechanism of transference as one by means of which treatment is made possible even though transference very frequently appears as a form of resistance to treatment, and very often, because of its negative implications, creates veritable obstacles to treatment.

Time and time again therapists have lost patients because they could not deal with the transference situation, and Freud, in his "Dora" case (30), describes his own difficulties in dealing with the negative transference. The patient interrupted the treatment since she transferred to Freud not only her erotic, incestuous thoughts of the father, but also her disappointment in the father in whose fidelity she could not believe, and whom, therefore, she could not fully trust.

During treatment the instinctual expressions of the patient, sexual or aggressive, become stronger and stronger and eventually the transference neurosis sets in which is understood to be the replica of the infantile neurosis which is the basis of the patient's adult neurosis.

In the earlier years of psychoanalytic history, the transference neurosis was understood primarily in oedipal terms. The patient was seen as repeating in the analysis earlier relationships to father and mother, and attempting to resolve the oedipal conflict. It soon became clear that the material included as well so-called pre-oedipal material, that is, data which could be understood as the replica of earlier relationships belonging to different instinctual phases of psychosexual development, and going far back into the early, often pre-verbal stages of the patient's life.

One might assume then that the line referred to as the *transference* line refers to different conditions of childhood, a curve of mental development, rather than constituting merely one point in the development of the child. The material is changing and we see it in terms of a deepened transference neurosis which expresses itself in stronger dependency, sometimes a struggle against dependency, in more and more primitive wishes and fears and hates, and frequently even in repetitions of early pre-verbal struggles stemming from a time when there was not yet established object- and self-constancy.

It is assumed that the deepening of the transference neurosis leads also to the conditions of the cure, because somewhere in this ideal representation of the process a turn of events takes place so that the interpretation of the transference and the transference neurosis brings about desirable changes by means of which it is thought possible to dissolve the transference neurosis. At the end of the treatment process the transference neurosis is dissolved and what is said to remain is a realistic relationship to the analyst. This, of course, is an ideal goal and is never fully reached. Remnants of the transference neurosis may remain, sometimes to disappear slowly after the analysis, perhaps through some self-analysis. It may be revived in further treatment or whenever an emotional upset occurs in the life of the patient. But even if it were possible to succeed fully through interpretation to dissolve the transference neurosis, we are nevertheless left with the question as to how it could be possible that the very same interpretive process which at first brings about a deepening of the transference neurosis (the essential ingredient of a successful treatment), would suddenly dissolve the transference neurosis that it had created. Are we to consider the treatment process comparable to climbing a mountain so that we would get higher and higher and then climb down the mountain after we have reached the height of a development? This simile will not lead us very far even though it is seductive. Menninger (31) suggested that a patient finally gets tired of his helplessness and dependency, puts himself under pressure, responds adaptively now to the process of interpretation, and is willing to give up the analyst. This may be true of an adolescent whose dependency on parents finally changes into his wish for independence.

Two additional lines in the graphic representation of treatment suggest a different understanding concerning the deepening and widening of the transference and the slowly developing readiness of the patient to turn the transference neurosis into a more normal growing-up and growing-away process which is to lead towards the solution of most of the infantile aspects of the transference experience. Freud (32) suggests that: "This struggle between the doctor and the patient, between intellect and instinctual life, between understanding and seeking to act, is played out almost exclusively in the phenomena of transference. It is on that field that the victory must be won—the victory whose expression is the permanent cure of the neurosis." The struggle of the analyst with the patient must not simply be understood as a struggle between one and the other, but must also be seen as a struggle that the two of them together carry out against the neurosis. The healthy part of the patient, the observing part of his ego, is allied with the analyst. This alliance has been referred to as psychotherapeutic alliance. Greenson (33) has referred to it as *the working alliance,* implying a special technical problem which must be resolved in order to allow the patient to work together with the analyst on the solution of the neurotic components of the transference.

The two other curved lines, one described through the letter "R," referring to *regression,* the other described through the letter "P," referring to *progression,* help to understand more fully what is involved in dealing with transference phenomena. The rhythm of life moves us back and forth between regression and progression, such as between falling asleep and awakening; or between the need for love and the need for work; or between passivity and activity, and the like. The material of the patient can then be understood in terms of its progressive and regressive meaning.

The patient ideally suited to the psychoanalytic process might well be characterized as the one whose two curves, the regression and the progression curves, develop at the same time in like strength. Both deepen simultaneously, grow in strength and in quality, and somehow oppose as well as supplement each other.

While the interpretations of the analyst strengthen the progressive side of the patient, his ego capacity to observe, to digest, to assimilate and to integrate, there are also set free regressive aspects which can now be viewed with less fear because there is capacity to observe, to control, and to adapt. One might say that only he can regress in a healthy way who can match the regression with progression. He who is capable of understanding his dreams will not have nightmares. He who can return to logical thinking is not afraid of regressive poetic fantasy.

It is then the interpretive work of the analyst which strengthens the ego, thus then being capable not only of *observing* regressive material coming to the surface, but of *enabling* it to come to the surface, as if to say that censorship, defense action, is only necessary whenever there is a weak ego to struggle against the regressive material.

Lewin (34) suggested once that the basic rule permits the patient to regress, to fall asleep, so to speak, while the interpretation of the analyst encourages, indeed forces, the patient to wake up and progress. The basic rule is a kind of indirect gratification and the interpretation is a demand.

One might be able to define certain diagnostic categories of patients in terms of the specific nature of their respective regressive and progressive curves which, of course, cannot be entirely guided by the analyst. Somehow they can be kept in control by him through tactful interpretation, that is, an interpretation which is given in tact at the right time and is offered in a non-confronting and acceptable way. Reik (35) has elaborated on this double meaning of the word "tactful."

For example, an obsessive compulsive patient could be illustrated through a strong progressive line so that the regressive aspects, particularly the aspects of affect, could never develop. This person would use free association mainly in the service of defense, and progression in his case would not serve adaptation but would serve as a strong wall against underlying regressive tendencies.

On the other hand, an hysterical patient, an acting-out patient, could be viewed through lines where the regression curve would be powerful and where it would not be matched by an equally strong progression curve. Another way of putting this would be simply to suggest that it is difficult for the hysterical patient, the acting-out patient, to think as fully as he should, and to have the thought serve as trial action, while the obsessive compulsive patient finds it difficult to feel and to directly experience as much as he should while being dominated by rumination.

If we are now to assume that the interpretive process has helped the patient to modify the interrelationship between progression and regression and to restore a normal rhythm, we now find it easier to understand that he must not rely on the auxiliary ego, the interpretive ego of the analyst, the new parent surrogate, but can rely on his own mature rhythm, the new synthesis between progression and regression. Seen in this light, Freud's definition of mental health as the capacity to love and to work, to need objects, to be independent of objects, and to be self-supporting, takes on a new dimension.

The interpretive function of the analyst is replaced by the newly acquired or restored *synthetic function* of the patient, a concept introduced into the literature by Hartmann (36).

Much progress of the patient can be understood in terms of his attempt to identify with the analyst, as in earlier years he had identified with his parents and other significant people in his environment. While in the beginning of the analysis he identified the analyst as a parent and projected into and onto him parental demands, he does not really identify with the analyst but identifies with what he has projected onto the analyst. The

Kleinian concept of projective identification characterizes this state of affairs quite well.

Much of what is projected onto the analyst is the projection of the past, the projection of all the self- and object-representations. But as the interpretive process goes on, the patient—in part because of the working alliance—identifies with the technical activity of the analyst, his observations, his interpretive stance, his way of working. He thus acquires a new psychic tool by means of which to turn projective identification into true, more mature identificatory processes. To what degree he identifies, not only with the analyst's interpretive methods but also with the other aspects of the analyst, is an open question. It depends on his degree of inner difficulties, his particular object search and object hunger, and, of course, on the quality of the analyst.

This leads us now to the upper part of the diagram, the part which refers to the analyst. The upper part of our model of psychoanalytic treatment is almost like a mirror image of the lower part which refers to the patient.

The analyst is pictured as having a diagnostic impression of the patient, this being the mirror image of the symptom picture that the patient represents. But the analyst sees not only symptoms. He also attempts to see the dynamics behind the symptoms. He creates in his mind a tentative model of the patient (37). In an ideally terminated process, he would come to a conclusion about the patient which would show the patient symptom-free and would permit the analyst to understand him in terms of his strength and/or weakness for progression and regression. Both progression and regression, as mentioned earlier, can be in the service of adaptation but are sometimes in the service of pathology.

In the upper part of our model, we have mirrored the same three lines referring to the patient's progression, regression and transference, in order to suggest that the analyst could be understood in terms of his technical activities through these three lines. He will develop a *countertransference* potential as he listens to the patient with freely suspended attention, the equivalent of free association. The requirement of *freely suspended attention* is that he will not only listen to the data but will permit his mind to wander around the data, to relate them to fantasies of his own, to previous material, and thus achieve touch with the preconscious of the patient while mobilizing his own preconscious.

Sometimes a fantasy that he has about the patient, a sudden feeling, anxiety, anger, hate, or positive feelings, even erotic notions, will really be his way of understanding the patient preconsciously. If he were not well analyzed, he may well slip into countertransference reactions which are neurotic in origin, may lead him to counter act out, may lead him to guide instead of interpret, may lead him to react to the patient rather than to understand the patient. But usually his countertransference potential is better understood through Reik's apt notion of *listening with the third ear* (38). His countertransference potential really will be tamed and sublimated empathy. He will not over-identify with the patient, he will not need to project his own internal conflicts or his past onto the patient, and he will neither need to be dominated by transference reactions towards the patient (such as experiencing him as a sibling or a competitor) nor countertransference reactions, such as having the material of the patient revive neurotic conflicts of his own.

The nature of this countertransference potential will also depend on the nature of the two lines which refer to his regression and progression potential. If he is well analyzed and well trained, we would assume him to be able to regress in the service of the therapeutic process, the interpretive interventions he must try. His capacity to have contact with the preconscious forces in himself, his own fantasy life, his capacity to observe himself and not only the patient, will lead him to use regression in the service of the therapeutic ego. His capacity to progress, to learn, to understand theory and technique, will strengthen his capacity to use empathy. It will be empathy tamed and sublimated through knowledge, experience, and theoretical strength.

This will allow him to develop a therapeutic style perhaps characteristic for him. We would hope that this therapeutic style be a flexible one, changeable from patient to patient, rather than a sterile technical line, as is so often true for the beginner who has not yet freed himself from his teachers; who must repeat what he has learned in inflexible ways where the thoughts of others, former teachers or his own analyst, are more important than his own thinking.

To introduce a concept which perhaps will explain more about the working alliance, we come to the concept of *transference health* and *countertransference health*.

When the patient regresses into transference neurosis, he does not merely arrive at early pathological states but also repeats an earlier edition of health or partial health. After all, the patient brings not only the infantile neurosis to be repeated in the transference neurosis, he also brings infantile choices, infantile solutions, infantile ways of observing and discovering. Much of what is worked through in an analysis is frequently worked through with the competent ego of the younger person. We may speak not only of the adult ego which observes the infantile neurosis but may understand the ego itself as a hierarchy of ego organizations. During the treatment process, different aspects of this ego, earlier and later representations, become dominant in the treatment process and help us in the observational task. Perhaps that is the reason why sometimes long stretches of the analysis of adult people are remindful of child analysis. Free association may be quite similar to the free play activity of the child. After all, isn't free association a play with thoughts rather than a committed thought? This play with thoughts will frequently take on early forms, not only in terms of the repetition of the neurosis but also in terms of the repetition of health. Therefore, the working alliance with the patient, that psychotherapeutic pact, will be carried out at times with a partner whose ego, while healthy, is the replica of an earlier healthy but infantile ego, etc.

A social metaphor will make this clear. Let us assume that a country, defeated by war, finding itself in utter chaos, is to benefit from a government. As is the case after every disaster, the government function will have to be primitive and controlling rather than the sophisticated function of checks and balances which we know from more advanced forms of human cooperation. This first government, a kind of benevolent police state, is the analogue to the earlier ego which can deal with its inner struggles only through methods which stem from earlier phases of maturation.

Similar observations could be made about other psychic functions, such as superego development, id development, object relations, forms of adaptation and dealing with reality, reality testing and perception itself, development of motor skills, etc.

But what is true for the patient is also true for the analyst. The analyst sometimes falls back on technical methods which can be seen as regressions to earlier phases of his learning, not really incompetent, but not on the level of his highest capacity for therapeutic work.

Sometimes our analytical work becomes stilted, less useful, and we do not seem to be fully understanding. We find ourselves working with methods which do not show us at our best, even though we are not effective with them.

Essentially, the development of the transference neurosis, its interpretation as well as the analysis of the resistances, leads to a state of affairs which permits the patient to create a better balance between regressive and progressive forces, and thus sets free energy for the solution of problems. The interpretation of the analyst leads to the strengthening of the synthetic function of the patient's ego. The past, rather than a burden expressing itself in symptoms, becomes a lesson for the use of tomorrow. Santayana's phrase about those who have forgotten their past and are now condemned to repeat it, could be turned around and we could suggest that those who remember their past are capable of learning from it, so that *the compulsion to repeat turns into the power for adaptation, that is,* the change of one's self and one's environment in the service of *self-realization.*

APPLICATION OF THEORY

This patient's treatment lasted almost five years and this case illustration, therefore, is no more than a token characterization of the work done.

My analysand, whom I shall call Dr. Brown, was 45 years old at the beginning of the treatment. He had come for psychoanalysis because of serious dissatisfactions with himself, his marriage, his functioning as a father and his functioning as a physician. Diagnostically, he would best be classified as suffering from an obsessive compulsive character disorder. Under stress he could not successfully use the best level of his obsessive compulsive adjustment and then would regress to severe anxiety states, while from time to time being overwhelmed by uncontrollable rage outbursts and being pushed into episodes of severe acting out. His wife had been in analytic treatment for years. There was emotional distance between him and his wife, the two children, as well as his own parents who lived in the East. His father was described as an angry and demanding person, while the mother tried to influence with hidden but relentless reproaches that for him were more difficult to take than the father's angry demands. Among his siblings was a brother who had also been in analysis. All through the analysis of his wife he had been playing with the thought of also having analysis, being partly motivated by envy and jealousy, and becoming more and more involved in a kind of fantasy triangle between himself, his wife's analyst, and his wife. An earlier attempt to arrange for analytic treatment with a lady analyst left him with a deep disappointment. He had thought that she had promised him time and felt rejected when she later told him that she had no time and wanted to refer him to another woman analyst. Some years passed and he finally came to see me upon finding himself in a deep anxiety state at a moment when he attempted to separate from an older professional partner.

The beginning of treatment can best be described through the developing transference atmosphere which is characterized by his attempt to establish a kind of double evidence. On the one hand he wanted to prove to himself and to me that to leave the older physician was the only thing to do because his partner had always exploited him, had given him poor financial deals, forced him to work more. Proof after proof was accumulated in order to show that the partner did things bordering on the incorrect.

On the other hand, the "evidence" that he collected about me, his analyst, was to confirm himself that he was wise to have waited for me as long as he did; that he was better off not going to any other analyst, and he claimed that I actually was the only one to help him. He collected all kinds of "news" about me such as discovering publicity concerning a professional lecture, a publication of mine, remarks of psychiatric friends about me, and all of it dominated by over-idealization, behind which, of course, one must suspect doubt, hostility, and criticism of the analyst as well as of the effectiveness of the analytic procedure. Strangely enough, this obsessive collecting of good news about me was devoid of affect and was expressed in terms of intellectual, logical conviction, somehow in the same vein that someone would have selected the best store or the best technician, and it had none of the usual emotional components in it. The split between the conniving, exploiting colleague and the image of the brilliant, well-known analyst was complete. All early attempts to confront him with these two images, to relate them to analysis and to earlier experiences, were met with the response that there must be something to the analyst's interpretation but he could neither feel its validity nor remember anything in his childhood which would indicate that the analyst might possibly be right. Insight was intellectualized, restricted by isolation, by avoidance, by denial and displacement.

It was also characteristic for this first phase of treatment that whatever "observations" he made about me or himself were via reports from other people. He would literally take cues from his wife who would make remarks to him about certain aspects of his behavior and explain to him, for example, that she thought he must be angry, and he would take this as evidence for his state of mind that otherwise he could not feel. His total behavior could be likened to someone who would constantly look into a mirror in order to take cues from his mirror image as to what kind of feelings he might possibly have. One must think of Freud's remark as early as 1895 that recollections without affect are almost always useless.

Dr. Brown would never miss an analytic hour, would always be exactly on time and would behave quite correctly. The flow of his life was dictated by minute routines from home to office, to the analytic session, twice a week to the tennis court, stereotype meetings with his friends. Sometimes this flow would be interrupted by violent outbursts of rage, usually after comparatively minor provocations. He then might throw things at his wife, "invite her to leave the bedroom," try to force her out of the house since he could not control himself otherwise. Similar incidents occurred vis-à-vis his son and his brother. Perhaps a fuller description of a therapy session or two, illustrative material from the flow of free association and interpretive interventions, will help us to understand the analytical process, the nature of the therapeutic struggle. The following hour is taken from somewhere in the mid-point in treatment when anxiety became more and more mobilized in the transference situation and seemed to break down the obsessive compulsive facade.

Dr. Brown opened the session today, out of breath, with a remark which was meant to be jocular that if he were to talk fast here he might make it. He referred to an obstetrics case whom he had sent to the hospital during the night and who might give birth any moment. He left word with the hospital to call him here and to interrupt the hour in case the birth process should start. He thought he could still make it, but he felt by obstetrics statistics he really should not be here in his analytic hour. He felt, however, that the twenty minutes it would take him to go from my office to the hospital, provided he could drive fast enough and find no obstacles on the street, might still make this safe. He dwelt on the thought as to how much he did for the analyst, but he questioned what the analyst was doing for him. He thought that under such emergency conditions it was very hard for him to say what occurred to him and instead of trying to probe his own mind he had one eye on his patient and the other on the clock for the analyst. It seemed to him that this time he came very close to a point when the hour should really have been omitted, having spoken frequently in the past about his expectation that he might have to cancel or interrupt certain early hours because of obstetrics cases. He then made an attempt at what he called genuine free association and spoke about the Russians who had a man in space, and he suggested that it would be ideal if he could recall the dream he had had.

The analyst commented at this point that here again was a situation in which the analysand expressed the feeling that to give himself to the analytic task would get him in conflict with medical duties and ethical consideration.

While the patient dwelt on the idea that this conflict was not really anxiety arousing, the analyst interpreted the material as the patient's attempt to describe a total situation where he was pulled between two forces— the woman to be helped and the analyst to be satisfied.

The patient then suggested that as the analyst rephrased his comment, it fitted for him, the patient. He described himself as taking calculated risks at times, and that in the practice of obstetrics there are always misses, such as the last case that he actually missed when they called him from the hospital at four o'clock in the morning. The telephone receiver was off the hook when they called, and finally a police officer appeared and told him about the obstetrics emergency. He was two minutes late but there was no special difficulty since another doctor had taken care of the patient. He suggested that a part of himself must have been unconscious, that after the last telephone call during the night he had not succeeded in putting the receiver back on the hook. He dwelt on the many factors that somehow innocently got between himself and the hospital situation, and for a considerable time he tried to create an alibi for himself, only to say finally that he still could not convince himself that missing the patient was entirely accidental. The analyst remarked that Dr. Brown did not seem to be overly eager to rush to his woman patient.

Dr. Brown then referred to his "other analyst, Jane," his wife, who, when she went to her course at the university last night, rushed everything at home and he had felt very much on edge. He had felt that the food was not well prepared and he had found the whole rush disconcerting. But for his wife that Tuesday night course was essential. While he did not like the food or his wife being away, he suggested that it is inconceivable for him that the taste might be disagreeable because of her leaving and he wanted to relate that to other dissatisfactions. He then went on to prove that all these connections really are without evidence and prove nothing.

The analyst suggested as the underlying theme of the hour that the patient was constantly playing with psychological interpretations as well as with a strong wish to debunk the very interpretations which either he offers or which are offered to him.

The material provides an interesting illustration as to the repetition of the triangle between himself, father and mother. In order to avoid the father's rage he must be on time, must not miss the analytic hour, and to enable him to respond to the hidden reproaches of the mother, he must rush as quickly as he can to be at her bedside. The anxiety is the signal of the inner conflict, of divided allegiance, and thus he would almost make it, that is, either be on time for the woman or produce in the analytic hour in order to meet the analyst's (father's) demands. The paralyzing effect of the anxiety does not really permit him to meet either condition, and he must now try to defeat the anxiety—albeit unsuccessfully—and obsessively deny the insight achieved actively (his own work) or received passively (the analyst's interpretation).

The material could also be looked at in terms of turning into the opposite what is described as his wish to help (the woman) and to meet the analyst's demand. Actually, does he not want the woman to help him and does he not want to make demands on the analyst?

The next few weeks constituted a rather active and stormy period. A few days after the anxiety attack around the conflict as to whether he ought to go to the hospital in order to be ready for his obstetrics case and help the woman, or whether he ought to go to the analytic hour and do for the analyst what he is expected to do, a powerful incident took place, a piece of acting out which was experienced at the time without feeling, without joy, and even without anxiety. He was driven to act as if the man of action was completely separated from the man of feeling, the man of reflection, even the man driven by anxiety. In one of these later hours he came rushing in and reported that he had been delayed by a house call that he had to make. He realized that he "might not make it," comparing this particular situation with the obstetrics case, but feeling that his medical practice ought to take priority. A woman patient whom he had seen in the past called him describing what seemed to be the flu and demanded a house call. He thought he ought to see her before his analytic hour. The examination did not reveal much but the woman noticed that he was in a rush, observed that he looked tired and depressed and that she did not want him to feel bad. She wanted to make him feel good and offered to perform fellatio. All this was reported in the way someone might describe how he looked up a telephone number. He let it happen—the activity was entirely the woman's activity. He felt nothing, indicated nothing, and then rushed off to his hour. The medical service emergency call had turned around, so to speak, and had serviced him, tranquilizing him. That, of course, was interpreted but he could hardly feel the transference meaning of that. He did not experience matters on a level of feeling, or even anxiety, but the bizarre acting out itself was somehow convincing. There was actually no emergency, no need to see the woman before his hour, and he could just as well have visited her later or suggested an office visit. It was only then that he gave some more information about this woman with whom there had been previous erotic contact. She was a woman who gravitated between short periods of employment, being a welfare recipient, prostituting herself, and being committed for petty crimes, and she had described to him her observations of prison sexuality which excited him greatly. All of these observations referred to activities between Lesbian women about which all the prisoners knew, although the guards were kept uninformed. It was actually the Lesbian activity itself which had excited him and had made him respond to her, as if he had now become a woman to be gratified by her. He could somehow accept the transference wish, displaced on that patient, to be passively tranquilized by the analyst and to try to achieve health, freedom from anxiety, freedom from rage, via the methods a small baby might use, being tranquilized by the giving mother who would not let him wait, would not reproach him, but would accept his own reproaches and become his sedative. His occasional use of drugs, his heavy drinking then became the focus of the material.

I will now quote in full a later hour which illustrates how the process moved and how the obsessive compulsive facade yielded in and through the analytic process. It thus allowed the discontinuity between thinking and feeling, between impulse and defense, between passivity and activity, to be replaced by an emerging continuity which at first made the transference experience into a true experience rather than an intellectual construction or a piece of displaced acting out.

In this session he spoke about his wish to cancel a certain hour since he had to go out of town. He felt it was a great advantage that now he could get to the point so quickly. He looked at this hour as "a virginal morning" and he was trying to keep his mind clear and wondered what he should discuss. Should he discuss his analyst's expected departure? Should he speak about his own departure? He said there "wasn't much floating through his mind." He had some thoughts about his former associate who wanted to paint the outside of the medical building which they still owned jointly, and he had expressed some readiness to share the expenses. His nurse had made the comment that the building was decrepit inside and the patient was reminded of the word "exploiting." He could not see how his former partner did these things unconsciously, the beautiful external facade and the neglected interior, and wondered if he did not plan them deliberately. Also, the former partner wanted to paint the patient's name off the building, and this again revived the old situation of separation since he would have his name erased from the partnership of more than ten years. He again felt that he was exploited and he wondered how he could separate himself from the "parent figure." The patient then made some remarks concerning the two areas that were to explain why he was "ostensibly" in analysis, namely the feeling of being exploited and the issue of separation.

The analyst wondered what had occurred to the patient about using the word "ostensibly."

The patient suggested that if someone were to ask him: "Why are you here?" he would mention the task of moving away from his former partner as the prime incident, the prime cause. He said he could not trace all this back to his childhood, but he could see these factors operating during the last ten years or so. He could not really recall as traumatic his own separation from home. He could see two triggering areas where the word "exploita-

tion" could be used, but whenever he wanted to apply it to the analysis itself, he could see no direct or indirect application for him. The word "ostensibly" simply meant to him that there must be better reasons than those he had found or that the analyst had offered as yet in the analysis.

The analyst wondered whether perhaps the word "apparently" would be a better choice and the patient now saw the word "ostensibly" as having a kind of questionable ring about it and not meaning the same as "apparently." He saw hidden in it the experience of doubt, of suspicion and of similar factors. He then said that a word occurred to him that would be a better motivating reason for his analysis, namely, the word "tranquility." He felt that there are many groups of analysts of different analytic schools, but in his case the choice was the Freudian group where he thought the word "tranquility" was something of a therapeutic goal. He used this word also in relation to his risk of narcotic addiction. The addicted person gets tranquility from the drug, which is a heavy price to pay.

The analyst suggested that the patient saw the analysis as a sort of tranquilizer. The patient suggested that there was also a human factor and that "tranquil" could be understood in the sense of dead, non-active, and "tranquility" has its variable shades. He wondered what else he was searching for in his analysis, but indeed this was one of the areas.

The analyst suggested that the patient saw the analysis, saw the analyst, as a tranquilizing drug, a soothing mother.

The patient wondered why he should not look at the analysis as a soothing mother. He recalled the remark of the lady analyst who did not take him as a patient, whom he experienced as a rejecting woman, and who wanted to recommend another woman analyst for him. He thought then that for him the reverse situation should be worked out, namely that he should work with a man. He thought he needed a soothing substitute for a parent; the analysis could well be that, not really a substitute but a working tool. He said that he now was starting to recognize feelings that are more intense, more shaded. He found himself trying to put these feelings into place. Treatment was seen as a placebo that fools the patient. He said that he has never used placebo with patients, unless perhaps there are certain shades of that type of placebo in certain injections which he has used for patients.

The analyst interpreted that the word "ostensibly" could be used for placebos, that some of the interpretations we see in terms of the placebo affect but do not seem to fully explain, do not seem to cure, do not seem to alleviate the pain and anxiety.

The patient quickly explained that "ostensibly" meant more for him. The analyst wondered whether the word "ostensibly" was a comment about the patient or about the analyst. The patient then said that this was why a part of the program (he always referred to his analysis as "the program") was still confusing to him. The analyst said something about what he, the patient, said and what he, the patient, had in mind, but there were much deeper areas which were, as yet, uncovered. It reminded him of a humorous remark that he had made once to his wife when he said to her: "Ekstein and I talk about termination." The wife then pricked up her ears and he added: "I am talking and he is listening." He then added: "My program, in comparison to other people, makes me feel that I have hardly scratched the surface and the word 'tranquility' would fit as a therapeutic goal."

The analyst interpreted that the patient must actually have had in mind the word "equanimity" which he then replaced unconsciously with the word "tranquility." The analyst referred to the acting out with the woman as an attempt to be tranquilized by a soothing woman, an attempt that did not create equanimity. The fellatio experience was then seen as a placebo, while interpretations would be the true, though thought-disturbing and feeling-arousing agent of change.

As the analytic process moved on, the patient could more fully experience the passive desires, the anxiety about these passive desires, the rage about desires not met, as they moved into the transference struggle. Behind the homosexual fears were the oral fears and the struggle to turn the non-giving mother into a nurturing partner. Essentially, of course, these were reflected in the struggle to improve the marriage which in many ways was a repetition of the early child/parent relationships.

All this took place some years ago. As I reflect on these notes I find it characteristic for my work that I tried to remain on the level of the patient's communication. For example, I navigated the road of semantics for a while as is indicated in this last hour. It was as if I had to use the obsessional struggle about the meaning of words and the misuse of words in order to get to the feeling.

The analysis ended with a fairly positive result. I have heard from the patient occasionally and he maintains a good level of functioning. Much of what was missing in his own early life was slowly turned into a professional asset. He is a helpful and competent physician, and the family life has improved considerably. While in the past he was a deeply disturbed man whose panics and rages broke through the obsessive compulsive facade, he could perhaps now be described as a somewhat compulsive person who functions well and who, instead of being dominated by panic and rage, is guided by a well-meaning heart and cautious, perhaps sometimes overcautious, thought, having better contact with himself and the world.

THE FUTURE OF PSYCHOANALYSIS

Where will psychoanalysis go? To a large degree the social effectiveness of psychoanalysis depends on the state of society. Many an insight of the past, a discovery in antiquity, an invention made during the middle ages or the renaissance, even techniques developed in our time, have been lost or may get lost whenever there is social regression and violent change. It may well be that we might suffer a kind of temporary social regression in which all individual psychotherapy might suffer. One-to-one psychotherapy may even be pushed from the social scene for a while. Civil war and war conditions are not conducive to the kind of effort that I have described in these pages. Such setbacks have taken place several times in the history of psychoanalysis, but psychoanalysis has always recovered. Our society now has a variety of options and it is hard to predict what option it might follow. If it follows the options of a *free society* which will include freedom and dignity, individualism integrated with social responsibility, *psychoanalysis* will have its *safe* place.

What will be its new direction? It has moved from instinct theory, from the theory of the unconscious, to include other considerations as well. We have moved towards the structural model, the study of ego and superego. We have moved to ego psychology and object-relations theory. More and more we have moved away from mechanical models to humanistic models. While at first there was only drive, now there is also the will. While at first there was only the blind struggle between opposing forces, now there is also the consideration of adaptation, of problem solving, of synthesis on different levels of consciousness.

In research we have moved from the case study to process study. We now study not only transference but also countertransference. More and more we have studied the psychoanalytic tool, the analyst himself, and we have developed better training and teaching techniques. We have moved from training for psychoanalysis to psychoanalytic education.

We have moved from psychoanalysis in isolation and in open warfare with academic psychology and medicine to new islands of full collaboration. We have maintained our identity but we have created bridges to other behavioral scientists.

Much of the original hostility on both sides has turned into mutual respect. Psychoanalytic thinking is used in other scientific disciplines and we have learned that we, too, must be accessible as well as have access to the general information explosion.

All predictions in this field, due to the uncertainty of our world, are at best self-fulfilling prophecies or magic thoughts of wish fulfillment. Therefore, rather than predicting, I would like to say what I believe would be a healthy development.

I should like to see the teachers of psychoanalysis develop a more open system of training. Psychoanalysis should overcome more fully the separation between medical practitioners and people who come from other fields and who are today admitted for psychoanalytic training only if they are research-minded. We need talents from all fields. Sometimes when one goes through the former interests of psychoanalysts, of lay analysts as well as of medical analysts, and particularly notes those who have richly contributed to the field, one realizes that their background may be statistics or English literature, physiology or pathology, art or pedagogy, economics or sociology, social work or clinical psychology, pediatrics or internal medicine; one finds that one should not exclude any talent and any avenue to the human mind which can contribute to its study.

Furthermore, I hope we can continue to give up the isolation of private institutes, and that psychoanalysis will be ready to return to the university. Psychoanalysis should have *independent psychoanalytic departments in the universities,* not dominated by any of the other disciplines but freely dedicated to the search for truth and the search for healthy application. Most of us who think along these lines have one foot in private practice, the other in clinical or teaching activity. Is it too much to ask for a utopian development that would put us back into the university so there could be islands of growth?

Whenever a science becomes accepted, and indeed analysis is accepted today in America in spite of some of the setbacks, it is in danger of becoming diluted. *Ecclesia militans* after having become *ecclesia triumphans* may become *ecclesia dilutans.* Unless there are islands of research, of constant questioning, of constant progress, of constant scientific doubt, psychoanalysis like other activities is in danger of becoming institutionalized. Can we create, however, psychoanalytic institutions which have built into them the task of scientific change? Can one see to it that the task of change, of constructive development, of *endless renewal,* become everybody's vested interest, a genuine part of our inner and institutional life?

I started this contribution with Freud's classical definition of psychoanalysis. I end it in identifying with his *reflections on the future of psychoanalysis*:

"By a process of development against which it would have been useless to struggle, the word 'psychoanalysis' has itself become ambiguous. While it was originally the name of a particular therapeutic method, it has now also become the name of a science—the science of unconscious mental processes. By itself this science is seldom able to deal with a problem completely, but it seems destined to give valuable contributory help in the most varied regions of knowledge. This fear of application of psychoanalysis extends as far as that of psychology, to which it forms a complement of the greatest moment.

"Looking back then over the patchwork of my life's labors, I can say that I have made many beginnings and thrown out many suggestions. Something will come of them in the future, though I cannot myself tell whether it will be much or little. However, I can express a hope that I have opened up a pathway for an important advance in our knowledge" (39).

REFERENCES

1. FREUD, S. & BREUER, J. (1895). Studies on hysteria. *Standard Edition*, 2, 1-305. London: Hogarth Press, 1955.
2. FREUD, S. (1904 [1903]). Freud's psychoanalytic procedure. *Standard Edition*, 7, 249-254. London: Hogarth Press, 1953.
3. RAPAPORT, D. & GILL, M. M. The points of view and assumptions of metapsychology. *International Journal of Psychoanalysis*, 40, 153-161, 1959.
4. WALLERSTEIN, R. S. & SAMPSON, H. Issues in research in the psychoanalytic process. *International Journal of Psycho-Analysis*, 52, 11-50, 1971.
5. GREENSON, R. R. *The Technique and Practice of Psychoanalysis*. New York: International Universities Press, 1967.
6. FREUD, S. (1919 [1918]). Lines of advance in psychoanalytic therapy. *Standard Edition*, 17, 157-168. London: Hogarth Press, 1965.
7. ALLPORT, G. W. *Personality. Psychological Interpretation*. New York: Henry Holt, 1937.
8. FREUD, S. (1932). New introductory lectures on psychoanalysis. *Standard Edition*, 22, 3-182. London: Hogarth Press, 1964.
9. FREUD, S. (1905). Three essays on the theory of sexuality. *Standard Edition*, 7, 123-243. London: Hogarth Press, 1953.
10. ERIKSON, E. H. (1950). *Childhood and Society*. New York: Norton, 1963. Pp. 219-234.
11. SPITZ, R. *The First Years of Life*. New York: International Universities Press, 1965.
12. FREUD, ANNA. *Normality and Pathology in Childhood: Assessments of Development*. New York: International Universities Press, 1965.
13. *Op. cit.*, 9.
14. *Op. cit.*, 12.
15. EKSTEIN, R. Psychological laws and human freedom. *Journal of Social Psychology*, 25, 181-191, 1947.
16. SKINNER, B. F. *Beyond Freedom and Dignity*. New York: Alfred A. Knopf, 1971.

17. FREUD, S. (1923). The ego and the id. *Standard Edition*, 19, 3-63, London: Hogarth Press, 1961.
18. WAELDER, R. The principle of multiple function: Observations on over-determinism. *Psychoanalytic Quarterly*, 1936, 5, 45-62.
19. EKSTEIN, R. The tower of babel in psychology and in psychiatry. *American Imago*, 1950, 7, 76-141.
20. *Op. cit.*, 17.
21. MENNINGER, K. *Theory of Psychoanalytic Technique*. New York: Basic Books, 1958.
22. EKSTEIN, R. Structural aspects of psychotherapy. *Psychoanalytic Review*, 39, 222-228, 1952.
23. STONE, L. *The Psychoanalytic Situation—An Examination of Its Development and Essential Nature*. New York: International Universities Press, 1961.
24. FREUD, ANNA (1936). *The Ego and Its Mechanisms of Defense*. London: Hogarth Press, 1937.
25. EKSTEIN, R. Working through and termination of analysis. *Journal of the American Psychoanalytic Association*, 13, 57-58, 1965.
26. LEWIN, B. D. The analytic situation: Topographic considerations. *Psychoanalytic Quarterly*, 28, 455-469, 1959.
27. FREUD, S. (1912). The dynamics of transference. *Standard Edition*, 13, 99-108. London: Hogarth Press, 1958.
28. FREUD, S. (1905). Fragment of an analysis of a case of hysteria. *Standard Edition*, 7, 7-14. London: Hogarth Press, 1953.
29. FREUD, S. (1937). Analysis terminable and interminable. *Standard Edition*, 23, 216-253. London: Hogarth Press, 1964.
30. *Op. cit.*, 28.
31. *Op. cit.*, 21.
32. *Op. cit.*, 27.
33. *Op. cit.*, 5.
34. LEWIN, B. D. Sleep, narcissistic neurosis and the analytic situation. *Psychoanalytic Quarterly*, 23, 487-510, 1954.
35. REIK, THEODORE. *Listening with the Third Ear—the Inner Experience of a Psychoanalyst*. New York: Farrer, Straus, 1949.
36. HARTMANN, H. (1939). *Ego Psychology and the Problem of Adaptation*. New York: International Universities Press, 1958.
37. *Op. cit.*, 5.
38. *Op. cit.*, 35.
39. FREUD, S. (1925). An autobiographical study. *Standard Edition*, 20, 3-74. London: Hogarth Press, 1959.

BIBLIOGRAPHY

BRENNER, CHARLES. *An Elementary Textbook of Psychoanalysis*. New York: International Universities Press, 1955.
ERIKSON, E. H. (1950). *Childhood and Society*. New York: Norton, 1963. Pp. 219-234.
FENICHEL, OTTO. *The Psychoanalytic Theory of Neurosis*. New York: W. W. Norton Co., Inc., 1945.
FREUD, ANNA. *The Ego and Its Mechanisms of Defense*. London: Hogarth Press, 1937.
FREUD, ANNA. *Normality and Pathology in Childhood: Assessments of Development*. New York: International Universities Press, 1965.

FREUD, S. (1900). Interpretation of dreams. *Standard Edition*, 4, 1-310; 5, 311-628. London: Hogarth Press, 1953.

FREUD, S. (1905). Three essays on the theory of sexuality. *Standard Edition*, 7, 123-243. London: Hogarth Press, 1953.

FREUD, S. (1905). Fragment of an analysis of a case of hysteria. *Standard Edition*, 7, 7-14. London: Hogarth Press, 1953.

FREUD, S. (1923). The ego and the id. *Standard Edition*, 19, 3-63. London: Hogarth Press, 1961.

FREUD, S. (1925). An autobiographical study. *Standard Edition*, 20, 3-74. London: Hogarth Press, 1959.

FREUD, S. & BREUER, J. (1895). Studies on hysteria. *Standard Edition*, 2, 1-305. London: Hogarth Press, 1955.

GREENSON, R. R. *The Technique and Practice of Psychoanalysis*. New York: International Universities Press, 1967.

HARTMANN, HEINZ (1939). *Ego Psychology and the Problem of Adaptation*. New York: International Universities Press, 1958.

MENNINGER, KARL. *Theory of Psychoanalytic Technique*. New York: Basic Books, 1958.

REIK, THEODORE. *Listening with the Third Ear—the Inner Experience of a Psychoanalyst*. New York: Farrar, Straus, 1949.

SPITZ, R. *The First Years of Life*. New York: International Universities Press, 1965.

STONE, LEO. *The Psychoanalytic Situation—An Examination of Its Development and Essential Nature*. New York: International Universities Press, 1961.

WAELDER, ROBERT. *Basic Theory of Psychoanalysis*. New York: International Universities Press, 1960.

C. G. Jung

3

Archetypal Theory:
C. G. Jung

by JAMES HILLMAN

> Every exposition cannot help
> but be an apology, a critique,
> and also a confession.

Prefatory Note: I shall be following Jung's own approach to theory. For him it was always related to therapy of the soul because ideas cannot be separated from life without damaging both. As we go along I shall be pointing out the therapeutic implications of the theories of archetypal psychology.

Calling Jung's psychology after its principal structural idea, the archetype, emphasizes the theoretical work of his mature and late periods (ca. 1928-1961, *aet.* 53-86). Usually his psychology is called "analytical," a term coined in the early days in relation with Freud's "psychoanalysis." But "archetypal" more adequately corresponds with his own construction as a whole and its wide range of concerns besides actual analysis. Also, "archetypal" more accurately describes Jung's approach to the fundaments of the psyche.

Throughout my account I use the word "understand." Understanding is perhaps the most operational of all Jungian concepts, implied throughout all others, and places Jung's approach within the tradition of *psychologies of understanding* (Dilthey, Nietzsche, Jaspers), rather than psychologies that are explanatory, descriptive or medical in the narrow sense. Jung set out from the beginning, not to compare or measure or explain or redeem personality, but to understand it and bring understanding to it. His was the myth of meaning (Jaffé 1971).

THE IDEA AND NATURE OF PERSONALITY

Individuality

Jung writes: "My life has been permeated and held together by one idea and one goal: namely, to penetrate into the secret of personality. Everything can be explained from this central point, and all my works relate to this one theme" (*MDR*, p. 206). Towards the end of his late essay on the plight of contemporary man, he asks the rhetorical question of each individual threatened with doomsday extinction: "Does the individual know that *he* [and she] is the makeweight that tips the scales?" (*CW* 10, §586). What happens to the individual and to the world at large depends on the individual personality. No other idea in Jung's work holds as much importance as does personality. "The sole and natural carrier of life is the individual, and this holds true throughout nature" (*CW* 16, §224). "All life is individual life, in which alone the ultimate meaning is to be found" (*CW* 10, §923).

Individuation

Jung coined the term "individuation" for the activity of personality realization, a term which "denotes the process by which a person becomes a psychological 'in-dividual,' that is, a separate entity or whole" (*CW* 9, i, §490). More simply he calls individuation the process by which a person "becomes what he really is" (*CW* 16, §11). Individuation is the supporting theoretical construct, or vision, from which proceeds a rich proliferation of other ideas about personality, some of which we shall now examine.

Jungian theory does not ask the question "What *is* personality?" as an entity to be defined and explained. Rather, it is dynamic and pragmatic in its questioning, asking "In what way can a person know who he is, discover his personality, develop and refine it, and become him- or herself?" Personality itself is given with the psychic reality of the questioner, so the idea of personality is taken for granted in the common dictionary sense of a "personal being," as distinct from an abstraction or a thing, and the organization of that being into a qualitatively differentiated unit. Where philosophers and churchmen account for the essence of personal being in their metaphysical language and embryologists and geneticists account for its origin in their physical language, Jung's hypotheses attempt to describe it and further it—psychologically.

Value

Part of this description is in terms of value. One way of giving value to personality is to connect it with transcendent factors, especially God. By doing so the Jungian idea of personality is in keeping with the Greek, Roman, and Judeo-Christian tradition. Each personality is potentially a self that embodies and reflects something more than itself. It is not self-sufficient, but in relation with others, both other persons and "the other" which is not personal and not human. The very word personality from the Greek, *persona,* implies a mask through which sounds something transcendent. Without this "other" which stands behind ego-consciousness, independent of it, yet makes personal consciousness possible, there would be no individualized personality, no subjective center to which events relate and become experiences. This inner conviction in oneself as a personality Jung also calls "vocation" (*CW* 17, §300 ff; cf. Grinnell 1970).

The condition clinically called depersonalization demonstrates what Jung here means. There can be a loss of personal reality and identity even if all ego functions remain intact; perception, orientation, memory, association, etc., are each undisturbed (Meyer [ed.] 1968). Depersonalization indicates that the sense of personality, the very belief and conviction in one's reality as an individual, depends on a factor transcendent to the ego-personality, beyond its sensorium and its powers of will. Sometimes Jung calls this factor, on which the individual depends, the "self." This term can be taken as a description of substance and as a description of value. I prefer the latter usage.

Self

The self in Jung refers to: (a) the fullest extension of the individual, and (b) experiences of the highest value and power beyond one's own extension, that is, experiences of the transcendent and other. Such experiences and images of great value and power have traditionally been given the names of Gods. By giving "self" this double meaning, both personal and transcendent, Jung suggests that each person is by definition connected to something transcendent, or even has a transcendent supreme value beyond his ego-personality. This gives worth to all manifestations of human nature. Even the most debased conditions have a wider significance and are not merely human faults because they point to transcendent collective, archetypal, and non-human factors. The double meaning of self suggests also that personality cannot be understood by a personal approach alone. One eye needs always to be focused upon the impersonal, non-human background.

Evil

This background is not only positive, not only good. Non-human means also inhuman. Personality reflects disorder, destruction, and shadow values as well. These powers are as effective in the psyche as the apparently creative, constructive ones, so they are psychologically just as real. Jung's position here in regard to the place of evil in personality is not at all moralistic, even if religious. This distinguishes his from other psychologies that are moralistic, but not religious.

Because the individual personality has such worth, because it is the locus of all values—consciousness, conscience, life, meaning, soul as well as destruction and evil—work with individuals, whether others or oneself, statistically insignificant as such work may be, remains nonetheless a most valuable kind of occupation.

Religion

These religious aspects of Jung's personality theory derive partly from his personal make-up and partly from his notion, gained through practice and research, that religion is constitutionally based on personality and no more an illusion than is sexuality. Further, the religious metaphors he uses belong to his style of giving value to psychic facts, just as other psychologists imply their value system by employing other kinds of transcendent metaphors such as "nature," "evolution," "authenticity," "maturity," etc. Jung's religious language in no way implies orthodoxy of creed, membership in church, or observance of ritual.

Psychic Reality

The world of reality that personality inhabits is *psychic reality*. In Jung "reality" finds an altogether different definition than in Freud, where the word refers mainly to what is external, social, and material and where psychic reality is decisive only in the realm of neuroses and psychoses (Casey 1972). Jung states: "Reality is simply what works in a human soul" (*CW* 6, §60). All sorts of things work in the soul—lies, hallucinations, political slogans, outmoded scientific ideas, superstitions—and so these events are real, whether true or not. Many other conscious events—good advice, historical facts, ethical codes, psychological interpretations—may not have any effect in the psyche's depth, and so these events may be considered as not real, whether true or not.

Fantasy Images

At the most basic level of psychic reality are fantasy images. These images are the primary activity of consciousness. This ongoing fantasy activity, a vital process that Jung states cannot be explained as mere "reflex action to sensory stimuli," is a continuously creative act—through fantasy "the psyche creates reality every day" (*CW* 6, §78).

Jung reverses the familiar theory that holds reality to be external, images to be the imprint of externals, and fantasies to be decayed or distorted impressions. He also departs from psychoanalytic colleagues who hold fantasy to be a substitute reality. Fantasy *is* reality, even creates it by giving instinctual conviction (Santayana's "animal faith") to whatever area of experience we believe is real. By creating reality into the shapes and notions that we actually perceive and by which we apprehend the world, formulate it and deal with it, fantasy is evidence of the negentropic activity of consciousness. Images are the only reality we perceive directly; they are the primary expression of mind and of its energy which we cannot know except through the images it presents. When we perceive a fantasy image we are looking into the mind of instinct, seeing the libido itself ("Fantasy as imaginative activity is identical with the flow of psychic energy"—*CW* 6, §722, cf. §§711, 723ff; *CW* 11, §§769, 889; *CW* 8, §389).

Instinct and Archetype

The primacy of images means that they are in the realm of cognition what instinctual activity is on the conative-affective level. In the realm of mind, instinct is perceived in images. In the realm of behavior, images are enacted in instinct. Behavior is always the enactment of a fantasy, and fantasy is not merely something going on privately in the head but presents itself in our behavioral stances. Psychic and behavioral events are distinct, but indivisible. One is not the sublimation of the other since they are co-existent. To conceive instinct independent of image-patterns is to make it blind, and to conceive images independent of instinct is to deprive them of vitality and necessity. Imagination becomes a sublimated luxury rather than the instrument of survival.

The principle which organizes imagery, the principle which gives psychic reality its specific patterns and habitual forms—universal, typical, regular, conservatively repetitive through centuries—Jung calls the "archetype." These same qualifiers apply to instinct, too. The energy of the archetype is instinctual because the archetype is instinct itself; the archetype is instinct's "pattern of behavior," its "meaning" or, as Jung says too, its "psychic equivalent" (*CW* 8, §§397ff).

Jung's analogy here is taken from animal behavior. He hypothesizes that every inborn release mechanism (or instinct) is both organized in a pattern and implicates a fantasy image that either releases it or represents its goal. Instinct misfires when there are disorders of imagery. Jung (*CW* 6, §765) defines instinct as "an impulse towards certain activities" which is compellingly necessary, inherited, reflex in character, uniform, regular, and unconscious (*CW* 8, §§267, 233ff, 378f). That instincts are so specific and typical points to a principle within them of order, meaning, and purposefulness. These are the archetypes. The psychic life of personality is governed by them.

The idea of the archetype is fruitful for therapy. Because fantasy is never merely a wisp of unreality, because it expresses personality's archaic, emotional and creative aspect and is a person's primary reality, by focus on fantasy we touch what really is at work in the soul. The qualitative transformations in fantasy such as go on in a long dream series or meditative discipline represent transformations of the archetypes that rule personality and thus its basic nature.

Schizophrenia

We also see such transformations in fantasy in the course of schizophrenic degeneration which point to changes in the basic nature of personality. Jung's theory of schizophrenia is based upon the same psycho-physical interaction. Even if we posit that psyche and body are one, our direct knowledge is only of psyche. Our knowledge of body always comes through psychic images. Although these images from all evidence depend on neurochemical systems, whatever we say about or do with these systems again depends on psychic images. We cannot reduce either one to the other. They are interdependent and interacting.

Jung was the first in modern psychiatry to suggest a psychological origin for schizophrenia. As early as 1907 (and as late as 1958) (*CW* 3) he considered schizophrenia to be an autointoxication, a metabolic disturbance owing to a pathogenic complex whose intense affects involve somatic processes. The archetype at the core of the complex would be that psychosomatic factor which induces both the psychological disorders and the somatic "toxin." Therapy of schizophrenia, also pioneered by Jung, focuses mainly upon these archetypal factors.

PERSONALITY IN ITS CONTEXT

Individuality presupposes something beside itself and within itself from which it differs. Individuality does not mean solidarity and so it cannot be considered alone, without its contexts.

Amplification

Jung calls his method for gathering the context *amplification*. The aim is not to reduce psychic data to its simplest element or single meaning, but to approach it from many sides until its meaning becomes stronger and fuller. *Nothing psychic means only one thing*. Ambivalence of value and ambiguity of content is basic to every piece of psychic data, and amplification is designed to show this. Personality is set within cultural, symbolic and historical processes. These impinge through the psyche's images. Personal associations to dream images are never enough because they are limited by the ego's bias and they return every image to the ego through the links of association. The ego personality can never by itself give full due to a dark tunnel or the lion or the image of a lake that appears in a dream. These images have an inexhaustible echo and yet have a highly specific significance.

Moreover, each dream belongs to a series of dreams which in turn is set within personality and its context. Extended, the idea of amplification means that no single consultation can diagnose in depth, nor even provide a competent opinion. It cannot do justice to the complexity of personality. At best one has gained information from only one contender (ego) and drawn conclusions in terms of its partiality.

Anamnesis

The context is gained just as in medical practice through a case history, an *anamnesis*. But an anamnesis does not equal the context, and this for several reasons. The anamnesis is mainly *conscious,* a record of what a person remembers in his ego personality. Depth psychology in general assumes that there is more to the context of a case than the string of chronologically presented memories. The anamnesis is mainly *external,* a record of what happened to one through life—family, education, work, illness. The context, however, includes internal events, as we shall soon explain. The anamnesis is *factual.* At its most simple level a case history begins with date of birth, height in inches and weight in pounds. It attempts to pare away interpretations and get to the factual core. But the context of personality includes shades of feeling, half-remembered and distorted events. These are aspects of one's personal complexity that are far from facts and hard to put into words. Finally, an anamnesis is *historical.* It refers to the past. But the context of personality is conditioned also by what lies ahead in the form of ambitions and anxieties, as well as avoidances in regard to the present.

Jungians also take the following factors into account in amplifying the basic case history.

1. *Ancestral.* "Family" in Jung's psychology includes more than the actual members one now lives with or the family one lived with as a child or as a parent (*CW* 17, §93). "Family" does indeed include these actual persons, but it extends as well to the circumstances of the parent's parents, for one is searching not only for the family history, but also the *family fantasy.* In my analyses I ask about grandparents and even their parents, what they did, what was odd about them, what they hoped for and died of. I ask about their interrelations with one another, the racial stock, religious belief, physical constitution, and economic position. I may ask an analysand to work out a family tree to uncover similarities in repetitive patterns or striking differences between the patient's life and that of the family, to see where he or she fits in with the family fantasy. By means of this investigation we are not looking for inherited psychic factors. Rather we are recreating a genealogy or a mythology of "my own" family. This helps create in an individual a sense of roots, a context within which his personality belongs and to which it has emotional affinities. This investigation of family, the respectful care one gives to every detail of fantasy and scrap of evidence (old photos, souvenirs) revivifies in a modern clinical setting a worldwide practice lost in our culture called ancestor worship.

Psychological Level. This amplification exposes as potential areas of stress any extreme disparities between personality parts. To the psychological level of a person belong: psychological age; quality of self-awareness, humor and insight; capacity for emotion, especially depression; intelligence quotient;

quality and quantity of imagination; the lacunae or holes (where we draw a blank); nature of sensuousness; gifts and accomplishments; area of fear; general culture in the use of language and relationship with symbolic modes, ranging from dreams to art, travel, music, crafts and skills, food and drink; tragic experiences undergone (war, death, disease, betrayal, failure, etc.).

The question here that comes to mind is: is a person living in general above or below his economic class, innate gifts, social milieu, cultural background, psychological age. The answer helps indicate where the shadow problems can be expected. Too far above one's level can point to strongly regressive counter-pulls and manic defenses to maintain the pitch. Too far below can mean that the presenting complaint may be a strong developmental urge in disguise.

Wholeness. Investigation of the person's psychological level makes operational in therapy the richness of personality posited in theory. By calling attention to human complexity through the theory of amplification Jungian therapy is obliged to amplify its attention to the whole warehouse of inventory that constitutes personality and to coax the whole crowd into the encounter, otherwise Jung's idea of wholeness remains an abstraction, a circle, an empty egg, the number four. Personality is revealed not merely by two persons in chairs talking problems. This shrinks personality, and psychology too, into the narrow boredom recorded by countless taped therapy sessions and textbooks. Jung's theory implies that therapy engages as many as possible of the partial personalities. This brings the confusion of life itself into the psychological container of therapy. "Individuation does not shut one out from the world, but gathers the world to oneself" (*CW* 8, §433). The alchemical description for this process was putting a *massa confusa* of active substances into a closed transparent vessel for the sake of soul-making.

Soul. Jungian theory presupposes an independent factor which once was called depth of soul. A personality may have attained a high educational or economic level and yet be a psychological dunce, below himself in culture, insight, sensuousness, emotional capacity, and so on. Depth analysis goes about soul-making through *deepening* psychic events, whether they be feelings, insights, pathological peculiarities, or fantasies. It fills up the holes and deepens the superficialities in a person's psychological level. Depth takes slowness and holding on, living things in as images more than acting them out onto others. It is in terms of disparities and shallownesses in psychological levels that Jung speaks when he fears for "modern man in search of a soul" as one of his books was called.

2. *The Actual.* One way Jung's psychology differed from Freud's was in

terms of past and present, Freud asking about early memories, Jung turning to the "here and now." Whether Jung was right or wrong in his characterization of Freud is less my point here than is his insistence upon the actual situation. Here Jung's thought precedes later schools—Existentialist, Rogerian, Gestalt, Encounter.

Compensation. First, actual means current. The present problem is explored in terms of its present significance: What is the problem interrupting? What does it (not you) want? What and how is it a *compensation?* Here we operate with the principle of *self-regulation*: Personality naturally attempts to balance itself between various opposing complexes. Every presenting complaint belongs to the present situation, fits into its archetypal meaning, and expresses an aspect of it in metaphorical language. All dreams, symptoms, emotional tangles, and failures are also asked the question of *finality*—what is their purpose and intention, what are they pointing towards—in preference to questions about causation.

The current situation has an archetypal significance. So the investigation of context must expand and deepen to the eternal actualities of human life. Amplification brings in the deeper context by turning to myth and religion, philosophy and fiction, art and folklore in order to give full value and psychological understanding to the archetypal significance.

Constellation. Secondly, actual means what works in the soul, psychic reality. Because what is actual to the soul is not always the same as what is literally actual, the focus of the context can be reduced immediately to what is psychologically pertinent. Much can be set aside—psychological tests, social workers' reports, previous physicians' opinions—if these are not working actually in the person's psychic reality. If one personality is in psychotherapy, then this therapy is the paramount actuality, for therapy is an archetypal situation designed to constellate (activate in dreams, moods, and life experience) the many complexes of personality. "Actual" in its fullest and most precise sense means the present constellation of specific archetypal images within archetypal situations.

3. *The Collective*. Personality is of course situated in a living concrete person, who gets up each morning in a specific room, leads a specific pattern of life among certain other persons, is surrounded by definite objects, and receives the input of subliminal information from social, political, and economic "forces," and so to sleep, and dream, where again personality is subject to immersion in a second collective with its specific scenes, friends and enemies, input and information. In both realms a personality acts and is acted upon. This interaction between the individual and the collective is a theme running through Jung's entire description.

On the plain naïve level of experience, there is an opposition between individual and collective: I can't be myself when doing crowd things, and the crowd can't function with a unified purpose if it must take into account each individual's style and needs. The philosophical antinomy between individual and universal (*CW* 16, §§1-5) is itself an archetypal situation that enacts in each person's life.

When Jung's idea is examined more carefully we find:

(a) Not all that is collective is actual. The psyche is highly selective as to what moves it. Only a small area of "the collective" impinges actually and is therefore psychically real. We shall return to this shortly.

(b) The collective is also the common, what we all hold in common and what holds us universally together as human beings. The hypothesis of the *collective unconscious* means for therapy that *all people can communicate on this commonly human level,* both today, and with the peoples of the past, in the language of emotion, fantasy, dream, and archetypal imagery and situation, despite individual differences of age, sex, sanity, culture. Similarly, the hypothesis of *collective consciousness* establishes community through roles (persona). We can understand our fellow citizen also in terms of his and her collective activity (postman, salesgirl, patient, nurse, etc.). These are also contexts in which personality is situated and by which it is made more understandable.

(c) The collective is neither only inside or outside, nor only subjective or objective. It is both. I am collectivized as much by the role of my outer job as by the mood of my anima complex. The moods and opinions of the lover, the salesman, the messianic hero or the therapeutic guru show little individual differences. All trippers, whether on a public bus tour or private drug session, bring back similar collective reports. Inwardness and outwardness can both be collective, and Jung shows in several papers (on flying saucers, on the Germany of Hitler) (*CW* 10) that the two collectives reflect each other. The *Zeitgeist* (spirit of the times) affects both inner and outer through archetypal images and emotions.

Therefore, to know individual personality means to know where it varies from its collective context. Deviations thus become cues to essence of individuality. This is also what it means in Jung's view *to be* an individualized personality: to be called into differentness. But this personality, ideally, will not have to deny collectivity, for it will have found a differentiated style of performing the roles. Adaptation in the Jungian view means not effacing individuality, but rather an innovative collectivity. Living a collective vocation in an individual manner is precisely the way in which the archetypal pattern that is one's myth can be fulfilled.

Mythology. To complete the collective context, personality is amplified by mythological parallels. Myths give another dimension to the present plight. For Jung, myths describe the behavior of the archetypes; they are dramatic descriptions in personified language of psychic processes. As universal presentations of psychological dilemmas, *myths are the basics of archetypal psychology.* Besides their drama, myths are dynamic, effectively moving personality out of its fixation on itself, its problems in isolation, and the desperate "hows" of immediate solutions. Besides giving a generally human background to one's particular mess, we discover that the archetypes in a myth are the selective factors which arrange the particular pattern in which one finds oneself. So to understand one's mess, one seeks the mythical pattern, for its mythical personalities (the archetypal figures) and their behavior give the clues to what is happening in our behavior. The ultimate context of personality are the myths which the personality is enacting.

STRUCTURE OF PERSONALITY

Descriptive Method

Jung's presentation of the structure of personality is radically original in one respect. His model is in terms of personality itself, that is, he describes the structure of the individual person as a composite of partial personalities. He thereby avoids the difficulties of transposing to human experiences biological, metaphysical, or mechanical models.

For Jung there is nothing more "basic" than the psyche itself. It is the only thing we experience directly and know immediately. All other fields are abstractions derived from psychic experiences. The concepts from other fields which some psychologies use to account for the structure of personality and its processes are secondary inventions. They are abstractions from primal images in the psyche at its pre-conceptual level.

Besides, models that rely upon analogies from other fields also tend to insinuate, for instance, a biological, or physical, or moral point of view towards psychological processes. If I conceive the parts of my personality as so many mathematical forces or instinctual drives or independent factors, I will understand myself accordingly, devising means of treatment for personality disturbances that will rely on the same sort of thinking. I will be abstract and mathematical, or like an animal trainer, or a preacher, or a census-taker of personality inventory.

By grasping the processes of any personality as the interaction and relation between different partial personalities, there is at once set up *through theory itself* a wholly psychological field, an interior community. There are relationships. There are contrasts and conflicts—not between traits or drives or forces or brain regions, but between individual persons, each as worthy of respect, each as complex and difficult to understand, each as influential in the body politic of the whole psyche as I (the ego personality). Jung's theories definitely do not present an ego-psychology, since the ego, too, is, and must always remain, but a partial personality by definition.

Opposites. These interior relationships call for psychological understanding within the community of each of our personalities: between masculine and feminine members, between superior developed parts and those that have been neglected and repressed, between healthy and sick, moralists and criminals, young new enthusiasms and old fears, high spiritual aims and savage physical impulses. These problems between all these parts Jung conceives as the struggle of opposites. But "the opposites" is merely a way of putting the tumultuous contention of persons that compose each individual human being.

Dream and Drama. Jung puts the same interior contention also in terms of drama. His theory of the dream states that it has a dramatic structure from opening scene, characters, plot, crisis, to resolution. Since he regards the dream as psychic reality laid bare, or the self-portrayal of the complexes, the psyche's structure is therefore a dramatic one. If psychic structure is fundamentally a dramatic process, then a person's whole life history is a story and personality cannot be grasped in any more accurate way than in narrational form. From this perspective, personality is a theater of archetypal figures, some downfront and center, others waiting in the wings, and the contests show heroic, commercial, comic, tragic, and farcical themes.

How the ego personality relates *internally* with the others, whose side it takes and whom it opposes, will also show in one's relations with the social environment. If I am repressively domineering toward my interior weaknesses, I will tend to be the same way to others, not listening to the needs of my associates and patients any more than my egoism is able to listen to my internal needs. If I play favorites, preferring inner companions that seduce and charm and flatter the ego, then chances are that I will drift into that same sort of milieu in the world at large, avoiding criticism and confrontation. In Jung's theory, the roles we play with each other are given by the partial personalities. *Interpersonal relations are based on intrapersonal relations.*

Personified Multiple Personalities

The *personified* (Hillman 1974) way of regarding personality structure is valuable for therapy, or, better said, it is already therapeutic in its effect.

"Drives," "processes," and "factors" remain abstract. They lend themselves to intellectual rationalizations and to defenses against direct experience. But with personifications I can communicate directly. In Jungian therapy the technique, "active imagination," does precisely that. It is an encounter between parts of the personality; it is a battle, a dialogue, a symposium, a drama, among the complexes.

However, before we move into the detailed account of personality structure, there are several theoretical consequences of a general nature to be considered. Of these, most important is Jung's idea that every *personality is essentially multiple* (CW 8, §§365f., 388f.). Multiple personality is human nature. Therefore, every personality is potentially dissociable into the partial personalities which compose it. This is both a regressive threat and progressive differentiation. Individuality (which in Jung's mind means undivided) is the counterpole of natural dissociability. Individual personality means a contained diversity, a differentiated unity that is neither single nor simple. Wholeness of personality means a highly complex tension of parts. Multiple, dissociable personality remains a lifelong tenet of Jung's theory. We see it in his early work on schizophrenia, his interest in parapsychology, in hallucinatory visions, and dissociation, as well as in his autobiographical account of himself in terms of personality number one and personality number two (MDR, pp. 45, 68).

Although the idea of partial personalities is a hypothetical construct and no less a metaphor than other such explanatory constructs as drive, factor, need, etc., the actual partial personalities are given directly to consciousness and are not only inferred. We meet these persons in our dreams and hear them as inner voices. We experience them in our peculiar reactions to which friends say "that isn't like you at all," in moments when we see ourselves looking exactly like mother or father, when we are out of ourselves or beside ourselves with rage, when we say what we do not intend to say, or cross ourselves up in any of a hundred ways. For Jung these partial personalities are also the foundation for the worldwide belief in spirits and demons (CW 8, §§570 ff.).

Archetypal Figures

Jung insists that his constructs be formulated in experiential terms and so he names the partial personalities in accordance with their imagery. His method is both that of phenomenology, sticking close to things as they present themselves, and that of naïve realism, taking psychic events at face value as fully real. He holds that primitive descriptions (personifying and demonizing) are the most empirically accurate way of talking about psychic facts. It is in the personifications of sweetly seductive nymphs that we experience what we learn to call "sexual desire" and in the shape of shaggy night demons that we meet what the textbook labels "anxiety."

The partial personalities are collected under the names shadow, persona, ego (hero), anima, animus, puer (eternal youth), senex (old wise man), trickster, great mother, significant animal, healer, divine child, self. On the one hand, these are the names of archetypes, that is, typical figures in myth, art, literature, and religion the world over. On the other hand, they are the typical figures in dreams, family roles, personal emotions, and pathologies patterning our behavior. They can be found wherever the human imagination elaborates its products, from religious dogma to delusional beliefs, from the sublimest art to a hallucinatory psychosis. These figures are the stances which each personality can assume when one or another of them dominates, and these are the viewpoints that rule our ideas and feelings about the world and ourselves. Of course all of them and their variations do not appear at once, so it is not a matter of memorizing the cast of a variety show in order to know the psychology of personality. But in Jung's view it is a matter of recognizing that personality is archetypally conditioned, or that personality is a dialectical scene where during a lifetime many imaginal characters play their part, have intercourse, and argue it out. [It is beyond our scope here to do anything more than sketch how the partial personalities generally work.] More detailed studies examine most of these figures, their phenomenology and pathology. Some of these recent studies, besides Jung's own, are Neumann 1955, *great mother;* Guggenbühl 1971, *shadow;* E. Jung 1957, Adler 1961, de Castillejo 1973, *animus;* E. Jung 1957, Hillman 1973, *anima;* v. Franz 1970, *puer;* Hillman 1970, Vitale 1973, *senex.* This by no means complete list offers a serviceable introduction to the archetypal figures and their effects on behavior.

Let us take the shadow as an example. It is the image of all sides of personality that I could become. In my dreams he may be a brother, a schoolfriend I feared or envied, an outcast or a success, or a professional colleague whose traits are those I most dislike—but which are closest to mine. Because of my identification with my ego personality, the shadow usually appears as inferior and as rejected by society. The development of one partial personality, the ego, builds a shadow at the same time. Ego development in our culture proceeds through choices between good and bad, right and wrong, like and dislike. The bad, the wrong, and the disliked then fall into the shadow, becoming fearful. Soon the suppressed side becomes the repressed side; the shadow archetype which is a potential of destructive values, an "instinct to evil" or "destrudo," is activated by the cast-off impulses of daily life. The more right I become, the more the shadow is fed with contrary motives until the extremes of a Dr. Jekyll and Mr. Hyde can result. Because the shadow is an archetypal figure, and not merely a cover-name for the repressed, it is a living personality with intentions, feelings, and ideas.

By keeping innocent and self-righteous in ego-consciousness, the shadow is forced into the dark, where he archetypally belongs anyway as the devil is depicted in hell and the criminal fantasied in the night. So, in dreams, he will show in ghettos, as a welfare case, an invalid, crippled or diseased. He appears also in the images of power politician, fake guru, street gang, or person of darker skin. It is easy to see how problems of society can be referred straight back to individual partial personalities.

The shadow also determines the ulterior motives in plans, the schemes for professional advancement, the nasty gossip, the sellouts, all beyond and in spite of our honest intentions. Although I have described him mainly in terms of ethics, the shadow can as well carry any incompatible aspect—one's unlived sexuality or primitivity and one's unlived potential achievements and cultural sensitivity. Especially, the shadow presents images of one's pathology: sadism, hypochondriacal complaining, or any of the various psychotic syndromes that reflect in caricature one's overall personality structure.

Therapeutic work cannot avoid meeting the shadow. An aim of Jungian therapy is a mutual accommodation of the two brothers, ego and shadow, and a relativization of their previous antagonistic attitudes, lightening the dark and darkening the light. However, the shadow is never wholly overcome any more than we ever achieve all that is potential in us or ever have done with the destructive and malevolent aspects of human nature. The shadow is particularly relevant for understanding the difficulties that can occur between doctor and patient. They can mutually project shadow on each other, so that one remains perpetually strong, healthy, and knowing, the other weak, self-destructive, and inferior (Guggenbühl 1971).

Archetypal Situations

Just as significant as archetypal figures are archetypal situations. Although not strictly a part of personality structure, they are basic for understanding behavior. By recognizing which archetypal situations a person is actually living, we are better able to understand what he or she is undergoing. As an example we might consider *initiation*. Many cultures have initiation rituals to help the individual pass from one stage of life to another. According to Jungian theory (Henderson 1967), a person without the psychological equivalent of initiation may well be at a loss when confronted with a transition for which he is not psychologically prepared. At such moments a massive regression can take place in which the entire personality seems to recoil from a critical task (examination, military service, marriage, parturition, menopause and mid-life, death of a beloved, one's own death). There can be an acute psychotic episode. When we look at the fantasies, fears, behavior, and dreams during this crisis they may show the person to be going through a psychological initiation, giving to the peculiar behavior a ritual import—the magnified fears of the physician, the fantasies of torture, the sense of isolation, the images of birth or transformation to a new condition, and the hallucinatory voices giving instruction, all may be appropriate to the archetypal situation of initiation. By confirming the events as archetypally significant, the person in close touch with the case may aid, not only in deterring senseless disintegration or suicide, but also in making the episode psychologically significant.

Another archetypal situation is the *temenos* (Greek for sacred precinct) or enclosed area in which overwhelming problems can be placed, a center of order can be experienced, or the personality itself be protected while vital changes are going on. Jung has illustrated the temenos with geometrical illustrations, mainly from Oriental *mandalas*. Their spontaneous appearance in extreme disintegrative stress and their relevance for understanding counterphobic rituals are only two aspects of their importance.

In the *descent*, another archetypal situation, there is often a depressive darkening or a confused clouding of consciousness, even a loss of orientation, for the sake of experiencing hitherto unknown aspects of personality. *Sacrifice* often helps clarify bizarre mutilations or feelings of radical deprivation. *Abandonment* is familiar clinically in emotions of separation, loneliness, and helplessness, which, as shown by the myths of Hercules, Moses, Jesus, etc., refer to a necessary precondition for the emergence of a new kind of strength which belongs archetypally to the same pattern.

Archetypal Substances and Processes

Alchemy. Many discussions of Jung find his alchemical writings an embarrassment. But to present him without this part of his theory would be a gross distortion. Jung devoted the last thirty years of his research to this subject, published perhaps a quarter of his printed pages on alchemical texts and themes, and said in his autobiography that it was alchemy which provided the true background to his psychology (*MDR*, pp. 205, 212, 221). Alchemy is thus not merely of scholarly interest and a separate field of research, nor is it Jung's quirk or private passion. It is in fact fundamental to his conception of personality structure. Jung saw alchemy as a prescientific psychology of personality disguised in metaphors. He understood four basic substances of alchemy (lead, salt, sulphur, mercury) to be archetypal components of the psyche. Individuation, or the full realization of personality, requires a long series of operations upon its basic stuff, expressed metaphorically by these substances. Personality is a specific combination of solid depressive lead with inflammable aggressive sulphur with bitterly wise salt with volatile evasive mercury. The alteration and integration of these experiences form phases in the combination of the two principal oppositions: gold and silver, sun and moon, king and queen, active consciousness and reflective unconsciousness. The alchemical formulations correspond with the archetypal figures mentioned above (anima, animus, senex, etc.) filling out with pathological detail and subtle psychological understanding those more general personifications.

The processes that go on in personality are also archetypally depicted in alchemy as a series of operations. The names of many of these have found their way into clinical psychology. Projection, dissolution, sublimation, fixation, and condensation were all alchemical terms. The two main processes—solution and coagulation—are another way of putting the main work of psychotherapy: taking apart and putting together, analyzing and synthesizing. Thus the methods which modern analysis believes it has invented for furthering personality development were already known to alchemy as descriptions of the autonomous movements of psychic processes. The goal of the alchemical work—and in Jung's mind goals are but signposts, to be valued for their impetus as ideals not meant to be attained literally (*CW* 17, §291)—is a series of unions of the various contending psychic substances. These unions he calls the "integration of personality" and the work, "individuation of the personality."

Types (A)—Introversion and Extraversion

Beyond the structures of personality is the overall characteristic tendency of its energy. Is its basic dynamic orientation outward, flowing towards its world and the things, people, and values in its surroundings? Or is its primary movement inward towards its subjectivity, the claims of its internal nature, images, and values? This distinction between the objective and subjective orientation of personality, between introversion and extraversion, is one of Jung's major contributions to psychological theory. It was soon employed by Hermann Rorschach, whose widely influential work began primarily as a further investigation through projective methods of the introvert-extravert polarity (Klopfer 1972), and it was developed in many publications by H. J. Eysenck, both theoretically and experimentally.

As so often happens with successful ideas (evolution, entropy, relativity), they become popularized. Thereby they lose much of their original precision and subtlety. It is now all too easy to characterize introverts as withdrawn and schizoid, extraverts as manic and superficial. We facilely believe introverts are maladapted and extraverts overadapted. This opinionated way of regarding the attitudes of personality itself derives from the prejudices of the observer and one's own typical attitude. Therefore, activity or object-dependency as keys to extraversion, or antisocial hostility and desire for power as keys to introversion may be quite deceptive. The introverted attitude requires a good deal of involvement with the world in order to draw stimulation for its subjectivity. And the extraverted personality may strongly turn against its environment, be shy at large social events, or be innovative in regard to ideas and systems. This behavior, though seemingly introverted, actually reflects an orientation toward the object and accurate appreciation of it. ("Toward" the world or "against" the world are movement in the same dimension; they are still in terms of the world, and therefore both reflect the predominance of extraversion.)

Because introversion and extraversion are energetic phenomena, it is best to think of them as "facts of nature," given with existence like right and left, expansion and contraction, morning and evening, each having its necessity.

Introversion and extraversion are concepts of practical value for diagnosis, treatment, and clinical prediction. Therapeutic measures always need to be relativized according to the attitude type of the patient—one man's meat is another man's poison. Sometimes Jung prescribes compensation through the opposite attitude, while at other times Jung hints that the treatment of choice is "more of the same." The preferred therapy of extreme introverted conditions, for instance, is less a forced extraversion to compensate than it is a thoroughgoing investigation of and empathy with the subjectivity of the patient through understanding the fantasies. The attitude types are also valuable conceptual tools for understanding people in all sorts of situations: work with colleagues, life with family, choice of scientific method and projects, leisure-time preferences. Even politics and religion come under the influence of the introverted-extraverted bias.

Types (B)—Functions

Besides these two fundamental attitudes describing energy movement there are also four functions: *thinking, feeling, sensation,* and *intuition.* These functions are theoretical constructs derived from the terminology of traditional psychology. Ever since Kant (1724-1804) and the modern psychology of the Enlightenment, functions (usually called faculties) of the human mind have been described by academic psychologists. Jung's work on types (1921; *CW* 6) offers the hypothesis that each personality functions preferentially, structurally and typically by means of one or another of these faculties. We are not merely typically extraverts or introverts; we are also typically introverted thinkers or feelers, say, or extraverted intuitive types. The four functions are *modes of consciousness,* whereas the attitudes or introversion and extraversion refer to the basic *energies of the person.* The four functions describe the way in which consciousness shapes experience. The function of sensation, for instance, tends to work mainly through perception, either inwardly of images and proprioceptions of the body, or extravertedly in accurate observation and esthetic sense. So, with thinking, feeling and intuition—each presents a typical modality, and a typical pathology, of consciousness.

In recent years a spate of publications (Marshall 1968; Shapiro 1972; v. Franz and Hillman 1971; Mann *et al.* 1972; Plaut 1972) express the recurrent interest, both clinical and experimental, in this aspect of Jungian personality theory. However, within Jung's work as a whole, the typology is only one of the twenty large books constituting his collected works and *typology remains but an introductory approach* to the complexities of personality. Typology is elementary, both in the sense of fundament and also in the sense of preliminary, merely a primary step into the nature of individual differences and into the theories of Jung.

Complexes

Association Experiment. Jung's most important theoretical construct is that of the complex. The term is his, and was first used by him and his co-workers at Burghölzli, the psychiatric clinic of Zurich University, to account for interferences in verbal associations in an experimental situation. A list of a hundred words—verbs, nouns, adjectives—is read, one by one, to a subject(S) who is asked to reply as quickly as possible with the first word (and only one word) that comes to mind. After recording the one hundred associations to test-words and the reaction time (in fifths of seconds) to each, the experimenter again goes down the list of the stimulus words, asking S

to repeat what was said the first time. Deviations between the first association and recall are also recorded. Patterns of disturbance are then examined
in the protocols, as, for example, prolonged reaction times, perseveration of
the same verbal reaction, forgetting of the original reaction the second-
time through, peculiar or bizarre associations, rhyming, or affective reactions, etc. (cf. *CW* 2; Hull and Lugoff 1921; Rapaport *et al.* 1946; Cramer
1968).

Jung hypothesized that disturbances in association reflect an unconscious
group of ideas, images, and memories, intertwined in an individual way,
permeated by a single feeling tone (longing, anxiety, anger, painfulness, etc.),
and charged with strong emotion. This he called the complex. Despite the
best intentions of the ego personality to pay attention and follow instructions, there were interferences. This experimental work that went on during
the first decade of the present century brought him into contact with
Freud. At that time experimental and clinical psychology and psychiatry
all worked closely together in fraternal felicity.

Jung's work gave Freud's theory of repression a second leg to stand on.
The first leg is anecdotally empirical, a collection of psychopathologies from
everyday life—slips of the tongue, parapraxes, forgetting, absent-mindedness.
But the second leg, disturbances of attention, can be shown experimentally.
The theory of repression was now on an empirical footing, and as well, the
wider conclusions drawn from it—a second system of mental functioning,
or the unconscious psyche. In this way Freud and Jung support each other.
Freud's idea of the unconscious used Jung's complex for its empirical grounding. Jung's idea of the complex used Freud's theory of repression and of
the unconscious for its theoretical account.

In all of the work of that period, especially in regard to psychopathology
(theory of schizophrenia), criminology (lie-detector test), and psychosomatics (psychogalvanic phenomena, or changes in the resistance of skin-
conductivity when complexes are struck), there is one paper particularly
relevant for personality theory (*CW* 2, §§793ff). There Jung shows the
connection between the content of the disturbance that appears in the
association experiment, the hysterical symptom, and the dream. All three
can be accounted for through the hypothesis of the complex. One and the
same complex disturbs the association, is the underlying meaning of the
symptom (as a bodily conversion of an emotionally charged bundle of
ideas and images), and appears as a personified figure in dreams. Jung's
vision of personality as a multiplicity of interacting partial personalities,
"splinter psyches" (*CW* 8, §203) or "little people" (*ibid.*, §209), can of

course be traced to his association experiments and the hypotheses of complexes, which for him are the basic realities, elements, nuclei of psychic life.

Experienced *figuratively*, the complex is a personality with feelings, motivations, and memories. Experienced *somatically*, the complex is a change in heart-rate, skin-color, sphincter control, genital tumescence, breathing, sweating, etc. Experienced *energetically*, the complex is a dynamic core, accumulating ever new particles to it, like a magnet, or coalescing with other atomic units, like a molecule. It produces tension, compulsions, charged situations, transformations, attractions, repulsions. Experienced *pathologically*, the complex is a psychic cancer growing autonomously, or an overvalued idea that first becomes delusional and then a paranoid delusional system, integrating to its core all dissuasive arguments.

Complex and Archetype

Analysis of any complex shows it composed of personal associations from personal experiences. But Jung recognized that the energy it could mobilize, the autonomy of its behavior, and the archaic, universal character of its imagery, could not be accounted for altogether through personal experiences. He thus hypothesized that the core of the complex is archetypal and that the personal material is clustered around and organized by an archetypal image and charged with instinctual energy at the somatic level. For example, my mother complex is built on my experiences with my mother and my associations to her world. But the patterning of those experiences and the immense emotional charge this pattern contains, refers to the archetypal great mother imago and to the instinctual desires, taboos, and magic involved in the mother-son relationship, together with the rich collective fantasies and roles to do with nature, nurturing, growth, protection, preventing, encompassing, smothering, etc. Therapy can disentangle much of the mother complex at the personal level, freeing the personality from projections of archetypal significance upon the ordinary citizen who is our actual mother. But the archetypal foundation of the mother complex and all its faces remains as long as life, belonging to all humankind.

PERSONALITY IN THERAPY

All along I have been pointing out the operational meanings of Jung's concepts. To draw these meanings together into short statements will be the focus of this conclusion.

1. Since fantasy-images are the fundament of consciousness, we seek for them in therapy. Fantasies may not appear as such. Patients often "have

no fantasies." The fantasy is then disguised in plans, in reports about themselves, in snatches of popular culture that especially fascinate them, in personal hatreds and desires. The therapist listens to this material metaphorically, imaginatively, trying to "hear through" to the fantasy, rather than to the literal content. This can be called *deliteralizing*.

2. Since individuation is defined as "a process of differentiation" (*CW* 6, §757), analysis attempts to separate and to distinguish between the parts of personality. We ask the parts to identify themselves. This both relieves identifications with complexes and aids in establishing intrapersonal connectedness, thus consolidating one's personal identity. We distinguish the parts of personality by asking each feeling, opinion, reaction to which complex it belongs. "Who is speaking now? Mother, Hero, Old Senex?" We attempt to develop individual self-knowledge through knowledge of the different collectivities that speak through the ego. Only as these are made distinct and identified is one able to discover who one is. This is *differentiating*.

3. Differentiating means also being different, just as individuality means being unique, and thus peculiar. So, we focus on the odd. The eccentric, that which does not fit in, occurs most evidently in psychopathological abnormalities. We see these rather as seeds of individuality than as faults to be rid of. We keep in relation with symptoms but do not focus upon them. We attempt to reconnect the various supposedly balanced or cured parts of personality with their odd aspects so as not to lose touch with (suppress) them. By keeping aware of psychopathology, which means the abnormal aspect of all so-called normalities, we hope to avoid pseudo-cures based on "therapeutic repressions." This is *pathologizing* (Hillman 1973).

4. Because the highest value in personality is expressed in Jung by the term *self* which is defined as partly transcendental and impersonal, we aim to move personality away from too personal relatedness, whether in transference or in relationships in general. Therapy works at developing relationship to impersonal affairs and at experiencing the *impersonal* aspect of relationships. We assume that the relationships in our contemporary humanistic culture are not humanly underdeveloped as much as overloaded with archetypal demands. What people expect of mothers and fathers, teachers and friends and lovers is far beyond the ability of personal human beings; people ask that archetypal qualities be present in each other which in other cultures are present only in Gods and Goddesses.

The movement towards impersonalizing relationships and relating to the impersonal is aided by the therapist in various ways: through selective attention, through interpretations, through the style of the therapeutic relationship which attempts to be both personal and impersonal, and through interest in dreams. We prefer not to translate the dream into psychodynamic explanations or concepts (even Jung's own terms—"anima," "shadow"—become misused as concepts). Instead, we reply to the dream in a similar language, even by telling a dream in return. We move away from the personal by moving towards the story-telling and the mythological, through talking imaginative, personified speech, through allusions to fictions of all sorts (films, fairytales, theater). By concentrating upon the images of the dream rather than their translation we hope to revitalize the imagination of the patient. This is *remythologizing*.

5. Since images and instinct are conceived as two aspects of one and the same archetypal structure (and not as a sublimation of the "lower" by the "higher"), emphasis in therapy upon fantasy images is also an emphasis upon instinct. Through active imagination instinctual disturbances are amenable to change: only symbols are as potent as symptoms. A direct approach through behavioral and body therapies is eschewed in favor of the psychological engagement with images, so that instinctual vitality and sophisticated psychic differentiation proceed hand in hand. This leads to a more immediate and passionate adaptation which is at the same time more culturally imaginative, whether achieved by means of music, painting or writing, or work on dreams, or opening the imaginative eye in daily life. This can be called *vitalizing*.

6. Jung's general theory of neurosis is simply "onesidedness." (He refused a specific theory of the neuroses other than occasional insights drawn from typology, complexes, and archetypal patterns.) Therapy of all neuroses of whatever sort aims at extending consciousness beyond the dominant onesidedness—usually of the ego—to the other partial personalities. The patient learns methods for carrying on the psychologizing process after therapy has ended. The patient does this either through intrapersonal dialogues between the parts of himself, or by reflection on dream images, carrying them around in the day, keeping them alive. Especially the changeless parts and unwelcome images that one is likely to repress are kept near. This continual work upon one's psychic ground, this familiarity with one's multiple personalities, gives increasing containment, inner space and depth to personality. It gives a sharper definition, unifying the looseness and loosening the onesided unity. This can be called *consolidating*.

APPLICATION OF THEORY

When I met Mrs. Carson she had already been with two other analysts, both elderly women, colleagues of mine. She had lasted with each about two months. She picked me as her third and "last chance in Zurich" because my fees were low and because I reminded her of her grandson from whom came no threat (I was 34 to her 69). I did not consult with her former analysts except to gain their "no objections."

Six months in Zurich had only exacerbated all her conditions. It seemed to me that this *pathologizing* was an improvement, for what had been half-recognized now stood out boldly and had brought her to grips with her actual psychic condition, so she felt worse. She was usually emotionally excited (suggestible, argumentative, impulsive, labile); she formed delusional ideas of paranoid self-reference (people schemed against her behind her back); she suffered from arthritis, teeth and eye troubles, high blood pressure, and social rejection. She lived at welfare level, having been divorced for years. Her fairly successful older and younger sisters were enemies and her children did not want Mrs. Carson in their homes. She had few letters from them and never any money. Her new acquaintances in Zurich kept their distance. Her extra savings were gone and she could find no physician here who would treat her ailments as she wanted. Her analyses had not worked. The Jung Institute had not met her expectations—expectations to be "saved." She had read Jung's books and had come "all the way to his city at great sacrifice to be redeemed through his teachings."

Mrs. Carson's case illustrates three points: 1) Deep analysis in the classical sense is possible in old age. 2) The *personal* relationship between analyst and analysand is not the crux of psychic change. 3) Change in outer reality depends primarily on internal changes.

Anamnesis

Her father had emigrated from Britain to the United States and followed a riotous up-and-down business career connected with the expansion of the West from the Civil War through the nineties. He was brilliant, inventive, harsh, and stupid. The stock was mixed Welsh, Irish and West Country English, Catholic and Protestant, both solid and passionate, healthy and unstable, imaginative, quick-witted, bossily egocentric and also given to morose silences. Father had disliked her from the beginning; she was a girl, small, awkward and dumb. His feelings shot back and forth between sentimental tenderness and sadistic punishments. Her parents' marriage had been for business reasons. The mother died when Mrs. Carson was in her late teens and the father and all three sisters idolized this weak suffering saint, whose goodness had no room for shadow and whose blessing actually cursed all subsequent feminine relations. Mother, as a death-bed command, had urged her daughter to marry quickly a professional man who was then courting, so as to be free of house and father. She did and the marriage was a repetition of her home, except that Mrs. Carson, unlike her saintly mother, survived—four children in quick succession, her husband fifteen years her senior, also a tyrant but without father's gifts, narrow in mind and mean in heart. They fought; her spirit broke. She resolved in silence to leave him one day, began to read, study, join classes in her spare time. This history is of course not "objective reality," the "facts" of which we can never know. But it is *psychic reality* and must be read as the fiction of her life, the myth of her personal development, how and why she fantasied that she became as she is.

She moved to Chicago with her three children (one had died), fell in love for the first time, continued a liaison, was dropped. She developed her first hysterical symptoms (loss of vision, spontaneous micturition) and underwent treatment. This was modern, psychologically advanced, and led her into remedial education as a field of work. Divorce ended the relationship but not the hatred for her husband.

In alchemical language, there was a preponderance of salt (bitterness) and sulphur (highly charged actings-out): sudden erotic connections, power-egoistic maneuvers to capitalize on her projects, cravings for food, vivid projections which so charged her mind that during the night they could become delusional systems of plans which others were stealing. Psychic reality and concrete reality were embroiled in a *massa confusa*. Her psychological level was excellent: an emotionally deep personality with tragic experiences, humor, fantasy, culture, and a rich pathologizing strain that kept her tangled in her complexes.

Analysis

She mounted the stairs to my third floor office, resentful over the climb. She wore a hat and bright clothes. She had a dumpy body, good facial features and large clear eyes. She had lots to say, mainly about previous failed analyses, and what was wrong everywhere. Then she told her dream (of two days previous): it was simply an image of a barren tree made only of fingernails. In telling it, she stretched out her fingers and clawed the air. To her, it was the image of her cold and bleak existence. To me, it was a meeting with the aggressive, clutching, taloned Mother. She accused me of "freezing her out"—and I did. But were that all, nothing would have happened, for within the cold distance that often constellated between us there was an archetypal pattern. Once she dreamed of my image as a

with new emotional reactions. The longdrawn experience with pain and suffering through the last six months had actually resulted in a new vital connection among the personified parts of the psyche which was at the same time "rain."

Now many things came together. She felt she was no longer little Annie but an adolescent girl. Our personal battles subsided and she wrote me a list of things she liked about me. She dreamed of a bouquet of old-fashioned flowers, and of a black psychological counselor. She found a place of retreat inside herself. Then came this dream: "My father is sitting in an armchair. The mood is different from anything ever previous. There is a homey, comfortable atmosphere in the room. Is it a library or living-room? My father wears a maroon smoking-jacket, and he is placidly smoking a pipe and carrying on pleasant conversations. He seems a man of education and culture who would be pleasant to know, not a man to be afraid of."

With this almost too-good movement within the father complex, there next came a new and most difficult phase.

Mother and Daughter

Mrs. Carson dreamed: "In bed with Binzie (her daughter) about six years old. The child calls, 'Mom.' I was sleepy and didn't want to wake up. I wanted to sleep and not be bothered and I felt guilty and I didn't answer."

Motherhood and guilt were so tied in one complex that to be free of guilt she had to refuse the call of the child. Facing this meant waking up to the archetypally shadow side of mothering. It meant "being-a-bad-mother," which her saintly mother image had made impossible, and thus had made her unconsciously live out. It also meant facing the idea that "remedial education" (which, by the way, she had internalized and practiced on herself with "little Annie") had it roots partly in the guilt over bad-mothering. She was unable to distinguish between the guilt to her actual children of the past and the internal younger personality, the daughter now calling.

The mother-daughter myth (Persephone-Demeter-Hecate) was the myth now constellating. This was the central religious and sexual mystery of Greek psychology, an initiation into the archetypal feminine cycle from maidenhood to old witchery and death. As a mystery it had to be "undergone" and not "explained," especially not by reductions to personal life.

Next she dreamed: "Women. All young women, mothers about 25 to 30 years old. All are playing with dolls, very seriously like little girls do." I took this dream too as a put-down, considering her attitude towards her children to have been one which treated them like dolls imbued only with the life of mother's wishful projecting psyche.

She left on "holiday" and did not come back when expected. A month passed since the last hour. She called to say she was ill again. She had refused my remark that she was partly responsible for "bewitching her daughter" (Binzie) who treated her so badly. And she had refused my view of the dolls. "You are just like all the other analysts; you don't understand."

I hadn't; she was right. I had interpreted personalistically from my mother-complex countertransference and thus done injustice to the archetypal nature of the process and its images. I had lost touch with the myth. We managed to make one meeting to talk about it again. This time we decided that the dolls were an imaginative way into mother, much as her imagination with little Annie. The circle of women were her young motherhood imagining how to mother, an attempt of the psyche to redeem the past within herself. She had indeed awakened from her sleep.

Ending

The hours during the last two months were scattered, partly she was away, partly I. The regularity and intensity of the first six months was over. She was secretly making plans to go back to America, but held this from me because "You would not let me go." Her desire to stay in Zurich had been put on to me, and split off from her. "Zurich was like a pilgrimage for me, like what old people do in the East." But she did not get what she came for. "Maybe what I got was more important?" "I feel I have been uncursed, but not redeemed."

One part of the personality wanted to leave, and to leave in thanks. Another part was afraid to leave, and yet another could leave only by cutting. The ending of the analysis as much as the beginning's *massa confusa* shows the multiplicity of personality, that a whole is made of many coexisting parts; pathologizing belongs. Unity of opposites means ambivalence. The paranoid fantasies were not gone, nor was the tree of clawing fingernails turned to sweet green leaves. But now, more or less, she was aware of the delusional tendency and the demands and could see through them by herself more readily. She had had practice, too short perhaps, in looking for the fantasy images within the emotional obsessions.

The indecision about return continued. She phoned, asking to see me at once. She came with a large paper sack and wanted all her dreams, all her drawings and letters back. She felt I was now bad for her: I had cooked her too long in the alchemical stove. "Who do you think you are to be so responsible for me!" She would not even sit down. I had the happy insight that this new wave of personal attack was the psyche's attempt to free herself from the transference dependency. And I told her so. She relaxed, and told me a new dream image: She saw Helen Hayes in a grey dress on the center of the stage in the play *Our Town*. Home it was, and the grey lady was still there, but now in the center of the stage.

She came to say goodbye. No hat, little make-up, but not altogether the grey lady: she had adjusted to this internal archetypal figure, but not identified with her. She had one more dream. "A baby about nine months old, in a high chair, about to be fed." She complimented me and even one of her former analysts. She had written to one of her children and apologized for an old score.

Some months later she wrote from Florida. Her children were adding to her monthly income, and one had let her visit for a long while. She mentioned a dream of a child with a mouth full of teeth, and cared for by two other women besides herself.

BIBLIOGRAPHY

JUNG, C. G. *The Collected Works*, Vols. 1-17. Princeton: Princeton Univ. Press, 1954-   . Abbreviated as *CW* with paragraph numbers, unless otherwise indicated.
JUNG, C. G. & JAFFE, A. *Memories, Dreams, Reflections*. New York: Pantheon, 1961. Abbreviated as *MDR*.

*   *   *

ADLER, G. *The Living Symbol*. New York: Pantheon, 1961.
CASEY, E. S. Freud's Theory of Reality: A Critical Account. *Rev. Metaphysics* XXV, 4, 1972, pp. 659-690.
CRAMER, P. *Word Association*. New York: Academic Press, 1968.
DE CASTILLEJO, I. C. *Knowing Woman*. New York: Putnam's, 1973.
GRINNELL, R. Reflections on the Archetype of Consciousness: Personality and Psychological Faith. *Spring 1970*, pp. 14-39.
GUGGENBUHL, A. *Power in the Helping Professions*. New York and Zurich: Spring Publications, 1971.
HENDERSON, J. *Thresholds of Initiation*. Middletown: Wesleyan Univ. Press, 1967.
HILLMAN, J. On Senex Consciousness. *Spring 1970*, pp. 146-165.
HILLMAN, J. *The Myth of Analysis*. Evanston: Northwestern Univ. Press, 1972.
HILLMAN, J. Anima. *Spring 1973*, pp. 97-132.
HILLMAN, J. The Terry Lectures, Yale University, 1972. In press for publication. New York: Harper and Row, 1974.
HULL, C. L. & LUGOFF, L. S. Complex Signs of Diagnostic Free Association. *J. Exper. Psychol.*, 4.
JAFFE, A. *The Myth of Meaning in the Work of C. G. Jung*. Trans. R. F. C. Hull. London: Hodder, 1970.

Jung, Emma. *Animus and Anima.* New York and Zurich: Spring Publications, 1957.

Klopfer, W. G. The Short History of Projective Techniques. *J. Hist. Behav. Sci.,* 9, 1, 1973, pp. 60-64.

Mann, H., Siegler, M., & Osmund, H. Four Types of Personalities and Four Ways of Perceiving Time. *Psychology Today,* 6, 7, 1972, pp. 76-84.

Marshall, I. N. The four functions: a conceptual analysis. *J. Analyt. Psychol.,* 13, 1, 1968, pp. 1-32.

Meyer, J.-E. (Ed.). *Depersonalisation* (fifteen papers by various hands). Darmstadt: Wiss. Buchgesellschaft, 1968.

Neumann, E. *The Origins and History of Consciousness.* New York: Pantheon, 1954.

Neumann, E. *The Great Mother, An Analysis of the Archetype.* New York: Pantheon, 1955.

Perry, J. The Messianic Hero. *J. Analyt. Psychol.,* 17, 2, 1972, pp. 184-198.

Plaut, A. (Ed.) et al. Typology. *J. Analyt. Psychol.,* 17, 1, 1972, pp. 111-151.

Rapaport, D., Gill, M. & Schafer, R. *Diagnostic Psychological Testing,* Vol. 2. Chicago: Yearbook Publ., 1946.

Shapiro, K. J. A Critique of Introversion. *Spring 1972,* pp. 60-73.

von Franz, M.-L. *The Problem of the Puer Aeternus.* New York and Zurich: Spring Publications, 1970.

von Franz, M.-L. & Hillman, J. *Lectures on Jung's Typology.* New York and Zurich: Spring Publications, 1971.

Vitale, A. Saturn: The Transformation of the Father, in *Fathers and Mothers.* New York and Zurich: Spring Publications, 1973.

NOTE: *Spring 197-* refers to *Spring 197-: An Annual of Archetypal Psychology and Jungian Thought.* New York and Zurich: Spring Publications.

Alfred Adler

4

Goal-Oriented Individual Psychology: Alfred Adler's Theory

by HEINZ L. ANSBACHER

When Alfred Adler presented his new theory of personality, psychopathology, and psychotherapy in 1912, at the age of 42, he named it Individual Psychology. This name presented difficulties from the start: it stands also for differential psychology or the psychology of individual differences, and it is easily mistaken for individualistic psychology, whereas it means nearly the opposite.

The Meaning of Individual Psychology

Adler chose the term individual in its original Latin sense of indivisible, thus designating a psychology which regards the person as an indivisible organic unity, a holistic psychology, in contrast to any psychology which presumes that a person can be meaningfully analyzed into parts or elements. But further important meanings can be inferred. When Adler formally introduced the name, Individual Psychology, he described the "individual," quoting from Rudolf Virchow (1958), as "a unified community in which all parts cooperate for a common purpose" (p. 124). This description in connection with "psychology" suggests a socially oriented teleological psychology. Yet the source of the description leads still further. Virchow was the great German 19th-century pathologist who from his youth on was also politically committed, on the liberal side, and became the founder of German public health or social medicine. Beyond this, Virchow, a contemporary of Ernst Brücke, Emil Du Bois-Raymond, and Hermann Helmholtz, was a staunch opponent of their reductionistic physicalism. He wrote in 1855, "It is high time that we give up the scientific prudery of regarding living processes as nothing more than the mechanical resultant of molecular forces inherent in the constitutive particles" (p. 22), and in 1895, "Life cannot be simply reduced to physical and chemical forces" (p. 22).

The principles attacked here by Virchow were those that were later embraced by Freud in his "metapsychology," his philosophy of science, which included strict determinism and a value-free approach as part of science. Yet even in the 19th century a more humanistic, holistic philosophy of science had its representatives, although only a few, such as Virchow. When Adler in introducing the name for his system referred to Virchow he did then in fact indicate that he was continuing the organismic humanistic tradition as opposed to the mechanistic one.

In psychotherapy this meant the abandonment of a causalistic disease model in favor of a teleological, educational one, in which mental symptoms were regarded as erroneous attempts of an active individual to solve problems of living. If children could be trained in a better way of living and problem-solving, mental disorders could be prevented. Thus Adler considered child guidance clinics a need of the first order and took it upon himself to fill this need in his own city of Vienna. In the 1920's he established numerous clinics connected with the public schools, staffed largely by volunter paraprofessionals of his own training. The counseling sessions were conducted as training sessions open to interested persons. There were over 30 such clinics when they were closed in 1934 by the Austrian fascist government which preceded the take-over of the country by Hitler.

To date it is in educational counseling, child guidance, and family education where Adlerian psychology shows particular strength. This has been largely the work of the late Rudolf Dreikurs, 1897-1972, who, building on Adler, specified techniques to an extent that they have become relatively easily teachable. Two of his books (1968; Dreikurs & Soltz 1964) are especially widely used and have been translated into numerous languages. Recently a book for parents by one of his students with a co-worker (Dinkmeyer & McKay 1973) has been well received. In an interview, Dinkmeyer made such clear statements as: "All behavior occurs for a purpose, and this includes what we call 'good behavior' like minding one's parents, as well as 'bad' behavior like lying or stealing. . . . So I urge parents to look beyond the child's behavior and ask themselves why the child is doing it. What does he hope to gain?" (Hansen, 1973).

Biographical Note

Alfred Adler was born in a Vienna suburb, February 7, 1870, the second son of a Jewish merchant who originated from a German-speaking part of Hungary. As a child Adler got along well with the other children in the neighborhood and he always considered himself a real Viennese, which indeed he was, from being able to speak the dialect to singing *Wienerlieder* and songs by Schubert. Adler graduated from the medical school in Vienna in 1895 and after military service established himself as a practitioner in a modest neighborhood.

During his student days he became interested in socialism, that is, the social rather than the economic or political side of it. The first publication by Adler (1898) was a pamphlet on the health of the tailoring trade in which he described the miserable, disease-producing living and working conditions of the independent small tailor, and called for a new social medicine and legislation to control the occupational diseases. In 1902 he published several further articles calling for social medicine "to make good medical care available to the poor" (Ellenberger 1970, pp. 601-602).

It was in 1902 also that Adler, together with three others, was invited by Freud to meet every Wednesday in Freud's house to discuss problems of neurosis. It was this small discussion circle which eventually grew into the Vienna Psychoanalytic Society. Adler became its president in 1910 but resigned from it a year later.

Two years after having joined Freud's small group, Adler (1904) published a paper on "The Physician as Educator," foreshadowing several aspects of his later writings. Adler stated that "confidence in their own strength" (p. 4) is the greatest factor in the intellectual development of children, and that weak and sickly children, as well as pampered children, are in particular danger of losing this self-confidence. An older child is likely to become jealous of a newly born. Parents should use affection to direct a child "toward ethically valuable tendencies" (p. 5). Children's questions about their origin should be answered so as to prepare an understanding of "the unity of organic life" (p. 9). "Under no circumstances may one scare a child. . . . A child's self-confidence, his personal courage, is his greatest fortune. Courageous children will later on not expect their fate to come from the outside, but from their own strength." In this last sentence one can recognize an original hypothesis of the current research on internal versus external control conducted by Rotter and his associates and reviewed by Lefcourt (1966).

In these years there were further papers preparing Adler's later holistic, teleological value theory of human behavior. Adler's (1907) well known *Study of Organ Inferiority* intended in part to show that not only sex but all organic functions have important psychological repercussions. A paper on "The Child's Need for Affection" (Adler 1908) makes a point against a simple, self-centered drive-reduction theory and speaks of "social feelings," showing that the child wants self-transcending contacts rather than being cannibalistic, and that the mother-child relationship is one of mutuality. The next year, Adler (1909) read a paper entitled "On the Psychology of Marxism."

In *Defiance and Obedience* Adler (1910) replaced conflict between two assumed antithetical forces, as in ambivalence, by a new conception, "following the laws of dialectics" (p. 86). Manifestly antithetical behaviors such as defiance and obedience can, he stated, serve the same purpose—to defeat authority. This argument, like the others, was pointed at Freud, who rejected dialectics, believing he was dealing with "real" antithetical forces while in fact working in the dialectical tradition (Rychlak 1968). This was Nietzsche's way of thinking, whom Adler had found "among all great philosophers . . . closest to our way of thinking," while Freud gave the assurance, "He does not know Nietzsche. . . . His ideas have had no influence on his own work" (Nunberg & Federn 1962, I, pp. 359-360; Ansbacher 1972a, p. 14).

Regarding ambivalence Adler (1912) added, "One must not, as is usually the case, see in it a reality of things, but . . . a form of perception which measures a thing, a force, an experience against its pre-arranged antithesis" (p. 51). This anticipated the idea of George A. Kelly (1955) of the "bipolar" way in which man "construes" his world (p. 106).

Particularly noteworthy is a discussion on suicide which Adler had arranged at the Psychoanalytic Society in 1910 (see Ansbacher 1968), the first English translation of which appeared a few years ago, edited by Paul Friedman (1967). Adler proposed a social intention theory of suicide—suicide as wanting to take revenge on someone. "One's own death is desired,

therapy, among the issues listed by Michael Wertheimer (1972), a turn of emphasis from determinism to free will; from objectivity to subjectivity, that is, from facts to the interpretation of the facts; from emphasis on the past to emphasis on the present, including the subjective present which includes the future; and from emphasis on nature to emphasis on nurture, that is, from drives to values; from psychology as a natural science toward psychology as a social science; and methodologically, a change from precision toward richness.

It so happens that Adler had moved consistently in that direction, since he made no pretense of wanting to be a "scientist" as generally understood in his day, but wanted to be a helper of mankind. In this endeavor he took his models from social medicine, philosophy, literature, and education.

Since the present trend is in this direction, one who understands Adler is immediately at home with the various representatives of this trend, some of whom recognize that among the founders of modern psychotherapy Adler came closest to what they are trying to express. Let us give some examples:

Existential and humanistic psychology both include essential characteristics of Individual Psychology (Ansbacher 1971a; Ansbacher, R. R. 1959; Stern 1958; van Dusen 1959). Harold Kelman (1962) concluded that "of existentialism there is least in Freud, somewhat more in Jung and Rank, and the most in Adler and Ferenczi" (p. 120). Viktor Frankl (1970) recognized in Adler "a fore-runner of the existential-psychiatric movement."

Sullivan's system of interpersonal relations parallels Adler's in many respects (Ansbacher, R. R. 1971). Brief psychotherapy, as originated by Franz Alexander, has taken up a large number of Adler's procedural points (Ansbacher 1972b). The trend toward community mental health, including especially the use of paraprofessionals, is completely in line with Adler's early efforts (Guerney 1970).

Albert Ellis (1971) observes: "Every time I reread Alfred Adler, I am amazed at the similarity between the main principles of Individual Psychology and my own theory and practice of Rational-Emotive Psychotherapy" (p. 50). Berne (1972), the originator of Transactional Analysis, noted, "Of all those who preceded it, Alfred Adler comes the closest to talking like a script analyst" (p. 58), and he follows this with a long quotation from Adler. Glasser's Reality Therapy as well has much in common with Individual Psychology, especially as applied in the classroom by Dreikurs (Ansbacher, R. R. 1969).

Behavior modification is also in line with the general trend. It is an outgrowth of behaviorism, with emphasis shifted from the past to the present and from the object to the subject in that one must first study the individual to determine what is a reinforcer to him and what goal he wants to attain. The new book by Krasner and Ullman (1973) represents a further step in this direction, thus including also many statements in line with Adler. Psychology is defined as a "biological *and* social science" (p. 14), not simply as a science, and personality as "a human behavior *in a social context*" (p. viii). Furthermore, "Human beings are not passive, robotlike recipients of influence but are responsible for the consequences of their choices" (p. 490). And since man makes choices, he needs directives of what is the good goal. These directives are the values. "Man is influenced; man influences his environment" (p. 499). This same sentence by Pestalozzi was used by Adler (1964, p. 321) on several occasions.

We may conclude this brief and incomplete survey of current developments in line with Adler's pioneering by pointing out that there are two features of his psychology which are to date still quite unique. These are: (1) a most consistent approach to all human behavior as goal-oriented. The therapist's question is always, "What is the patient trying to accomplish?" rather than, "How did he get that way?"; and (2) the assumption of an innate aptitude for social living and concern, social interest, which when developed also becomes a normative concept.

With these two conceptions, we feel that Individual Psychology has still a good deal to offer to the future of psychology and the advancement of man.

GENERAL PERSONALITY THEORY

Function of the Theory

Today it is widely accepted that a theory is not an absolute, but a human construction for a human purpose. In the words of James Conant (1953), "A scientific theory is not . . . a map; . . . it is a policy—an economical and fruitful guide to action by scientific investigators" (p. 97). With Adler it was to be a guide for therapists, and ultimately for everybody, to improve the quality of living. He constructed his theory quite consciously not for the purpose of establishing any absolute truth about human nature, nor to stimulate research. Adler (1964) believed he had succeeded in this aim in comparison with other theories. He wrote, "There may be more venerable theories of an older academic science. There may be newer more sophisticated theories. But there is certainly none which could bring greater gain to all people" (p. 364n).

Adler (1929b) attempted to found a "science of living," the title of one of his books. In its opening paragraph we find, together with a citation of William James, "In a science which is directly related to life, theory and practice become almost inseparable. The science of life . . . becomes a science of living" (p. 1).

Following this general program, Adler adapted his constructs to what one finds and must deal with in actual life, including the therapy situation. The criterion for a construct is its applicability and usefulness. When, among the various fundamental issues in psychology (Wertheimer 1972), Adler consistently selected the non-mechanistic alternatives, as mentioned above, these are at the same time also those more helpful in psychotherapy. The conception of an all-pervasive sex drive, for example, did not meet this criterion. "The detection of transposed sexual elements in a variety of manifestations is not very practically useful, even if it is possible" (Adler 1929a, p. 46). Such an explanation would only confirm to the patient that there are forces within him which are beyond his control, incapacitate him, or make him do things he does not want to do—most likely the nature of his complaint in the first place.

Adler regarded his concepts or explanations as not necessarily referring to actual facts, but as potentially useful working concepts. For example, regarding the inferiority complex which had quickly become the popular mark of Individual Psychology, Adler (1937) explained, it "has never been in the consciousness or unconsciousness of the patient but only in my own consciousness, and [I] have used it rather for illumination so that the patient could see his attitude in the right coherence" (p. 776). On another occasion he said, "The inferiority complex is only an idea given by me to the patient. He behaves 'as if' he had an inferiority complex. After we tell him that, he has a new concept to work with" (Ansbacher 1965, p. 349).

It follows from his aim that his theory should be practically applicable to life situations and from his view that life in its sociocultural aspects is continuously evolving, that Adler (1930) was satisfied if his theory was applicable to present conditions. "Individual Psychology claims no more for itself than to be taken as a theory which does justice to the present condition of civilization, and to our present knowledge of man and his psychological condition, and which does so better than other theories" (p. 47).

Unity of the Individual

The concept of the unity of the individual is foremost in Adler's system. In fact, as we have seen initially, Adler chose the name for his system to indicate the individual as a unified organism in which the parts work together and adapt to each other for a common purpose. As in Gestalt psychology the organization of the whole figure determines how the parts will be perceived, so in Individual Psychology the organization of the whole person influences all his partial functions. Even apparent antitheses are only different aspects of the same person. As Adler (1929) stated it, "Individual Psychology distinguishes in the conscious and the unconscious, not separate and conflicting entities, but complementary and cooperating parts of one and the same reality" (p. 29). Earlier Adler (1912) had written, "My observations regarding the unity of personality signify a lasting psychological gain which has solved the puzzles of *double vie,* polarity, ambivalence (Bleuler)" (p. 30).

The unity is to be understood not only cross-sectionally, but also longitudinally, over time. Thus Adler (1912) also stated, "We must regard each single life manifestation as if traces of the past, the present and the future, together with the superordinated guiding idea were present in it at the same time" (p. 25).

The conception of the unity corresponds exactly to the reality of the treatment situation. All the therapist has before him is one individual and what he discloses about himself. Even the therapist's inferences about the "unconscious" are based on what the patient offers him to observe, orally or visually. There are no other methods of investigation. And even what the patient says about his past, his present, and his future, all comes from the present individual and is essentially channeled through and directed from his highest nerve centers. It is all channeled through the individual.

The Individual, Part of Larger Systems

With a holistic attitude such as Adler's, man is seen not only as an organism, a system, but as a part of larger systems. "In addition to regarding an individual's life as a unity, we must also take it together with its context of social relations. . . . The style or the pattern of a child's life cannot be understood without reference to the persons who look after him. . . . The child has interlocking relations with the mother and family, which could never be understood if we confined our analysis to the periphery of the child's physical being in space. The individuality of the child cuts across his physical individuality, it involves a whole context of social relations" (Adler 1956, p. 127).

Adler (1930) often spoke of "the relationships between man and earth, community, and bisexuality" (p. 47), from which arise the three life problems of work, friendship, and love-and-marriage. All these problems are or become social problems and can be best solved through cooperation. One's social system then becomes most important, and Individual Psychology becomes the study of interpersonal transactions.

In therapy this conception becomes immediately effective in steering the therapist toward understanding the patient's present social situation and the attitudes he brings to it. The patient always behaves in a social setting and for a purpose. "The opponent of the game, *Gegenspieler*, is never absent" (Adler 1956, p. 388). We see here the starting point for the conception of family therapy: in the original clinics of Adler the parent(s) and the child's teacher were seen, with the child coming in at the end. The concept of man in his social system is of course basic to milieu therapy as well as group therapy.

Creativity and Self-Determination

In an organismic model of man such as Adler's, man is seen as active and an initiator of actions, not as a passive S-R mechanism. He actively uses the stimulus material with which he is presented for his purposes. In this sense everybody is creative. The criterion is the capacity to formulate, consciously or most often unknowingly, a goal of success for one's endeavors and to develop organized procedures for attaining the goal, i.e., a life plan under which all life processes become a self-consistent organization. Only in the truly feebleminded is such purposeful creative power absent (Adler 1964, pp. 46-47).

The presupposition is that man is not completely determined by heredity and environment, but that once he has been brought into existence, he develops the capability of influencing and creating events, as witnessed by the cultural products all around us, beginning with language, which are all man's creations. Heredity and environment merely supply the raw material, the equipment, which man uses for his purposes through his creative power. "The important thing is not what one is born with, but what use one makes of that equipment" (Adler 1964, p. 86).

The healthy person "is and wants to be the master of his fate" (p. 156), he takes the responsibility for his actions. Mental disorder is also the individual's creation, but for the sake of escaping responsibility and blaming forces beyond his control. The patient thus feels as if he were powerless. He feels as we all should feel if we lived by the principle of determinism which is generally taught as the only really scientific approach.

The patient's complaints are about what happens to him, what others and fate do to him, with himself but a passive victim. The assumption of self-determination becomes extremely useful here. It causes, e.g., Dreikurs (1967) to ask and explore at all times, "And what did you do?" When a wife complains, "My husband comes home late at night," the question, "And what did you do?" may elicit the answer, "I scolded him." Thereby her eyes are opened to the fact that she "is not merely a victim . . . but an active participant" (p. 269). Once she understands that she does act, she will also accept the fact that she could act differently. She could be friendly toward her husband, her "opponent in the game." While she cannot change his behavior directly, she can change her own response, thereby changing the balance of the interactional system, and changing his behavior indirectly. Such a demonstration is enormously encouraging to the patient, and initiates a movement in the situation.

Goal Striving

A concept of man as a unitary organism requires a unitary dynamic principle. This Adler derived directly from life itself. All forms of life are characterized by movement in the direction of growth and expansion. In addition to participating in this general biological process man has the capacity to anticipate the future, including his growth, development and decline. He also has the capacity to make choices, as we have seen. Thus he creates ideals and goals, toward which he wants to develop, and these supply him with criteria for making the innumerable choices with which he is confronted in his daily living, the values which function as guideposts.

The movement in the lower life forms can be explained in a mechanistic way through drives and feedback systems, a causal explanation, which is of course what Freud attempted also for man. But man, in general and as one meets him in therapy, is concerned with problems of living, his self-esteem, his future, always the improvement of a situation, a goal. Thus Adler replaced causal explanation with explanation in terms of goals, or teleological explanation. He found the latter more in accordance with the actual situation and more helpful in actual practice.

How can one change actual causes, supposedly objective events that happened in the past and are unalterable? Obviously one cannot, but it is possible to influence goals and values which the patient holds in the present. These are, like beliefs and attitudes, mental constructs available for reconstruction.

This does not mean that Adler denied causality. But he subordinated it in man to value and goal factors. In other words, objective causal events are still open to interpretation and utilization by the individual according to his attitudes toward them. Adler (1956) wrote, "We do assume the validity of the principle of causality, but we recognize that it is inadequate to solve a mental problem and even to enable us to predict the adoption of a particular attitude of mind. Thus we regard man *as if* nothing in his life were causally determined and *as if* every phenomenon could have been different" (p. 91, italics added). The *as if* characterizes this statement as a working hypothesis.

"The most important question of the healthy and the diseased mental life is not whence? but, whither? Only when we know the effective direction-giving goal of a person may we try to understand his movements" (p. 91). According to Viktor Frankl (1970), what Adler achieved by this change from whence to whither, "was no less than a Copernican switch. No longer could man be considered as the product, pawn and victim of drives and instincts; on the contrary, drives and instincts form the material that serves man in expression and in action" (p. 12).

Inferiority-Superiority Dynamic

The goal striving always takes the form of a movement from a relative minus to a relative plus situation—from a feeling of inferiority to a goal of superiority. This goal can take an infinite variety of forms. Yet they all include, to be a worthy human being. Therefore, "the sense of worth of the self shall not be allowed to be diminished." Adler (1956) called this "the supreme law of life" (p. 358).

Inferiority feeling and compensation seem to have lost their primary importance for Adler over the years in favor of the goal striving, making for a better, open-ended theory. Logically, where there is no prior conception of what one would want to be, there can be no inferiority feeling—if my goal concept does not include being a good cook, I will hardly feel inferior about not knowing how to cook. But even beyond this shift Adler (1964) in his late papers de-emphasized the term "inferiority feelings." He notes that against the background of goal striving "the feeling of incompletion, of insecurity, of inferiority, is always to be found" (p. 53). By listing inferiority feelings last in this series Adler would seem to indicate that he intended a broader concept and wanted to prevent "inferiority feelings" from becoming a shibboleth.

Parallel to this development the terms "goal of superiority," let alone of "power," fell more and more into disuse. Instead, Adler (1964) spoke increasingly of "a goal of success" (p. 88) depending on the individual's own interpretation of what constitutes success, or "a goal of perfection, security, completion" (p. 51), or most broadly, applicable to all forms of life, a goal of overcoming. "Striving towards a goal, towards an objective, we find everywhere in life. Everything grows 'as if' it were striving to overcome all imperfections and achieve perfection. This urge toward perfection we call the goal of overcoming, that is, the striving to overcome" (p. 86).

The movement from inferiority to superiority, or in whatever other terms the two poles of this movement dimension are described, is a dialectical conception. In this Adler (1912) was undoubtedly influenced by Nietzsche. "Nietzsche's 'will to power' . . . includes much of our understanding" (p. 32). And just as will to power meant for Nietzsche, according to Kaufman (1968, pp. 251-252), not primarily domination over others but the dynamics toward self-mastery, self-conquest, and self-perfection, so for Adler (1956, p. 114) power meant overcoming difficulties, with personal power over others representing only one type likely to be found among patients.

The dialectic is particularly well presented in the following from Adler (1929b): "Every symptom . . . is expressed in a movement—in a progress. Thus the symptom may be said to have a past and a future. Now the future is tied up with our striving and with our goal, while the past represents the state of inferiority or inadequacy which we are trying to overcome. This is why . . . we should not be astonished if in the cases where we see an inferiority complex we find a superiority complex more or less hidden. On the other hand, if we inquire into a superiority complex . . . we can always find a more or less hidden inferiority complex. . . . If we look at things this way, it takes away the apparent paradox of two contradictory tendencies . . . existing in the same individual. For it is obvious that as normal sentiments the striving for superiority and the feeling of inferiority are naturally complementary. We should not strive to be superior and to succeed if we did not feel a certain lack in our present condition. . . . The striving for superiority never ceases. It constitutes in fact the mind, the psyche of the individual" (pp. 27-28).

If some Adlerians have stressed toward their patients or counselees "the courage to be imperfect" (e.g., Dreikurs 1968, pp. 126, 258), this is only an apparent contradiction to the above. It is actually a dialectical therapeutic device to enable the patient to give up certain escapist perfectionisms to free him for greater success and perfection, on matters which really count.

Life-Style

For Adler (1964) life-style represented the organismic ideas of the individual as a self-consistent unity, an actor and creator rather than an object and mere reactor, his goal directedness—all this as it manifests itself concretely in the unique individual case. It includes the person's conception of his goal of success, the content of which is "left to the opinion of the individual" (p. 24).

"The unity in each individual—in his thinking, feeling, acting, in his so-called conscious and unconscious—in every expression of his personality—we call the 'life-style' of the individual. What is frequently labeled the ego is nothing more than the style of the individual" (p. 175). "This style is the creation of the child, who uses inheritance and impressions of the environment as bricks in building his particular avenue for success—success according to his own interpretation" (p. 175).

"The goal of superiority with each individual is personal and unique. It depends upon the meaning he gives to life. This meaning is not a matter of words. It is built up in his style of life and runs through it like a strange melody of his own creation. In his style of life, he does not express his goal so that we can formulate it for all times. He expresses it vaguely, so that we must guess at it from the indications he gives" (Adler 1956, p. 181).

The coordination of all processes under the life-style includes also the organic functions. "This is notably the case with the lungs, the heart, the stomach, the organs of excretion and the sexual organs. The disturbance of these functions expresses the direction which an individual is taking to attain his goal. I have called these disturbances the organ dialect, or organ jargon, since the organs are revealing in their own most expressive language the intention of the individual totality. The dialect of the sexual organs is especially expressive" (Adler 1929a, p. 156).

The concept of life-style, an outgrowth of Adler's finalistic or teleological conception, is particularly helpful in making the therapeutic process more economical and efficient. Sullivan, who otherwise has a great deal in common with Adler, believed, according to Mullahy (1970), that "the more relevant and significant information the investigator can obtain . . . the more accurate is his picture of the interpersonal influences that molded the patient's life" (p. 203). For Sullivan a complete inventory is the ideal, whereas a sampling is sufficient for Adler, who wants merely to arrive at a conceptualization of the particular fashion in which an individual uses all his experiences for his particular purposes. Also, "We can begin wherever we choose: every expression will lead us in the same direction—towards the one motive, the one melody, around which the personality is built" (Adler 1956, p. 332). It is like understanding the style of a certain composer. Once you have understood the style, you don't have to study each of his compositions. In fact, you will be able to "predict" how he would have handled a certain melody.

Personality Development

A unitary holistic theory of personality can have little use for an approach to development in terms of stages. They would artificially divide the life cycle into discrete steps and raise self-fulfilling expectations for the various steps as described. Instead, personality, that is the life-style, is seen as emerging gradually and as a whole. "In the first four or five years the child builds up its own prototype, by adjusting its inherited abilities to its earliest impressions, and lays the irrevocable foundation of its style of life" (Adler 1929a, p. 31).

Since Adler (1956) stresses "the free creative power of the individual in his earliest childhood" (p. 186), the influences on the child function as more or less strong probabilities of steering the development in one direction or another. Adler points to three main conditions with regard to their possible negative influence on self-esteem and social interest, the two cardinal personality traits. These unfavorable conditions are:

1. *Imperfect organs and childhood diseases.* "Such children may turn in upon themselves, lose hope of playing a useful part in our common life, and consider themselves humiliated" (p. 368). However, "The outcome depends on the creative power of the individual which expands according to no rule except that the determing goal always is success, that is, what constitutes success for him" (p. 368).

2. *Pampering.* A pampered child "has been trained to receive without giving . . . He has lost his independence and does not know that he can do things for himself. . . . When faced with difficulties he has only one method of meeting them, that is to make demands on others. . . . Every pampered child becomes a hated child. Our civilization is such that neither society nor the family wishes to continue the pampering process indefinitely" (pp. 369-370).

3. *Neglect.* The neglected, hated, or unwanted child "has found society cold to him and will expect it always to be cold. . . . He will be suspicious of others and unable to trust himself . . . Many failures in life come from orphans or illegitimate children" (pp. 370-371). Such a child's "goal is to escape and to get at a safe distance from others. . . . The unusual tension of their life makes these children postulate a higher goal of security and superiority than that of the average child" (Adler 1929a, pp. 36-37).

Adler (1956) saw it as the mother's particular task to give her child the proper start in life. "The mother represents the greatest experience of love and fellowship which the child will ever have. Her task is to relate the growing child to herself psychologically, as he was formerly related to her physically. But she must also nourish the child's growing consciousness with true and normal conceptions of society, of work, and of love. In this way she gradually transforms the child's love for her and dependence upon her into a benevolent, confident, and responsible attitude towards society and the whole environment. This is the two-fold function of motherhood: to give the child the completest possible experience of human fellowship, and then to widen it into a life-attitude towards others" (p. 372).

THEORY OF MENTAL HEALTH AND PSYCHOPATHOLOGY

Social Interest

Adler's crowning theoretical achievement was the concept of community feeling, *Gemeinschaftsgefühl*, often translated as social feeling or social interest. In one of his last papers Adler (1937) stated, "Degree of social interest is the main characteristic of each person and is involved in all his actions" (p. 774).

Adler started from the simple fact that man, after all, is outstandingly a social being. Our outstanding trait is the ability to express our thoughts in language and to communicate in this way with other human beings. Language is a communal invention, and we acquire it through human interaction. Through language we become a member of the human kind and its cultural development. Through the division of labor and through the fact that even sexual gratification is most satisfactory in partnership with a member of the other sex, all the important problems in our lives become social problems. These are the problems of work, friendship, and love and marriage, mentioned earlier.

Without disturbing his basic assumption of the unity of the individual and the master dynamics of striving from a minus to a plus situation, Adler (1929a) simply postulated that man is endowed with an aptitude for social living, since he normally does live this way and has collectively created languages, societies, cultures. This he called an innate aptitude for social interest or for communal feeling which, however, "has to be *consciously* developed"(p. 31, italics added). This is in accordance with the cognitive, rational emphasis in Adler's psychology which led Ellenberger (1970, p. 628) to regard it as in the tradition of the Enlightenment.

Social interest is not an innate altruistic motive, opposed to a selfish motive. This would be a motivational dualism, quite foreign to a holistic theory. Nor is social interest the equivalent of conformity or passive adaptation. It is rather an active interest in the interests of man from a broad future perspective. It thus may well lead to disagreement with any contemporary group or society. The man with a strong social interest will not blindly conform with wrongs done by his own social group, but will resist them and work on improving the situation.

The concept of a natural potentiality for social interest facilitates therapy in that it does not raise negative expectations in the therapist, as is the case with the assumption of innate destructive tendencies. It supports the conviction that harmonious social living is theoretically possible and can thus become a reasonable therapeutic goal, all existing contrary behavior notwithstanding. Such behavior is explained by lack of development of social interest. The concept of social interest creates in the therapist a basic trust in human nature, replacing the basic distrust the therapist must have when he assumes destructive primary processes which have to be managed by the person through a precarious balance between repression and acting out, under the strictures of a more or less severe superego.

Mental Health—Developed Social Interest

According to a disease model of mental disorder, the therapist's task would be accomplished once he has eradicated the disease. This is achieved by bringing the hidden psychogenic causes from the past out into the open and thereby rendering them ineffective. The therapist is not concerned with the patient's actual life. Therefore it is conceivable that the patient is formally "cured" while he still does not know how to live a satisfactory life.

In Adler's educational model, mental disorder is an erroneous way of living, a mistaken life-style, including a mistaken goal of success and underdeveloped social interest. Due to these mistakes the patient is not the sufferer from a disease but a "failure" in solving his life problems. Psychotherapy "teaches" him a more suitable approach so that he may succeed. Adler's (1929a) aim was "to replace the great mistakes by small ones . . . Big mistakes can produce neuroses, but little mistakes a nearly normal person" (p. 62). The normal person is more successful in solving his problems in that he is at the same time making a contribution, whereas the failure is a liability not only to himself but also to others.

Thus social usefulness became for Adler the criterion of mental health. "By useful I mean in the interest of mankind generally. The most sensible estimate of the value of any activity is its helpfulness to all mankind, present and future, a criterion that applies not only to that which subserves the immediate preservation of life, but also to higher activities such as religion, science, and art" (p. 78). A self-centered goal of success is bound to be limited and precarious, whereas a goal which includes general usefulness has the greatest validity attainable.

Such usefulness is the outcome of a well developed social interest or social feeling. "It is almost impossible to exaggerate the value of an increase in social feeling. The mind improves, for intelligence is a communal function. The feeling of worth and value is heightened, giving courage and an optimistic view, and there is a sense of acquiescence in the common advantages and drawbacks of our lot. The individual feels at home in life and feels his existence to be worthwhile just so far as he is useful to others and is overcoming common instead of private feelings of inferiority. Not only the ethical nature, but the right attitude in aesthetics, the best understanding of the beautiful and the ugly will always be founded upon the truest social feeling" (p. 79).

Adler (1929b) was a pragmatist, and to such an extent an operationalist that he defined the normal man as "an individual who lives in society and whose mode of life is so adapted that *whether he wants it or not* society derives a certain advantage from his work" (p. 41, italics added). Also, he meets his "problems and difficulties as they come along."

A similar passage by Adler (1929a) reads: "Courage, an optimistic attitude, common sense, and the feeling of being at home upon the crust of the earth, will enable him to face advantages and disadvantages with equal firmness. His goal of superiority will be identified with ideas of serving the human race and of overcoming its difficulties by his creative power" (pp. 47-48). The person who has been well prepared for social life through development of his social interest potential will also "solve all love problems with loyalty to the partner and responsibility to society" (p. 47).

Psychopathology

Everyone lives in a world of his own construction, in accordance with his own "schema of apperception." While the "absolute truth" eludes us, we can discern between greater and lesser errors, that is, between "private sense" (also private intelligence and private logic), characteristic of mental disorder, and "common sense," an aspect of social interest, characteristic of mental health (Adler 1956, pp. 253-254). The private intelligence is uncompromising, "unreasonable." The neurotic wants "everything or nothing" and "success at the beginning," which is the intelligence of the failures (p. 150).

Behind this, one always finds a high goal of personal superiority, compensating for strong inferiority feelings. This combination precludes the development of a healthy interest in others. "The striving for personal superiority and the nondevelopment of social interest . . . are one and the same mistake" (pp. 240-241). Thus the individual will have difficulty meeting his life problems which always require social interest for their solution. He will retreat from tasks, the failure which he fears might "injure his vanity and interfere with his striving for personal superiority" (pp. 293-294). The neurotic symptoms are the individual's "arrangements" (p. 284) to serve as excuses for not meeting his life problems and to protect his self-esteem.

The neurotic life-style. This is essentially the life-style of the pampered child. "Such a child experienced, developed, and secured for himself during several years of his life an . . . elevated position by obtaining everything easily, with the help of others, and by expecting everything from others. . . . Extreme discouragement, continuous hesitation, oversensitivity, impatience . . . physical and psychological disturbances showing the signs of weakness and need for support" (pp. 241-242), are always evidence of the pampered life-style. While the pampering situation mentioned earlier is most likely to induce a pampered life-style, Adler reminds us that, "The pampered style of life as a living phenomenon is the creation of the child. . . . Consequently it can be found occasionally in cases where we cannot speak with any justification of pampering, but where on the contrary, we find neglect" (p. 242).

About cases of neglect, Adler (1926) contends that such a child will not be able to make the transition from a self-contained attitude to one of putting himself in context with human society and regarding himself as a part of it. "This transition can fail if the child has no mother . . . [and] in the case of foster children who are . . . pushed from one place to another. . . . They necessarily seek a form of life in which they are alone, because they always believe that the others are hostile towards them. . . . Himself always pushed . . . always treated harshly, such a child will grow up as if in enemy country" (p. 12).

In a neurotic life-style, "we must always suspect an opponent [in the game], and note who suffers most because of the patient's condition. Usually this is a member of the family, and sometimes a person of the other sex, though there are cases in which the illness is an attack upon society as a whole. There is always this element of concealed accusation in neurosis, the patient feeling as though he were deprived of his *right*—i.e., of the center of attention—and wanting to fix the responsibility and blame upon someone. By such hidden vengeance and accusation, by excluding social activity while fighting against persons and rules the problem child and the neurotic find some relief from their dissatisfaction" (Adler 1929a, p. 81).

The nature and function of symptoms. Symptoms are the patient's "arrangements" to serve as excuse for not meeting his life problems and to protect his self-esteem. "The life plan of the neurotic demands categorically that if he fails, it should be through someone else's fault and that he should be freed from personal responsibility; or that, if his triumph is prevented, it should be by a fatal detail only. The common human element in this desire is striking. When the individual helps it along with his devices, then the entire content of life is permeated by the reassuring, anesthetizing stream of the life-lie which safeguards the self-esteem" (Adler 1956, p. 271). Later, Adler most often used the term self-deception instead of life-lie. This idea was taken up by Sartre in his concept of "bad faith" (*mauvaise foi*) (Stern 1958).

Exogenous factor. Adler (1956) adds, however, the important principle, "Every neurotic is partly right" (p. 334). He is "right" in that there were "traumas" and all sorts of "frustrations" in his life, which can easily be construed as adverse "causes." But he is only "partly right" in that he was not obligated to construct his life in the inexpedient way in which he did. Others with similar experiences did differently.

An individual with a neurotic life-style could still go through life without actually coming to a crisis, if the conditions surrounding him were so favorable that he would never be put to a test. By the same token Adler assumes that for any crisis to develop, there must be a confrontation with such a test, or a task—the exogenous factor. "The exogenous factor, the proximity of a task that demands cooperation and fellowship, is always the exciting factor of the symptoms, the behavior problem, the neurosis, the suicide, the crime, the drug addiction, and the sexual perversion" (pp. 297-298).

Specific disorders. The dynamics described here for the neurotic are, according to Adler, the same for all mental disorders. He makes, however, one fundamental distinction, namely, between the neurotic and the psychotic: the former recognizes the common sense, while the latter does not. The neurotic formula is "yes—but." The "yes" is the recognition of the common sense. In the "but," "you find the whole strength of the neurotic symptoms. They are much stronger than what is represented by the 'yes. . . .' [But the neurotic] understands social interest, and that makes him different from the psychotic" (pp. 302-303).

Adler (1964) makes a further distinction between disorders, namely with regard to "degree of activity." This he finds lowest in anxiety neurosis and schizophrenia, higher in compulsion neurosis and depression, and still somewhat higher in suicide and alcoholism. In view of our case report we want to mention, "The activity [in cases of suicide] has a particular curve in that it runs apart from social life and against it, and that it harms the individual himself, not without giving pain and sorrow to others" (p. 250). Cases of suicide show "a life-style which attempted to influence others through increased complaining, sadness, and suffering." There is also "increased ambition, vanity, and consciousness of their value to others . . . a belief . . . usually acquired from the pampering situation of their childhood" (p. 251). "We find in the suicide the type who thinks too much of himself, too little of others, and who is unable sufficiently to play, function, live, and die with others" (p. 252).

Compulsion neurosis—neurotic prototype. As hysteria, with its emphasis on the emotions, was prototypical for Freud's conception of the neuroses, so compulsion neurosis, in which the rational aspect is most strongly stressed, is prototypical for Adler's understanding of the neuroses. Adler wrote more on this form of neurosis than any other. Leonhard Seif (1926), one of Adler's prominent co-workers in the 1920's, found the dynamics of the compulsion neurosis so essential to all neuroses that "one could call virtually any neurosis a 'compulsion neurosis.' "

Adler's (1964) summary on compulsion neurosis includes: "Compulsion neurosis is a striving for personal superiority which, from fear of betraying an actual inferiority, is diverted into easy and generally useless channels. . . . It occurs in the face of actual situations (problems of social living, occupation, or love), where the dread of failure or a blow to vanity leads to a hesitating attitude. This hesitating attitude finds expression in killing time, in seeking out and repeating a single routine or expressive movement or idea which will preclude further contact with the terrifying problems of life. . . . The construction of compulsion neurosis is identical with the structure of the entire life-style. . . . The compulsion does not reside in the compulsive actions themselves, but originates in the demands of social living, which the patient feels as a . . . threat to his prestige. . . The feelings of guilt or humility almost always present . . . are elaborations of the effort to kill time. The prognosis of compulsion neurosis is fundamentally the same as that on any other neurosis. . . . The cure can come about only when there is a reconciliation with the problems of life" (pp. 135-138).

In recent years Leon Salzman (1968), member of the William Alanson White Institute, has arrived at very similar views. "The obsessive-compulsive personality type is today's most prevalent neurotic character structure. . . . The obsessional defensive mechanism provides the most widespread technique for enabling man to achieve some illusion of safety and security in an uncertain world . . . never exposes an individual to . . . failure and thus avoids the awareness of imperfection, fallibility, and humanness" (pp. vii-viii).

The schizophrenic life-style. Adler saw the schizophrenic essentially as human as everyone else. The main difference he found in schizophrenics is that their goal is loftier and more godlike than that of neurotics, and, in turn, that of normals, compensating for their abysmally low self-esteem. A concomitant to this is increased distance from the others—the break with common sense. Most of the bizarre symptoms of the schizophrenic are the result of his godlike goal. When confronted with the tasks of life and the threat of failure, he breaks with the real world to safeguard his self-esteem. His world becomes a rigid, barren, private construction, in the service of the goal.

The important ingredient in Adler's treatment here, as in general, is encouragement, by which he meant in fact (a) letting the patient demonstrate his own strength and pointing this out to him, and (b) demonstrating to the patient by your own friendliness that the world is not altogether as hostile toward him as the patient had assumed. Adler (1931) reported the successful treatment of a girl who had been psychotic for eight years. As her courage had come back to some degree, Adler tells, "she hit me. . . . I let her hit me and looked friendly. . . . It took away every challenge from her. She still did not know what to do with her reawakened courage. She broke my window and cut her hand on the glass. I did not reproach her, but bandaged her hand. . . . Let them do it. There is no other possibility of helping them" (pp. 256-257).

The life-style of the schizophrenic has been described by Kurt Adler (1958). A book by Bernard Shulman (1968) presents the Adlerian viewpoint on schizophrenia, giving many practical examples of treatment which could be followed, regardless of the therapist's theoretical orientation. Alexandra Adler (1966) recommends with "severely affected, chronic paranoid, and paranoid-catatonic patients" drug therapy, without simultaneously attempting involved interpretations of behavior. The patient's whole life situation must be considered, every effort must be made to keep him out of a hospital, and he must be given "opportunity for continued socialization, in particular through work or . . . other group activities." The borderline schizophrenic is treated much like the neurotic, helping him "to gain courage, to assert himself and to develop social feelings" (Papanek 1954).

Psychotherapy

Adlerian psychotherapy is essentially (a) to recognize and conceptualize the basic mistakes in the patient's way of living and (b) to convey this understanding to him in a manner which he can accept. From this, three or four phases of therapy have been variously identified. They can be described as follows:

1. *Establishing and maintaining a good relationship with the patient.* "Psychotherapy is an exercise in cooperation and a test of cooperation"

(Adler 1956, p. 340). It is equally an exercise in encouragement, activating the patient's resources.

2. *Gathering data.* Every record about, and every expression by the patient helps in discerning and conceptualizing the patient's life-style or method of living. What has been found especially useful is an account of the patient's early formative years, his family setting at that time, and how he expresses himself about it today. This includes his account of his sibling relationship and particularly his early recollections in general, as well as his dreams. These data will show the patient's opinion of himself and the world as well as his hypothetical goal, as relative constants throughout his life span.

3. *Interpretation.* As the therapist gains his own understanding of the patient's life-style, he conveys this to the patient. The therapist generally listens to the patient dialectically; that is, he asks himself what opposite could be paired with a certain statement. "While he [the patient] looks at his obstacles, we must look at his attempt to protect his fictive superiority and rescue his ambition" (Adler 1964, p. 199). Interpretations are also given through concretizing or operationalizing a statement. For example, in the case of "guilt feelings," the patient implicitly feels virtuous about his remorse, yet generally does nothing to remedy the actual situation.

4. *Active reconstruction.* The therapist actively directs the patient toward alternative ways of regarding himself and his circumstances. The patient generally sees himself as a victim of forces beyond his control; his attention is then turned to his own responses to the situation, and possible alternative responses, more effective and generally useful, are pointed out to him. "The cure is brought about by . . . the unequivocal acceptance of a mature picture of the world" (Adler 1956, p. 333). "As soon as the patient can connect himself with his fellow men on an equal and cooperative footing, he is cured" (p. 347). Part of this active reconstruction is confrontation, as described by Shulman (1971) and by Garner (1972).

Adlerian psychotherapy is most extensively dealt with by Dreikurs (1967). Adlerian techniques of psychotherapy with transcripts of demonstrations are reported in the proceedings of a special conference on this topic (Ansbacher 1972c).

APPLICATION OF THEORY

To demonstrate the application of Adlerian theory to the understanding of a life-style we shall use the case of Marilyn Monroe. As an extraordinary case that has remained enigmatic, it lends itself particularly well to illustration of Adlerian concepts. If, furthermore, we assume that her suicidal attempt had not succeeded, we can follow our interpretation with therapeutic considerations.

My particular interest in the case of Marilyn Monroe was aroused through two early recollections she gave in her interview in *Life* (Monroe 1962) published two days before her death, and her childhood dream published in *Time,* August 10, 1962. These are given below as ERs 7, 8 and 5. Through these three items with the basic data about her, reported by the press at the time of her death, I felt that I understood her very well—although I had never met her.

I reported my view of the case for the first and only previous time briefly in an article on Adler in *Psychology Today* (Ansbacher 1970b). I arrived then at the conclusion that as a child living in foster homes "she had set herself a godlike goal. Her misfortune was that as a sex goddess she achieved that goal" (p. 66) to a fantastic extent. Pampered by her circumstances as she was, she never gained a mature outlook and remained unprepared to meet the tasks of life as a human being. Her suicide is, so to speak, a confirmation that she had no place in this world.

Only for the present paper did I read the biography by Guiles (1969) and found in it much support for my hypothesis. The biography by Mailer (1973) appeared as I was well along with this paper, so that I decided not to use it, but only after a cursory examination had satisfied me that it did not conflict with my hypothesis—quite apart from the speculative and controversial aspects of the book.

Objective Account

Marilyn Monroe died in her home in Hollywood from an overdose of sleeping pills on August 5, 1962. To indicate her onetime immense popularity, at the height of her career fans would write her 5,000 letters a week. Her 23 films since 1950 grossed about $200 million.

During her last years she had suffered severe setbacks. Two months earlier she had been dismissed by 20th Century-Fox for unjustifiable absence during filming. Her previous two films had been box office disappointments. Two years earlier she was divorced from Arthur Miller after four years. Two previous marriages had ended in divorce. After her dismissal she pleaded with Fox to let her return to work.

Although her success was based on her unusual sexual attraction, in her own life she had not succeeded in marriage, and it is questionable how much she was interested in sex altogether. According to one biographer, Fred Guiles

(1969), "Marilyn was too self-absorbed to respond to men much of the time" (p. 82). As a child she was considered a tomboy (p. 20), liked to lose herself in group sports such as baseball (p. 28), was not interested in feminine skills (p. 27), and was always considered a good athlete and a good sport (p. 36). Physiologically too there were difficulties with the feminine role. She had suffered at least two miscarriages and was never able to have a child. When under stress, she would become sick to her stomach.

What further characteristics have been attributed to her? On the positive side, people who knew her well from living and working with her, most often described her as warm (warm hearted, full of warmth, etc.), likeable (affable, *not* hard, tart, malicious, mean, capricious), and good-humored, amusing and witty. She was also considered generous, conscientious, healthy, zestful, and relaxed.

On the negative side, her most exasperating characteristic was her truancy and tardiness through which she finally lost her contract, since the studio could no longer afford the enormous expense this caused. On one occasion, in 32 days on the set she showed up only 12 times, made only 7½ usable minutes of film. She was from 1 to 24 hours late for appointments. She would spend four hours on her make-up knowing that reporters waited in the living room. She was also considered self-absorbed, self-dedicated, lacking self-control and self-discipline, having a bad temper, rages, and private furies, and, most frequently, nervous, scared, and unsure of herself. One publicity man, according to Martin (1957), thought "Marilyn had a tremendous inferiority complex" (p. 61).

As to habits, it was reported, "The urge to go nude was her most public whim" (*Time* 1962). While she was still an unknown starlet she posed for a widely distributed nude calendar photograph, at a time when this was by far more unusual than it would be today. In a later interview she said she was not ashamed about this: "I was behind in my rent" (Martin 1957, p. 74). She spent her last day sunbathing, glancing over filmscripts, playing with cloth dolls. She went to bed early. With all this she had been considered a sex symbol, a contemporary Venus.

Early History

Marilyn was born in Los Angeles on June 1, 1926, to a lower middle-class mother. The mother had been married and divorced and her two previous children were not in her custody. Marilyn's father never entered the picture. For the first seven years Marilyn remained at one foster home where she was kept, with up to four other boarding children, strictly but rather well, in a religious atmosphere. Her mother visited her on weekends, and she saw her grandmother more frequently until the latter was committed to a mental institution.

This was followed by two years when her mother tried to look after Marilyn; by two years in an orphanage of 50 boys and girls, 1935 to 1937; and by various other placements until her first marriage in 1942. The marriage had been arranged and suggested by friends as a way of finding a home for Marilyn. Jim Dougherty was a simple and good young man. But toward the end of the war and after it, he was away with the Maritime Service. During this time Marilyn lived with her in-laws, and took a job in a parachute plant at which she was an ambitious and productive worker.

It was there that she was "discovered" through an army photographer-reporter who was sent to the plant to do an essay on women in war work. This was the beginning of her way to modeling and the moving pictures, the realization of a lifelong ambition. "When I was five, I started wanting to be an actress . . . I wanted to play" (Monroe 1962, p. 33). In this ambition she was encouraged by one of her mother's best friends who told her "day after day": "Don't worry. You're going to be a beautiful girl when you get big. You're going to be a movie star. Oh, I feel it in my bones" (*N. Y. Times* 1962, p. 13:1). Although she actually liked Jim, she divorced him in 1946, feeling that marriage would stand in the way of a film career. "She had a growing fanaticism about her final success. Everything started and ended with that" (Guiles 1969, p. 59).

About her early childhood Marilyn later in life liked to convey the impression of herself as an "Oliver Twist in girl's clothing." But actually her situation was not quite that of a neglected and unwanted child. There was also some pampering. Her grandmother, who lived across the street from Marilyn's first foster-home, occasionally interfered when Marilyn was disciplined and took her to her house for the afternoon once or twice a week. Her mother also spoiled Marilyn on her weekly Saturday visits. "Discipline was nonexistent at such times" (Guiles 1969, p. 12).

The Adlerian Approach

We have heard of Marilyn's early decision and strong ambition to become an actress. In this she did indeed succeed beyond her wildest dreams. But why could she not succeed in her life? Why the contradictory characteristics we mentioned? Why the shyness, the inferiority feelings?

As to hereditary and environmental causal explanations, true, her maternal grandparents and her mother were eventually committed to mental institutions, and an uncle committed suicide. True also that she did not have a childhood home of her own. But these factors explain her failure no better than they explain her ambition and success. Nor, and this is most important, can we see in such explanations any application to psychotherapy.

Marilyn saw several psychoanalysts in her later life and up to the end. A few hints by her confirm our guess as to what their explanations may have been. "We are all born sexual creatures [infantile sexuality]. But it is a pity so many people despise and crush this natural gift [repression]. Art, real art, comes from it—everything [libido, sublimation]" (Monroe 1962, p. 36:2). At first she thought the treatment helped. "I'm beginning to understand myself . . . I've spent most of my life running away from myself . . . I don't feel as hopeless as I did . . . I've read a little of Freud . . . I think he was on the right track" (Martin 1957, pp. 62-63). But in the end it was, "I have never quite understood it—this sex symbol" (Monroe 1962, p. 36:2). In some people's opinion, "Her preoccupation with her 'emotional memory' . . . triggered a disintegration process, a fracturing of an ego that had only been reassembled . . . a few years earlier" (Guiles 1969, p. 175).

The holistic Adlerian approach proceeds phenomenologically and teleologically to arrive at explanations. The crucial heuristic device is the working hypothesis of an overall goal, a guiding image toward which the person strives and of which he is not really aware, yet from the viewpoint of which all his actions "make sense," although often only private rather than common sense. When the nature of the goal and the opinion of oneself and the world are somewhat correctly inferred, even contradictory phenomena will fall into place without unresolved basic contradictions—in contrast to the usual assumption of "inner conflicts" and ambivalences. The therapy would attempt to modify the goal, which would also involve opinion of the self and the world, in order to attain more self-transcending, contributive, and satisfactory behavior.

Early Recollections (ERs)

Marilyn's world view and goal may of course be inferred to some extent from the story so far. But these inferences become much more palpable from an examination of her early recollections, the most specifically Adlerian technique. A remembered childhood dream is included, as are ERs that may be more or less fantasy, or are based on stories retold to the subject by others. Fortunately we are supplied with a series of such ERs.

ER 1. When at her grandmother's at the age of one, she told her husband Arthur Miller, "I remember waking up from my nap fighting for my life.

Something was pressed against my face. It could have been a pillow. I fought with all my strength" (Guiles 1969, p. 12).

ER 2. Also at a very young age at her foster home, with the Bolenders, there was a boy, Lester, two months her junior. One day, she recalled, she and Lester shed their clothes in the front yard, and were surprised to find a difference between themselves. She was shouted at, while Lester escaped punishment (p. 13).

ER 3. Lester and Marilyn shared a tricycle. One day she pushed it over with Lester on it, bumping his head. She got a whipping with a razor strap. "I got into more trouble than the other kids" (p. 16).

ER 4. "While I was in the second grade, the public school chose me to appear in the Easter sunrise service at Hollywood Bowl. . . . All we children were arranged in the form of a cross. Just when the sun rose we were given a signal to throw off the black robes [we wore white tunics underneath] and that changed the cross from black to white. I got so interested in watching the sky, I did not . . . see the signal. I was the only child who forgot to throw off the black robe. I was the only black mark on a white cross" (Zolotow 1960, p. 106).

ER 5. She related the following childhood dream: "When I was maybe 6 or 7, I dreamed I was standing up in church without any clothes on, and all the people there were lying at my feet on the floor, and I walked naked, with a sense of freedom, being careful not to step on anyone" (*Time*, 1962).

ER 6. At the age of 7 or 8 she recalled having been seduced by an elderly star boarder who wore a heavy golden watch chain over the wide expanse of his vest, and that he gave her a nickel "not to tell." When she nevertheless did tell, her foster mother at the time severely punished her for making up lies about the "fine man" (Luce 1964, p. 72).

ER 7. From this period she also remembered: "Some of my foster families used to send me to the movies to get me out of the house and there I'd sit all day and way into the night—up in front, there with the screen so big, a little kid all alone, and I loved it" (Monroe 1962, p. 33:2).

ER 8. From the time she was 11 she remembered: "The whole world which was always closed to me suddenly opened up. Even the girls paid attention to me because they thought, 'She is to be dealt with.' I had this long walk—2½ miles to school, 2½ miles back—it was sheer pleasure. Every fellow honked his horn. . . . The world became friendly. All the newspaper boys when they delivered the paper would come around to where I lived. I used to hang from a limb of a tree, and I had a sort of a sweatshirt on. . . . Here they'd come with their bicycles and I'd get these free papers and the family liked that and they'd all pull their bicycles up around the

the tree and I'd be hanging. I was a little too shy to come down. I did get down to the curb . . . mostly listening. . . . I used to laugh so loud and so gay. . . . It was just this sudden freedom, because I would ask the boys, 'Can I ride your bike now?' and they'd say, 'Sure.' Then I'd go zooming, laughing in the wind, riding down the block laughing, and they'd all stand around, and wait till I came back, but I loved the wind; it caressed me" (Monroe 1962, p. 33:2).

Interpretation and Therapy

Although earlier we distinguished between interpretation and reconstruction as stages 3 and 4 of therapy, in actual treatment these stages go hand in hand. In the following we shall after each interpretative generalization insert therapeutic comments. These are made visible through indentation.

ERs, dreams, and other behaviors are considered samples of the individual's life-style. He does not understand them because he does not see them in their context. Interpretation is based on doing just this. In many respects interpretation is similar to that of H. A. Murray with TAT stories. Mosak (1958) has described ERs as a projective technique.

1. *The goal of superiority.* We have seen before, that Marilyn was from age 5 on resolved to become an actress, was encouraged in this goal, and pursued it with great resolution. Once she told a member of the Fox Studio legal staff, "I don't care about money. I just want to be wonderful." And the legal person wondered, "What do you suppose she meant by that?" (Martin 1957, p. 19).

From ER 5 we learn how she actually dreamt her goal of success to be. It is expressed metaphorically, yet quite concretely, while some of the metaphors are actually those of our daily language. In church she stands up, while "all the people there were lying at my feet on the floor." How could one depict more starkly the idea of absolute superiority? With all the people at her feet in church, she becomes almost immediately a goddess, or at least an angel, and her nudity in this context seems to be more an expression of sublimity than of sexuality. This is also the impression she made on some, later in life. In one of her late roles, "she seemed an exhausted angel trapped among earthlings" (Guiles 1969, p. 267).

In ER 8 we have again the picture of being above the crowd. When she does come down from the tree it is not to join the crowd; she is aloof, "mostly listening." But, with all her "shyness," she makes demands and gets what she wants—a bicycle. This she uses to leave the others behind. "I loved the wind; it caressed me." Only a natural phenomenon, the wind, not a human, is good enough for her—making her in fact superhuman.

> These and all the following interpretations would be given to her. One might add: "Isn't there some truth in this? But you are only a mortal, and you can't get well until you have completely reconciled yourself to this fact. Unless you accept this cheerfully, you can't live at all."

2. *Conquest through vulnerability*. Without clothes, one is at a disadvantage in a world where clothes are worn, and in any event, one is literally more exposed, more vulnerable. Yet in ER 5 she has all the people at her feet while she is naked. That she is venerated in all her innocent vulnerability heightens her triumph. This gives her "a sense of freedom"—from any responsibility. Fitting with her state of vulnerability, she is "careful not to step on anyone."

This cautiously evasive manner is also reflected in her nickname, "the mouse." It was given to her in her early teens when she lived with her mother's best friend. "She often appeared in a room, listened intently to whatever conversation might be going on there, but never announced her presence by so much as a cough" (Guiles 1969, p. 31).

It was through her nudity that she actually attempted to and did conquer the world. She also wanted to secure her immortality through her body. Twice shortly before her death she had nearly-nude and nude photographs taken of herself, saying, "I want the world to see my body" (*Time* 1962). She also was found nude upon her deathbed.

> In therapy one could have confronted her with this entire idea of nudity by saying: "Now you are 36 years old. How much longer do you want to have your picture taken in the nude? You don't have permanent youth and beauty; you are perishable like the rest of us. The sooner you accept this, the better for you. What do you think about this?"
> This would have shown her the immaturity which is also reflected in her having played with cloth dolls on her last day. By awakening her to a more mature outlook one would automatically have detracted from her self-centeredness and increased her social interest.

3. *The will to conquer—masculine protest*. Yet the "angel trapped among earthlings" was also an active, fighting, and athletic girl who did not like her role as a woman. Her ER 1 sets the tone. The first thing she remembers is having to fight for her own life, and she credits herself with, "I fought with all my strength." As an active child she also remembers having gotten

"into more trouble than the other kids" (ER 3). Climbing trees, riding a bicycle, the pleasant memory of her long walk to school (ER 8) round out the picture of a tomboy who later also had difficulties with her feminine physiological functions. Guiles (1969) attributed a "restless energy" to her. In the parachute plant where she worked in 1944 after her husband was sent overseas she soon "won a commendation from her employers . . . an 'E' certificate for excellence on the job" (p. 48). This, she felt, diminished still further her already low popularity with her women co-workers with whom she rarely spoke.

All this corresponds quite well to Adler's (1956) description of the masculine protest in woman. "Fighting, climbing, excessive achievements in sports . . . point to dissatisfaction with the feminine role and to the masculine protest" (p. 49). We only need to substitute "excessive achievements at the plant" for "in sports." In these cases one may indeed also find "frigidity, few children" (p. 49) and other difficulties with the feminine functions.

Human beings, however, operate dialectically, so that, e.g., defiance may be expressed through excessive obedience (pp. 52-54). In fact, "The masculine protest in women is usually covered up and transformed, seeking its triumph with feminine means" (p. 49). When the army photographer discovered Marilyn's great talent as a model, she immediately pursued this opportunity of realizing her old ambition with the vigor characteristic of her. It also was the start of her transformation toward "seeking triumph with feminine means." As to mark this transformation, she changed her name from Norma Jean Mortensen to Marilyn Monroe.

If we regard her transformation as merely a change of means, from "masculine" to "feminine" means—and we have seen that she was able to utilize both—while she actually saw life as a fight requiring "all my strength," then we have the resolution of the apparent contradiction that the "sex symbol" was unable to stay married and probably also was not a good lover. It would also reconcile Marilyn's traits of being warm-hearted and affable with her inclination toward temper, rages, and private furies. Either way she was a lone fighter. "I have always had a pride in the fact that I was on my own" (Monroe 1962, p. 33).

> In therapy we might have explained to her that she is not really the "born sexual creature" which she had come to believe she was, but that she was merely determined to succeed in her immature way and use her femininity to achieve the greatest personal triumphs. True sexuality is a form of cooperation and contribution. When she said, "I now live in my work and in a few relationships with the few people I can really count on" (Monroe 1962, 38:2), we would have asked: "Do

you know what I think you mean by 'people I can count on'? I think you mean people whom you can completely dominate."

4. *Lack of social interest*. Not one of her ERs indicates that Marilyn believes goals can be attained through cooperating on an equal footing with others, as a fellow human being. She is either above others (ERs 5 and 8), getting something for nothing (ER 8), fighting alone for her life (ER 1), being different from others (ERs 2 and 4), alone (ER 7); or being victimized by being punished for something she did (ER 3), or being punished unfairly (ERs 2 and 6), or being sexually seduced (ER 6).

Marilyn can certainly be considered to have been a neglected child in the sense that her mother was unable to introduce her to the world as a friendly place where people essentially cooperate. For such individuals the probability is great that they will "seek a form of life in which they are alone," believing the others to be their enemies. Their goal of success will be, to be on top—alone. And in fact, Marilyn was described as "a queen surrounded by courtiers" (Guiles 1969, p. 267).

Some critics sensed this in her art. Bosley Crowther (1962) wrote: "Marilyn Monroe was not generally regarded as an artist submerged in her art. She was popularly looked on and thought of as a lustrous, free body that floated above and only occasionally came in contact with the artistic element of the screen" (p. 13:4).

When social interest is underdeveloped every life situation will be approached from a self-centered viewpoint rather than one of mutuality. Her following description of her marriage to Arthur Miller would be a good illustration. "I love being married. . . . Now for the first time . . . I have a feeling of being sheltered. It's as if I have come in out of the cold . . . I mean just being together" (Luce 1964, p. 74:1).

> The therapeutic confrontation would be: "And what, do you think, you did for Arthur Miller? After all, a marriage is a cooperation between two equal partners." Numerous confrontations suggest themselves on the other items in this section.

5. *The antithetical mode of apperception*. The Adlerian dialectic inferiority-superiority dynamics is greatly accentuated if social interest remains underdeveloped and the striving is one for personal superiority. This sharply polarized mode of apperception is shown in ER 7 where Marilyn is sitting in the movies, "up in front, there with the screen so big, a little kid all alone," the people on the big screen representing her dream of the future.

At the height of her acclaim when she was so-to-speak at the other end

of the continuum she still retained this polarized view, simply because everything with her remained self-referent. She did not mature. In 1962 she was
asked to appear at President Kennedy's birthday rally in Madison Square
Garden. "There was a hush," she told, "over the whole place when I came
on to sing *Happy Birthday*. . . . A hush like that from the people warms me.
It's sort of like an embrace. . . . When I turned to the microphone I looked
all the way up and back and I thought, 'That's where I'd be—way up there
under one of those rafters . . . after I paid my $2' " (Monroe 1962, p. 36:1).

Since she saw herself at any time in this "all or nothing" dimension, her
success, when it was attained and as it faded, did not seem real. "I used to
get the feeling, and sometimes I still get it, that sometimes I was fooling
somebody, I don't know who or what—maybe myself" (p. 34:1). And
again, "Fame to me certainly is only temporary and a partial happiness—
even for a waif and I was brought up a waif" (p. 38:1). "Then you're at
the finish line and you sort of sigh—you've made it! But you never have—
you have to start all over again" (p. 38:2).

It would be possible to point out to Marilyn how in her polarizing
way of perceiving any situation, she deprives it of its real, greater meaning, and thereby ultimately deprives also herself of a greater satisfaction.
At the President's birthday celebration she could have taken the greater
and more real pride and satisfaction in being a part of an important
national event, rather than the narrow pride in how far she had gotten.

By measuring everything in terms of her own person, while disregard-
ing the larger situation of which she is a part, she arrives at the above
melancholy reflections. "You have to start all over again," probably
refers to her decision to become a Broadway actress. In this connection
one could have told her: "You are no longer the little waif with big
dreams. You have made a great name for yourself, you are *somebody*
and might as well admit it."

This would have been encouragement for her while at the same time
holding her responsible. Then one would continue, "At this point you
don't have to become 'one of the greatest actresses this country has
ever seen' (Bacon 1962), as Paula Strasberg, your coach, wants you to.
Why should anybody want a second time to reach the pinnacle of such
a precarious profession as you have accomplished once? Just be a good
actress, if this is what you want to do now, and enjoy yourself as
well as the rest of the cast with whom you are playing. What do you
think of that?"

All this is aimed at increasing her "common sense" and decreasing
her "private intelligence." As early as 1952 some reporters reflected:
"With all Hollywood at her feet, she is obsessed by an irrational childhood ambition: she wants very much to become an actress" (Martin
1957, p. 126). It is this private intelligence which led her also to the

rather poor metaphor, "A hush . . . from the people warms me. It's sort of an embrace." We would have confronted her with: "What a chimera! Like the wind caressing you! Let yourself be caressed, embraced and warmed by a man, to whom you could reciprocate! What do you think about that?"

6. *The pampered life-style.* While Marilyn had to some extent been a neglected child, there was also some pampering. Once she had achieved initial successes, the pampering took on gigantic dimensions. The difficulty with attaining so much for relatively little is that the elevated position is not accompanied by a corresponding feeling of personal growth, competence, and self-confidence. Since this disproportionate personal success was, however, all she had and cared about, and since through her pampered position this became increasingly precarious for her, she developed her various symptoms as excuses and safeguards for her self-esteem.

It is characteristic of the pampered life-style that in any serious problem situation the person has no other resort than to put the blame on others and to increase his demands. This is strikingly illustrated by Marilyn in her last interview. Instead of showing any understanding for the fact that with her tardiness she really had caused tremendous losses to the studio, she blames the motion picture industry for not taking good enough care of its famous actors. "This industry should behave like a mother whose child has just run out in front of a car. But instead of clasping the child to them, they start punishing the child" (Monroe 1962, p. 34:2). That is, she believes herself to be entitled to act irresponsibly like a little child, and in return to be pampered all the more by a doting parent. To be made to suffer the logical consequences for her actions as any sensible parent would do, she considers a grave injustice. This unreasonable demand and accusation express the error in her life-style which therapy would have to correct by getting her to see what she is really doing, namely behaving as if she were not subject to the common human order of living.

ER 8 reflects her wanting to be pampered. She receives newspapers and a bicycle ride free, without giving anything in return, and instead, going off on her own. Even letting others wait, this important part of her, is included in this ER. "The boys would all stand around and *wait till I came back*" (italics added). This was introduced with: "The whole world . . . suddenly opened up. Even the girls paid attention to me."

When once asked why she was usually late, she replied: "If I knew, I'd get over it" (Martin 1957, p. 67). In therapy one would explain to her the full meaning of the above memory, and of her lateness, as being: "The boys had been nice to you and made you feel good. In return, you rode off alone and let them wait till you came back. They did not seem to mind. That you had the magic power—with all your shyness and innocence—to get away with this, was your understanding of 'the world became friendly.' Isn't this exactly what you are still doing, letting the boys wait till you come? Could it not be that each time you are late you are testing how much magic power you can exert?

"When you learned that the old magic no longer worked as it used to, this was the end for you. But this is nonsense, just as the magic was nonsense, as you know yourself. Now you can stop fooling others and yourself and start to do something real. You are an expert in what it means to be a waif. Perhaps you would like to help other waifs to get along better. Or, you are interested in the human body: Perhaps you can do something with this interest, in fashions, undergarments, cosmetics, or physical culture? What do you think about this?"

Postscript on therapy. We have given a number of examples of Adlerian interpretation and confrontation which may have sounded very simple. But it should be remembered that in this hypothetical treatment we could only illustrate the method, and even in that we remained sketchy. In reality, therapy is difficult and in the case of Marilyn may not have been successful.

As mentioned earlier, for Adler the neurotic formula was "yes—but," with the "yes" representing the common sense and the "but," the private logic. Prognosis depends on the strength of the "but." As if to confirm the Adlerian understanding, Marilyn, in brief succession, expressed herself twice in terms of this formula. "I *would* like a bit more control so that it would be a little easier for me. . . . But everybody is always tugging at you" (Monroe 1962, p. 34:2). And again: "I would like to become more disciplined within my work. But I'm . . . not to be disciplined by a studio! . . . I'm not in a military school . . . not just a manufacturing establishment" (*ibid.*).

We do not wish to guess from this at the strength of her "but" in our hypothetical therapy. Instead, we want to conclude with a quotation from Adler (1956): "In every case there is a 'yes' that emphasizes the pressure of social interest, but this is invariably followed by a 'but' that possesses greater strength and prevents the necessary increase of social interest. This 'but' in all cases, whether typical or particular, will have an individual nuance. The difficulty of a cure is in proportion to the strength of the 'but.' It is strongest in suicide and in psychosis . . . in which the 'yes' almost disappears" (p. 157).

Summary of the Case

More could be said on Marilyn's tardiness and wasting of time, stammering, somatic disturbances, her "private intelligence," her good intentions, her ER 6 and other wrongs she had to suffer, her feeling of always being the helpless victim and later blaming Hollywood, the press, the whole system, to whom after all she owed her fame. However, the reader will have gotten a sufficient sketch of her life-style, and how we would attempt to modify her erroneous goals and evaluations, to get a fair idea of how Adlerian concepts and techniques would be applied to a particular case.

Matching the case of Marilyn Monroe against Adler's description of the potential suicide, we may say: Marilyn was an active person with extraordinary ambition and little thought of others. She tried, however, to enlist their sympathy and kept herself in a mood of self-pity, by dwelling on her unfortunate childhood situation, making it appear darker than it was. As long as she was at the beginning of her movement from minus to plus, as she had construed it, she was merely a determined fighter for her ends, be it by masculine or feminine means. But as she advanced toward the plus side, two things happened. She was rewarded by society out of all proportion, and at the same time she felt increasingly threatened in her vanity and personal superiority because she had enough tacit "common sense" to feel the "unreal" foundation of it all. All her symptoms and her suicide can be seen as attempts to maintain her exalted and erroneous opinion of herself. The exogenous factor for the suicide was the cancellation of her contract, a situation which she was quite unprepared to meet. Having presented herself and pitied herself all her life as a victim of cruel circumstances, her suicide is also to be seen as an accusation of and perhaps revenge on persons close to her who did not fulfill her "insatiable demand for limitless love" (Luce 1964, p. 78:1) and the world at large which she blamed for not treating her fairly. And, indeed, her suicide was taken by many as an indictment of the environment in which she lived and worked.

The task of therapy would have been to modify her opinions in the direction of common sense by demonstrating to her in a friendly way, step by step, her present mistaken ways. She would then recognize her over-life-size secret goal of success, her personal ambition, her disregard for the larger social context of her life, her lack of social interest. She would then also understand and accept that her difficulties are not "caused" by anything in her past, nor by any present malice of particular persons or the system, with herself as the helpless victim, but by her goal and consequent actions. She would realize that she is in fact a very active and forceful person, and could begin to use her resources to live in a more cooperative, constructive and all-around more satisfactory way in which she would no longer need her symptoms.

Therapy starting from these considerations would still not be an easy task. But the therapist would at least have a basis of positive realities and would have gained objectives on which he could focus his efforts.

SUMMARY

Adler's Individual Psychology is a theory of personality, psychopathology and psychotherapy constructed on a scientifically sound basis for the main purpose of being useful in psychotherapy and in improving mental health in general.

With this aim Adler consistently selected among the fundamental issues in psychology those alternatives which would be more helpful in effecting change toward more satisfactory behavior. In line with this he also selected his concepts and terminology so that they would be as much as possible directly applicable with patients.

This resulted in an apparent simplicity which is, however, an expression of Adler's great sophistication—the "disciplined naivete" (MacLeod 1947) of the phenomenologist who limited his inferences to such as would open alternatives to the patient.

The chief principles of Individual Psychology are (a) the assumption of the unity and creative activity of the individual, and the recognition of his embeddedness in larger systems; (b) a consistently goal-oriented, teleological approach to all psychological phenomena; (c) the conception of all human dynamics, in accordance with life in general, as a striving from a felt minus to a felt plus situation (overcoming, completion, goal of superiority, of success); (d) the individual uniqueness of such striving, the individual's law of movement (style of life); (e) a definition of mental health as a striving which is in concordance with the general striving of mankind in its societal evolution (communal feeling, social interest, *Gemeinschaftgefühl*); (f) a definition of mental disorder (the failures in life) as a striving in a narrow, self-centered way from which the larger whole derives no benefit (the symptom as a striving on the "useless side of life").

Psychotherapy is the science and art of getting the patient to see and acknowledge the error in his life-style so that he can select alternative behavior which will be more satisfactory to himself as well as to his fellow men. This is illustrated by the case of Marilyn Monroe and her hypothetical treatment.

BIBLIOGRAPHY

ADLER, ALEXANDRA. Office treatment of the chronic schizophrenic patient. In H. Hoch & J. Zubin (Eds.), *Psychopathology of Schizophrenia*. New York: Grune & Stratton, 1966. Pp. 366-371.

ADLER, ALFRED. *Gesundheitsbuch für das Schneidergewerbe.* Berlin: Heymanns, 1898.

ADLER, ALFRED. Der Arzt als Erzieher (1904). In Alfred Adler & Carl Furtmüller (Eds.), *Heilen und Bilden.* Munich: Reinhardt, 1914. Pp. 1-10.

ADLER, ALFRED. *Study of Organ Inferiority and Its Psychical Compensation: A Contribution to Clinical Medicine* (1907). Transl. by S. E. Jeliffe. New York: Nervous and Mental Disease Publication Co., 1917.

ADLER, ALFRED. Das Zärtlichkeitsbedürfnis des Kindes (1908). In Alfred Adler & Carl Furtmüller (Eds.), *Heilen und Bilden.* Munich: Reinhardt, 1914. Pp. 50-53.

ADLER, ALFRED. On the psychology of Marxism (1909). In Hermann Nunberg & Ernst Federn (Eds.), *Minutes of the Vienna Psychoanalytic Society.* Vol. 2, 1908-1910. New York: Int. Univer. Press, 1967. Pp. 172-174.

ADLER, ALFRED. Trotz und Gehorsam (1910). In Alfred Adler & Carl Furtmüller (Eds.), *Heilen und Bilden.* Munich: Reinhardt, 1914. Pp. 84-93.

ADLER, ALFRED. *Über den nervösen Charakter* (1912). Frankfurt am Main: Fischer Taschenbuch Verlag, 1972.

ADLER, ALFRED. *The Practice and Theory of Individual Psychology* (1920). Totowa, N. J.: Littlefield, Adams, 1969.

ADLER, ALFRED. *Schwer erziehbare Kinder.* Dresden: Am andern Ufer, 1926.

ADLER, ALFRED. *Problems of Neurosis* (1929). New York: Harper & Row, 1964. (a)

ADLER, ALFRED. *The Science of Living* (1929). Garden City, N. Y.: Doubleday Anchor Books, 1969. (b)

ADLER, ALFRED. Fundamentals of Individual Psychology (1930). *Journal of Individual Psychology,* 26. 36-49, 1970.

ADLER, ALFRED. *What Life Should Mean to You* (1931). New York: Capricorn Books, 1958.

ADLER, ALFRED. Psychiatric aspects regarding individual and social disorganization. *American Journal of Sociology,* 42, 773-780, 1937.

ADLER, ALFRED. *The Individual Psychology of Alfred Adler.* Ed. by Heinz L. & Rowena R. Ansbacher. New York: Basic Books, 1956.

ADLER, ALFRED. *Superiority and Social Interest: A Collection of Later Writings* (1964). Ed. by Heinz L. & Rowena R. Ansbacher. 3rd ed. New York: Viking Compass Book, 1973.

ADLER, KURT A. Life style in schizophrenia. *Journal of Individual Psychology,* 14, 68-72, 1958.

ANSBACHER, HEINZ L. The structure of Individual Psychology. In Benjamin B. Wolman (Ed.), *Scientific Psychology.* New York: Basic Books, 1965. Pp. 340-364.

ANSBACHER, HEINZ L. Adler and the 1910 Vienna symposium on suicide. *Journal of Individual Psychology,* 24, 181-191, 1968.

ANSBACHER, HEINZ L. Alfred Adler: A historical perspective. *American Journal of Psychiatry,* 127(6), 777-782, 1970. (a)

ANSBACHER, HEINZ L. Alfred Adler, Individual Psychology, and Marilyn Monroe. *Psychology Today,* 3(10), 42-44, 46, Feb. 1970. (b)

ANSBACHER, HEINZ L. Alfred Adler and humanistic psychology. *Journal of Humanistic Psychology,* 11, 53-63, 1971. (a)

ANSBACHER, HEINZ L. Alfred Adler and G. Stanley Hall: Correspondence and general relationship. *Journal of the History of the Behavioral Sciences,* 7, 337-352, 1971. (b)

ANSBACHER, HEINZ L. Adler's "striving for power," in relation to Nietzsche. *Journal of Individual Psychology,* 28, 12-24, 1972. (a)

ANSBACHER, HEINZ L. Adlerian psychology: The tradition of brief psychotherapy. *Journal of Individual Psychology*, 28, 137-151, 1972. (b)

ANSBACHER, HEINZ L. (Ed.). Adlerian Techniques of Psychotherapy. *Journal of Individual Psychology*, 28, 119-266, 1972. (c)

ANSBACHER, HEINZ L. The first critique of Freud's metapsychology. *Bulletin of the Menninger Clinic*, 38, 78-84, 1974.

ANSBACHER, ROWENA R. The third Viennese school of psychotherapy. *Journal of Individual Psychology*, 15, 236-237, 1959.

ANSBACHER, ROWENA R. Reality therapy and Individual Psychology in the classroom. *Journal of Individual Psychology*, 25, 106-111, 1969.

ANSBACHER, ROWENA R. Sullivan's interpersonal psychiatry and Adler's Individual Psychology. *Journal of Individual Psychology*, 27, 85-98, 1971.

BACON, JAMES. *Associated Press—Free Press*, Burlington, Vt., August 6, 1962, 15.

BERNE, ERIC. *What Do You Say After You Say Hello?* New York: Grove Press, 1972.

BOTTOME, PHYLLIS. *Alfred Adler: Portrait from Life*. New York: Vanguard, 1957.

CONANT, JAMES B. *Modern Science and Modern Man*. Garden City, N. Y.: Doubleday Anchor Books, 1953.

CROWTHER, BOSLEY. Actress as a symbol. *New York Times*, August 6, 1962, 13:4-5.

DINKMEYER, DON & McKAY, GARY D. *Raising a Responsible Child: Practical Steps to Successful Family Relationships*. New York: Simon & Schuster, 1973.

DOBZHANSKY, THEODOSIUS. Darwin versus Copernicus. In Bernard Landis and Edward S. Tauber (Eds.), *In the Name of Life: Essays in Honor of Erich Fromm*. New York: Holt, Rinehart & Winston, 1971. Pp. 130-142.

DREIKURS, RUDOLF. *Psychodynamics, Psychotherapy, and Counseling: Collected Papers*. Chicago: Alfred Adler Inst., 1967.

DREIKURS, RUDOLF. *Psychology in the Classroom*. 2nd ed. New York: Harper & Row, 1968.

DREIKURS, RUDOLF & SOLTZ, VICKI. *Children: The Challenge*. New York: Duell, Sloan & Pearce, 1964.

ELLENBERGER, HENRI F. Alfred Adler and Individual Psychology. In *The Discovery of the Unconscious*. New York: Basic Books, 1970. Pp. 571-656.

ELLIS, ALBERT. Reason and emotion in the Individual Psychology of Adler. *Journal of Individual Psychology*, 27, 50-64, 1971.

FRANKL, VIKTOR E. Tribute to Alfred Adler. *Journal of Individual Psychology*, 26, 12, 1970.

FREUD, SIGMUND. On the history of the psychoanalytic movement (1914). In *Collected Papers*. Vol. 1. London: Hogarth, 1953. Pp. 287-359.

FREUD, SIGMUND. Mourning and melancholia (1917). In *Collected Papers*. Vol. 4. London: Hogarth, 1953. Pp. 152-170.

FRIEDMAN, PAUL (Ed.). *On Suicide, with Particular Reference to Suicide Among Young Students—1910*. New York: Int. Univer. Press, 1967.

FURTMULLER, CARL. Alfred Adler: A biographical essay. In Alfred Adler, *Superiority and Social Interest* (1964). 3rd ed. Ed. by H. L. and Rowena R. Ansbacher. New York: Viking Compass, 1973. Pp. 309-394.

GARNER, H. H. The confrontation problem-solving technique: Applicability to Adlerian psychotherapy. *Journal of Individual Psychology*, 28, 248-259, 1972.

GUERNEY, G., JR. Alfred Adler and the current mental health revolution. *Journal of Individual Psychology*, 26, 124-134, 1970.

GUILES, FRED L. *Norma Jean: The Life of Marilyn Monroe*. New York: McGraw-Hill, 1969.

HANSEN, LINDA. *Gannett Service—Free Press*, Burlington, Vt., June 20, 1973.

KANKELEIT. 5. Internationaler Kongress für Individualpsychologie in Berlin vom 26. bis 28. September 1930. *Archiv für Psychiatrie und Nervenkrankheiten*, 93, 261-336, 1931.

KAUFMANN, WALTER. *Nietzsche: Philosopher, Psychologist, Antichrist*. 3rd ed. New York: Random House Vintage Books, 1968.

KELLY, GEORGE A. *The Psychology of Personal Constructs*. Vol. 1. New York: Norton, 1955.

KELMAN, HAROLD. Psychoanalysis and existentialism. In L. Salzman & J. H. Masserman (Eds.), *Modern Concepts of Psychoanalysis*. New York: Phil. Lib., 1962. Pp. 115-126.

KLEIN, GEORGE S. Two theories or one? *Bulletin of the Menninger Clinic*, 37(2), 102-132, 1973.

KRASNER, LEONARD & ULLMAN, LEONARD P. *Behavior Influence and Personality: The Social Matrix of Human Action*. New York: Holt, Rinehart and Winston, 1973.

LEFCOURT, H. M. Internal versus external control of reinforcements: A review. *Psychological Bulletin*, 65, 206-220, 1966.

LUCE, CLAIRE BOOTHE. What really killed Marilyn? *Life*, 68-74, 77-78, August 7, 1964.

MACLEOD, ROBERT B. The phenomenological approach in social psychology. *Psychological Review*, 54, 193-210, 1947.

MAILER, NORMAN. *Marilyn: A Biography*. New York: Grosset & Dunlap, 1973.

MARTIN, PETE. *Will Acting Spoil Marilyn Monroe?* New York: Pocket Books, 1957.

MASLOW, ABRAHAM H., ANSBACHER, HEINZ L., & FEDERN, ERNST. Was Adler a disciple of Freud? *Journal of Individual Psychology*, 18, 125; 126-135, 1962; 19, 80-81, 1963.

MONROE, MARILYN. Interview with Richard Meryman. *Life*, 31-34, 36, 38, August 3, 1962.

MOSAK, HAROLD, H. Early recollections as a projective technique. *Journal of Projective Techniques*, 22, 302-311, 1958.

MULLAHY, PATRICK. *Psychoanalysis and Interpersonal Psychiatry: The Contributions of Harry Stack Sullivan*. New York: Science House, 1970.

NUNBERG, HERMANN, & FEDERN, ERNST (Eds.). *Minutes of the Vienna Psychoanalytic Society*. Vol. 1, 1906-1908. Vol. 2, 1908-1910. New York: Int. Univ. Press, 1962, 1967.

ORGLER, HERTHA. *Alfred Adler: The Man and His Work* (1963). New York: Mentor New Amer. Lib., 1972.

PAPANEK, HELENE. Dynamics and treatment of borderline schizophrenia from the Adlerian viewpoint. *American Journal of Individual Psychology*, 11, 60-70, 1954.

RYCHLAK, JOSEPH F. *A Philosophy of Science for Personality Theory*. Boston: Houghton Mifflin, 1968.

SALZMAN, LEON. *The Obsessive Personality: Origins, Dynamics and Therapy*. New York: Science House, 1968.

SEIF, LEONHARD. Die Zwangsneurose. In Erwin Wexberg (Ed.), *Handbuch der Individualpsychologie*. Vol. 1 (1926). Amsterdam: Bonset, 1966. Pp. 507-531.

SHULMAN, BERNARD H. *Essays in Schizophrenia*. Baltimore, Md.: Williams & Wilkins, 1968.

SHULMAN, BERNARD, H. Confrontation techniques in Adlerian psychology. *Journal of Individual Psychology*, 27, 167-175, 1971.

STERN, ALFRED. Existential psychoanalysis and Individual Psychology. *Journal of Individual Psychology*, 14, 38-50, 1958.

Time Magazine, August 10, 1962.

VAN DUSEN, WILSON. Adler and existential analysis. *Journal of Individual Psychology*, 15, 100-111, 1959.

VIRCHOW, RUDOLF. *Disease, Life, and Man: Selected Essays*. Ed. by L. J. Rather. Stanford, Calif.: Stanford Univ. Press, 1958.

WERTHEIMER, MICHAEL. *Fundamental Issues in Psychology*. New York: Holt, Rinehart & Winston, 1972.

ZOLOTOW, MAURICE. *Marilyn Monroe*. New York: Harcourt, Brace, Jovanovich, 1960.

Harry Stack Sullivan

5

Interpersonal Theory:
Harry Stack Sullivan

by HILDE BRUCH

It is hardly possible to overestimate Sullivan's influence on psychiatric thinking and practice. Yet he is rarely given credit for his stimulating and evocative contributions, though interest in his work has been steadily increasing. Over and over, some development that is announced as representing a "radical departure" in psychiatric thinking can be traced to his teaching. As a matter of fact, his influence has been so persuasive, and his ideas have been so effectively incorporated into modern psychiatry, that some even raise the question, "What is so special about Sullivan? These are things we all do and know about." Whether we speak of milieu therapy, or the whole field of social psychiatry, or whether we are engaged in detailed family studies, or express modern psychoanalytic thinking as "object relationship theory," or whether we show interest in linguistics and the significance of communication, the roots of these and many other developments can readily be recognized in Sullivan's work. There is another reason for Sullivan not getting the recognition he deserves: many find that he is difficult to understand; that reading his books is hard work.

Though a prolific writer on a variety of topics, with publications in various and not always easily accessible journals, he did not publish a comprehensive exposition of his theory in book form during his lifetime. In the early 30's he made an effort at formulating his new theory, and the manuscript, "Personal Psychopathology," was mimeographed and circulated privately but not published as a book until quite recently. A series of lectures, "Conceptions of Modern Psychiatry," given in 1939, were published in the journal *Psychiatry* in 1940, and then republished as a text for students in 1947. Sullivan himself considered these lectures "grossly inadequate" and did not want a formal publication. All other books published under his name are based on lectures and seminars which he gave after he resumed teaching in 1943. They represent his continuous effort at redefining and clarifying his own concepts. He was concerned with being misunderstood, or with not being clear enough in his formulations, or with not differentiating himself decisively enough from the then current psychoanalytic theory. He would not say one word in his lectures and seminars without having a recording machine going, always in the hope that in interchange with people he might express some formulation that was clearer and more succinct than what he would write, and he traveled around with whatever recording equipment was available during the 1940's. It is unfortunate that this continuous effort at perfect clarity resulted in the rather cumbersome repetitiousness of style which distracts from the basic lucidity and consistency of his theory. The efforts of some of his most devoted students to see in each variation of presentation, or in some varied illustrative material, a change in theoretical or philosophical concept, has not helped matters either.

Having had the good fortune to have Sullivan as a supervisor during this whole period, I shall present here my understanding of his theory as it came across in clinical work. In contrast to his elaborate effort during lectures, he was exceedingly clear and direct as a supervisor, and these more succinct formulations were of help to me in listening to his lectures. The book, *The Interpersonal Theory of Psychiatry,* published in 1953, is based on recordings of lectures I attended in 1947. I also kept brief notes of what I considered the basic points of his theory, and I shall use these notes as the outline for my presentation here.

BIOGRAPHICAL DATA

Harry Stack Sullivan was born on February 21, 1892, and died on January 14, 1949, a month short of his 57th birthday. He grew up on a farm in upstate New York, an only and lonely child, with a taciturn farmer father, and a mother who emphasized the importance of her family's professional status. I recall the many times he referred to his bewilderment as a child when being told that being a Stack rather than a Sullivan was of special significance. In his isolation on the farm he developed a great interest in nature and became a voracious reader of many topics and issues, a habit he continued throughout life. This is illustrated by the wide range of references and footnotes in his writings. He had wanted to become a physicist, but then changed to the study of medicine with psychiatry as the goal. His work reflects his knowledge of modern physics in the structure of his conceptual approach, though he continuously warned against the misplaced ambition to validate psychiatric observations by the methods of the natural sciences. After graduation from medical school in 1917 he served in the Armed Forces and became involved in problems of rehabilitation of veterans. In 1920, when 28 years old, he was assigned to the St. Elizabeth's Hospital in Washington, D. C., where he came under the influence of William Alanson White, who encouraged his interest in psychoanalysis and also his efforts to pursue independent studies. In 1923 he began his association with the Sheppard and Enoch Pratt Hospital where he began, as one of the first American psychiatrists, to treat schizophrenics psychotherapeutically. He became director of clinical research, and finally developed a special ward for the treatment of young schizophrenics. This was the first attempt to use the total setting as the matrix in which psychotherapy takes place. He rated the experiences of the "other 23 hours" as of the same importance as, if not greater than, what might transpire during the therapeutic sessions. The recovery rate of his patients was unusually high and he acquired an awesome reputation as being able to do something with schizophrenics nobody else could do. He began his work along traditional psychoanalytic lines, but soon recognized the shortcoming of this theory when applied to psychotics. During these years, around 1930, he made the most decisive innovations for rethinking the basic aspects of psychiatric investigation and these conceptions gradually matured into his Interpersonal Theory. In his work with schizophrenics he had recognized the close relationship to obsessive compulsive neurosis. Subsequently he was engaged in private practice in New York and acquired a similar awesome reputation of being successful with obsessives, who had been recognized as unusually resistant towards psychoanalytic treatment. With the beginning of World War II he moved back to the Washington area and became actively concerned with problems of the Selective Service. During these years he also began his remarkable teaching career.

Personal Contact

My first contact with Sullivan coincided with his resuming his teaching career. After having been a pediatrician, I was at that time a psychiatric resident at the Phipps Clinic, in psychoanalysis with Frieda Fromm-Reichmann, and participated in one of her psychoanalytic seminars. One day she asked me to present a case of compulsive neurosis to a guest teacher whom she had invited to conduct a seminar and who, she felt, had important contributions to make. Much later she told me that she had asked me to present the case because I was the only participant in the seminar who at that time did not know enough to be overawed by the reputation of the guest, Harry Stack Sullivan. I accepted the assignment and volunteered to become the therapist of a young woman with a severe handwashing compulsion whose therapist was on the point of leaving. She became my patient on a Saturday. I studied her voluminous case records over the weekend, and then presented her in the next seminar on Monday evening, in March, 1943. She had been sick and in treatment for over five years, had been in the clinic for a year and a half, having spent most of the time on the ward for disturbed patients because she felt she needed constant help to feel protected against her panicky fear of passing "germs" on to other people. She spoke with much pressure and urgency, with many details about her early life, preoccupations with sex, and constant anxiety of being harmful to others. Study of her treatment history revealed that she had told exactly the same story, with the same sense of urgency and of divulging of secrets, but with increasing complexity, and with the encouragement of her earlier therapists.

In my presentation I summarized this, with the expression that reading her history was like listening to a "broken record," and this term aroused Sullivan's attention and approval. He enlarged on the obsessive's tendency to use verbal maneuvers to keep from dealing with underlying problems. By focusing on the minute examination of her symptoms in the hope of learning her unconscious meaning, the previous treatment efforts had only reinforced this tendency, and had not only not relieved the underlying anxiety but had resulted in increasingly fruitless ruminations. Sullivan suggested a change of focus, which he spelled out in great detail, that might help her to deal with her problems of living. After she had told her past history and current symptoms and worries in minutest details, with her knowing that they had been properly recorded, she should not be permitted to repeat what she had already told—only new things could be added to the script. After that all discussions should concentrate on how she conducted her life at the moment, and how she felt about people and events now. He advised formulating this to the patient as "We talk only about things about which you or I can know something." This implied speaking about her experiences with people around her, her fellow patients or the nurses on the ward, and on the factual exchanges with her family.

She was reluctant to follow this suggestion as not dealing with the deeper problems, and found it difficult to talk along the new line. She was unable to give any realistic descriptions, neither of her folks at home nor of the people on the ward. But she began to pay attention to the people around her, became more detailed and objective about them as individuals, and how she reacted to them. There was also the beginning awareness of her own feelings. Until then she had spoken of disliking a great many people, was critical of all of them, and appeared to be vaguely irritable without any apparent reason. By being asked to focus on the details of what was going on, she began to be more genuinely interested in other people. Within a month she appeared more outgoing, then became friendly with several patients who until then had shunned her because of her incessant talking about her "germs." Her discussion of her family, and of the problems and circumstances that had resulted in her illness, also became more realistic.

She was slow to recognize any feelings stirring in her, except for intense rage and hate. For a while she was quite confused about her own emotional reactions, often unable to differentiate between like and dislike, love and hate, or irritation and friendly interest. The diffuse feelings of hatred for everyone became gradually more differentiated, with awareness of justified anger for specific events or mishaps. Simultaneously, memories of congenial and loving experiences began to come up. This development was aided by several visits from members of her family, and a visit to her home to attend her sister's wedding; this involved a lengthy railway trip. During this visit she recognized how much resentment she harbored towards her mother for having been belittling towards the father. But this feeling was mixed with compassion and pity for the difficult life she had led. She also recognized how the hatred towards an uncle, who had played a great role in the family's affairs after her father's death, was mixed with a desire for his approval. The wedding of her sister gave her an opportunity to discuss her concepts of sex and marriage, her anxieties about them, in factual terms.

She had a completely unrealistic concept that "love" was some magic happening which would take care of a lucky girl forever after. She had for the first time an inkling that it involved a give and take relationship in which she would need to express a true interest in another person. As her overt symptoms diminished she was able to review her whole development in much more realistic language. Most of her life she had been continuously worried about what other people thought of her. That is why she had always been conscientious, always doing homework to perfection, never staying away from school; but she had never felt good about anything she did, nor had she ever felt satisfied that it was alright.

Until this new review of her development, she had never dared to say anything of this openly. With all her previous therapists she had talked in general terms about the things she felt they expected her to talk about, namely about her hostility, and about sex. Now she became increasingly detailed and realistic in giving short descriptions of the various family members and of what had happened between them. She could even openly express the criticism that she felt she had been pushed around by too many people.

Her scope of activities increased greatly and rapidly. Within six weeks after the change in treatment approach she felt so much better that she moved to the open ward. Then she began to work in the administrative office where she proved herself a very competent secretary. A month later she began to attend evening classes in mechanical drawing, for which she showed great aptitude and which she enjoyed. She became more active in taking part in various social and athletic activities at the hospital. After having lived in the hospital for such a long time she was at first frightened at the idea of living on the outside, and even more so about going back to her home. However, she was able to leave the hospital four months after the change in treatment approach, and she returned to her home after one month as an out-patient. She kept in touch with me for some time to let me know that her improvement persisted.

Needless to say, I was impressed by the effectiveness of Sullivan's suggestions, though I came to appreciate the underlying theoretical conception only later. I asked him for regular supervision of a young catatonic schizophrenic who recovered under our joint effort. I learned from him how to understand the schizophrenic mode of communication, and also how to use it as a guide towards exploration of the reality entanglements that had precipitated the schizophrenic withdrawal. Subsequently, while I was in private practice, I had the benefit of Sullivan's supervision of several obsessive patients and his wisdom as a consultant for five more years, practically until the time of his death. During these five or six years I attended almost every seminar and lecture course he gave in New York and in the Washington area. I could use the clarity of his communication as a supervisor like a thread guiding me through the labyrinth of his elaborate and over-explicit style as a lecturer.

HISTORICAL PERSPECTIVE

To fully appreciate Sullivan's contributions one must examine them against the background of psychiatric and psychoanalytic thinking of the time when he formulated his most substantial innovations—the late 1920's and early 1930's. Sullivan was one of the early American psychoanalysts who was greatly appreciative of Freud's contribution for having drawn attention to the fact that abnormal mental phenomena were capable of being understood, for having focused our interest on the individual person suffering from mental disorder, and for having developed a therapeutic method. However, his own experiences with schizophrenics soon convinced him that Freud's theoretical elaborations did not agree with his own deductions about the genesis of their difficulties.

It is difficult to reconstruct today the atmosphere that surrounded psychoanalytic thinking of the time, the heat and rancor with which theoretical points were proclaimed and defended. Freud had elaborated a theory of instincts, also called libido theory, and had presented his fundamental concepts in the picturesque language of analogies and metaphors. It was unavoidable that the first draft presented the concepts in an over-general and incomplete way. Throughout his life Freud struggled to revise his theory, and he remained critical of all his efforts to formulate a fixed theory of instincts; yet many of his early followers accepted his theoretical assumptions as proven facts.

There were only a few psychoanalysts in the United States, most of whom had gone for their training to Europe. The German and Austrian refugee analysts had not yet arrived. On the whole, psychoanalysis was treated like some mystical and secret knowledge which was passed on to devoted and privileged disciples. The 1930's saw the beginning of the revisions with its broadening of psychoanalytic concepts, as we know them today, though disagreeing with the established theory was never treated generously in psychoanalysis. Sullivan's involved language, his continuous effort to define every concept as carefully as possible, needs to be understood, in part at least, as a reaction against this rejecting climate.

I present here the assumptions underlying classic psychoanalytic theory in a deliberately oversimplified form. In its imagery it conceives of the infant as born equipped with instincts that, if they were allowed to flourish and were not deformed through the vicissitudes of the repressive culture, would guide an individual to a healthy, non-neurotic life. The sexual instinct, the libido, in particular, was conceived of as suffering from such damaging interferences, thus becoming fixated at various levels of psychosexual development. These instinctual repressions lead to unconscious conflicts which became manifest as neurotic symptoms. Psychoanalytic therapy, in this classic frame of thinking, consisted of uncovering the repressed conflicts, invariably of a sexual nature, and of the psychic trauma that had caused them, and thereby liberating the libido. Making such unconscious conflicts conscious, by working through the transference and resistance, would bring about a cure through insight. Under extremely unfavorable conditions the libido was conceived of as not attaching itself to any "object," that is to another human being, but would remain fixated on the self, and "narcissism," the essence of psychotic isolation, would result. Since the transference of former libidinal attachments is essential for psychoanalytic therapy, psychotics were considered untreatable by analysis.

How literally these concepts were understood is probably best expressed by the fact that they were also applied as preventive child rearing. It is difficult to reconstruct with our 1970 mentality the naïve enthusiasm with which such new "insights" were taught and applied during the era of permissive child care.

By that time psychoanalysts in Europe began to openly express their concern with the inadequacies of the theory. Freud himself had redefined the importance of anxiety for the development of neurosis during the 1920's. Other milestones in the re-evaluation of psychoanalytic theory and practice were Anna Freud's book on the defense mechanisms, Reich's book on character analysis, and Hartmann's work on adaptation. Such contributions were published during the 1930's in German, but they made their way to America only slowly, and integration into psychoanalytic teaching took even longer. A decade later, Erikson emphasized more definitely the developmental importance of interaction with the environment, and how the achievement of shortcomings during one phase would influence subsequent developmental steps.

These contributions were integrated into the changing formulations of psychoanalytic theory, whereas Sullivan's work was not. Yet modern psychoanalysis, with its emphasis on "narcissistic character," the "self" and "object-relationship theory," is scarcely distinguishable in point of focus from what Sullivan taught 30 or 40 years ago. The significant point of difference lies in the fact that these authors, and the many others who contributed to the elaboration of these newer concepts, stayed essentially within the conceptual framework and terminology of the original theory. In contrast, Sullivan presented his contributions as a radical departure in basic conceptual assumptions.

CONCEPTUAL PRINCIPLES

The outer manifestations of Sullivan's departure from the fold was his no longer referring to his own work as "psychoanalysis." He also discarded the whole psychoanalytic terminology as misleading neologisms based on unprovable assumptions. He felt that such preconceived notions interfered with clarifying the patient's problems, and he was unsparing in expressing this. In a paper published in 1931, in which he referred to his own approach as "modified psychoanalytic treatment," he made pithy comments like "the psychiatrist filled with the holy light of his recent analysis," and "The analytic zealot knows so many things that are not so that the patient never makes a beginning."* Subsequently he referred to his own work as contributions to modern psychiatry, and went to great lengths in his over-careful formulations to differentiate himself from the pseudocertainty of the early psychoanalytic theory.

It has been said that the main difference of his theory is a matter of semantics, that he took Freud's concepts and attached new terms to them. Sullivan always objected strenuously to any attempt to translate his definitions into psychoanalytic terminology, since they had been constructed in a different frame of conceptual thinking. His essential innovation does not rest in his agreeing or disagreeing with one or the other aspect of psychoanalytic theory, but in his knowingly employing a conceptual framework derived from developments in modern physics which had led to broad changes in the general approach to scientific problems. In this new orientation, phenomena can no longer be explained as occurring in an isolated organism, a closed entity, and according to the deterministic, one cause/one effect mechanisms of old time physics. This deterministic conceptual frame underlies the orthodox psychoanalytic theory. Sullivan stressed that such concepts were no longer tenable in view of the changes in scientific thinking which at that time had been formulated as field theory, and which the life sciences had taken over from the physical sciences. This change in theoretical orientation implied that human behavior could not be studied

---

* The modified psychoanalytic treatment of schizophrenia. *Am. J. Psych.*, 11, 519-540.

in terms of isolated events, but needed to be approached in terms of processes resulting from the interaction of multiple forces within the prevailing field. The need for reformulation of terms is inherent in such a change in conceptual thinking. It is not so much a question of a change of content, or of what behavior needs to be investigated, but of an approach from a different dimension.

Sullivan defined observations of processes that take place in the interpersonal field as the legitimate area of study of psychiatry, and insisted that "immutable private" intrapsychic experiences were not accessible to observation by someone else. Many objections against Sullivan are related to his so-called denial of human individuality. This attitude expresses a misunderstanding of what he actually said. He did not deny the existence of an individual identity, and of an intrapsychic life, but insisted that intrapsychic processes could not be legitimate objects of study. Only what is expressed through the "public" communicative processes can be observed and studied. Even a person reporting about his inner life, including dreams and fantasies, transforms them by the process of communication from the absolutely private into something public. Furthermore, most intrapsychic preoccupations deal with experiences with other people, usually "eidetic people," the "personifications" of former experiences with people, to use Sullivan's expression.

Similarly, with this process-oriented approach, Sullivan felt that in the study of human development an individual could not be conceived of as existing at any time in isolation. He emphasized that the human condition, by its very definition, was at all times a communal existence, and that all development took place in interaction with others.

THE INTERPERSONAL THEORY OF
PERSONALITY DEVELOPMENT

Sullivan conceived of "personality" not as a static or stable entity but as an abstraction, referring to "the relatively enduring patterns of recurrent interpersonal situations which characterize the human life." If these patterns change in significant ways, what is apparent as personality also changes. Some of these changes occur with great regularity in man's progress from birth to maturity; others are by no means universal, and represent the fortunate or unfortunate differences in an individual's development. The organization and integration of such patterns begin practically at the moment of birth and signify the transformation of the newborn, the purely physiological human organism whom Sullivan calls "man the animal," into a person.

He considered the human neonate to be endowed with a viable physiological organization which though immature has the full potential for mature adaptive development. The organization is, however, remarkably labile, and therefore continuously subject to changes by experience. He stressed the contrast of his view to the theory based on the assumption of "human instincts." Individual biological differences were rated as relatively less important, and as becoming less and less governing the further away one goes from birth, in comparison to the significance of the interpersonal influences for the development of the personality. Though dependent on, and limited by, inborn biological factors, the *significant* differences in human personality are predominantly determined by nongenetic factors that shape the human career line.

In view of his immaturity and nearly total helplessness, the infant's survival depends on the ministration of the "mothering one," to use Sullivan's expression. The infant's cry is his contribution to his survival. It is his first tool, his action to achieve satisfaction of his needs. Though the cry itself contributes nothing to the relief of the discomfort, it succeeds by inducing tension in the mother, which she experiences as tenderness, a compulsive need to relieve the infant's distress, an interactional link which Sullivan considered so important that he called it the "Theorem of Tenderness." Since his cry leads to a desired and needed action, the infant is considered to have power in relation to the other person.

The fulfillment of the infant's needs has from birth rested on two components. One is concerned with achievement of *satisfaction*, the relief of bodily tension, experienced as need for food, drink, warmth, sleep, and physical closeness. The other is the experience of a sense of *security*, which has to do with the need to feel accepted and approved by the person providing this relief. The absence of this sense of security is a highly unpleasant sensation, namely *anxiety*, which is disruptive, interferes with other pursuits, and may stand in direct opposition to the satisfaction of other concurrent needs. The pursuit of security is the more important factor in shaping the personality and it modifies in many ways the needs for satisfaction. It has to do with the development of the human potential in a social cultural setting, with the development of self-esteem, the feeling that one enjoys the respect of others, and the assurance of competence in pursuing one's goals.

Sullivan made a sharp distinction between the experience of *anxiety*, the internal threat to self-esteem which is related to the interpersonal field, and *fear*, which is felt as a reaction to a threat to the biological organization—a threat which is concretely definable, comes more or less from the outside, and thus may be avoided or removed. In contrast, anxiety is an internal experience, and it often cannot be escaped since the interpersonal entanglements usually persist. Quite early in life it becomes labeled "to be avoided." The need to maintain security is so important that only those patterns of behavior develop that succeed in avoiding anxiety. Only those processes which have this effect become integrated into the symbolic organization and make up what is in awareness.

Important for understanding of developmental data is the concept of *experience,* the inner component of any event and of anything that is undergone and lived, and which mediates our contact with the world. The quality and symbolic meaning of experience is not the same as the event in which the organism participates. In reconstructing a life history the difference between the "outer event" and "inner experience" is often overlooked, and even more, the way the experience becomes integrated into the mental organization. Sullivan postulated that this integration of experiences occurs in different modes, depending on the state of maturity and also the quality of the interpersonal relatedness, whereby severe anxiety, and also fatigue, may be interfering factors.

These modes of experience appear serially, but overlap to some extent, and remnants of earlier forms may intrude later on. The earliest mode of experience, the least elaborate form, with the infant not yet feeling differentiated from others, and without any verbal representations, was called the *prototaxic* mode. Later in life, this mode is found only during marked disturbances, the uncanny component of terror states.

Experiences from about three or four months on, persisting until the third year of life and beyond, are made in the *parataxic* mode. Experiences are related to individual events, but without recognition of their continuity and logical sequence, and the infant begins to experience himself as a separate unit. This also is the time of earliest language learning which is still, to a large extent, autistic and magical in its application. Though with increasing maturity this mode is superseded, parataxic components can be recognized in many and various manifestations later in life, particularly during mental disturbances.

The next level is represented by what Sullivan called the *syntaxic* mode of experience, capable of "consensual validation," whereby events and meanings are checked with others, and what one observes and experiences is brought in agreement with that of others and results in mutually understandable communication. Mature and rational assessments of events and interactions with others occur in this mode. A large part of therapy is taken up with recognizing and correcting parataxic distortions that interfere with realistic self-appraisal of events and of oneself in relation to others.

The earliest experiences are made in a mode that is not capable of later recall, and knowledge about the inner experiences of infants rests at best on inferences, though it is beyond question that these earliest experiences leave a lasting impact on the developing personality. Sullivan went to great length to reconstruct in detail the patterns of fulfillment, or of difficulties, in the interaction with the environment. He felt that at no time could an infant be considered apart from the setting in which he lived. Direct observations of child development in the perspective of mother-child interaction were practically nonexistent at that time. The extent to which subsequent direct observations have borne out his deduction is remarkable though he underrated, or did not discuss, the possible positive influences of the environment.

Practically from birth on, the infant, in an unknown way for which Sullivan used the term "empathy," perceives the feeling tone of the mother, and becomes anxious when she is tense and upset. It is thus that the way the mother performs her task of relieving the infant's tension states has an effect in shaping his reaction. Her ways of handling him are an expression of her own personality, but also of socially and culturally patterned attitudes. Impulses and biological strivings become thus socially conditioned from infancy on. There is no real dichotomy between the biology of the human being and cultural influences; they are closely interwoven. The mother herself does not live in isolation, and persons other than the mother exert an influence on the infant long before they enter into direct interpersonal relation to him.

If satisfaction is attained through relaxed warm tenderness, it is associated with a feeling of well-being and security, and the child will grow up relatively free from the restricting effects of anxiety. But if the mother is tense and anxious when handling the child, anxiety is induced in him, and thus may interfere with his needs for satisfaction. Conflictual situations develop. The mother's tension and anxiety do not need to be related to the infant, though he will experience them as if they were, and the infant's distress will make the mother more anxious still. The inner conceptualization when things are relaxed and peaceful will become that of "good mother," whereas when contact arouses anxiety and discomfort, the personification will be that of "bad mother." The "mother" about which the patient reports will reflect these early integrations, and may bear little resemblance to the real mother.

Sullivan considered the experience of anxiety, and its relevance in an interpersonal setting, as the dynamic force in molding each individual, along with his given biology and heredity, into a definite personality. Only those expressions of his actions, motivations, thoughts, desires and drives that meet with approval from significant people, and thus do not provoke the disintegrating experience of anxiety, develop within range of awareness, mature, and become capable of rational usage. This part of the personality which is experienced as "I" or "myself" represents the self; Sullivan called it the "self system," or "self dynamism," since it has a functional existence, that of screening the permissible and approved from the forbidden and disapproved. Everybody develops a sort of tubular vision early in life, surrounded by an aura of anxiety that excludes and distorts; what is outside its field is noticed only in a vague and foggy way, or not at all. In the inner integration of one's self concept, that which is approved and associated with a sense of security becomes personified as "good me"; those aspects that are still within awareness, but labeled as disapproved, become "bad me," and need to be held in check or concealed. Those impulses, feelings and needs that arouse severe anxiety, and which remain completely outside of awareness, are disasssociated and experienced as "not me." However, they are not nonexistent but are expressed in many unwitting acts and unconscious motivations that interfere with the rational and mature conduct of one's life.

The self, then, is not an inborn tendency or a static trait that comes suddenly into existence. It is the dynamic functional capacity to view and deal with others which has developed out of the interaction with significant people. In a way, it is not original with the individual but is the "reflective appraisal" of others. This dynamic concept serves to explain the wide differences of personality development under a training that is in many ways uniform and culturally determined, and its tendency to continue its development in the same direction.

Under fortunate circumstances the person's "self," that is, the field of awareness of himself and the world around him, will develop with a wide range of possibilities for the pursuit of satisfaction and security, and only few aspects of the personality will be disassociated. Such an individual has a feeling of belonging, with self-respect and confidence in his capacities, and is able to handle new situations without undue anxiety. If, however, a child has been exposed, from earliest infancy on, to the influence of severe and mechanical training, without consistent attention to his needs and the level of his capacities, with punishment and disapproval for failure, the self dynamism will develop into a harsh and rigid instrument, hemmed in by anxiety at every step, excluding from awareness corrective and broadening experiences that are essential for healthy progress of personality growth. Such a person will suffer from a low self-esteem and will have a great capacity for finding fault with himself and others.

Under certain unfortunate conditions, a development takes place that Sullivan had called the "malevolent transformation of personality." If expressions of need for tenderness have frequently been rebuffed or ridiculed, then manifestations of the need for tenderness come to be associated with anticipation of pain and anxiety. Instead of showing his need for tenderness, such a child will manifest behavior characteristic of his "bad me" component, something that provokes unpleasantness. The most common manifestation will be a tendency to tear everybody down and then to become anxious. At first his behavior may be rated as "mischievous," but he gradually develops into a bully; he will always feel surrounded by enemies, and show paranoid traits as time progresses. He makes it practically impossible for anyone to like him or treat him kindly; he beats them to it, so to speak, by the display of his negative attitude.

According to these concepts all possible transitions may occur from mental health to neurosis and to the most severe form of psychosis. Sullivan was opposed to rigid classification of mental illness and personality traits; he felt that the differences between various states of mental health were determined by an individual's characteristic *patterns* of energy transformation and interpersonal situations. Pattern was defined as "the envelope of insignificant but particular differences" which had developed out of the interaction of biological and interpersonal experiences, with a tendency to recur whenever new situations carried elements of the original anxiety provoking situation. People involved in the new experience are approached as if they were personifications of people of the past who had aroused so much discomfort.

Sullivan elaborated in great detail the significance and possible vicissitudes of interpersonal experiences during infancy and early childhood. However, he did not feel that patterns of personality were fixed at this early level, though severe anxiety narrowed the possibility of benefiting from later experiences. He divided the stages of personality development from birth to maturity according to the capacity for communication and integration of new interpersonal experiences. He felt that each phase was shaped by the experiences of the previous one, but also contained elements for widening and corrective experiences. Increasing maturity enables a child to interact, communicate, and comprehend differently at different levels.

Sullivan recognized as of particular importance for such corrective experiences the *juvenile* and *preadolescent* era, the phase that has been called "latency" in classical analysis, as if nothing relevant happened there. This is the time of the child's meeting the world beyond the family, when he enters school and can gratify his need for contact with peers. If anxiety makes him helpless, then there is danger of his becoming "lonely," and he may live in fear of ostracism when denied favorable evaluation by others. If not so severely handicapped, the experience of intimacy in a meaningful friendship becomes of crucial importance. In association with a chum he can find himself, emerge from the family bonds and develop a more realistic and competent self concept. The quality of these experiences determines to a large extent the way he will be able to meet the tasks of adolescence, with the need to develop the capacity for intimacy with a member of the opposite sex, which then becomes integrated into the capacity for shared sexual experiences. Under favorable circumstances, old and restrictive patterns and their association with anxiety will be reevaluated during these years. If at this stage the adolescent's insight and awareness are broadened, the danger of the personality solidifying into permanent patterns of maladjustment may be prevented.

PSYCHOTHERAPEUTIC IMPLICATIONS

Sullivan was first and foremost a clinician, and the need for theoretical reformulations arose from his therapeutic experiences with schizophrenics and obsessives. In 1931, reporting on his by then already extensive experience, he called his approach "intimately related to the psychoanalytic method of Sigmund Freud." He added: "No argument will be offered as to the propriety of the use of 'psychoanalytic' in referring to a definite variation from Dr. Freud's technique. The choice of a word must be made a matter of personal opinion." Subsequently, he no longer expressed concern about the question whether or not his therapeutic approach was called psychoanalysis. He found it irrelevant as compared to the real issue, namely, whether treatment was effective. His indifference about this question did not keep some of his most devoted followers and co-workers, who also had strong emotional investment in being psychoanalysts, from proving that Sullivan's approach fulfilled the essential requirements of psychoanalysis: that he dealt with unconscious mental processes, was deeply concerned with the significance of early infantile development, and that his emphasis on clarification of the interpersonal processes during treatment was identical with the analysis of transference and resistance.

Sullivan was very much aware of the points of departure in his approach. Here again, the changes are expressed through fundamental issues, namely in his redefinition of the doctor-patient relationship, on the style of the therapeutic investigation, and not on one or other point of technique or content. Some of this has been illustrated, by implication, through the earlier case report.

Sullivan defined the role of the therapist as that of a *participant observer,* alert not only to the overt and covert behavior of the patient, but also to his own reactions and behavior, in contrast to the "blank mirror" image of the classical psychoanalyst. He conceived of the therapeutic situation as a particular kind of interpersonal relationship which differed from other intimate relationships by its *purpose*—that "something useful" should come out of this that would insure increased skills of living for the patient. The special skill of the psychiatrist was his alert awareness of phenomena that distorted the ongoing processes, and he paid much attention to differentiating between behavior and responses appropriate to a given situation, and expressions which were inappropriate and irrational and reflected "parataxic distortions." The patient brings into the therapeutic situation his habitual patterns of living, preconceptions and fantasies, and the therapeutic investigation is primarily concerned with clarification of the context of the established patterns. Sullivan considered it advisable to study some current situation, outside of treatment, to find out the precise patterns of the ongoing difficulties. Only then should one attempt to clarify whether and how the same patterns manifested themselves in relation to more significant people, and in particular in relation to the therapist.

Sullivan's emphasis was on how to achieve clarification of underlying disturbances, and in his lectures and in supervision he was quite specific in describing how to go about this business, how to look and where to look, but without emphasis on what one would find, which he expected to differ from one individual to the other. His fight against excessive theorizing was related to his observation that such preconceptions would stand in the way of observing the significant and novel for a particular patient. In this process of clarifying relevant problematic areas, patient and therapist would begin with mutually unknown assumptions, and an important aspect of treatment would be how to attain consensual validation, which if successful is apt to be accompanied by a lessening of anxiety and improvement in interpersonal relations. In the course of this inquiry, with emphasis on marginal thoughts and undirected recall, conflicts and emotions that had been thus far inadmissable to consciousness would come into the range of awareness, and would also be experienced in relation to the therapist. Such conflicts usually had their roots in the early family constellation, though they might manifest themselves in many different areas, and attention needed to be focused on the specific aspects in the distortions of certain relationships.

In the uncovering process of disassociated current and past distorted experiences, *minor manifestations of anxiety* serve as the significant guide. Sullivan was quite explicit in discussing how to use the minor manifestations of anxiety, such as change in voice, change of the subject, or just stopping, and other overt and covert expressions, as stimulus for relevant and useful inquiry. He warned against precipitation of severe anxiety by premature confrontation with what the therapist had inferred. He defined the psychiatrist's expertise as his alertness to minor manifestations of anxiety, in the patient and himself, often manifested as inattention or annoyance. The therapist's skillful attention to what is going on gives the patient some hint of what psychiatry is able to do.

A reflection of this alert attention to anxiety is the needed consideration for a patient's particular sensitivities and low self-esteem. Sullivan was meticulous about being respectful to the individuality of each patient, and warned against using humiliating comments like calling behavior "immature" or "childish." In particular, tact was needed to discourage a patient from showing himself as overconforming when agreeing with the therapist. Annoying, irritating, and "hostile" expressions need to be respected as signaling severe underlying anxiety, or a conviction of inner worthlessness. Sullivan's basic humanistic approach was probably best revealed by his speaking of people whose whole development had been distorted by their conviction of their inner badness as "we are all more human than otherwise."

BOOKS BY HARRY STACK SULLIVAN

1. *Schizophrenia as a Human Process.* (Reprints of papers from 1924-1935) Introduction and Commentaries by H. S. Perry. New York: Norton and Co., 1962.
2. *Personal Psychopathology: Early Formulations* (ca. 1932). New York: Norton and Co., 1972.
3. *Conceptions of Modern Psychiatry.* The First William Alanson White Memorial Lectures. *Psychiatry*, 3:1-117, 1940. Republished New York: Norton and Co., 1953.
4. *The Interpersonal Theory of Psychiatry.* H. S. Perry and M. L. Gawel, (Eds.). New York: Norton and Co., 1953.
5. *The Psychiatric Interview.* H. S. Perry and M. L. Gawel (Eds.). New York: Norton and Co., 1954.
6. *Clinical Studies in Psychiatry.* H. S. Perry, M. L. Gawel, and M. Gibbon (Eds.). New York: Norton and Co., 1956.
7. *The Fusion of Psychiatry and Social Science.* (Reprints of papers from 1934-1949) Introduction and Commentaries by H. S. Perry. New York: Norton and Co., 1964.

Ludwig Binswanger   *Ronald D. Laing*

6

Existential and Humanistic Theories:
Ludwig Binswanger and
Ronald D. Laing

by ARTHUR BURTON

I. LUDWIG BINSWANGER

Ludwig Binswanger was born in Kreuzlingen, Switzerland, on the Swiss-German border, April 13, 1881 and matriculated at the Universities of Lausanne, Heidelberg, and Zurich where he studied medicine. He began his psychiatric career with Eugen Bleuler, the man who among other things coined the word schizophrenia, and C. G. Jung, the Clinical Director, at the Burgholzli mental hospital in Zurich, the psychiatric department of the University of Zurich. From there he went to a psychiatric clinic in Jena, where his uncle was medical director. He eventually returned to head the

Sanatorium Bellevue, in Kreuzlingen, where his father was director and where he stayed for the rest of his life. He died there February 5, 1966 (1).

I met Ludwig Binswanger twice on pilgrimages to Kreuzlingen. This was after his "Case of Ellen West" had been published in Rollo May's, *Existence* (2), and when I was highly motivated to meet the man who could write such an unusual case history. He was at that time over 70 years of age and had yielded the directorship of Sanatorium Bellevue to his son, Wolfgang, who is still there.

Dr. Binswanger was a moderately large man with a leonine head crowned by a full shock of grey hair. The thought then crossed my mind that such a man could have intuited Ellen West's specifically human dilemma. He was gracious in manner, given to humor, and was perhaps more interested in what the visitor brought to him than his own "message." He was astonished at the popularity of existentialism and voiced some apprehension that his life work might be misinterpreted, if not misappropriated, by others. I offered him the comment I had heard made by a famous psychiatrist that *Ellen West* was perhaps more drama than clinical psychiatry! He laughed at this and said that drama was what life was all about. With this opening, he then disclaimed Sartre as paternal influence while extolling Heidegger with an almost reverential awe.

Helm Stierlin, who describes family theory in this book, was a staff member at Kreuzlingen from 1962 to 1964 and has this to say about Binswanger, his former mentor (3):

> When I met Binswanger he was close to 80, very impressive looking, the epitome of a philosopher-sage (Heidegger, in contrast, looked more mundane, more like a farmer from Germany's Black Forest from which he actually came). As I indicated in my chapter in *Twelve Therapists*, one could easily talk with Binswanger for hours about a great range of subjects. He liked to talk about Freud and would often contrast the modest beginnings in Vienna with the world-wide organization that since has come into being. He said repeatedly that Freud would have disliked what has become of the analytic movement. He then would quote some disparaging comments of Freud on America—very much like those which Paul Roszen has written about. There was an adolescent quality about him. . . . Almost up to the time of his death he took a lively interest in certain patients of the hospital. But when we talked about these patients, I feel often we were not sharing a common focus of attention. I thought then that he had a much more abstract notion of psychodynamics than I had.

In formulating the thesis of this essay as to how phenomenology and existentialism influenced classical psychoanalysis, it would have been easy to select any of a number of psychoanalysts for this purpose. Eugene Minkowski, Erwin Strauss, Medard Boss, Viktor Frankl, Viktor E. von Gebsattel, and even Rollo May come immediately to mind. They all have in common—with the exception of May who is a Ph.D.—that they are doctors of medicine, are formally trained in psychoanalysis, and all felt sufficiently uncomfortable over the years with Freudian theory that they allowed phenomenological and existential concepts to divert them from Freud. All of them are grounded in philosophy as well, and for them the model prototype is Karl Jaspers, who was both an eminent psychiatrist as well as an eminent philosopher. Hegel was for them more than ready for interment, and when Heidegger published his revolutionary *Being and Time,* all of them saw in this work a new basis for understanding the human condition.

Binswanger was a logical choice since not only did he publish more assiduously than the others, but more of what he wrote has been translated into English. Not only that, Binswanger found the case or life history method a most salubrious way of presenting his newer existential analytic conceptualizations, and this fits well with the American clinical temperament which demands a case file. His writing is also more integral than the others, and if a systematic set of new personality constructs could be found here, they would most certainly be manifested in Binswanger's work.

Before, however, taking up existential psychoanalysis proper, it is necessary to recapitulate for the student what existentialism is all about, and why it assumed the importance it did at the time it did. It is now being replaced in the United States by what is called humanistic psychology, but its origins are of first importance. It is no easy task to do this because a background in philosophy is indicated which few American students in the behavioral and social sciences have. Even the most motivated of students find the philosophical convolutions of Heidegger and Sartre hard going, partly because *written* scientific German (and French) have a peculiar context which is not found when the languages are spoken, and because philosophers themselves seem to enjoy certain logical and lexical subtleties which escape others. This essay, then, assumes merely a personality theory background and not a philosophical one. (But I have not eschewed philosophy altogether.)

Existentialism arose as a counter-reaction to a certain aridity in the conceptualization of man which was best capsulated by the works of Hegel, who was to 19th century philosophy what Freud was to 20th century psychiatry. A psychiatrist once said to me that he believed that no thinking person of this century could successfully escape Hegel. The problem with Hegelian philosophy was that in its most purified forms it left man *qua* man out of its deliberations. There was hardly room for dread in Hegel's system! It was a romantically idealistic philosophy which involved the search for absolutes. Hegel's assumptions were such that the pure understanding of reason and thought would deliver man himself to the philosopher. Man's essence, we should say, would lead the way to his existence. But a world soon to be driven to its nethermost limits by several World Wars, Auschwitz, atomic fission, etc., could not singularly accommodate the armchair Hegel in this way.

It was Kierkegaard who became restive with the inauthentic Christians all about him—and even more so with the Church hierarchy. He could not somehow exchange a Christian salvation for the personal one he needed. He wanted a return to Christian fundamentals in the manner of the ancient church at the founding of Christianity. In so doing, he described man's emotional plight in a most insightful way.

Nietzsche was another insightful observer of man's growing despair and the failure of his personal fulfillment. But he sought a solution in "a man above man"—a superman who could ride above his alienation by a self-generated power. This is why, by contrast, Heidegger's concept of Sorge—the interdependence of man—came as a blow to the solar plexus of philosophers. What business had the world's greatest living philosopher writing about the basic social interest of one person in another—about man's angst and the difficulty of finding his being? Heidegger had returned ontology to the common man.

The situation of Western science was not more salubrious. The fathers of logical positivism were determined that truth should be discovered in an explicit way, and that it be replicated and redemonstrated by anyone who wanted to take the time and trouble. They were impressed by Mach's writings in physics and Wittgenstein's in logic. Mathematical precision became the word, and elegance of design its hallmark. The greater such elegance, the greater the potential beauty of the truth which could be discovered. The logical positivists felt that knowledge had been unduly burdened by divine revelation, and complained of gnosticism and the rarefied inner searchings of Kant and Hegel. Whatever its shortcomings the world has certainly profited by the scentific method their philosophy derived.

It was not to be expected that Schlick, Carnap and the others of the *Wienerkreis* could project that the ultimate outcome of their new thesis would be Einstein and the splitting of the atom. Their "truth" was to set men free rather than to bind them by mechanism and affluence. They did not appreciate that the new science would pose for itself more and more minuscule "pure" problems while the growing personal and social problems of man would cry out for attention. And they never could have predicted as humane men themselves that the scientist would lose a certain humanity for the purpose of his experiments. Skinnerian psychology and the more recent stereotaxic surgery of the brain for the behavioral control of human beings are unfortunately the outcomes of logical positivism.

The positive gains which we can ascribe to Western science—health and longevity, economic well being, motility, universal education, efficient use of land, etc.—had a curiously paradoxical effect in the 20th century. The more such progress manifested itself, the less joy man found in his existence. Not only that, the myths and symbols by which he had formerly lived now lost their dynamic, and he lost meaning in life. If God were dead, the nuclear family no longer viable, and the myth of the early return no longer tenable, where were the heroes to come from? However the scientist depreciated institutionalized religion, and the psychologist the nuclear family, they certainly brought a kind of wholeness and meaning to its members. Where such traditional collective investments were no longer available, a substitute had to be found, for the energy principle demanded it. Always at hand was *love,* that state of personal being which transcends all. Alas, people now found that they could not love either, or no one wanted to love them, and sex in new abundance did not satisfy. The conditions were thus set for the modern manifestations of alienation, autism, and loss of meaning. Anxiety, dread, depression and despair, formerly the province of the mentally ill, now became part and parcel of Everyman. Psychiatric literature, in novel form, regularly became best sellers as a form of reader self-cure. Schizophrenia, once a rarefied clinical problem and regularly relegated to back wards of asylums, was offered as merely a cop-out life-style or mode-of-being. What Lopez-Ibor calls "schizophrenics at liberty" became the regular thing, and they began to close the large mental hospitals. Psychiatry and psychoanalysis found themselves unable to cope with these new social phenomena, and encounter, gestalt and transactional group therapies rushed in to fill the public vacuum.

It is therefore no happenstance that Heidegger, Camus, Sartre and others began writing about Nothingness, the obverse ontological polarity of *being,* which everyone had heretofore avoided as unsayable. And they wrote with a viciousness and joylessness which highlighted the social loss of joy in the world. Sartre's *nausea* was a most fitting epithet, and by the arousal of unpleasant gastric association, it did not once again permit the intellectualization of the growing dilemma of dehumanization. This, I believe, more than anything labeled Sartre an existentialist.

The more sensitive and poetic of the psychoanalysts could not long tolerate the growing numbers of people who presented themselves at their consulting rooms but who were not sick in the usual psychoanalytic sense. The consulting room found the world encroaching on it! Such patients were lonely, depressed, anxious, felt empty, despairing, and above all, they could not love according to their expectations and wishes. They seemed to want an archetypal friend, or a Socrates, rather than a psychoanalyst. Wheelis sensed this very early and his novels deal cynically with the problem.

The patient wasn't even sure that his problem was a mental or a psychological one, or that he had a problem at all. Those psychoanalysts who had always had room somewhere for a soulful metapsychology or logos became increasingly unhappy with Freud's rigid constructs, and with the couch as the technique of corrective self-realization, Hartmann rushed in with an ego-psychology, but it was too little and too late. Indeed, the patient began to refuse the analytic posture: "He wanted to rap." A few found a partial answer in C. G. Jung, who could not accept the causality and drive theories of Freud. It is an interesting point that although Binswanger was for several years a student and colleague of Jung—at the time Jung was doing his most creative work—he never became a Jungian himself even though he employed many Jungians on the staff of the Sanatorium Bellevue. He rarely refers to Jung in his writings (4). My guess is that Jung always seemed to stop short of a new and fundamental doctrine of man which Binswanger sought and then found in Heidegger. But Binswanger was never critical of Jung, just as he was not critical of Freud.

Existentialism is an attempt to return emotional substance to the intellectualized life of the individual. Thus, Heidegger's aphorism "that the anguish of man lies in his existence," means that in anguish lies the quality of life. But the goal of science has been to cleanse man of anguish. Yet by so doing, it simultaneously deprived him of a feeling-dimension which countered his loneliness, alienation and loss of meaning. Existentialism we might say is becoming an adult without the customary screens of "power" and "flesh." It gives the appearance of pessimism because it looks at the bedrock of existence and refuses to be comforted by superficialities. It interiorizes rather than exteriorizes, and by so doing extols the subjective life. Indeed, it claims that the inner creative life is necessary to any fulfillment. The greatest interiorizers of record were Sigmund Freud and Marcel Proust, and in this sense they were great and fulfilled existentialists. Both asked unanswerable questions about man—and to do so is to be by definition an existentialist. But the process involved is so indigeneous to life that this is perhaps why Jaspers, Sartre, Heidegger and Marcel all deny they are existentialists, or even refuse to admit they know what it is. There are also existentialists who find the existential salvation of man in God as did Kierkegaard. They pose the problem of the human condition, the being of man, as do all existentialists; but they solve man's problems by a theistic resolution to a higher order of things. Marcel and Bultmann are primary examples with Buber not far behind. Most psychoanalysts, following the personal example of Freud himself, reject a saving godhead, and place the responsibility for existence directly upon man himself. Seeking an ameliorating God is considered childlike and a refusal to be "thrown into the world." No psychoanalyst will permit man to escape himself in this way unless he has himself escaped by this means—a rarity.

Man by this definition lives an existential lie, and the psychoneurosis constitutes the worst life lie of all. Caruso describes it in the following succinct way (5):

> It is, incidentally, one of the central symptoms of neurosis that the unrelated and hypertrophied individual cannot inwardly recognize any Providence, and being of little faith wishes to be secure against all the world and against himself. In the neurotic world where everything has become an object, man himself is the central "object," which in his fright he worships like an idol.

Neurosis is only one example of the bad faith we clinically label narcissism and self-paranoia. All men of inauthenticity suffer from identical disabilities so that one does not have to be labeled neurotic to know that one suffers. The child is taught by his mother to conceal his anguish, and psychoanalysis comforts itself by categorizing behavior as abnormal rather than facing up to the condition of Everyman. The existentially anxious, depressed, and guilty are not grist for the psychiatric mill unless they can offer a certain recognized and accepted symptom complex. This is true even though by general admission more than 70% of the people in psychotherapy have existential problems. Existentialism, on the other hand, considers all people as patients who have the misery and dread of this century.

The Holy Grail of scientific objectivity obscured the now known fact that every success and failure in science has both a causal determinative and a value surrounding it. Both are indigeneous to stimulus-response and cannot be artificially split. Nothing involved in a scientific experiment is objective except perhaps the monotheic design itself. The scientist *qua* human being suffers from the same subjectivity as any person, and if he does not have humanity he probably has difficulty finding a meaningful problem to investigate. Objectification was the false lure which promised a precision that only atoms can have. And even there, atoms and particles are turning out to be a matter of probability as well. The personal situation of the scientist became by reaction formation the search for a penultimate objectivity in his science he could not have in his life.

The energy principle copied from the new physics and applied to psychic functions by Freud and others soon began to spring a leak. The deflection of life energy from its goal could help explain some of the symptom formation in the neurosis, but it failed in those positive states we call well-being, joy, and ecstasy. The attempt to establish brain models on analogues of physics worked well up to a point but broke down in *gestalt* states where there was no point-to-point localization. In an earlier publication I said that one has to have good organ health to be neurotic—that one needs to be in good health to have neurotic phobias, obsessions, compulsions, and the like. My neurotic patients are surprisingly healthy! If neurosis is not then a disease in the medical model sense of the word, but a failure of the opportunities for existence, Heidegger's *dasein,* how can energetic models help us to understand and change inauthenticity? While psychoanalysis and psychoanalytic psychotherapy certainly do help neurotics, it is not necessarily on the basis of the Freudian model that this occurs. All therapeutic systems help, and they seem to do so by a phenomenological humanism which sneaks in the back door of the cognitively-oriented treatment.

The concept of "human nature" is a much abused one. Even Freud used it as a whipping boy. It is used to describe a certain supposed uniformity, consistency, and invariability in man. Human nature has been employed as apologetics by such diverse people as Heraclitis, Rousseau, and Freud. But what is human nature? In the behavioral science sense it is a construction interpreting man's relationship to the natural world, his place in it, and how far he may deviate from it subjectively. But the derivation of the concept is an obstruction, and the assumption is made that anyone departing from the biological or natural is on dangerous ground. Alas, nature shows little regard for the joys of the individual, and has precisely that indifference which denies man his subjectivity. Nature is for man birth and death, and in neither of these events is he the master. Instinct as a central phenomenon is always claimed by those who prattle on about nature, and sooner or later instinct or libido becomes the central focus of that particular school of thought. Internecine intellectual wars have raged over the question of instincts, which divided the good friends Freud and Jung, and has had a recent reincarnation in Skinner and Wolpe.

Instinct formulations are the easy way out for a scientist because the drive or propelling aspects of the instinct serve to detract from the need to understand the content of the drive. The propelling energy is not the same as the content or meaning of the going-toward an object or person. Human reflexes do not tell us much about the purposiveness or goals of the behavior itself. Men, we know, have choices which bees do not. Instinct theory has been reified into a monolith which usurps any possibility of understanding the life within. But in observing behavior itself, and certainly on the higher primate level, the diffusion or negation of an instinct for a higher-order goal is more than a rarity. But it is invariably discounted as a pathological mutation of a kind. Food, sex, self-preservation, and the like are certainly primary, but after a certain point, secondary motives take over. Operant conditioning, for example, has difficulty interpreting the heroic, the comic, saintliness, and suicide. But existentialism can fully account for such events.

*   *   *

The essence of existentialism can now perhaps best be further described by its central themes. The more important of them are briefly noted.

Alienation

More than any other single factor, existentialism was created because of the growing alienation of modern man. Men felt cut off from their ancient roots, from their God, and from their institutions. In the face of increasing distraction, pleasure, and tangible objects, their desuetude grew. Work no longer gave them Calvinistic satisfaction and recreation began to fall into mechanized patterns. The age of golf and bowling were upon us! But more than this, the interpersonal, that is, love and intimacy, became frozen in a frigidity and impotence. The more people tried to shake alienation the more alienated they became.

The alienation was not merely from the Other, but more so from the Self. The Self became a conglomeration of parts, with little communication between its many aspects. In the extremest forms dissociation came into the picture so that a split between cognition and affect took place. The person could in this way retreat into his deepest Self without regard to the objective world outside.

Both Kierkegaard and Heidegger founded their philosophical systems on man's growing estrangement from himself. They particularly understood the new ritualization of society, the meaninglessness of man's goals, and the loss of the inner spirit and creativity. For Kierkegaard, alienation was an incorrect relationship of man to his God; but Heidegger interpreted it rather as a breakdown of a basic morality in which man cared for his brother. Together, they finally doomed the hopes and illusions of Plato, Aristotle, and Hegel that a healing Absolute could be found in the mind.

Sartre and Camus, employing the novel and dramatic forms, portrayed the existential dilemma in a way the layman could quickly recognize. Camus' *The Stranger* and *The Plague,* and Sartre's *Nausea* and *No Exit,* brought the message home in a way no philosophical tract could ever do.

The man on the street, fed by his loneliness and alienation, began a personal assessment of himself of an intensity never before known in history. The Judeo-Christian conception of individuality was perhaps never intended to go this far in self-searching. Not only did psychoanalysis then find a fertile market in a way which even surprised Sigmund Freud, but it gave rise as well to what I call the Esalen phenomenon: the sensitivity and encounter movements, aided and abetted by Eric Berne's transactional games and operations. But there was simultaneously a return to Jesus, Buddha, Lao-Tzu, and similar sages. Chemicals to evoke a wider consciousness became the thing and everyone worth his salt began to write his autobiography. In all of this, the always difficult borderland of normality and abnormality became a very confused thing. Who was to be hospitalized then became the question. The radical psychiatry movement attacked the conventional outlook and methodology of clinical psychiatry and, indeed, the vested interests of the psychoanalyst himself. Self-realization and self-fulfillment became the watchwords, but very few of the millions of people who were hurting wanted to become identified as patients. In all of this, alienation from Self and Other became the neurosis of our time.

Authenticity

The search for an authenticity became garbed in a set of metaphoric terms ranging from Jung's individuated state to Maslow's self-realization (6). The saving methodology—personal and professional—took on a multi-hued persona. But no one could say with any precision how one was to find realization, or even what one was to be realized for. Those with their eyes on heaven saw salvation in a return to religious fundamentalism; those impressed by psychoanalytic theory sought new, shorter, or more vital forms of conflict resolution; some, like Alexander Lowen, following upon Wilhelm Reich, advocated a return to the primacy of the body; still others sought the fount of authenticity in creative projects, magical manipulation, or in a descension to the unconscious even unknown to Jung. None of these approaches could claim a greater validity than others so the decision was left to a personal face validity. But everywhere was rebellion against authority, social institutions, the family, and science. Then in greater numbers they turned to astrology, ESP, hypnotism, the I Ching, reincarnation, the occult, and the phenomena science had refused point blank to examine.

A kind of nausea with the absurdity of life, its paradoxes, became the basis for the new pervasive existential neurosis, with boredom, loneliness, alienation, and meaninglessness as the central symptomatology. The physician's personality, his placebo effect, rather than his medications or healing techniques became the source of his cure. Binswanger was one of the first to realize the magnitude of the healing revolution and to attempt to alter psychoanalytic concepts to meet the new cultural phenomena.

It at any rate became clear that to become authentic one must, so to speak, "cast his fate to the wind." That is, one had to take risks beyond his nature and style, and then accept the responsibility for what happened. He was thrown back squarely on his Self and could not look to the Other to be rescued. The unconscious flight into ambulatory schizophrenia could no longer be taken with such secondary delight, so that the person had for the first time to face his refusal to take risks. Any psychoanalyst will testify that the most excruciating point of the analytic process for the patient is precisely that place in which the patient discovers his *mea culpa* and must then take new and extraordinary measures to change it. The majority of course refuse. But those who do, accept "thrownness-into-the-world," and then proceed to construct a varied life-style or existence. Such insight, that one is one's own victim, comes as an earth-shattering feeling, and its shadow aspect is a hovering close to death. Interestingly enough, the more gifted, sensitive, and endowed the patient, the more difficult such leap into reality is. The pundits are returning to morality—J. D. Frank now speaks of demoralizing as the cause of neurosis, and Erik Erikson has come to hope and ideals as intervening variables.

The subject-object split in modern man cries out for a basic return to the subjective. He must apparently find his authenticity not in the pleasure principle but in the inner evolvement of Self which is *his* reality principle. Freud's reality always meant accepting biological and social limits. But we now know these are again and again transcended in every way. The "pull" to find one's Self is seen in the many people who endlessly go from one encounter group to another, or still others who have been in psychoanalysis for 20 or more years.

Anonymity

The dread of the personality is that of becoming the anonymous or faceless one. Self-esteem, meaning, and creative recognition are the drives of today. But these are no longer to be found in corporate power or government but in a humanistic idealism. Management realizes that wages and even profit-making are only minor incentives in the motives of men and are bringing a new humanism to the assembly line.

If the dehumanizing experience is cast into a world mold, the problem of anonymity offers itself for inspection. Man requires recognition as man—he cannot be an ant, not even a productive one. For most of us, it is not sufficient to find identity in fantasy, for fantasy lacks certain integrative properties which are found only in the motorized parts of the person. Yet everything in society seems to deprive the person of such distinction, to hold him down, and it seems he must wrest it from culture by force. The Horatio Alger story of a half-century ago brought the hero from poverty to riches. This must now be reversed to mean converting riches to poverty, in the way of Buddha, Saint Francis, and others. The cry of the ecologist is that nature is being defiled. By this he means that even a Rousseauian return to the pristine life is becoming closed as a way out. The possibilities of passion are sadly reduced in the modern world. Passion counters anonymity. Sexuality and pleasure only lead to more of the same. But passion is also a task, a burden, and not a simple desire. The neurotic is a passionate person, but he cannot implement passion. He finds distinction at first only in his neuroticism, and in the "shoulds" which drive him. Existentialism calls above all else for a return to passion and in this way a surrender of one's neuroticism. It may even see death as a better solution than neurosis or psychosis. The satisfying life over the long haul is a constructive rebellion which both sunders and reconstructs society. No man can any longer be an island or live anonymously.

Dread and Despair

Dread and her half-sister despair occupy a prominent place in existential literature. Kierkegaard made dread the central concept in the human condition, and Sartre applied it more directly to the individual problems of existence. Anxiety was, on the Freudian model, always an overly simplistic conception to describe man's situation. Dread and despair serve much better in this regard coupled, of course, with anxiety. But dread needs to be distinguished from anxiety on the one hand, and fear on the other.

In another connection (7), I described dread as follows:

> Dread is the subjective and symbolic statement of fear, and anxiety is its phenomenological manifestation. Dread is more long range, more encompassing, and less situational than fear. Dread is in a sense the fear of fear. Here is what Ellen West had to say about her dread:
>
> "This is the horrible part of my life: It is filled with dread. Dread of eating, dread of hunger, dread of the dread. Only death can save me

from this dread. Every day is like walking on a dizzying ridge, an eternal balancing on cliffs. It is useless to have analysis tell me that I want precisely this dread, this tension. It sounds brilliant, but it does not help my aching heart. Who wants this tension, who, what? I see nothing any more, everything is blurred, all the threads are tangled."

The dread of the chronic alcoholic is seen in every sign or symbol of a cocktail bar, a liquor store, and even a liquor bottle. The homosexual finds dread in every sexually attractive man, in the cop on the vice beat, and in women who challenge his erotic situation. But in essence there are only two basic dreads: the dread of self and the dread of death. It is the self one dreads most for that self can at times take over cognition, perception, and feeling, and put obsession, anxiety, and compulsion in their place. The normal symbols of food, drink, sexuality, and similar others become transmuted into dangers with fear and anxiety as their accompaniment. Dread becomes pervasive and the personality attempts to dissociate the self from it-self. All behavior then becomes the escape from dread.

The basic dread is that of dying. This is man's chief repression. Whether Eros is in a constant dialogue with Thanatos, as Freud believed, is an open question; but no man lives without that great question of finality which hangs over him. The appearance of institutional religions was purposely designed to help him with this problem. Dread may be considered the imbalance between the id, the ego, and super-ego. By this we mean, between the creative forces and the extinction of that creativity. Eros and Thanatos, by their intercurrent power, shift the polarity of that balance and, the closer one comes to the appreciation of death, the greater the dread."

Dread becomes the apprehensive quality of existence and the freedom from joy. But it is also the leading edge of existence, for there is no growth without dread. Subjectivity has dread as its content and suffering is more a dread than a pain.

Despair is dread pushed to its furthermost limits. It is its summative function. Despair finds only a closed circle with no way to freedom possible. It seeks a way out and, not finding it, may turn to suicide, self-castration, or starvation. Despair leads to depression, which is the act of punishment for the despair itself, but also for the possibilities of its resolution into growth. Despair comes in waves, and it employs obsessional ideation as its apperceived structures. It is temporarily relieved by the closeness of others—by a dependence on them—but despair can only find its own conclusion and not in the conclusions of others (8).

Temporality and Spatiality

Dread, despair, and anxiety have the quality of shrinking one's world. There are any number of cases on record in which neurotics have lived out their entire lives within a highly circumscribed geographical radius. The past and the future are subsidized by the present in such states of constriction. Personal history should not capture the psyche by irrational fixation on a historical event, nor should the present be lived only in the future promise of a heaven, nirvana, or reincarnation.

Heidegger demonstrated that time and space have personal meaning to man beyond their physical properties. They may eventually turn out to be the core of all the neuroses. It is certainly true that one sees the most elaborate distortions of temporality and spatiality in schizophrenia. Being able to live in *our* time, and in *our* space, is the best single sign of the acceptance of one's being and culture. Ellen West both shrank and dilated time, expanded and contracted her life space, and lived perpetually in a dread-full world which would not retain its physical or temporal boundaries. The self refers to it-self for space and time orientation. If these "givens" lack normalization, a bizarre effect is introduced into experience.

The present moment, the past event, the "becoming" future—one's size and shape, world contours, constancy, the reachability of the perceptual world, etc., all then become porous. Finally, time and space may be largely given up, as is done in the catatonic and hebephrenic. Compare, for example, the meaning of 50 minutes to a psychoanalyst, and to a hospitalized schizophrenic patient. For the former, 50 minutes is an inviolate existential premise which provides for the transition from one patient to the next, and is related fundamentally to the production of his income and to his life style. For the patient, 50 minutes is like 5 to 100 or 1000 minutes, and has as well no social, work, or creative meaning. Concepts such as "nothing" "forever," "never," etc., mean more to the patient than 50 minutes, or any other similar quantum.

Heidegger challenged the universal acceptance of time and space as physical constants and disclosed their personal and existential referents. Most neurotics in treatment are bored as well as sick. And even in those people we call psychotic one finds a curious unconscious willingness to depart from reality rather than to be endlessly bored. Fantasy has the chief goal of changing one's space. Dream material invariably involves physical concepts of falling, moving, rising, eating, etc., and rarer, of displacement in time as well. From this we must conclude that while a man is "thrown into a place at a certain time," he must then go on to construct a world on the basis of his "thrown epoch." Most patients would prefer to live in another century. Authentic people find time and space a functional framework for joy. This is directly antipodal to what we find in the psychopathological states.

Commitment

Existentialism is the interesting paradox of a highly subjective inner world which demands motor decision and commitment. The most famous of the existentialists were swashbucklers of a sort, and Camus, for example, died in a sports car traveling very fast. There is a distinction to be made between the man who internalizes and subjectifies every nuance of the mental life—say, Proust—and the man who uses his inner life as a prelude to action—say, Hemingway. Mental stasis is the order of the day in the first.

The modern manifestation of the automobile is not the need for transportation but the avoidance of physical stasis. It comes as a shocking surprise to all in a long term psychoanalysis how unwilling the patient is to take new and daring action. The order of the day is to hold on to existing security, and even Freud was chagrined at this in the case of Emmy O. and others. To change a basic character pattern in oneself is truly a heroic event.

Existentialism stipulates that mental work which has no actional component is a kind of self-defeating behavior. Ideas *qua* ideas are useless unless put to the test of implementation. Existentialism is not a thesis of success for it urges failure just as often as success. But the man who moves in some direction is more fulfilled than the man who does not. Existentialists are, by virtue of this, creative expressionists of the highest order.

It is therefore necessary to commit oneself for authenticity. The joyful ones in our society are the committed ones. Even a commitment to alcohol has certain redeeming features. One can therefore understand why suffering is inherent in finding authenticity. Commitment is meaning, but the social value of that meaning is a relatively unimportant thing.

Experiencing is commitment and leads to further experiencing. Formal social procedures, such as psychoanalysis, fundamentalist religions, universities, etc., offer experiencing but within a narrower format. "Care" is a call to interpersonal action and loving is ontic thrust.

Joy

Very few pundits can define the good life. Philosophers have tried for eons. For the devout Christian, it might be a life without sin; for the voluptuary, a life brimming with pleasure; for the sado-masochist, the opportunity to inflict and receive pain, etc. Individual styles of life evolve more as freedom from discomfort and dis-ease than from positivistic goals. Existentialism insists joy and suffering are goals of man. While it has been in the past accused of being pessimistic, of seeing principally the dark side of man, this is true only in the sense that man is finite and that he mourns his finiteness. Joy can only be in dialogue with suffering.

We need a new idealism for life. The old values of money and power no longer suffice. The new values are a kind of "letting-be," an inner quietude or peace, and the revitalization of the ideas of brotherhood and love. The campus revolts seem to have run their course and have changed very little. Only those personal reorganizations which bring an inner numinousness with "soul" seem generally to hold. Joy is then the beauty of being man, of exercising passion and creativity, and of finding meaning in life through commitment. It is a feeling of always being present, of being human, and of being in deep communion with others.

Death

The greatest exponent of Eros, Sigmund Freud, was eventually forced into the recognition of death as an instinct. He then gave it parity with Eros. Man hates to die; he sees no reason for it. He represses his vulnerability to Thanatos and it becomes his agony. While it can be debated whether or not Thanatos is an instinct, its influence on living men is not debatable.

Existentialists live (or write) closer to the borderlands of death, and Sartre, Camus, and Bonhoeffer knew what it was like to be condemned to death. Indeed, it is their thesis that we all live under a sentence of death. It is how man faces and uses his contingency which structures his being. Thanatos is the hidden tension behind art, drama, literature, and actually all social creation. Art attempts to solve the problem of death and to ward it off at the same time. Those cultures—say, Spain a century ago—which lived closer to it, were more natural and authentic cultures. In a certain psychological sense commitment to death is necessary, which like the commitment to life, balances things up as an Eros/Thanatos equation. But while longevity has now been extended into the eighth decade, and the possibilities of Thanatos considerably diminished, psychic misery and meaninglessness abound as never before. It is also precisely those who live beyond their years who are the most miserable (9).

The literature on death has jumped from nothing to a sizable library in the last 10 years. This has been due to existentialism. The purpose of all this is to vitalize death, to return it to consciousness from the repressed, and even to make it a choice where individually indicated.

*   *   *

The historical appearance of existential psychoanalysis upon the psychiatric scene was presaged by Caruso (10) when he said:

> These new paths had already been paved by the extreme psychology of consciousness, which equated all mental activity with consciousness, so that its opponents compared it to the caricature of a man with a gigantic thinker's head on a tiny body. In answer it might have been said that the great pioneers of depth psychology themselves, in paying attention exclusively to the unconscious and regarding man's consciousness as unimportant, were also caricaturing man, but this time by standing on his head.

Psychoanalysis, and all healing methodologies based upon it, had fallen into a crisis, but one only depthfully apparent. This crisis had a number of facets, including the failure to reproduce the analytic kind, but principally that the biological determinism of psychoanalysis was not in tune with the new freedom of the times, and the patient was rapidly losing the needed docility and receptivity for the transference. The goals of psychoanalysis seemed also to be shifting away from disease to training or to self-realization or to the ego, which left all of the analysts trained in symptom removal somewhat at a loss. The best statistics available about psychoanalytic results and outcomes revealed a shocking inefficiency of the cure. Mountains of labor, time, pain, and money very often produced a cured mouse. Revisionary attempts to treat people in groups, to produce a brief psychoanalysis, and to create variant and more efficient ego forms had not been spectacularly successful. Hartmann was revered, but by analysts only. The public's—particularly the young—return to Jung and Adler on newly reevaluated bases had not yet gathered momentum and did not at any rate promise to hold the remedies sought. There was not only a crisis of faith at large, but a crisis of faith in psychoanalysis as well. There was the strange social paradox of ever more and more patients but also increased lampooning and derision in the slick intellectual magazines and films as well.

There were two very important theoretical problems in all of this upon which the issue rode. The first was Freud's libido theory; the second, Descartes' *cogito ergo sum*. We know that Freud fought bitterly (and successfully) not to seriously alter the theory of the id. His conviction, held at great personal cost, must have involved his own personality needs and reinforced itself daily, for otherwise the whole thing becomes irrational.

Now, the postulation of an id was a great step forward in understanding the psychopathology of the ego. Freud was neither the first nor the last to posit a set of instincts—but he was the only one to fit them precisely into a total philosophy of man. (One thinks here of McDougal and his hormic psychology!) But the libido theory began to break down internally when repression was no longer culturally necessary—as it indeed was in *fin de siecle* Vienna—and when open pleasure was available in great abundance. Psychoanalysis then perhaps became a style of life for both the analyst and patient, and one often wanted, and needed, to make a catholicism of it.

The difficulties with libido theory today have now been so explicitly stated and repeated as to constitute a bore (11). At any rate, in the practice of psychoanalysis, and in its psychotherapeutic derivatives, psychosomatic and anxiety defenses seemed to have lost their ability to quiet the conflict, to reduce the basic anxiety, or our methods had become subtly and unknowingly altered for the worse. It occurred with increasing frequency that long-term analysis left both the analyst and the analysand dissatisfied with the results. The milieu in which the analysis took place, society, did not seem to fit with the theory that was being applied. And the patients wanted to participate in dialogue and not lie on a couch unheard, as I said earlier. The analyst was forcibly retreating into his classical history.

I do not demean the great discoveries of Freud by which millions have come to understanding and fruition, and by which a whole culture has been changed. Psychoanalysis today is still a viable and growing healing function, as well as the key to basic understanding of man. But Freud never claimed to have found that universal and alchemical secret by which man would grow and change for all times. Indeed, were he alive today, I would predict that he would have revised his libido theory in the direction of Binswanger or Jung. Freud detested the mystical and kept it out of his formulations, but man presumably needs a bit of mysticism, and it often transforms him as an inner truth even though it may remain mythic scientifically. Further, I have known scientists who consider Freud himself a magician or worse. The pleasure principle, the most primitive of man's behavioral concepts, is now an insufficient basis for understanding man's reality. Had Freud been willing to abridge the fundamental drive-organization of pleasure, existential psychoanalysis might never have been created.

The healing experience is certainly that the patient has an id centered about pleasure and sex. But sexuality and pleasure are no longer as formative and critical in his life, and the repression of a traumatic sexual event or fantasy can no longer account for the neurotic symptomatology which develops. Hysteria has vanished from the scene. In fact, psychoanalysis never could explain the origins and flowering of schizophrenia, and even now it has very little to offer in understanding the existential neuroses. If one includes paranoia, the character disorders, and psychotic depressions, then psychoanalytic theory is a highly limited thing which has been generalized way beyond its data. It was never really intended as a philosophy of man, and Freud wanted only to be the healer. But society needed psychoanalysis as a philosophy at the time just as it seems now to be rejecting it as a philosophy of man.

Another great man casts his shadow over men today. Descartes was a curious paradox in that he was the godfather of the mathematic-deterministic viewpoint of man, but at the same time saw this as the proper approach to God. The two opposed attitudes never seemed to produce a conflict in him, at least insofar as we know. Descartes' position is usually summed up by his now famous *cogito ergo sum*. By this Descartes meant that the primacy of man was to be found in his cognition and perception, but not in his being. The fact that man can reason makes him man. More correctly the formula must now become: *sum ergo cogito—because I am, I think*. Being and ontology have primacy, existence itself, and thought and perception are latecomers to the scene. Psychoanalysis and psychiatry are still strongly fettered by Cartesian doctrine. The categorization of the patient (diagnosis), the emphasis on cognition (thinking disorder), the concept of will ("you want to be sick"), the search for a universal coccus pathogen (organic deficiency), the psyche as brain disorder (psychosurgery), and similar others are part of the Cartesian inheritance.

Cultural psychoanalysis became the "analytic attitude," and all mental operations were subjected to a fractionization process. Synthesizing or gestalting was more difficult and assumed to be inherent in a proper analytic job, that is, synthesis would appear spontaneously at the proper time. Ideas, wishes, impulses, images, affects, etc., were all fed into this analytic mill and came out compressed into a few formulative pellets. Quite often psychoanalysis ended with the case note: "Has arrived at a fundamental insight into her conflict but is unfortunately not yet able to act upon it."

Binswanger, as I have pointed out earlier, was only too painfully aware of the inability of psychoanalysis to meet man's deepest needs in a changed world. Nothing forces one to such a fateful recognition as does the psychosis generally, and schizophrenia particularly, and Kreuzlingen specialized in treating refractory schizophrenics. The advent of Heidegger as an ontologist freed Binswanger from Freudian shackles and permitted earlier conceptions he had absorbed from Kierkegaard and Nietzsche to become perceptually central. He began creating a "new" psychoanalysis, but he accepted the truth that the basic discoveries of Freud had to remain in force. Ontology, and the philosophical and psychological bases of being, were to be coupled to psychoanalysis in a new gestalt as Karl Jaspers had decades ago attempted to do. The fact that Binswanger has been only partially successful in this quest is not the question here. Existential psychoanalysis has been a most significant force in the revival of humanistic values in psychiatry, and one of its important by-products has been the death knell of the "warehouse" type of mental hospital.

At any rate, Binswanger set out to do the following in his new existential psychoanalysis:

1. To experience the patient phenomenologically rather than categorically.
2. To change the goals of psychoanalysis so as to be more syntonic with the patient's "interval" existence and less with the needs of the analyst.
3. To give the subjective, or dynamic, being of the patient parity with organic postulations in formulating diagnosis and prognosis.
4. To deny psychopathological manifestations as culturally or personally special and to return them to the human condition.
5. To recognize the splitting in schizophrenia as a reaction to untenable life modes and to the world as less than an idealistic experience.
6. To make possible personal freedom and rebellion in the sphere of the mental.
7. To demythologize transference and resistance as sole healing conceptions in psychoanalytic treatment.
8. To focus on the patient's interpersonal moment, its passion and meaning, rather than on the historical trauma, or fantasy of trauma, in treatment.
9. To establish newer concepts of existential anxiety, guilt and depression, and relate them more exactly to the total human condition.
10. To refuse to provide the analyst professional refuge from his own humanity, and to force him into the interpersonal human condition at large.
11. To rephrase the fundamental analytic question of mental conflict to one of "to be or not to be."
12. To give new and personal meaning to the world of time and space, creating new personal dimensions or modes of fatness, thinness, mania, delusion, love, and similar others as analytically viable.
13. To recast libido theory to include pleasure as only one mode of the ego being-in-the-world and to provide room for needs dominated by spirit, soul, or meaning.
14. To reinterpret the neuroses as the self-surrender of *dasein*.
15. To refuse genetic, organic, and hereditary interpretations of existence across the board as analytically self-serving.
16. To interpret consciousness and intentionality as specifically *human* consciousness.

The existential analysis of Binswanger is a mixture of Freudian and Heideggerian concepts which often lack clarity and certainly fall down at points of systematization. This seems also to be true of other existential systems such as those by Boss (12), Frankl (13), Caruso (14), and May (15). The gaps and holes are so serious that the reader is left with the feeling that this is a grafting rather than a new species. None of it really satisfies in a new way or in the way Freud first seized upon people (16). In the case histories as well, the descriptions seem more analytic than existential, and one doesn't really know to what to ascribe the causality of the diseases. Perhaps it is too early to expect from Binswanger what it required Freud more than 50 years to do.

What seems of the greatest importance here is the new and fresh attitude toward the patient—the new incentive for the analyst. Binswanger never repudiated the sexual basis of the neuroses as Jung and Adler had done. His purpose was to place ontology in a more proper perspective to psychoanalysis. Freud was basically a moralist who for all of his self-abnegation freed man from culture to find his pleasure and sexuality. Binswanger's contribution, as I see it, was to place a personal value on the pleasure, and to relate it to the deeper spiritual and religious needs of the person. Freud saw psychic suffering as an individually pathological matter based upon a few well-formulated clinical concepts; Binswanger saw such suffering as related to all men, and sometimes transcending and chosen. He did not rush in to cure. Freud's stars were contained in the Eros/Thanatos, Truth/Fiction, and Good/Evil polarities. Binswanger rather demonstrated that truth is relative to the seeker—fantasy is truth and truth fantasy—being rises above good and evil—below-consciousness is also above-consciousness—and that Eros and Thanatos are values as well as biological aspects of man. Binswanger never hesitates to employ a metapsychological construct in the way Freud could not do, if it aided his thesis. This makes the anti-philosophical reject Binswanger. But Binswanger never stops being the psychoanalyst, and his fundamental goal is the cure or betterment of the patient. He is a healer in every sense of the word and not a philosopher as such. There is something psychiatrically sobering in the fact that Ellen West committed suicide, and that Binswanger was satisfied with her treatment. This means for me that Binswanger understands, as Freud did not, that we all head toward some ultimate fate or destiny, and that such goal is not necessarily a sickness.

Dasein

Heidegger's (17) basic conception of the *dasein* is a confusing one for the American student, and Sartre's (18) paraphrasing of it doesn't help much. In part the matter is linguistic. *Dasein,* on its simplest, most elementary level, means *being there;* that is, the person being in life. This is strange because we know we are here! But Heidegger makes a more formal thing of it by revealing degrees of "being here." Being "out of it" or being "in it" are everyday parlance, but the *dasein* is not the presence or absence of a certain consciousness, but rather a "being thrown" (at birth) into a set of distinctive human circumstances. One is, so to speak, caught "being a a human being." This humanness then involves other people, love, biological needs, the fact of death, etc. It is perhaps like being thrown into the sea where one must either swim or die forever. Something like this must happen with the newborn child, and Gesell and Spock seem to miss the dynamic aspects of this "thrownness" or *dasein* experience.

Being "thrown into the world" implies a counterforce of not wanting "to be thrown." One's *dasein* is always a fluid one and is perpetually being searched by the ego for joy and satisfaction. Certain psychological defenses, described more fully in the next section—existential anxiety, existential depression, and existential guilt—monitor being when it gets severely off course from its *dasein.* Suicide (or homicide) reveals that the despair of the *dasein* is so great that self-preservation is no longer tenable for it, and dread is the constant apprehension of despair. The neuroses are not so much a manifestation of instinctual conflict—to have an evil pleasure or not to have it—as the demonstration that the *dasein* has not fulfilled, and is not fulfilling, itself. The farther reaches of the psychosis, on the other hand, reveal that *dasein* is attempting to make a *new and perverse dasein* for itself.

It must be understood that *being* and *dasein* are not identical. Being is a construct to notate the fact of a personality existent; *dasein,* on the other hand, is a statement of a commitment to an intercurrent human dilemma, a history, and a problematic future. The former often leads to a *trait* description of the individual and, ultimately, to sophisticated assessment devices such as the Minnesota Multiphasic Inventory or even Rorschach Test. But the *dasein* can never be a summation of traits, impulses, needs, or even potentialities. The former is static; the latter the quality of life in its most painful and interpersonal aspects.

Dasein is not an instinct; it is the supreme fact of being man. It leads to a central purpose and style of life, and from it the meaning of existence is constructed. This necessary action depends initially not only on the circumstances or ambience one is in but also on the endowment one has. But the basic opportunity for authenticity is inherent in the Self not because of money, aptitude, or even intelligence, but because one has had the opportunity of being "thrown in," and is therefore a person with great possibilities.

structure which arises, including the psychosomatic situation, then becomes unrecognizable from the usual neurosis and can even be treated similarly.

Existential guilt is not the guilt of behavioral commission but of life omission. One feels guilty for missing the critical choice points in life by which life might have been fulfilled. This feeling of missing the chance to be heroic is described by Camus in *The Fall,* and it leads to his protagonist's ultimate mental downfall. The guilt arises not because of impropriety to another, but because of impropriety to the self. Aggression is always a self-design, and has its principal projected image there. O. H. Mowrer's emphasis on restitution to the victim in the neurosis fails to account for the fact that the neurotic is the greatest victim of all of himself.

The various patients Binswanger has written about—Lola Voss, Suzanne Urban, Jurg Zund, Ellen West, and others—all reveal high quanta of existential guilt. They feel guilty about their eating, their clothes, their sex, their religion, etc., but underneath it all there is the concern that they are inauthentic people and unworthy of regard. They do not feel they deserve good fortune and unconsciously punish themselves should it come. They are guilty for their pseudo-humanity and their fear of becoming.

The A-Priori Structure

All phenomenologists, and not the least among them, Binswanger, fall back upon inherent perceptual structures which are the given of mental life. That is, we might say that all knowledge has as its function the evolutionary extension of the species and that cognitive processes are shaped to further this function. The empirical findings on perceptual constancy, gestalt integrity of percept, verticality, among others, all illustrate this. These may be related to brain and neurophysiological functions, or they may involve these coupled with the dynamic needs of the person as well.

Binswanger makes frequent reference to a concept he calls the *a-priori* ontological structure. Certain functions of man, say, language, are rather late comers to the scene of existence and would not be considered an *a-priori* ontological structure. What, then, would qualify? The answer is the bedrock of man's existence, that is, his very essence itself. In the world of nature, the fact of *being present* is the greatest fact of all, and this is an *a-priori.* The manner in which one is present then becomes a secondary event to the fact itself of being present. A certain religious or spiritual attitude which all men have would be another *a-priori.* Binswanger says (21).

I found myself forced to recognize in man something like a basic religious category; that, in any case, it was impossible for me to admit that the religious was a phenomenon that could somehow be derived from something else. I was thinking, of course, not of the origin of a particular religion, nor even of religion in general, but of something that I have since learned to call the religious I-Thou relationship.

Not only the basic I-Thou, but the fact of personhood, and of being thrown into the world are the *a-prioris* upon which all higher questions of social existence are predicated. These are not instincts or archetypes but universal givens inherent in the being of man. They cannot be easily shown to have antecedents.

*   *   *

We have now to ask how existential psychoanalysis operates as a treatment modality. In what sense is it an improvement upon psychoanalysis? Here the following statements from Caruso and Binswanger help us.

> If Freud repeatedly finds that Mankind, like the individual, "lives beyond his means," this does not mean that the pleasure principle dominates human life in its entirety, but only that man in his everyday life takes his existence too lightly, that the Dasein makes light of itself (22).

And, from Binswanger (23):

> While clinical psychiatry strives to make such comparison possible on the grounds of the similarity or dissimilarity of symptoms and syndromes, *Daseinanalyse* provides us with a different kind of systematic comparison—one based, namely, on certain existential processes and determinations. Instead of a disease unit consisting of a small and perhaps also clinically and symptomatically rather varied class, we have here a unity of definite existential structures and processes.

The clinical problem thus becomes the clarification of being, the analysis of the dasein, and the bringing together of the gestalted elements of existence. Nowhere does existential analysis get caught up with the establishment's attitude toward disease in the usual way. As in Rogerian psychology, the patient has the responsibility for his own dasein, and there is nothing, as such, to be cured. No analyst arrogates to himself the belief that he knows "the way" because he is a physician. With the exception of the Jungians, many psychoanalysts have become so indoctrinated in Freud that they lack the breadth of culture and education which an existential psychoanalysis calls for. To be an existential analyst one must be a poet and artist as well as a doctor, for otherwise the point of ontology might be missed. Existential analysis is not a new methodology so much as a freedom for the patient to work out his fate collaboratively. Wherever a person's existence is concerned, we deal not with the objective facts but with a highly subjective and internal life which emphatically responds to a similar subjectivity in the healer.

If one documents Binswanger's published case histories, then a number of existential concepts appear again and again, albeit in unsystematic fashion. They are merely cited here with one-line referents for the student.

1. *Inconsistency*
   The holes in the existence of the patient.

2. *Chasing the Ideal*
   The moral need of the patient for a more sublime world.

3. *Laying Aside of Oneself*
   The dasein's refusal to accept the leap into life.

4. *The Either/Or Split*
   The dasein ambivalence which can become schizophrenia.

5. *Disembodiment*
   The mind supreme without an attached sensualism or bodily referent.

6. *Fallenness*
   The dasein which has lost its thrownness.

7. *The Uncanny*
   The experience perception of unexplained psychic events beyond the borderlands of cognition.

8. *The Horrid*
   The loss of beauty in continued despair.

9. *The Terrible*
   The impossibility of a way out for the dasein.

10. *The Wearing Away of Existence*
    The grinding down of the dasein so that suicide becomes plausible and desirable.

11. *Feeling Betrayed*
    The dasein which has failed to live up to its promise of fulfillment.

12. *Paradise Lost*
    Proust said about this, "The only true paradise is always the paradise we have lost."

13. *Dread*
The presence of psychic danger in every possible act of pleasure.

14. *Despair*
The dasein being closed in upon itself.

Existential psychoanalysis for its method follows the psychoanalytic model by the transference and its analysis. Even the resistances which develop there are worked through in the usual way. The neurotic conflict is analyzed as mental conflict but from there one goes on to the existential anxiety, existential depression, and existential guilt. Freedom from neurosis is not enough, for existential analysis proper begins when the patient is no longer symptomatically neurotic as such. The ego, the body, and the spiritual or religious then blend into a necessary unity. In this work the existential analyst is more of a process model than the Freudian analyst can ever be, or allow himself to be.

REFERENCES

1. Memorial Services Booklet, Kreuzlingen, February 8, 1966.
2. MAY, R., ANGEL, E., & ELLENBERGER, H. F. (Eds.): *Existence. A New Dimension in Psychiatry and Psychology*. New York: Basic Books, Inc., 1958.
3. Personal communication, March 27, 1973.
4. Binswanger comments very briefly on his "Jungian dilemma" in *Being in the World*. New York: Basic Books, 1963, p. 246.
5. CARUSO, I. A. *Existential Psychology*. New York: Herder & Herder, 1964.
6. BURTON, A. A commentary on the fully-analyzed person. *Am. J. Psychoanalysis*, 32, 186-194, 1972.
7. BURTON, A., LOPEZ-IBOR, J. J., & MENDEL, W. *Schizophrenia as Life Style*. New York: Springer, 1974.
8. BURTON, A., ET AL. *Ibid.*
9. DE BEAUVOIR, S. *The Coming of Age*. New York: Warner Paperback Library, 1973.
10. CARUSO, I. A. *Op. cit.*, p. 112.
11. See my extended comments on this in Burton, A., *Modern Humanistic Psychotherapy*. San Francisco: Jossey-Bass Publishing Co., 1967.
12. BOSS, M. *Psychoanalysis and Daseinanalysis*. New York: Basic Books, 1963.
13. FRANKL, V. E. *The Doctor and the Soul* (Rev. Ed.). New York: Knopf, 1965.
14. CARUSO, I. *Op. cit.*
15. MAY, R., ET AL. *Op. cit.*
16. DEUTSCH, H. *Confrontations with Myself*. New York: Norton, 1973.
17. HEIDEGGER, H. *Being and Time*. New York: Harper & Row, 1962.
18. SARTRE, J. P. *Being and Nothingness*. London: Methuen and Co., 1957.
19. SEARLES, H. F. *The Non-Human Environment in Normal Development and in Schizophrenia*. New York: International Universities Press, 1960.
20. FRANKL, V. E. *Op. cit.*

21. BINSWANGER, L. *Being-in-the-World, op. cit.*, p. 183.
22. CARUSO, I. A. *Op. cit.*, p. 177.
23. BINSWANGER, L. *Ibid.*, p. 251.

BINSWANGER READING BIBLIOGRAPHY

1. The Existential Analysis School of Thought, in R. May, *et al.* (Eds.), *Existence.* New York: Basic Books, 1958.
2. The Case of Ellen West in R. May, *et al.* (Eds.), *Existence.* New York: Basic Books, 1958.
3. *Being-in-the-World. Selected Papers of Ludwig Binswanger.* New York: Basic Books, 1963.

II

RONALD D. LAING

Ronald D. Laing is a Scottish psychiatrist who did his creatively formative incubation work at the Tavistock Clinic in London where so much fine psychiatric theory has been spun. He has also been associated with the Tavistock Institute of Human Relations, Glasgow University, Glasgow Royal Mental Hospital, the Langham Clinic, and, most recently, the Kingsley Hall Clinic. Like the complex doctrine he espouses—he does not call himself an existentialist—he is a man of many talents and many interests, and is comparatively youthful. He has now replaced Fritz Perls charismatically with those under 30, and is also popular with all people who would like to see psychiatry radically revised or even abolished. He is, paradoxically, a psychiatrist who is anti-psychiatry.

Dr. Laing has two manifest interests at the moment. The first, and most important for us, is schizophrenia; the second, the liberalization and humanization of the human nexus through family, social, and political change. In this essay, which has the theory of personality as its focus, we will have to largely ignore the second, while placing the spotlight on the first.

Unlike Ludwig Binswanger, with whom he shares a more or less common outlook on schizophrenia, Laing seems unsophisticated in philosophy, quotes Heidegger and Kierkegaard less and Sartre more, and like the majority of healers, comes to his philosophical position on an experiential basis, and on a "learning from the patients" rather than from the study of "philosophical tracts." There is much that is unsystematic, even chaotic, about Laing— possibly only the systematization of his own inner model counts with him —and he borrows, appropriates, and uses whatever makes his thesis or social point. He states that he has no basic disagreement with Freud, whom he accepts as a genius, and as one who showed us things we didn't see before. When asked recently whether he was working in the same vineyard with Freud, he said (1):

> . . . A great deal of human suffering caused by errors, delusions and deception—having sold oneself and other people down the river. If one can actually revert to the truth, then a great deal of one's suffering can be eased—because a great deal of one's suffering is based on sheer lies. A great deal of guilt, and shame, and humiliation, anxiety, envy, jealousy, revenge and many painful feelings we have are based on a false self. If our realization of the truth could penetrate deeply enough —I mean into our guts, into our physiology, into our chemical, hormonal, endocrine procedures—then a great deal of what we're suffering about just evaporates. It's not so much the conflict as the resolve. The truth brings with it a great measure of absolution, always.

This would indicate that Laing's objectives for the common mental weal are the same as Freud's, but he obviously does not share Freud's interest in metapsychology.

Laingian psychology uses few conceptions, but employs them cogently and brilliantly. Most of Laing's ideas about schizophrenia are, at the time of writing, to be found in his two earliest books, *The Self and Others* and *The Divided Self,* which originally were a single manuscript. Some additional case material on families with schizophrenic members is to be found in *Sanity, Madness, and the Family.* For Laing, schizophrenia has been the mine whose high grade ore has given him a fundamental insight into the total human condition. He disagrees with Freud's ideas about the "narcissistic neuroses" and does not define schizophrenia as an id unable to project itself in its deep fixation upon itself. Most of all he refutes the organic pessimism of German-Viennese psychiatry which ultimately condemns the schizophrenic to the back ward of the mental hospital.

Laing follows Binswanger's earlier discomfort with traditional psychoanalysis and psychiatry, particularly as it applies to schizophrenia. He sees psychiatric categories as disguising the fact that the patient is first of all a person, and cannot see that categorization of patients even serves the best interests of a healing science. He is suspicious of the psychiatric use of diagnosis, and even of psychiatric linguistics proper, but he never has claimed, as Szasz does, that there is no mental illness, or that mental health practitioners are corrupt in certain ways. He believes that as far as schizophrenia is concerned—and the implication is that this would hold for all forms of psychological problems—the causes, if not the answers, are to be found in the family structure and, beyond this, in the society in which the family is embedded. These are the pertinent nexes of human life.

Now, for one in such a rejecting psychiatric mood, there exists a philosophical point of view, a system of psychology, we will say, which is still not a system, called phenomenology. It is tempting for the revisionist to reach for it, and if one takes Sartre, Minkowski, Camus, and others seriously, as does Laing, then one is almost ordained to become a phenomenologist. What then is phenomenology?

Without belabored allusions to the founders of phenomenology, citing Dilthey and Husserl, it is possible to say that within a psychiatric framework phenomenology has the following properties:

1. Phenomenology concerns itself directly with the experiencing of the person without intervening variables of any kind.

2. Phenomenology resists refraction and discontinuity in experience and retains its holistic and gestalt qualities.

3. Phenomenology retains the emotional penumbra which accompanies experience and behavior and focuses upon them as desirable.

4. Phenomenology accords temporality and spatiality, as private experience, a special recognition and relates them to birth and death, the perception of time, fantasy, dream life, and the inward meaning of time in one's made space.

5. Phenomenology reduces language and logical processes to communicational vehicles and does not place them at the center of existence itself as does modern philosophy.

6. The individuation of the person becomes an intensity in phenomenology so that existential qualities of dread, despair, guilt, loneliness, social ideals, etc., are given center stage as the qualia of ontology.

7. The pathogen in behavior, whether bacterial, protein, or of other nature, is reduced in scientific value, and the social context or gestalt in which dis-ease manifests itself becomes the more important determiner of inhibition.

8. Phenomenology dilates the S-R bond by recognizing the stimulus as a pattern rather than a point, and the response as a dilated experience rather than a reflex.

9. Phenomenology seeks less to change nature than to relate to her and to understand her; it finds inherent beauty in all natural processes.

10. The findings of the Gestalt psychologists, Kohler, Wertheimer, Kaffka and others, on the nature of perception, and such phenomenologists as Strauss

and Van den Berg, are extended to all of life as revealing a natural coherence of experience into joy in the absence of artificial social barriers.

11. Reality is interpreted as *realities* in that personal experience has consensual meaning regardless of its autistic quality. No one reality is privileged, and certainly not the statistical reality.

12. Phenomenology teaches that the inherent world is full of meaning, and even objects may be said to have an existence.

13. Phenomenology claims that man and his world are so intertwined that they cannot be separated, say, for example, by an arbitrary psychiatric examination of a patient.

14. A Cartesian body-mind dualism is totally impossible in phenomenology.

15. Phenomenology attempts to solve problems reflectively by making the problem openly speak for itself by its "standing forthness."

Van den Berg puts it this way (2):

> Phenomenology is a method; it could be called an attitude. The method is a way of observing, new in science; new, for instance, in psychology, not at all new in general life. On the contrary, the phenomenologist wants to observe in the way one usually observes. He has an unshakable. faith in the every-day observation of objects, of the body, of the people around him and of time, because the answers to stated questions are based on the results of this sort of observation. On the other hand, he distrusts theoretical and objective observations, observations at a closer inspection, the kind of observations made by the physicist. He distrusts standard opinions, quickly formed opinions like projection, conversion, transference and mythicizing. He is convinced that this kind of opinion mystifies reality with an easy, but incorrect, and as a rule obscure, theory. He wishes to hold back his opinion (for he, too, has to express one) until later and listen to what the incidents, the phenomena, tells him. His science is called phenomenology. His story tries to be the interpretation of what he observes: hears, sees, smells and feels.

Laing takes phenomenology seriously, for its lessons serve as a needed corrective in psychiatry, but also perhaps because of his deep anarchistic needs. Some of his rebellion on the socio-political level smacks of the need to limit institutional organizations which press men into conformance. He thus tends to interpret schizophrenia as a wild outburst of freedom. Freud, of course, also feared society's imposition on man's basic needs. Laing says, "If the set and the setting can be changed (from the mental hospital model), the experience of psychosis may be so transformed that it no longer need be regarded as 'psychotic' at all" (3). In this sense he empathizes deeply with the schizophrenic and sees in him a blood brother. Laing has not yet come to the position of denying the psychosis a conceptual validity, but I predict he will soon (4). He goes as far as to say, "Whatever it is that clinically is diagnosed as acute schizophrenia or schizophrenic-form breakdown, may itself be a resource a human being calls upon when all else seems impossible" (5).

If one seriously departs from the medical model, at least in something as historical as schizophrenia, then the pathogen—if we may call it that— must be sought in two principal areas of experience. The first is what Laing calls *ontological insecurity;* and the second, the *family nexus.* In both, it should be noted, Laing has been anticipated by a whole host of people.

By ontological insecurity Laing means not the insecurity of the garden-variety neurosis but a basic rift in the feeling of being human—of existing, or being. Thus, in connection with schizoid behavior he says (6):

> The term schizoid refers to an individual the totality of whose experi-
> ence is split in two main ways: in the first place, there is a rent in
> his relation with his world and, in the second, there is a disruption of
> his relation with himself. Such a person is not able to experience himself
> "together with" others or "at home in" the world, but, on the contrary,
> he experiences himself in despairing aloneness and isolation; moreover,
> he does not experience himself as a complete person but rather as
> "split" in various ways, perhaps as a mind more or less tenuously linked
> to a body, as two or more selves, and so on.

But these are not just the felt signs of the schizoid or the schizophrenic. They represent ontological insecurity wherever it exists, and engulfment, implosion, and petrifaction are its specific accompaniments. Like Erikson's "basic trust," Laing considers that one must come into, or be-in-the-world, with a basic feeling of belonging, of a feeling of being whole, with a need for interpersonal trust, and with an essential comfort in being in a human skin. The privacy of self is the basis of a genuine relationship; but the person whom we call schizoid feels more exposed, more vulnerable, and more isolated.

It is interesting that Laing uses the term "anxiety" very sparsely, and this seems generally the case with the existentially oriented. Anxiety is now a badly abused word in psychopathology and, at any rate, fails to describe the more ontic quality of the despair involved in the anxious life. To say that one is anxious about one's death is like spitting into the ocean to provide more water. To say, instead, that one ontologically dreads death, rings the coin of existence more solidly. Thus it is that a great many new descriptive epithets are employed by Laing—as by Binswanger—to set the tone and meaning of being-in-distress rather than of being sick. This has the effect of placing psychiatric phenomena within the realm of the "normal,"

breaking down the differentiation between sane and insane, and also re-
fusing to absolve the "sick" person of responsibility for himself and society.
Thus, self, being, loneliness, alienation, despair, dread, guilt, disembodiment,
split, death, unease, existence, risk, discontent, meaning, individuation,
archetype, and similar others are prominent in Laing's essays, but conventional psychiatric terminology is mostly absent.

Laing's theoretical outlook is of course a self theory, and here he has
much in common with Rogers, Jung, and Maslow. Marcel's statement of
man being encumbered with himself comes to mind! Ontological insecurity,
no matter how defined, is simply a self not at home to it-self. The actualized
self is all-of-a-piece and, with proper subdifferentiation, has a fundamental
relatedness to its vehicle body, meaningfully encounters other selves, works
up to its creative limits, and feels all of the human pain and pleasure of
full awareness. A precise definition of self is hard to come by and *examples*
of actualized selves are easier to isolate. The self which Laing postulates as
healthy is an inner seeker, a doer, realistic, alive, sensual, free, unsplit, and
identified. Such a person is known by his projects rather than by his
obsessions. No force, neurotic or otherwise, can deny the pushing upward
of life's growth in him. Of course, as I have implied, self theory is still at
this time defined by its deficiencies or deviations rather than by the normative or ecstatic aspects of it. This is true of Laing as well.

The second aspect of Laing's personality theory, the social, has Laing
saying this (7): "I began to see that I was involved in the study of
situations and not simply individuals." And he goes on, "A person does not
exist without a context. . . . For us, on the contrary, the etiology of schizophrenia has come to be sought through the studies of social situations, of
social circumstances under which this attribution [schizophrenia] is brought
into play" (8). In dealing with schizophrenia this point of view has forced
Laing into the intimate dynamics of the family, what has been called by
others family therapy, and on the social scene it has projected him into the
understanding of the "politics of experience" (9), the "politics of the
family" (10), and into other social engineering mechanisms.

Laing enjoys the use of the case history approach as a teaching method.
One of his earliest books was a volume of case studies of families with
schizophrenic members (11). In commenting on the case of Maya Abbott
he says (12):

> In respect of depersonalization, catatonic and paranoid symptoms, im-
> poverishment of affect, autistic withdrawal and auditory hallucinations,
> confusion of "ego boundaries," it seems to us, in this case, more likely
> that they are the outcome of her inter-experience and interaction with

her parents. They seem to be quite in keeping with the social reality in which she lived.

It might be argued as regards our historical reconstructions that her parents might have been reacting in an abnormal way to the presence of an abnormal child. The data hardly support this thesis. Her mother and father reveal plainly, *in the present*, that what they regard most as symptoms of illness are what we regard as developing personalization, realization, autonomy, spontaneity, etc. On their own testimony, everything points to this being the case in the past as well. Her parents felt as stress not so much the loss but the development of her self.

Laing is not here speaking about double-binds or similar communicational difficulties between parent and child. Nor does he anywhere posit what goes wrong psychopathologically in such family development. He is more concerned with establishing the point that the identified carrier of the "pathogen" is intimately connected with some unique family need or family idea of growth and development of the child. The patient is so integral with this kind of family that he never integrates his self or the family's needs. He says, "We believe that the shift of point of view that these descriptions both embody and demand has an historical significance no less radical than the shift from a demonological to a clinical viewpoint three hundred years ago" (13). Presumably, the extension of such family "malevolence" involves a projection and carrying forward into society which Laing has more and more shown an aptitude for.

The family is a system, perhaps the most vital system the person ever encounters, and it is the "internalized" family rather than the *de facto* family which counts. Fantasy plays a central part in Laing's ideas, and family-fantasy experiences are highly determinative. Temporality and spatiality become organized around family personages and events, so that the cheated personal ego must certainly be family ego as well. Relations and images, not people, are introjected in the family, and Laing can then speak of an *incarnate group structure*.

The *deus ex machina* of family intervention is the transpersonal defense of attempting to regulate the inner life of the Other in order to preserve family integrity. There is a shared structure which is the basis of self-identity, and Laing says, "To be in the same family is to feel the family inside." Maturational problems develop if a dilemma arises which may be stated this way: "If I do not destroy my family, will it destroy me? But I cannot destroy my family without destroying myself." The family becomes the defense against total collapse, disintegration, emptiness, despair, guilt, dread, and terror. Most schizophrenics I have treated never get more than 50 miles from their families because of such ambivalence. Its protectionist properties can best be seen, for example, in the Sicilian culture where family honor, pride, and defense are frequent stimuli for murder or, less often, mayhem. Some families can allow additions to it, but cannot on any basis countenance departures. No one ever leaves the Mafia family!

Summatively, the sensitized family member finds himself more imprisoned by his circumstances than if he were behind bars.

Family members mystify each other and there is a concerted family resistance to discovering what is going on. This is what is so frustrating about doing family therapy with them. Laing says that their "complicated stratagems to keep everyone in the dark, and in the dark they are in the dark." Some of the vital parameters of self which are in this way mystified are:

1. Inside and outside
2. Pleasure and pain (pleasant-unpleasant)
3. Real and not-real
4. Good and bad
5. Me and not-me
6. Here and there
7. Then and now
8. Body and no-body.

The confusion which arises between such polarities, the failure of the thesis-antithesis dialogue, all lead to confusions and distortions of Self and Other relationships. There are, in addition, the more covert mechanisms of denial, splitting, displacement, somatization, projection, introjection, rationalization, repression, regression, identification, mystification, and reversal.

It must by now be apparent that Laing's theory of personality is a self theory which has many analogues to Rogers and Jung, even though they are rarely mentioned in Laing's books. The instincts are reduced in value—Laing rarely uses the word sex—and the superego is lodged in the immediate family (and society) rather than in the primordial or mythological. To this conception of the self as an inner-organizing, meaning-producing, body-integrating person are added some of the infra-existential findings of Sartre and others as an overlayer. These involve freedom of choice and self as a goal, but with acknowledgment of the dread and despair of finding it. Will and decision rather than conditioning, imprinting, reflex, and instinct are the modes of actualization. Love is the central focus of the personality operation but difficulties enter, in that others respond incompletely and not often enough. The world has to be constructed, and in its worst form it can be schizophrenia when the press for freedom is so great and the realization possibilities so small that the real world is then finally relinquished for fantasy. The self must avoid becoming not-self, or divided, and it seems all social groupings more or less conspire to break the intactness of the self. Becoming one's own being is the desideratum, and Laing implies that not only is this the responsibility of the individual but that it is his sole task and analysts can help only slightly.

A word must be said about Laing's treatment methods to finalize this essay. Laing is a humanistic psychotherapist in that he gives the patient central focus in the treatment, self-effaces himself to the greatest degree, yet seeks and obtains a deep emotional encounter with the patient. He says (10):

> When the other is a patient, existential phenomenology becomes the attempt to reconstruct the patient's way of being himself in the world, although in the therapeutic relationship, the focus may be on the patient's way of being with me. . . . The task in psychotherapy was to make, using Jasper's expression, an appeal to the freedom of the patient.

The split in personality, disembodiment, extreme departures from reality testing, the unavailability of love, loneliness, despair, ontological insecurity are all matters for Laing which require healing. Traditional psychiatric nosology is mostly absent from Laing's accounts of treatment or are downgraded. For him the viable interpersonal factors of the human condition which lead to despair and alienation are the meat of the analyst's work.

Of course, much of Laing's current treatment efforts with schizophrenics are centered in group "live-in" arrangements as, for example, Kingsley Hall. These are new to England, but have been in existence in the United States for some time. He has yet to publish his findings on these experiments (15), but since more and more of them are being formed, the implication is that they have been helpful.

In Kingsley Hall, and in similar treatment centers, there is, first, no intent to treat, and second, no psychiatrist to do the treating. It is a group of people with a certain existential outlook and a style of life who live together to share their fantasies and realities in an attempt to find more joy in life. The intent is the deepest look possible yet at the conscious in a setting of peers in which critical judgment is held to a minimum because all participants are, so to speak, in the same boat. The group leader, the psychiatrist, is simply one who keeps the boat from rocking too violently and from going on the shoals. Carnations and reincarnations regularly take place in such setting. Schizophrenics become leveled off to merely the atypical.

Laing's psychotherapy is becoming less dyadic, less drug-oriented, and more and more sociological. But his ultimate therapeutic goal is a less or greater revision of society itself. He believes that the paradoxes, the ironies, and absurdities of our society leave many individuals little recourse but to descend into a hell of psychopathology. They sometimes prefer schizophrenia to the absurdities of the nexus they live in. The goal is a society which puts less strain on its members and permits a more honest dialogue than is presently afforded. Not individual release of repression but honesty and love are the desiderata for the person who becomes an identified patient. People have the answers to their own problems of living if only they will band together and resolve them.

Laing's position as an existential phenomenologist, his description of himself, is still not historically clear. He belongs to that select group of people who see in the logical categorization of phenomena its violation or destruction, and who will not subscribe to the sanity-insanity nonsense as a categorical imperative for psychiatry. His concern is always the being or ontology of the person and his final message is identical to that of Binswanger: love is the essence of being human.

REFERENCES

1. *Human Behavior*, 2, 16-23, 1973.
2. VAN DEN BERG, J. H. *A Different Existence. Principles of Phenomenological Psychopathology.* Pittsburgh: Duquesne Univ. Press, 1972, p. 77.
3. LAING, R. D. "Metanoia: Some Experiences at Kingsley Hall, London," in H. M. Ruitenbeck (Ed.), *Going Crazy. The Radical Therapy of R. D. Laing and Others.* New York: Bantam Books, 1972, p. 12.
4. See in this connection the writer's comments in Burton, A., J. J. Lopez-Ibor, and W. Mendel, *Schizophrenia as Life Style., op. cit.*
5. LAING, R. D. *Op. cit.*
6. LAING, R. D. *The Divided Self.* Baltimore: Penguin Books, 1965, p. 17.
7. LAING, R. D. *Op. cit.,* p. 113.
8. *Ibid.,* p. 13.
9. LAING, R. D. *The Politics of Experience.* New York: Pantheon, 1967.
10. LAING, R. D. *The Politics of the Family and Other Essays.* New York: Vintage Books, 1972.
11. LAING, R. D. & ESTERSON, A. *Sanity, Madness, and the Family.* Vol. I. *Families of Schizophrenics.* London: Tavistock Publications, 1964.
12. *Ibid.,* p. 32.
13. *Ibid.,* p. 13.
14. LAING, R. D. *The Divided Self,* p. 25.
15. Laing has made some documentary films and the one I have recently seen was called *Asylum.*

LAING READING BIBLIOGRAPHY

1. *The Politics of Experience.* New York: Penguin Books, 1967.
2. *Sanity, Madness and the Family* (Vol. I). (With A. Esterson.) New York: Basic Books, 1965.
3. *The Self and Others.* New York: Tavistock Publications, 1961.
4. *The Divided Self.* New York: Tavistock Publications, 1960.

III

APPLICATION OF THEORY

Some of the conceptions of Laing and Binswanger discussed above are best illustrated in my treatment of a 21-year-old Berkeley student. In an interesting coincidence, the case of Joseph W., my patient, has parallels to Laing's Julie, which he describes in *The Divided Self.*

Joseph W. came to me about a year ago because he had, for all intents and purposes, terminated his life except to "drum." He was more than a fair drummer and sometimes played with "rock" bands. Like Gunter Grass' *Tin Drummer,* he could only march to the tune he drummed, for all else in his life was nihilism. He was from an upper-middle-class family but was 3,000 miles from home and had rejected its values as well as its personnel. He had a general air of dread about him, a preoccupied distractedness, and from time to time his despair knew no bounds.

Joseph had a "filter" in his mind which talked to him almost incessantly. He called it a filter because it seemed to screen out everything important he wanted to feel and do. The constant dialogues with the filter were despairing ones, for he had never once bested the filter before coming to treatment. In its most aggravated form it could make him conform by bringing on a depression, and by intensifying his usual dread. His only freedom from the filter was at rare peak periods of drumming. He put the essence of his problem aphoristically, of which the three following are random samples.

(1) "I was always deadly in analyzing myself."
(2) "I was disarmed by repeated fantasy."
(3) "Schizophrenia is the neutralization of meaning."

Joseph's father had reached the top of his profession but Joseph hardly considered him a man. At home he used alcohol to excess, which served to further infantilize him in his son's eyes. They were Jewish and their life-style was that described so well by Philip Roth and Bernard Malamud in their various novels. Joseph has two siblings, two older sisters, and I was fortunate enough to hold one conjoint session with Joseph and the father and each of the sisters in turn. All of them had apparently paid a penalty for middle-class affluence, for "making it," for they all revealed existential or neurotic symptoms and were troubled people.

Joseph's father was a large man who verbally radiated success, lived uneasily with the discrepancy of a lion in the courtroom and a lamb at home, and which he mitigated somewhat by dissociating himself at home for his inferiorities and lack of respect.

Of course, Joseph's mother was the key to the household. After 200 hours of analytic therapy, and considerable manifested growth, Joseph drew a picture of his mother which in its unreality aspects can be called the actress, Liv Ullman. But his mother was never like this; it was only the way he wanted to or had to recall her. But, you see, she died of cancer of the ovary when Joseph was 14, a death which need not have occurred had a certain watchfulness been maintained. Joseph does not believe she is dead—he accepts it intellectually—even though his father forced him to look at her dead in the casket. Our analytic work has in a sense been involved in disinterring her and burying her properly in a way that Joseph can mourn her as he should.

Like Laing's Julie, Joseph was a model child and never gave any hint of psychopathology. His sisters were taken to psychiatrists, but not he. All developmental data were normative.

1. "Delivery was normal."
2. "No weaning problems."
3. "No nervous habits."
4. "No bowel problems."
5. "He was never demanding."
6. "He was no trouble."
7. "He did what he was told."

It must be apparent that if we need a diagnosis, Joseph is an ambulatory schizophrenic. A number of LSD experiences confirmed him in this understanding, and I concurred. I could spend pages justifying this diagnosis but this would be a bizarre thing to do in an essay such as this.

Joseph was denying his dasein, not really alive, and had a split between his cognitive and affective processes "a mile wide." Now, schizophrenia, in my understanding, is a life style and not a disease—a way of existence based upon a long history of residues of dasein avoidance and dissociation (1), and its treatment is assisting the patient to recognize and accept his ontological choices and then to be responsible for them. This statement seems retrospectively vacuous, for the difficulties of attaining it are almost insurmountable. But Jung said that the schizophrenic ceases to be so when he meets someone by whom he feels understood. The treatment of Joseph was an encounter of Jung's sort.

Too much has already been made in psychoanalysis of Sophocles' *Oedipus Rex,* and Oedipus' affectional need for his mother. But it is anyway apparent that Joseph and his mother lived as one and shared a common dasein. It was a pooling of misery—the father's inadequacy—rather than a sexual attraction as such. Joseph wrote this about his family:

> My parents strained to always present the proper image. All our activities were geared to fit a preconceived notion. We hardly ever had fun. My father told the same stories a thousand times and slurped his soup like a moron. He was the straight-man for our highly developed sarcascastic wit. My mother was much too straight to have fun very often. She would have been as appalled as my father was last month when he observed my step-brothers and step-sister pretending they were vacuum cleaners. Imagination was frowned upon if it was not properly channeled (school work, etc.).

About a year after his mother died, his father remarried, and now his stepmother, whom Joseph likes very much, is also dying of cancer.

> "I can't help feeling," he says, "that the family and my father especially are cancerous. We present a happy, smiling face to the world, but inside each of us feels alone and rotten. My mothers had to fight my father day by day until their strength was so weakened that their cases of the family disease became fatal."

Does Joseph also believe he will die of cancer?

Now, interestingly enough, if there is a villain for me in this piece it is not dad but Joseph's mother. She traded on Joseph's ontological insecurity, made a willing husband-companion-lover out of him, and thoroughly submerged his dasein while using it against her husband. So well did this unconsciously adjust things that there was never in Joseph any appreciation of strain except to feel unease in his father's presence.

But the strain was really his mother's and she may have died to avoid the denoument certain to come. The implied covenant was that the relationship would go on forever, which is itself by definition an existential failure, for nothing goes on forever.

Joseph's filter is his symbolic mother, in Melanie Klein's "good and bad aspects." Here is what Joseph W. wrote about it.

> By means of a kind of filter, I'm not altogether here—there's a kind of delay mechanism in my head, through which everything I experience has to go. I have a feeling it was, you know, originally set up as a defense to protect me from things that would hurt me, because I could protect myself from what was trying to harm me by delaying its impact and by kind of rationalizing it. That's what the filter does. I think the filter takes the form of a voice. In kind of mild instances—I could be

taking a test, and I'd be wanting to do well, and all the time in my head I'd be hearing, "You got to do well. You got to follow directions. Try hard. Do well. Pay attention. Read all the directions." And this kind of thing. I'd be hearing so much *noise* in my head that I really never did all that well. The voice would be giving me so much advice that I couldn't really participate in the test. I was never really tested so much on what I *knew* as on my, you know, ability to be there and actually be taking the test.

I think, though, where it, you know, served me well is kind of the reason it came into being, too. . . . If I were undergoing a kind of painful experience, this filter would kind of lessen the pain. I can remember my parents doing something that would hurt me, or, well, specifically like my sister. I can remember her beating me up and, like, the filter was like a mature voice, a rational voice, a voice of reason —kind of reminds me of my father—and it told me that, "you know, she's just physically beating you up, but that doesn't matter, like, 'cause you know what's happening and you know she's being childish and that you're right, you've got right on your side, and so it really doesn't matter." I think the voice was always telling me, you know, it doesn't matter; tell me things like, "Don't show how you feel. Don't let 'em know. Don't let them know how you feel. That's your strength." And so the voice was kind of like a guide, a guide in the world.

The purpose of any filter is to screen. In Joseph's case, the filter asks him not to do what would displease his mother, and the fact that she is for him not yet psychologically dead makes the job of a filter necessary. But the therapist refused to share his illusion that she was still alive, and kept insisting that she be properly buried, and then suitably mourned. Joseph could never cry—and he certainly cannot cry for his mother. It has been a great event in therapy when we have cried together. Our therapeutic work puts Joseph in a bind: it depreciates the "aliveness" of his mother at the same time it extols the beauty of life and experiencing outside of her. It urges him to choose and partake of that life.

Two months ago he stopped "drumming" after giving me a demonstration in my office, and now only "drums" more appropriately at rare band engagements. (He recently gave up the opportunity of joining a nationally known band.) He no longer wants to be a Buddy Rich or Gene Krupa. He is now all for human relationships and is thinking of a graduate curriculum in clinical psychology. In the meantime he is spending the summer as a psychiatric aide at a medical school psychiatric hospital. He found a girl, lived (and fornicated) with her for several months. She wanted to get married but he decided she was not the kind of wife he needed.

Joseph demonstrates in his psyche all of Binswanger's metaphoric items given above in, of course, varying degrees. He is symbolically Jurg Zund,

Ellen West, and all of the others, and is in good company. He feels betrayed by a cause to which he devoted his dasein, family love, and he has covert murderous designs which corrupt his being. There never was a better boy, I am told, in all of "Raintree County," a docile, loving, gentle youth who didn't even know that sex was dirty, or that there was sex. He was promised Paradise Forever and it became Paradise Lost when his mother died. He lives both in hope and fear that she will at any moment still honor the contract between them.

His dasein was gradually worn away by honest conformity, affection, and the maintenance of harmony. Only his sister, Hepzibah, plagued him for his goodness by calling him a fag, resented his usurpation of their mother, and became herself a "tomboy" in turn. Today, at a moderately advanced age, she is on the point of being married to someone not unlike Joseph. It remains to be seen whether she can make the transition to womanhood.

Joseph keeps the same company of dread as did Ellen West, but he does not have her overt periods of madness and has never been hospitalized. He loses his self among a few others, but he does not flee into his schizophrenia anymore. But his social idealism needs his self-hatred, and the split in his cognition-affect is the same. At first there was a social paranoia, but it is now a cynicism and who can fault it with Watergate in the headlines at this time. He fears that he will never be allowed to actualize himself —that some authority will intervene and prevent it—and he fears Thanatos. But being a hipster, and being on the drug scene, was not enough. It gave him a release and at times beautiful visions, but his excellent intelligence told him that he could not sustain his dasein this way. His dread overcomes him at times. Then he is lost and "out of it" in the dialogue with his voices. More recently the voice has been playing Beethoven symphonies to him, and this change has encouraged him. He now takes piano lessons to improve his knowledge of music as well.

The saddest moment of his despair brings up finitude. Joseph has not to my knowledge made any attempt to die but he has thought of it. At these times he sees a certain beauty in Thanatos. Of course, the purpose would be to join his beloved mother if only he could be sure she was there. He remembers that in the coffin she looked "Grecian," after the embalmer got through with her. By "Grecian" he of course means a goddess—say, Hera, Diana, or Persephone. The mythic in schizophrenia is always close to the surface.

But I stand against him for the beauty and purpose of the dasein, of the centeredness and glory of life, and I will not have descension to Hell.

At such times, I also tell him of my own periodic despair and even of my own mother and my problems with her.

Joseph W. is a Fallen Man. This is not a fall from grace, a descent into theological sin, but rather a falling away from the dasein and Heidegger's Care for people. No one gives him absolution. And he cannot give it to himself. He recently had a fortnight entirely free from his filter and said it was the first time he had ever really read a book, "seen" a girl, and experienced nature. It was for him a miracle! Of course, this was only a small victory in the total campaign for his being. For that period, at any rate, the "Fallen One" rose, and he played with tremendous feeling at the rock concert that night.

Joseph rarely complains, now, in therapy, except about his father. His sense of the Horrid and the Terrible are rather the falling away from the social ideals in our time and as they reflect on him. He is the true egalitarian, and cannot and will not exploit anything or anyone. The Terrible is the validity of Camus' Absurd, the low state of meaning and purpose in man today, and the paradox between man's brilliant scientific attainments and the destruction of his environment. Joseph needs the true brotherhood of man, agape and Eros, and it is Horrid that love, which is free, is in such short supply. It is the schizophrenic search for the Ideal? Camus said "man in our time was torn between the nostalgia of the heart for truth and justice and the unreasoning silence of a murderous world." This is the Terrible and the Horrid for Joseph.

His body lacks significance, but his face (beautifully bearded) is Michelangelo. It has grace, beauty, and wisdom; it is Aristotelian in magnificence. He takes karate to buttress his weak structures, but regularly is knocked insensible by more coordinated or faster opponents. But he persists. His orifices seem without passion and are simply biological. No gourmet or Don Juan he. Joseph is not disembodied in Laing's sense, but his body is not part of a conceivable dasein. He walks as though he could not push the atmosphere aside, and as a compensation takes overscrupulous care of his car, which he loves. He jousts with other drivers on the highway in a way he cannot do on foot.

The existential problem we are treating is, as Camus puts it, "that the best living is the most living, and revolt and passion and intellectual lucidity can provide the vitalness to keep the Absurd tension from doing us all in." This is Joseph's goal. We are on the way to it. Soon his filter will stop entirely.

REFERENCE

1. BURTON, A., LOPEZ-IBOR, J. J., & MENDEL, W. *Schizophrenia as a Life Style.* New York: Springer, 1974.

Carl R. Rogers

7

Client-Centered Theory: Carl R. Rogers

by CARL R. ROGERS and JOHN K. WOOD

I* would willingly throw away all the words of this manuscript if I could, somehow, effectively *point* to the experience which is therapy. It is a process, a thing-in-itself, an experience, a relationship, a dynamic. It is not what this book says about it, nor what another books says about it, any more than a flower is the botanist's description of it or the poet's ecstasy over it. If this book serves as a large signpost pointing to an experience which is open to our senses of hearing and sight and

---

* This chapter is jointly produced by the two authors, yet is written in the first person. In some places "I" represents one author, sometimes the other. The reason for utilizing the first person is that it helps to keep the material in a human perspective. This chapter is not a statement of a closed theory. It is the personal perspective of two men with wide experience in carrying on therapy, yet congenial in their working approach, and in the tentative formulations they draw from their work.

to our capacity for emotional experience, and if it captures the interest of some and causes them to explore more deeply this thing-in-itself, it will have accomplished its purpose. If, on the other hand, this book adds to the already staggering pile of words about words, if its readers get from it the notion that truth is words and that the printed page is all, then it will have sadly failed to achieve its purpose. And if it suffers that final degradation of becoming "classroom knowledge"— where the dead words of an author are dissected and poured into the minds of passive students, so that live individuals carry about the dead and dissected portions of what were once living thoughts and experiences, without even the awareness that they were once living— then better by far that the book had never been written.

This statement prefaced the book *Client-Centered Therapy* (Rogers 1951, p. ix), the first major formulation of the theory underlying the client-centered approach to interpersonal relations.

Since then, the social impact of client-centered therapy has gone far beyond our expectations. From their early beginnings shaping a radical new approach to psychotherapy, client-centered principles today reach far out into education, business, interpersonal relations, and have even been applied to such unusual situations as an intensive group experience aimed at facilitating communications between warring factions in Northern Ireland.

I fear now that client-centered theory has too quickly and too easily become a closed book of truth, in spite of my warnings against this. The theory has been dissected, analyzed, memorized, until it has in fact suffered the degradation of becoming "classroom knowledge," and regarded as dogma.

In psychotherapy it has become a part of the underlying assumptions for psychological counseling—probably for all effective therapy. This is based in part on the fact that for more than three decades many different therapists have worked with many kinds of clients to provide ample evidence that significantly positive changes tend to occur in the client's behavior, attitudes, feelings, and personality after even a relatively short time in a client-centered therapeutic climate. This kind of professional acceptance, based on experience, seems sound. But because there have been widely varied applications of the principles to all kinds of interpersonal relations in our society— a healthy trend in itself—the theory has often been taught superficially, and absorbed in the same way. This is what I object to.

Because of this superficial understanding of the principles by psychotherapists, prospective psychotherapists and others, there has often been a tendency to overlook their deeper implications. There is little appreciation of the precision of client-centered therapy. Its theoretical base is probably stated in a more precise manner than that of any other therapy (Rogers, 1959).

There is also a failure to appreciate its radical and revolutionary philosophy.

Actually a client-centered philosophy does not fit comfortably into a technologically-oriented society. Even psychotherapy is coming more and more to value "efficiency." Proper diagnosis, reliance on immediate cause and effect theories, and other linear constructs are seen as ways "to find out what is wrong and cure it," *quickly*. Client-centered therapy, lacking flashy methods and techniques, relying upon the evocation of the client's strengths, flowing at the client's pace, seems to many naïve and inefficient. It does not fit into a "fix-it" culture.

In this chapter I hope to aid in the appreciation of client-centered theory. I want to "point" to the experience which is client-centered therapy. I will try to outline some of my struggles in arriving at the tentative conclusions that make up the present theory. I hope you will be encouraged to integrate your own approach to therapy from your own experiences—the same way this theory was constructed. I hope this chapter will also help you answer, "What does client-centered therapy—in all the sea of theories—have to do with me as I face my client or a troubled friend?"

Characteristics

Client-centered theory is still growing, not as a "school" or dogma, but as a set of tentative principles. In fact, I believe that as our knowledge of the therapy process expands, the so-called schools of therapy will fade into a unified approach to healing.

Some characteristics which currently distinguish the client-centered approach from other points of view are:

1. The continued belief in the *client's* responsibility and capacity to devise the steps which will lead him to a more potent encounter with *his* reality. The client is the only one who has the potentiality of knowing fully the dynamics of his behavior and his perceptions of reality, and hence of discovering more appropriate behaviors for himself. It is not the goal of this therapy to help a person adjust to "society." In fact, a counseling student told me recently that this therapy does not even work in this regard. "In my internship at a county rehabilitation center," he said, "I used the client-centered approach and my clients did not change, so I switched to behavior modification and they began to conform to the agency's expectations." Client-centered therapy, with its emphasis on working for the client's goals, was, in this case, at cross purposes with the agency needs that had ordered these clients to therapy and specified their desired end behavior.

2. A continued focus on the phenomenal world of the client—the therapist attempting to see the client's world as he sees it.

3. The hypothesis that the same principles of psychotherapy apply to all persons whether they are labeled as "normal," "neurotic," or "psychotic."

4. A view of psychotherapy as one specialized example of all constructive interpersonal relationships. It is in the relationship—where another person helps him do what he cannot do alone—that the client experiences psychotherapeutic growth.

5. The developing hypothesis that certain attitudes of the person designated as "therapist" constitute the necessary and sufficient conditions of therapeutic effectiveness and change in the person designated "client."

6. The developing concept of the therapist's function as that of being immediately present and accessible to his client and relying on his moment-to-moment experiencing in the relationship to facilitate therapeutic movement.

7. A developing theory that views the therapeutic process as a continuing change in the client's manner of experiencing—with his increasing ability to live more fully in the immediate moment.

8. A concern with the "how" of the process of personality change rather than the "why" of personality structure.

9. An emphasis on the need for continued research to acquire essential learnings regarding psychotherapy. A determination to build all theoretical formulations from their roots in experience instead of squeezing experience to fit a pre-formed theoretical construct.

Client-centered therapy is best characterized as an approach, an attitude, a way of being, not a technique—"nondirective," "reflective," or otherwise. The first prerequisite for doing therapy is not a theory or a dogma, but a way of being with persons that is facilitative. The theory is growing out of thousands of hours of experience in counseling and clinical observations, changing as new research sheds new light on our formulations.

CLIENT-CENTERED PHILOSOPHY

A tentative conclusion, which I have reached after years of experience with troubled individuals in psychotherapy, is that man has an inherent tendency to develop all his capabilities in ways which serve to maintain or enhance his organism—the total person, mind and body. This is the single basic postulate of client-centered therapy.

I view this as a reliable tendency which, when free to operate, moves the individual toward the process called growth, maturity, life-enrichment. Need reduction, tension reduction, drive reduction, as well as growth motivation are all included in this one concept.

Contrary to the views that see man's deepest instincts as destructive, I have found that when man is truly free to become what he most deeply is (as in the safe climate of therapy), when he is free to be his nature as a being capable of awareness, then he clearly moves toward wholeness and integration. As I have said elsewhere (Rogers, 1961a, p. 105):

> [When man] is most fully man, when he is his complete organism, when awareness of experience, that peculiarly human attribute, is most fully operating, then he is to be trusted, then his behavior is constructive. It is not always conventional. It will not always be conforming. It will be individualized. But it will also be socialized.

"Socialized," in this context, means "in cooperation with other persons and oneself," not necessarily in accordance with "society." In a very oppressive society the life-affirming person may very well be classed as an outlaw.

A person's behavior can be counted on to be in the direction of maintaining, enhancing, and reproducing self—toward autonomy and away from external control by external forces. This is true whether the stimulus arises from within or without, whether the environment is favorable or unfavorable. This is the very essence of the process we call living.

A biological experiment with sea urchins illustrates my concept of this tendency toward growth. Scientists know how to tease apart the two cells which are formed after the first division of the fertilized sea urchin egg. If they are left to develop normally, each of these two cells will grow into a portion of a sea urchin larva—both contributing to form a whole creature. It may seem, then, that when the two cells are skillfully separated, each, if it grows, will simply develop into some portion of a sea urchin. This reasoning overlooks the directional or "actualizing tendency," characteristic of all organic growth. In fact, each cell, if it is kept alive, develops into a *whole* sea urchin larva—smaller than usual, but normal and complete.

This tendency toward wholeness expresses itself in humans in a wide range of behaviors and in response to a wide variety of needs. The tendency of the organism, at one moment, may lead to seeking food or sexual gratification. Yet, unless these needs are overpoweringly great, their satisfaction will be sought in ways which enhance, rather than diminish, the need for self-esteem, for example. Other fulfillments, such as the need to explore, produce, change, and play, are basically "motivated" by the actualizing tendency.

The actualizing tendency, expressed through the total experiencing of the individual, can be trusted as a reliable referent for behavior. I believe that man is wiser than his intellect alone and that well-functioning persons learn to trust their experiencing as the most satisfying and wisest indication of appropriate behavior. When consciousness participates in a coordinated, rather than competitive fashion with his actualizing tendency, the person is engaged in an exciting, adaptive, and changing encounter with life and its challenges. He makes mistakes, but he also has the best possible mode of correcting them.

As a therapist I act on my belief in these natural processes by respecting my client's right and capacity for self-direction and growth. I trust his ability to deal with his psychological situation and with himself. One veteran therapist, for example, experiences this trust in her clients as a continual learning process. When she runs out of new directions or approaches with a client, she "waits" on him. "Always when I can wait on my client and do not feel that I have to cure him immediately or rush his growth, when I fall back on the person himself for direction, he inevitably begins to grow and make progress."

THE BEGINNING OF A THEORY: PROCESS IN THE CLIENT

> I wanted only to try to live in accord with the promptings which came from my true self. Why was that so very difficult?
>   HERMANN HESSE (Demian)

If each individual possesses the capacity to devise the steps which will lead him to a more mature and potent relationship with his reality, what happens to reduce the effectiveness and quality of life for some? Why do some people seek the help of a psychotherapist, and what can he or she do to help?

From my direct experience, being in therapeutic relationships with my clients, I have begun to shape an explanation of the process of therapy. (A theory of personality has also been developed, but it has always been of secondary interest.) My concern in a theory of the therapeutic process has been in descriptions of the "how" rather than the "why" of change. There is no need for a theory until there are observable phenomena, changes, which call for explanation. First there is experiencing, then there is a theory. In thus attempting to understand and explain what has happened and formulating testable hypotheses about future experiences, our effectiveness in therapy is advanced.

A Primitive Theory

To date, three successive major formulations of the therapy process have been developed. The earliest description of client-centered therapy pictured the process of therapy as composed primarily of three steps. There is first a release of expression by the client, a release of personal feelings. Following this emotional catharsis, the client tends to develop insight into the origin and nature of his difficulties. Such awareness is followed by the making of positive choices and decisions in regard to the various problems he faces in his life. This practice leads to the client's increased capacity for self-direction.

Research studies (Snyder 1945; Seeman 1949) confirmed this description and it is still one way to look at the therapeutic process.

A Self Theory

Although my first description seems modestly adequate, another approach was forced on me by my clients. They frequently focus on their problems and progress in terms of self. "I feel I'm not being my real self." "It felt good to let myself go and just *be* myself here."

From the raw data of electrically recorded therapy sessions I noticed a change in how the self was perceived by clients over the course of their therapy. A theory of this process began to emerge regarding the person's self-concept and its relation to the actualizing tendency. I came to see the troubled individual as one whose self-concept has become structured in ways incongruent—at odds—with his total experiencing.

Let us see how this comes about. The infant lives in a phenomenal field —his life space—which includes all that is experienced by his organism, whether consciously or not. (Even as adults only a portion of our many sensory and visceral reactions are realized consciously, or put into thoughts and words.) Out of all that is going on in his life space the infant gradually becomes aware of experiences which he discriminates as being "me." Slowly, an organized, consistent conceptual gestalt forms. The perceptions of the "me" or "I" are figure and the perceptions of the relationship of this "I" to the outside world and to others are ground.

These perceptions of "I" have values attached to them, but some of these values come from others. Love by the parent or significant other is conditional. In order to be perceived as worthwhile and receive love, the infant must introject some of their values as his own. Since these introjected values become part of the self-concept and are not part of the child's normal process of evaluating his experience, the resulting constructs are rigid and static—often experienced as "shoulds" or "oughts." He tends to disregard his own experiencing process whenever it conflicts with these constructs. In other words, the person tries to be the self others want him to be instead of the self he really is. Because of this, family and other institutional relationships in our culture seem to supply some of the breeding grounds for psychological "illness."

The self-concept, then, becomes an organization of perceptual maps for meeting life. It may or may not be effective in satisfying the person's needs. The person reacts to his reality as he perceives and defines it, guided by his concept of himself. An individual may see himself as strong or weak, intelligent or stupid, beautiful or homely. The way he sees himself affects, in turn, his perception of reality and therefore his behavior. Thus, to the confident, successful student, an examination may be seen as an opportunity to demonstrate mastery of the subject. To an unsure student the same experience may be faced with dread and fear—a proof of his inadequacy.

All experiencing may not be in awareness but is viscerally available and affects behavior. We "know" things emotively which we do not know cognitively. The student who feels unconfident may, instead of being aware of fear, suddenly get a headache and be unable to take the exam. If his feelings are more remote or denied to awareness, he may "forget" the exam completely and fail to attend class that day.

Every aspect of experience is dealt with as it relates to the self. Some phenomena are ignored as having no significance to the self. Other phenomena are perceived consciously and organized into the self-structure. Some even seem to call themselves into awareness. For example, I have a friend who bought a relatively rare foreign motor car. He never noticed this make of car before becoming an owner. Now he spots them everywhere he goes—they seem to jump into focus. They have meaning to him. Still other phenomena are denied or distorted because they threaten the organized perception of self—to accept them the person would have to change his idea of who he is. As long as the self-gestalt is firmly organized and no contradictory material is perceived in the phenomenal field, positive self feelings may exist, the self may be seen as worthy and acceptable and conscious tension is minimal. The individual perceives himself as functioning adequately.

When the organized self-structure is no longer effective in meeting the individual's needs or when he notices discrepancies in himself, his behavior seems out of control. "I just don't feel like myself," is a frequent complaint. As a simple example, a mother sees herself as a kind and loving parent, yet, at the same time has feelings of rejection toward her child. Her concept

more of a trend or goal, than something which is fully achieved. It is a description of the "fully functioning person" (Rogers, 1961a, Chapter 9).

At this level the person is no longer fearful of experiencing feelings with immediacy and richness of detail. This occurs in outside relationships as well as in therapy. This welling up of experiencing in the moment constitutes a referent by which the individual is able to know who he is, what he wants, and what his attitudes, both positive and negative, are. He accepts himself and trusts his own organismic process, which is wiser than his mind alone (or body alone). Each experience determines its own meaning, and is not interpreted as a past construct. His self is the subjective awareness of what he is experiencing at the moment. He has become congruent, with his experiencing matched by the symbols he gives it in his awareness, and he is able to communicate this unity.

This, then, is a brief account of the process continuum which grew out of observations of clients who were experiencing what it meant to change from fixity to fluidity. It is an account of transformations which can be both observed and experienced as a person moves toward psychological maturity in a growthful and therapeutic relationship.

THERAPEUTIC CLIMATE: PROCESS IN THE THERAPIST

What then are the conditions for this therapeutic climate? How can the therapist optimally facilitate movement along the process continuum?

The research on client-centered therapy seems to suggest that personality change—positive movement on the process scale—is initiated by *attitudes* which exist in the therapist rather than primarily by his knowledge, his theories, or his techniques (Rioch, 1960; Truax & Mitchell, 1971).

This is the central theorem of client-centered therapy and is formally stated in a "process equation" (Rogers, 1961b, p. 40):

> The more the client perceives the therapist as real or genuine, as empathic, as having an unconditional regard for him, the more the client will move away from a static, unfeeling, fixed, impersonal type of functioning and the more he will move toward a way of functioning which is marked by a fluid, changing, acceptant experiencing of differentiated personal feelings.

Several research studies have been concerned with the relationship of therapist attitudes to effective therapy. Halkides (1958) used objective judges to listen to recorded therapy interviews in order to test these "necessary and sufficient conditions" (Rogers, 1957) for therapeutic change. Her study supports the above hypothesis.

Barrett-Lennard (1959), using a paper and pencil report with counseling center clients, found these same three attitudes on the part of the therapist to be a predictor of success in therapy.

Van der Veen (1970) found that hospitalized schizophrenic clients whose therapists were judged to provide more of the three conditions in the therapy interview showed greater process movement than clients of therapists who provided lower conditions. The amount of movement in therapy was found to be a function of both perceived and actual therapist conditions.

Truax and Mitchell (1971), after reviewing the published evidence dealing with the effectiveness of psychotherapy, conclude that although, on the average, the therapeutic endeavor is quite ineffective, therapists with the three attitudinal characteristics mentioned earlier *are* effective. They state that a four-year study of psychotherapy with sixteen hospitalized schizophrenic clients at the University of Wisconsin indicated that patients whose therapists offered high levels of nonpossessive warmth, genuineness, and accurate empathic understanding showed significant positive personality and behavior change on a wide variety of indices, while patients whose therapists offered relatively low levels of these characteristics during therapy exhibited deterioration in personality and behavior. Truax and Mitchell further conclude that a wide spectrum of therapists, regardless of their training or theoretical orientation, working with a wide range of clients including college underachievers, juvenile delinquents, hospitalized schizophrenics, college counselees, outpatient neurotics, and a mixed variety of hospitalized patients, are effective when they are accurately empathic, nonpossessively warm, and genuine. This seems true even in a wide variety of therapeutic contexts including individual and group therapy.

When these attitudes are communicated to (verbally or nonverbally, but not by explanation) and perceived by the client, they are considered to be the crucial determinants of therapeutic progress and constructive changes in personality.

Because of the significance of therapist attitudes to effective psychotherapy I shall present each characteristic in more detail.

Genuineness or Congruence—Realness.

Effective therapy is most likely to occur when I am who I am in the relationship with my client without being phony or defensive. This means that what I am feeling at the moment at an experiential or visceral level is clearly present in my awareness and is available for direct communication to my client when appropriate. Not only are my feelings and experiences available to me, but I am able to live and be these feelings in the relationship. I am in direct personal encounter with my client, meeting with him on a person-to-person basis. I am *being* myself, not denying myself. It is obviously not easy, nor always possible, to be so transparently real.

This stress on realness, deeply contrary to earlier ideas of the therapeutic relationship, sometimes involves statements such as, "I'm not listening to you very well this morning because there are some problems on my mind and I can't concentrate." "I'm afraid of you at this moment—afraid of what you might do to me." "I feel uncomfortable with what you just said." In each instance I would be expressing a feeling within myself, not a fact, or supposed fact or judgment about my client. To say, "I feel bored at the moment. I wish I didn't feel this way but I do," does not pass judgment on my client as a boring individual. It merely adds the basic data of my own feelings to the relationship. As I share this boredom and sense of remoteness from him, my feelings change. I certainly am not feeling bored as I try to communicate myself in this way. I am, in fact, likely to be quite sensitively eager to hear my client's response. As contact with him returns, my empathic understanding begins again to be experienced. To be real is to reduce barriers in the relationship. My client is now likely to find himself speaking more congruently because I have dared to be real with him. It now becomes a genuine person-to-person relationship between two imperfect human beings.

This concept is liable to possible misunderstanding. Being real certainly does not mean that I burden my client with all of my problems or attitudes. It does not mean that I blurt out impulsively any feelings that I experience. It does mean, however, that I do not deny to myself the feelings that I am experiencing, and I am willing to be and to express any *persistent* feelings that I have in the relationship. It means I do not hide behind a mask of professionalism. What I say to my client does not contradict what I am feeling toward him. I don't use practiced or contrived phrases or professional mannerisms with my client. My lack of defensiveness, my realness is essential to establish and keep a trusting relationship alive.

Being genuine has several effects upon my therapeutic relationships. It helps to guide me in my responses or interventions. (In this connection it is well to keep in mind Gendlin's statement [1970] that "respond" may mean "understand," or "point to" or even "want to know about.") I note that my client often feels relief when I respond exactly to his "felt meaning." When he can put an exact word or label on the visceral experiencing going on within him, he feels a physical sense of release. Thus when I experience his sense of forward movement, of getting more closely in touch with his own experiencing, I know I am on the right track.

It is important to me to assist my client to carry forward his own experiential process (Hart 1970)—allowing him to recognize, accept, and own his feelings and assign the meanings to them that are real to him. Thus my responses, if effective, help him as he attempts to move, in his experiential process, beyond his "hangups." His struggle to carry forward his search for felt meanings is the very struggle I wish to assist by my responses. I find it both natural and helpful in this process to share my feelings, to give answers to questions if that is my genuine desire, to mention wild thoughts or fantasies about my client or our relationship, if those persist.

If my responses bring no shift or movement—have no meaning to my client's struggle—I will quickly focus back on his experiential flow. If, for example, I comment on the way I hear his expression or push out beyond the edge of his awareness and he says something like, "Yes, that sounds like what I must be doing," I can correct my distraction by saying, for example, "It sounds right, but it doesn't quite fit your feelings. You had just mentioned . . ." bringing him back to his flow of feelings . . . his experiencing. The process is like trying to negotiate a maze. I try one path and if that deadends, I go back to the junction and try another.

By way of contrast, being unreal or non-genuine is definitely not helpful. Expressions which are unnatural—using someone else's style or technique —can have dire consequences to the therapy relationship and to the therapist's personal development. One counselor told me of an experience he had while in training. He was counseling, under supervision, a very nonverbal client. His evaluators told him he was talking too much (when he was natural) and so he adopted a "nondirective technique." He decided to wait for his client to talk. He waited and the young lady waited. He squirmed and she squirmed, both very uncomfortable, until near the end of the session the skin on her neck began to break out in large red blotches. He was withholding his real feelings and her discomfort was literally seeping out through her skin.

Between this very embarrassing session and the next, the therapist attended his first encounter group. In the climate of a group of people trying to live their feelings in relationship, he discovered that he could safely be in real personal contact—be genuine with people. This was a profound experience and when he returned to his training program he had a completely different attitude about being in relationship with another person. He was more willing to be real, more accepting, more natural and content to allow himself to be present and to permit his client's natural tendency toward growth to do the healing. The next session with the young nonverbal woman he felt really "present" and the change in their relationship and her progress was remarkable. He no longer had any need to be directive nor did he now need to play at being nondirective. He simply was himself. His client was able to move in her own experiencing when he, the therapist, was confident in his own experiencing—when he was real.

Another experience of learning the value of realness is conveyed in this account by a young trainee counselor of his awkward beginning as a psychotherapist: "The very first time a client came to me with a heavy personal problem, my first 'case,' I was struck with the question, 'Who am I to help this person?' All the theories I had learned just crumbled and nothing emerged. I felt lost in a sea that I had created. I had studied a lot of processes of people I know and of myself, but to be in on the processes of someone who was a complete stranger, I just felt lost. I don't feel lost now. I even got over being lost in that first interview. . . . Once I had waded in, in that first interview, my theory of counseling escaped me and I fell back on a kind of automatic value system. I hadn't planned it that way. I don't even consider myself 'nondirective' or 'reflective,' but when I got into trouble I began to listen to my client, I tried to understand and help her clarify her feelings. These were values I had learned in childhood. The first few minutes when I was feeling lost I was only thinking about myself—how I was going to be, what I was going to do. One thing I was sure of was that that was not what I wanted to be doing. I began to tune in to what my client was saying. Not too well at first, but I told her I would do the best I could. By the end of the interview we were both more comfortable and we had both put some things about ourselves together." He is learning to trust being himself—real—in relationship and that this attitude helps to bring about the change he and his client desire.

To be genuine is to be myself, who I am, in the relationship without a facade and to share with the other person my felt perceptions, responding out of my own ongoing experiencing process to keep in focus my client's search for felt meaning.

Caring or Unconditional Positive Regard

The therapeutic process is enhanced when the therapist both experiences and communicates to his client a deep and genuine caring for him as a person with many constructive potentialities. When this caring is uncontaminated by evaluations and judgments of the client's thoughts, feelings, or behavior, when he does not accept some feelings and disapprove of others, it deserves the expression "unconditional positive regard."

As a therapist I do not encourage "self-pity" or "confidence," nor do I "reinforce" any particular feelings or behavior. I encourage and accept the free expression of all feelings. My attitude is neither paternalistic nor sentimental nor superficially sociable or agreeable—I am not in a role. My attitude is outgoing, positive, nonpossessively warm, without reservations and without evaluations. I accept what *is*. When I am in this kind of experience —creating this climate—clients say that they are able to talk about what really bothers them. They can explore the "terrible places" within themselves, not just the safe territory next to the real issues.

It is difficult not to make judgments. The attitude I am describing involves as much feelings of acceptance for the client's expressions of defensive, hostile, negative, painful feelings as for his expression of loving, mature, or positive feelings. For many therapists it is more difficult to accept the positive joyful feelings than the negative, because therapists tend to look upon these with suspicion, feeling they may be defensive.

In many ways I am gullible, accepting my client as he says he is, without lurking suspicion that he may be otherwise. I accept what *is* in my client, not what *should* be. As one person said, "You always let me just be myself here. I never worry about acting appropriately. And, you know, I always feel a lot more creative when I leave—and that feeling continues afterward."

It seems that accepting a person where he says he is allows him to explore himself more deeply. One client wanted to talk about his guilt feelings toward his children. First, though, he wanted me to understand that he was successful in the way he was living his life and this was not a major problem to him. I accepted his feelings of that moment. A short time later, as he was allowed to explore other feelings (without the threat that I might not believe him or disapprove), he was able to own and admit into full awareness his complex feelings of sadness and resentment about his children.

A question which arises frequently is, "Suppose, as a therapist, I *feel* strongly judgmental of my client?" Seeman (1954) found that success in therapy is closely associated with a strong and growing mutual liking and respect between client and therapist. Another study, by Dittes (1957), shows how sensitive this relationship is. Using the psychogalvanic reflex to measure anxious or threatened or alerted reactions in the client, Dittes showed that whenever the therapist's attitudes changed even slightly in the direction of lesser degree of acceptance, the number of abrupt GSR significantly increased. When the relationship is experienced as less acceptant the organism organizes against threat, even at the physiological level. This points out not only the importance of acceptance in the relationship but also the congruence of the therapist. Since the client senses these less acceptant feelings, they should be dealt with openly in the relationship.

When the therapist is unable to accept his client, the therapeutic relationship is threatened. The only way through this difficulty is to share his reactions with his client. By admitting these evaluative feelings (which his client probably senses) and working on the problem together, they may be able to resume and even enhance an effective therapeutic process.

If therapist judgmental responses occur too often, the effectiveness of the therapeutic process may be lost. Truax (1971, p. 330), reporting on the previously mentioned study of schizophrenic clients, concluded that, "When the therapists are possessive in the sense of making frequent evaluative statements, they are destructive in their effects on their patients." The therapist who finds himself frequently judgmental may need to explore his feelings with a colleague or enter therapy himself. The therapist's ability to feel warm and accepting feelings for his client probably depends on how accepting and warmly he feels toward himself.

Another dimension of this attitude of caring and acceptance toward his client seems to involve a willingness on the part of the therapist to plunge to the depths of fear with his client and trust that they return. I face the unknown in my client and in myself without a complete assurance of, but a trust in, a positive outcome.

The following example illustrates an unusual way of communicating caring to another person. A friend of mine, deeply depressed over her lingering illness and immobility, feeling no one could possibly understand or accept her feelings of discouragement, finally "gave up." For two days she lay motionless in bed, did not speak, nor eat, nor sleep for that matter—almost like a coma. I said to her that I thought I understood how she must feel, that I cared, and that I was saddened by her decision not to go on living. I tried to imagine how she felt right that minute and gave speculatively empathic responses. She registered no reaction to my words. She did not hear me. I didn't even think about what I should be doing, but was completely with my friend. I knew I wanted to communicate my feelings to her. I cared a great deal whether she lived or died and I also respected her feelings and responsibility for her own life. I put on her favorite music and picked a flower from her garden outside and floated it in a saucer full of water. Without speaking I placed the saucer next to her head. For the first time she moved from that fixed stare. Her eyes moistened as she glimpsed the flower. My friend loves food and many times we have shared a simple health food lunch with matzo crackers. I brought her bottle of vitamin C, a small piece of cracker, and a label from her favorite cookies. She began to move her body ever so slightly and broke into quiet sobbing. I then took the morning paper and cut out pictures of children playing, young girls, baby animals—life—and built a collage of my fantasy of the way she ordinarily views life. When I brought this to her, she burst into tears and heavy sobbing with what I thought was a laugh now and then. By this time I was weeping also and we sat for ten or fifteen minutes crying together. After a total of nearly two hours together, without speaking, she was able to talk about her experience and we were able to explore her feelings. Weeks later my friend said, "I was literally kept from dying by one person who cared about me and wasn't afraid to go with me to the depths of my fear and despair."

I hope no one puts together from this the latest suicide prevention kit, consisting of a flower, matzo cracker, and a flannel board collage for eclectic therapists. I hope it is understood that this illustration is a special case of the infinite variety of ways I may be and communicate my caring for another person.

This nonpossessive caring—where I have no need to tell my client what's best for him or control him, where I can accept all his varied feelings, accepting him exactly where he is, creates a nonthreatening climate where he can explore and even dare to admit the "awful" feelings he is experiencing, the deeply shrouded elements of himself.

Accurate Empathic Understanding

In the moment-to-moment encounter of psychotherapy the "work" of the therapist is his ability, accurately and sensitively, to understand the experiences and feelings of the client and the meanings they have for him. The level of accurate empathy in the therapist has been shown to be related to the client's self-exploration and the degree of improvement (Truax and Mitchell, 1971, p. 330).

This empathic understanding means that the therapist is at home in the phenomenal world of his client. It is an immediate sensitivity in the here and now, sensing the client's inner universe of private personal meanings "as if" it were the therapist's own, but without ever losing the "as if" quality.

Understanding the phenomenal world of my client requires more of me than merely understanding his words. I must immerse myself in the world of complex meanings my client is expressing with his tone of voice and bodily gestures as well. At its best such understanding is expressed by comments which reflect not only what the client is fully aware of but also areas at the hazy edge of awareness. This moving forward of the client's experiencing is aided by my own ability to be in *my* experiencing—in touch with my own feelings. By being in the client's universe as if it were my own and being sensitive to my own experiencing and sharing my feeling, I sometimes communicate the felt meaning my client is only vaguely aware of. He is increasingly able to permit into awareness more of his actual, organic, "gut level" experiencing.

To be understood in this deep and thoroughgoing and accepting sense is a very affirming experience. It is as though the client can now say, "It seems okay to me, even this tentative new me which is emerging, since it seems understandable and acceptable to my therapist." And what feelings are not understandable? It should be made clear that this empathic understanding is not for the purpose of making a diagnostic or therapeutic interpretation. The experience of being understood in the here and now—immediate moment—is itself a powerfully growthful experience.

Though an accurate empathic understanding is by far the most helpful, even the intent to understand can itself be of value. This has been found particularly true in the psychotic individual where to realize that someone is trying to understand his bizarre, confused, uncertain statements, both encourages him to communicate more of himself and helps him to realize that the therapist perceives his feelings and meanings as being worth understanding. He realizes that he, therefore, is worthwhile.

Here is a commonsense test as to whether empathy is accurately sensitive. If the therapist has communicated a superficial understanding of his client's expression, the client's inner response, and perhaps his verbal response, will be: "Of course. That's what I just said." Clearly this has not advanced his self-exploration. When the therapist has communicated an effectively empathic response the client's reaction is likely to be, "That's exactly right! I didn't suppose anyone could understand what I really meant. Now I want to tell you more." When the therapist is exceptionally sensitive and has caught the subtle meanings on the edge of the client's awareness, the client's reaction is likely to be first a pause, then a gradual appreciation: "Yes, perhaps that *is* what I've been saying. Yes, I think you're right! I had never thought of it in just that way before, but that *is* what I've been feeling and experiencing." Here the therapist has definitely helped to move his client forward in his awareness of unknown aspects of his experiencing —of himself.

Probing the edge of awareness is a delicate process. Too bold a thrust by the therapist, too far beyond the edge of awareness, tends to be perceived by the client as evaluation or judgment. In this exploration the client is like a child venturing out into the darkness for the first time. He is easily frightened and quickly withdraws until he becomes familiar with this new world. In suggesting that he knows more about the world than the client, the therapist may easily threaten the tentative child-like yearning to explore dangerous parts of himself.

The following example from an encounter group illustrates the dramatic difference between clinical probing and an empathic type of response and the freeing nature of being at last understood.

Doug, a thirty-eight-year-old professional man, has just told the group about losing his business, wife, family, and credibility in his community, and then, after several years of painful struggle, slowly rebuilding his business and working his way back to solvency.

Group Member: "You mentioned the divorce and being separated from your children and the sadness that brings you. It seems like you have some hang-ups you aren't telling us about."

Doug: "Well, that just happened to be a very painful experience in my life and I was just trying to relate that that's what happened. To me it was very sad and it will always be very sad, but I feel like I was able to go through that experience and am a better man for it."

Member: "Do you feel that it was a lack of strength that caused this breakup?"

(Doug begins squirming and frowning.)

Member: "I feel like you are carrying a burden from that event that's holding you back. Like you have not made your peace with this—a scar that you keep rubbing. It seems like you have a lot of hurt under the surface."

(Doug crosses his legs, folds his arms across his chest, and then lights a cigarette. He looks detached and uninterested in the interaction.)

Doug: "You are probably right in a way. I am a very volatile person." (In a very low voice . . .) "I still feel very guilty about my children, coming from a puritanical background."

Member: "I wonder how much you let yourself feel your hurt . . . just let yourself feel it fully?"

(The group is fishing and probing, trying to get him to express his "obvious" pain or feelings. Doug is not, at this point, close to his felt meanings. He is, instead, becoming more and more defended and further from exposing his deepest feelings to the group.)

Member: "Did your wife leave you? Did she walk away from you?"

Member: "What feelings do you have about that?"

Doug: (Without affect . . .) "Well, we had some hard times."

Member: "Why did she leave you?"

Doug: "I lost all my money and she didn't feel like she could stay in the community and face the creditors, so she split. . . . I chose to stay and pay back all the money we owed—to rebuild. She had her feelings about a certain life-style. Social acceptance was very important to her—more important than me."

Member: "You still seem to have a lot of pain. It seems essential to your being. You haven't let it out."

Member: "How long ago did this happen?"

Doug: "Four years ago."

Member: "Wow! A long time to carry it (the pain) around."

Member: "Have you had any other relationships?"

Doug: "Yes."

Member: "How are they going?"

Doug: "Fine." (Very defensively . . .) "I think the group is right about my anger and pain. But I feel good. I've dealt with my ex-wife and I've dealt with the anger. I don't feel I am so bad off as you are suggesting."

Bringing the flow back to where Doug seemed to lose his felt meanings and catching some of those feelings empathically, the therapist remarks: "It must have taken tremendous courage and strength to fight your way back and build your life after being so devastated."

Doug: "Well, you know, it was *damn* painful (his eyes grow moist), the emotional and physical pain. My whole world collapsed . . . rejected by the community . . . after she left me. Just the sheer damn *effort* of a couple of years fighting back . . . (sobbing now and relating the story again . . .). It's just been the last year that I've been able to laugh and feel secure financially. (With anger. . . .) And I supported my children all through that period and still do."

Simply understanding Doug's feelings brought the release that the group could not shake out of him, no matter how well meaning their intentions.

I would like to end this section with an illustrative example of what surprises may be in store for the therapist who looks at another's private world from the other's perspective. John Shlien, in *New Directions in Client-Centered Therapy* (1970), tells the story of a psychologist who, on the invitation of concerned parents, observed a "troubled" youngster. The boy was quiet, sensitive, lonely, nervous, afraid of and highly excited by other children. The child stammered in front of strangers and was becoming more and more withdrawn. The psychologist watched, unseen, as the child played by himself in the garden at home. The boy sat pensively, listening to neigh-boring children shout. He frowned, rolled over on his stomach and kicked his white shoes against the grass. He sat up and looked at his stained shoes. Then he saw an earthworm. He stretched it out on the flagstone, found a sharp-edged chip of stone and began to saw the worm in half. At this point the psychologist began to make some tentative mental notes to the effect: "Seems isolated and angry, perhaps over-aggressive, or sadistic, should be watched closely when playing with other children, not have knives or pets." Then he noticed that the boy was talking to himself. He leaned closer and strained to hear as the boy finished separating the worm. The child's frown disappeared as he said, "There, now you have a friend." The difference between the external judgment and the internal world is sometimes striking.

Priority of Therapist Attitudes

When it comes to speculating on an ordering of importance for the three therapist attitudes of genuineness, caring, and empathy, the authors disagree.

Carl: Presently I feel that of the three attitudes of the therapist, genuine-ness, or congruence, is the most basic. As a therapist I must achieve a strong empathy to do the "work" of therapy. But such sensitivity to the moment-to-moment "being" of another person requires that I must accept, and to some degree prize, the other person. Neither of these conditions, how-ever, can be meaningful unless they are real, so I must first of all be integrated and genuine within the therapeutic encounter.

John: The most essential therapist attitude to me, thinking as a client, the one thing I cannot get in most friendships and other relationships, is unconditional positive regard. This type of nonjudgmental caring allows me to explore my deepest and most guarded feelings. The three therapist conditions have been shown to have a high degree of relatedness. They are perhaps three dimensions of one underlying factor. My hunch is that the client-centered therapist's trust and respect in his client's natural tendency toward actualization and self-determination is that underlying factor. This factor is closest, for me, to the attitude of acceptance, to "grokking"—Robert Heinlein's term for understanding and accepting so completely that you be-come one with the person you are perceiving.

Empirical evidence has yet to confirm either of our speculations. All that is known at this point is that therapy appears to be optimally effective when all three attitudes—realness, acceptance, and accurate empathy—are present in a high degree in the therapist.

To summarize this section: As the client finds someone listening to him with consistent acceptance while he expresses his thoughts and feelings, he little by little becomes increasingly able to listen to communications from within himself; he comes to realize that he *is* angry; or that he *is* frightened; or that he *is* experiencing feelings of love. Gradually, he becomes able to listen to feelings within himself which have previously seemed so bizarre, so terrible, or so disorganizing that they had been shut off completely from awareness. As he reveals these hidden and "terrible" aspects of himself, he finds that the therapist's regard for him remains unshaken. And, slowly, he moves toward adopting this same attitude toward himself, toward accepting himself as he is, and thus prepares to forward his process of becoming. Finally, as the client is able to listen to more of himself, he moves toward greater congruence, toward expressing all of himself, openly. He is, at last, free to change and grow in directions which are natural to the maturing human organism.

Psychotherapy is a process whereby man becomes his experiencing, without self-deception, without distortion. He returns to his basic sensory and visceral experience in a knowing way. It is a personal exploration process captured in this T. S. Eliot passage, "And the end of all our exploring will be to arrive where we started and know the place for the first time."

APPLICATION OF THEORY

In 1964 Carl was filmed in a half-hour interview with Gloria, an attractive thirty-year-old divorcee. Because the filmed interview contains all of the elements of client-centered therapy discussed in this chapter, and is available for purchase or rental, giving the reader the opportunity to see and hear client-centered therapy in action, it is presented here for study. (The film is Film #1, *Client-Centered Therapy*, in E. Shostrom (Ed.), *Three Approaches to Psychotherapy*, 1965.)

This is an example of how one client-centered therapist, Carl Rogers, implements his attitudes. Though the interview lasts only a brief thirty minutes, it is evident that the client moves along the predicted process continuum. Here, then, is that interview with occasional theoretical remarks.

Therapist: Good morning. I'm Dr. Rogers, you must be Gloria.

Client: Yes, I am.

Therapist: Won't you have a chair? Now then, we have half an hour together and I really don't know what we will be able to make of it but I hope we can make something of it. I'd be glad to know whatever concerns you.

Client: Well, right now I'm nervous but I feel more comfortable the way you are talking in a low voice and I don't feel like you'll be so harsh on me. But. . . . (*See Comment 1 below.*)

Therapist: I hear the tremor in your voice so. . . .

Client: Well, the main thing I want to talk to you about is, I'm just newly divorced and I had gone in therapy before and I felt comfortable when I left, and all of a sudden now the biggest change is adjusting to my single life. And one of the things that bothers me the most is especially men, and having men to the house and how it affects the children. (*See Comment 2.*) The biggest thing I want—the thing that keeps coming to my mind I want to tell you about is that I have a daughter, nine, who at one time I felt had a lot of emotional problems. I wish I could stop shaking. (*See Comment 3.*) And I'm real conscious of things affecting her. I don't want her to get upset, I don't want to shock her. I want so badly for her to accept me. And we're real open with each other especially about sex. And the other day she saw a girl that was single but pregnant and she asked me all about "can girls get pregnant if they are single?" And the conversation was fine and I wasn't ill at ease at all with her until she asked me if I had ever made love to a man since I left her daddy and I lied to her. (*See Comment 2.*) And ever since that, it keeps coming up to my mind because I feel so guilty lying to her because I never lie (*see Comment 4*) and I want her to trust me. And I almost want an answer from you. I want you to tell me if it would affect her wrong if I told her the truth, or what. (*See Comment 5.*)

*   *   *

A few process comments that can be made up to this point are:

1. At the very beginning the therapist communicates a caring which is perceived by the client.
2. The client in these early stages of the interview is not owning her feelings completely, ". . . one of the *things* that bothered me . . ." "*it* keeps coming up to my mind."
3. She sees her problems as with her daughter—outside herself. She is nervous, but is not being in the immediate experiencing of her feelings, focusing on issues instead of feelings.
4. Some of her personal constructs are rigid, ". . . I never lie."
5. Asking the therapist to tell her what to do about her problem and continuing to perceive and treat him as an authority avoids any personal encounter.

These remarks describe the client's then current behavior. This doesn't mean that this is the kind of person she is, nor that she always behaves in these characteristic ways. This is how she is right now. In terms of personality theory, the bifurcated nature of the actualizing tendency may also be seen here. The actualizing tendency supports, on the one hand, the natural striving to meet her needs through sexual expression; on the other hand it tries to actualize the self—the picture she has of herself as a person with "proper" sexual behavior. In order to look good—to actualize the self—she lies about her actions. Now she is in a real bind since part of her self-concept is also that of a person who never lies.

*   *   *

Therapist: And it's this concern about her and the fact that you really aren't—that this open relationship that has existed between you, now you feel it's kind of vanished? (*See Comment 8 below.*)

Client: Yes, I feel like I have to be on guard about that because I remember when I was a little girl, when I first found out my mother and father made love, that was dirty and terrible, and I didn't like her any more for awhile. And I don't want to lie to Pammy either and I don't know. . . . (*See Comment 6.*)

Therapist: I sure wish I could give you the answer as to what you should tell her. (*See Comment 7.*)

Client: I was afraid you were going to say that.

Therapist: Because what you really want *is* an answer.

Client: I want to especially know if it would affect her if I was completely honest and open with her or if it would affect her because I lied. I feel like it is bound to make a strain because I lied to her.

Therapist: You feel she'll suspect that, or she'll know something is not quite right? (*See Comment 8.*)

Client: I feel that in time she will distrust me, yes. And also I thought well, gee, what about when she gets a little older and she finds herself in touchy situations. She probably wouldn't want to admit it to me because she thinks I'm so good and so sweet. And yet I'm afraid she could think I'm really a devil. And I want so bad for her to accept me. And I don't know how much a nine-year-old can take.

Therapist: And really both alternatives concern you. That she may think you're too good or better than you really are. (*See Comment 8.*)

Client: Yes.

Therapist: Or she may think you are worse than you are.

Client: Not worse than I am. I don't know if she can accept me the *way*

I am. I think I paint a picture that I'm all sweet and motherly. I'm a little ashamed of my shady side too.

Therapist: I see. It really cuts a little deeper. If she really knew you, would she, could she accept you? (*See Comment 8.*)

Client: This is what I don't know. I don't want her to turn away from me. I don't even know how I feel about it because there are times when I feel so guilty like when I have a man over, I even try to make a special set-up so that if I were ever alone with him, the children would never catch me in that sort of thing. Because I'm real leery about it. And yet I also know that I have these desires. (*See Comment 9.*)

Therapist: And so it is quite clear that it isn't only her problem or the relationship with her, it's in you as well. (*See Comment 10.*)

Client: In my guilt. I feel guilty so often.

Therapist: "What can I accept myself as doing?" And you realize that with these sort of subterfuges, so as to make sure that you're not caught or something, you realize that you are acting from guilt, is that it?

Client: Yes, and I don't like the . . . I would like to feel comfortable with whatever I do. If I choose not to tell Pammy the truth, to feel comfortable that she can handle it, and I don't. I want to be honest, and yet I feel there are some areas that *I* don't even accept. (*See Comment 10.*)

Therapist: And if you can't accept them in yourself, how could you possibly be comfortable in telling them to her? (*See Comment 8.*)

Client: Right.

Therapist: And yet, as you say, you do have these desires and you do have your feelings, but you don't feel good about them. (*See Comment 8.*)

Client: Right. I have a feeling that you are just going to sit there and let me stew in it and I want more. I want you to help me get rid of my guilt feelings. If I can get rid of my guilt feelings about lying or going to bed with a single man, any of that, just so I can feel more comfortable.

Therapist: And I guess I'd like to say, "No, I don't want to let you stew in your feelings," but on the other hand, I also feel that this is the kind of very private thing that I couldn't possibly answer *for* you. But I sure as anything will try to help you work toward your own answer. I don't know whether that makes any sense to you, but I mean it. (*See Comment 7.*)

*   *   *

6. The client is being guided by an old construct. Instead of letting her new experience assign its own meaning she gives it an old meaning, "I didn't like my mother when I found out she had sex, so, my daughter won't like me if she finds out about me."

7. The therapist doesn't ignore her direct questions. He expresses concern and understanding of her dilemma and demonstrates his faith in her responsibility and capacity for self-direction and at the same time offers to help her find the answers within herself.
8. The therapist, in his responses, is adequately empathic and doesn't use safe professional language or mannerisms in his replies. He enters the relationship as a real person without analyzing or evaluating. He keeps focused on the client's felt meanings, allowing her to go deeper and deeper in her self-exploration.
9. As she explores herself and her relationships she recognizes the disparities between her self-structure and her experience, "I feel so guilty when I have a man over . . . yet I also know that I have these desires."
10. When the therapist makes an empathic response which is slightly beyond the client's awareness, ". . . it isn't only her problem or the relationship with her, it's in you as well," the only way she can relate to the problem is that, ". . . *it* is in my guilt (not in me)." Later, however, she begins to realize "it" is in her, ". . . I feel there are some areas (in me) that *I* don't even accept."

*   *   *

Client: Well, I appreciate you saying that. You sound like you mean it. (*See Comment 11 below.*) But I don't know where to go. I don't begin to know where to go. I thought that I had pretty well worked over most of my guilt, and now that this is coming up I'm disappointed in myself. I really am. I like it when I feel that no matter what I do, even if it's against my own morals or my upbringing, that I can still feel good about me. And now I don't. Like there's a girl at work who sort of mothers me and I think she thinks I'm all sweet, and I sure don't want to show my more ornery devilish side with her. I want to be sweet and it's so hard for me to—this all seems so new again and it's so disappointing.

Therapist: Yes, I get the disappointment—that here, a lot of these things that you thought you'd worked through, and now the guilts and the feeling that only a part of you is acceptable to anybody else.

Client: Yes.

Therapist: That keeps coming out. I guess I do catch the real deep puzzlement that you feel as to "What the hell shall I do?"

Client: Yes, and do you know what I can find, doctor, is that everything I start to do that's impulsive, seems natural to tell Pamela, or to go out on a date or something, I am comfortable until I think of how I was affected as a child and the minute that comes up, then I'm all haywire. (*See*

Comment 12.) Like I want to be a good mother so bad, and I feel like I am a good mother, but then there's those little exceptions. Like my guilts with working. I want to work and it's so much fun having the extra money. I like to work nights, but the minute I think I'm not being real good to the children or giving them enough time, then I start feeling guilty again. Then, that's why it is (what do they call it?) a double bind. That's just what it feels like. I want to do this and it feels right, but after all I'm not being a good mother and I want to be both. I am becoming more and more aware of what a perfectionist I am. That is what it seems I want to be—so perfect. Either I want to become perfect in my standards, or not have that need anymore.

Therapist: Or, I guess I hear it a little differently—that what you want is to seem perfect, but it means a great—it's a matter of great importance to you to be a good mother and you want to seem to be a good mother, even if some of your actual feelings differ from that. Is that catching it or not? (*See Comment 14.*)

Client: Gee, I don't feel like I am saying that. No, that isn't what I feel, really, I want to approve of me always, but my actions won't let me. (*See Comment 13.*) I want to approve of me.

Therapist: I realize. . . . You sound as though your actions were outside of you. You want to approve of you but what you do somehow won't let you approve of yourself. (*See Comment 14.*)

Client: Right. Like I feel that I can't approve of myself regarding, for example, my sex life. This is the big thing. If I really fell in love with a man and I respected him and I adored him, I don't think I would feel so guilty going to bed with him and I don't think I would have to make up any excuses to the children because they could see my natural caring for him. But when I have the physical desires and I'll say, "Oh well, why not," and I want to anyway, but I feel guilty afterwards. I hate facing the kids, I don't like looking at myself, and I rarely enjoy it. And this is what I mean. If the circumstances would be different, I don't think I'd feel so guilty because I'd feel right about it.

Therapist: I guess I hear you saying, "If what I was doing, when I went to bed with a man, was really genuine and full of love and respect and so on, I wouldn't feel guilty in relation to Pam. I really would be comfortable about the situation."

Client: That's how I feel, yeh. And I know that sounds like I want a perfect situation, but that is how I feel, and in the meantime, I can't stop these desires. I tried that also. I have tried saying, "O.K., I don't like myself when I do that so I won't do it anymore." But then I resent the children. I think, why should they stop me from doing what I want, and it is really not that bad.

Therapist: But I guess I heard you saying too, that it isn't only the children, but *you* don't like it as well when it isn't really. . . .

Client: Right. I'm sure that—I know that's it, probably even more so than I'm aware of, but I only notice it so much when I pick it up in the children. Then I can also notice it in myself.

Therapist: And somehow, sometimes, you kind of feel like blaming them for the feeling you have. I mean, why should they cut you out from a normal sex life?

Client: Well, a sex life, I could say, not normal because there is something about me that says that's not very healthy—to just go into sex because you feel physically attracted or something, or a physical need. Something about it tells me that that's not quite right anyway.

Therapist: But you feel, really, that at times you are acting in ways that are not in accord with your own inner standards. (*See Comment 15.*)

Client: Right. Right.

Therapist: But you were also saying, a minute ago, that you feel you can't help that either.

Client: I wished I could. That's it, and I can't—now I feel like I can't control myself as well as I could have before. For a specific reason now, I can't. I just let go and there are too many things I do wrong that I have to feel guilty for, and I sure don't like that. I want you very much to give me a direct answer, and I'm going to ask it, and I don't expect a direct answer, but I want to know. Do you feel that—to me the most important thing is to be open and honest, and if I can be open and honest with my children, do you feel that it could harm them? If for example, I could say to Pammy, "I felt bad lying to you, Pammy, and I want to tell you the truth now," and if I tell her the truth and she is shocked at me and she is upset, if that could bother her more? I want to get rid of my guilts and that will help me, but I don't want to put them on her.

Therapist: That's right.

Client: Do you feel that that could hurt her?

Therapist: I guess—I am sure this will sound evasive to you, but it seems to me that perhaps the person you are not being fully honest with is you. Because I was very much struck by the fact that you were saying, "If I feel all right about what I have done, whether it's going to bed with a man or what, if I really feel all right about it, then I do not have any concern about what I would tell Pam or my relationship with her." (*See Comment 16.*)

Client: Right. All right. Now I hear what you are saying. Then all right, then I want to work on accepting me, then. I want to work on feeling all right about it. That makes sense. That will come natural and then I won't have to worry about Pammy. But when things do seem so wrong for me and I have an impulse to do them, how can I accept that?

* * *

11. The client perceives the therapist as genuine and accepting in the relationship. Already in the interview the therapeutic climate is established by the therapist's attitudes and perceived by the client—the therapeutic relationship is forming.

12. She is struggling to put her own meanings to her experiencing but references her meanings to fixed constructs and these rigid constructs seem to guide her life, "I am comfortable until I think of how I was affected as a child. . . ." She is sort of saying, "It feels right and I *want* to do it, but I really *should* be a good mother."

13. Here is the actualizing tendency "causing" neurotic behavior, "I want to approve of me . . . but my actions won't let me."

14. This comment by the therapist, in light of the client's response, could be interpreted as reflecting a low order of empathy or even being slightly evaluative. However, in the context of the interaction and the material introduced by the client up to this point, I think the remark is very empathic but goes slightly beyond the edge of her awareness. When she says, in reply, "Gee, I don't feel like I am saying that," he accepts this response and sensitively returns to *her* thread of felt meaning in his next response. (In exploring new territory which is not understood, a client is often timid and frightened. Sometimes the therapist can repeat the exact words and the client still may not agree or hear himself saying those words.) In returning to the flow of the client's feelings the therapist accurately and delicately captures the essence of her meanings— seeing her world as she sees it at this moment.

15. The therapist continues to facilitate her self-exploration with accurate empathic responses.

16. He catches, exactly, the subtle meaning right on the edge of her awareness, "Right. All right. Now I hear what you are saying. Then all right, then I want to work on accepting me, then." She realizes now that the problem and its solution are within her. She assimilates a real insight and begins to communicate more freely in terms of self, focusing on her internal conflict.

* * *

Therapist: What you'd like to do is to feel more accepting toward yourself when you do things that you feel are wrong. Is that right?

Client: Right.

Therapist (smiling): It sounds like a tough assignment.

Client: I feel like you are going to say, "Now why do you think they are wrong?" and I have mixed feelings there too. Through therapy I will say, "Now look, I know this is natural. Women feel it—sure, we don't talk about it lots socially but all women feel it and it's very natural." I have had sex for the last 11 years and I am, of course, going to want it, but I still think it is wrong unless you are really, truly in love with a man, and my body doesn't seem to agree. And so I don't know how to accept it.

Therapist: It sounds like a triangle to me, isn't it? You feel that I, or therapists in general, or other people say, "It is all right, it is all right, it is natural enough, go ahead," and I guess you feel your body sort of winds up on that side of the picture. But something in you says, "But I don't like it that way, not unless it is really right."

Client: Right. (Long pause.)

Client (In a slower, somber way): I have a hopeless feeling. I mean, these are all the things that I sort of feel myself, and I feel—O.K., now what?

Therapist: You feel this is the conflict and it's just insoluble, therefore it is hopeless and here you look to me and I don't seem to give you any help.

Client: Right. I really know you can't answer for me, and I have to figure it out myself, but I want you to guide me or show me where to start or—so it won't look so hopeless. I know I can keep living with this conflict and I know eventually things will work out, but I'd like feeling more comfortable with the way I live—and I'm not.

Therapist: One thing I might ask, what is it you wish I would say to you? (*See Comment 17 below.*)

Client: I wish you would say to me to be honest and take the risk that Pammy is going to accept me. And I also have a feeling if I could risk it with Pammy, of all people, that I'd be able to say, "Here's this little kid who can accept me, and I'm really not that bad." If she really knows what a demon I am and still loves me and accepts me, it seems like it would help me to accept me more—like it's really not that bad. I want you to say to go ahead and be honest, but I don't want the responsibility that it would upset her. That is where I don't want to take responsibility.

Therapist: You know very well what you'd like to do in the relationship. You would like to be yourself and you'd like to have her know that you're not perfect and do things that maybe even she wouldn't approve of, and that you disapprove of to some degree yourself, but that somehow she would love you and accept you as an imperfect person.

Client: Yes. Like I wonder if my mother had been more open with me, maybe I wouldn't have had such a narrow attitude about sex. If I would have thought that she could be, you know, pretty sexy and ornery, and devilish too, that I wouldn't look at her as being such a sweet mother, that she could also be the other side. But she didn't talk about that. Maybe that's where I got my picture. I don't know, but I want Pammy to see me as a full woman, but also accept me.

Therapist: You don't sound so uncertain. (*See Comment 18.*)

Client: I don't? What do you mean?

Therapist: What I mean is you have been sitting there telling me just what you would like to do in that relationship with Pam.

Client: I would, but I don't want to quite take the risk of doing it unless an authority tells me that. . . .

Therapist (Eyes moistening):I guess one thing that I feel very keenly is that it's an awful risky thing to live. (*See Comment 19.*) You'd be taking a chance on your relationship with her and taking a chance on letting her know who you are, really.

Client: Yes. But then if I don't take the chance, if I feel loved and accepted by her, I'd never feel so good about it anyway.

Therapist: If her love and acceptance of you is based on a false picture of you, what the hell is the good of that? Is that what you are saying?

Client: Yes, that is what I mean, but I also feel there is a lot of responsibility with being a mother. I don't want to feel like I have caused any big traumas in the children. I don't *like* all that responsibility. I think that's it. I don't like it, feeling it could be my fault.

Therapist: I guess that's what I meant when I said, "Life is risky." To take the responsibility for being the person you would like to be with her is a hell of a responsibility.

Client: It is.

Therapist: A very frightening one.

Client: And you know, I look at it two ways. (*See Comment 20.*) I like to see myself as being so honest with the kids, and really being proud of myself so that no matter what I told them or no matter how bad they think I was, I was honest and down deep it is going to be a much more wholesome relationship, and yet you know, I get jealous like when they are with their daddy. I feel he is more flip, he is not quite as real, he is not quite as honest, but nevertheless they see a sweet picture of their dad. You know, he is all goodness and light, and I am envious of that too. I want them to see me just as sweet as they see him and yet I know he is not quite as real with them. (*See Comment 20.*) So it seems like I've got to swap the one for the other, and I know this is really what I want the most, but I miss some of that glory. (*See Comment 20.*)

Therapist: You sort of feel, I want them to have just as nice a picture of me as they have of their dad and if his is a little phony, then mine will have to be too. I think that's putting it a little too strongly.

Client: But that is close. That's what I mean. But I know she can't have that neat a picture of me, if I were honest. Besides that, I do feel that I am a little more ornery than their dad anyway. (*See Comment 20.*) I'm likely to do more things that they would disapprove of.

Therapist: Then you do really find it quite hard to believe that they would really love you if they knew you?

Client: That's right. You know that's exactly it. Before therapy, I would have definitely chosen the other area. I am going to get respect from them no matter what—even if I have to lie.

Therapist: I see.

Client: But right now, I know that's not true and I'm not positive they'll accept me. Something tells me they will. I know they will, but I am not positive. I want reassurance. I keep wanting these things.

Therapist: And now you are kind of in a no-man's-land of probably shifting from one point of view toward them to another, but boy you'd sure like somebody to say, "That's right, you go ahead and do it."

Client: Yes. That's why I get encouraged when I read in a book from somebody I respect and admire, that this is the right thing no matter what—honesty will win out. Well, then that keeps giving me confidence—by gosh, I'm right but. . . .

Therapist: It is so damned hard to really choose something on your own, isn't it? (*See Comment 19.*)

Client: Which makes me feel very immature. I don't like this in me. I wish I were grown up enough or mature enough to make my decisions and stick by them, but I need somebody to help me on—somebody to push me.

Therapist: So you kind of reproach yourself for that. I guess you feel, "Why if I was anybody, or if I was grown up, I'd be mature enough to decide things like this for myself."

Client: Right. And take more *risks.* I wish I would take more risks. I wish that I could just go ahead and be this and say, however the children grow up, I've done my best. I wouldn't have to constantly have this conflict. And I'd like, in later years, to say, "No matter what you asked me kids, at least I told you the truth. You may not have liked it, but it's been the truth." That, somehow, I can admire. I disrespect people that lie. I hate it so, you see what a double bind I am in. I hate myself if I'm bad, but I also hate myself if I lie. So, it's accepting. I want to become more accepting.

Therapist: I guess, judging from your tone of voice, you sound as though you hate yourself more when you lie than you do in terms of things you disapprove of.

Client: I do. I do because this has really bothered me. This happened with Pammy about a month ago and it keeps coming to my mind. I don't know whether to go back and talk to her about it or wait. She may have even forgotten what she asked me, but. . . .

Therapist: The point is, you haven't forgotten.

Client: I haven't forgotten. No. I haven't and I would like, at least, to be able to tell her that I remember lying and I am sorry I lied and it has been driving me bugs because I did. Now I feel like—now that's solved— and I didn't even solve a thing, but I feel relieved. (*See Comment 21.*) I do feel like you have been saying to me—you are not giving me advice, but I do feel like you are saying, "You know what pattern you want to follow, and go ahead and follow it." I sort of feel a backing up from you.

Therapist: I guess the way I sense it, you've been telling me that you know what you want to do and yes, I do believe in backing up people in what they want to do. It's a little different slant than the way it seems to you.

*   *   *

17. This question is illustrative of a strictly intuitive response. The therapist, deeply immersed in the relationship, completely present to his client, trusts the strength of this brief relationship enough to follow his own intuitive flow when the client's experiential flow deadends. As you can see, his question sparks an immediate reply in the client revealing to her the direction *she* wants to take and showing her again that the answers are within her. There is a Sufi expression that captures this wisdom in simple words, "He who has made a door and a lock, has also made a key" (Shah 1968, p. 111).

18. The therapist responds here, as in other places, to the client's tone, to the total communication, rather than only to the content.

19. In reply to the client's plea for an authority, the therapist with obvious intensity expresses what he is deeply feeling at the moment, being in his experiencing. He doesn't tell her she doesn't need an authority (as an authority might be tempted to do) but simply expresses his own feelings which at the moment are very close to hers.

20. Earlier the client did not see herself as wanting to *seem* perfect to her children. Now, realizing it on her own, she says, "And you know, I look at it two ways . . . I want them to see me just as sweet . . . I miss some of the glory." Then, "But I know she can't have that neat picture of me if I were honest. Besides that, I do feel that I'm a little more ornery than their dad anyway."

21. She is now focusing on her inner conflict and inner valuing process and bringing to awareness her inner experiencing. "Now I feel like—now that's solved—and I didn't even solve a thing, but I feel relieved." She feels relief—the felt meaning—before the meaning is symbolized in thoughts or words. She feels relief—settled—and yet hasn't made a conscious decision. This is a beautiful example of the meaning of the term "experiencing." An event has taken place in her. She knows this. She even knows it is a solution, though she doesn't know what that is. But she can return to this inner event when she needs to, and discover more and more of its meaning.

The therapist doesn't need to know what her decision is, because it seems clear that it is something integrative and satisfying to her. She also senses fully his empathic understanding and unconditional regard, remarking, "I feel a backing up from you."

*   *   *

Client: Are you telling me. . . .

Therapist: You see, one thing that concerns me is, it's no damn good to do something that you haven't really chosen to do. That is why I am trying to help you find out what your own inner choices are.

Client: But then there's also a conflict there because I am not really positive what I want to do. The lying part, yes, but I am not positive what I want to do when I go against myself. (*See Comment 22 below.*) Like when I bring a man to the house. I am not sure I want to do that. If I feel guilty afterward, I must not have really wanted to.

Therapist: I am interested that you say—I'm not just sure which words you used—but you don't like yourself or don't approve of it when you do something against *yourself.*

Client: Yes, you know this is so different. Now this kind of thing we are talking about now, it isn't just knowing whether you want to do something or not. If I want to go to work in the morning or if I don't want to go to work, that's easy. But when I find myself doing something I don't feel comfortable with, I automatically say, "If you are not comfortable, it is not right. Something is wrong." All right now. What I want to ask you is, how can I know which is the strongest? Because I do it, does that mean it's the strongest? (*See Comment 22.*) And yet, if I disapproved, that's just part of the thing that has to go along with it? You see, it sounds like I'm picking up a contradiction. I am not following.

Therapist: It sounds like you are feeling a contradiction in yourself too, although what I heard you saying in part is, the way you like it is when you feel really comfortable about what you are doing.

Client: Yes, and I have at times, when I have made a decision. Now that seems right. That seems perfectly right—no conflict—but then there are times I do things that I feel uncomfortable with. So that there is a conflict there. It's not the same at all. What I'm saying is, how do I really know when I am following my true feelings, if I have conflicts afterwards or guilt afterwards?

Therapist: I see. Because in the moment, it may seem like your true feelings.

Client: Yes. Like if I am starting to do it—O.K.

Therapist: But there really is . . . if you feel comfortable in the moment about it, but then afterwards don't feel at all comfortable, which course of action was really the one you should have followed.

Client: You know, the most outstanding thing—I don't know if you are following me, what I am saying about this conflict—the one thing I know is that I have wanted, for example, to leave my husband for quite a few years. I never did it. I kept thinking how nice it would be, or how scary it would be, but I never did it. And all of a sudden when I did, it felt right. I didn't feel mean toward him. (*See Comment 23.*) I just knew this was what I had to do. That's when I know I am following myself. I am following my feelings completely. I have no conflict there. Some unhappy things came from it, but I still have no conflict. That, to me, is when I am following my feelings. And in everyday life, the small little decisions, the small little things to do don't come out that clear at all. So many conflicts come with them. Is this natural?

Therapist: Although you are saying—I expect it is—but you are saying too that you know perfectly well the feeling within yourself that occurs when you are really doing something that's right for you.

Client: I do. I do and I miss that feeling other times. It's right away a clue to me.

Therapist: You can really listen to yourself sometimes and realize, "Oh no, this isn't the right feeling. This isn't the way I would feel if I was doing what I really wanted to do."

Client: But yet, many times I will go along and do it anyway and say, "Oh well, I'm in the situation now, I'll just remember next time." I mentioned this word a lot in therapy and most therapists grin at me or giggle or something when I say "utopia," but when I do follow a feeling and I feel this good feeling inside of me, that's sort of utopia. That's what I mean. That's the way I like to feel whether it's a bad thing or a good thing. But I feel right about me. (*See Comment 24.*)

Therapist: I sense that in those utopian moments, you really feel kind of whole. You feel all in one piece.

Client: Yes, it gives me a choked up feeling when you say that because I don't get that as often as I'd like. I like that whole feeling. That's real precious to me.

Therapist: I expect none of us get it as often as we'd like, but I really do understand it. (Pause. Tears come to her eyes.) That really does touch you, doesn't it?

Client: Yes, and you know what else I was just thinking? I—a dumb thing—that all of a sudden while I was talking to you I thought, "Gee, how nice I can talk to you and I want you to approve of me and I respect you, but I miss that my father couldn't talk to me like you are." I mean, I'd like to say, "Gee, I'd like you for my father." I don't even know why that came to me. (*See Comment 25.*)

Therapist: You look to me like a pretty nice daughter. But you really do miss the fact that you couldn't be open with your own dad.

*   *   *

22. It is surprising—and unusual—for a client to sense so clearly what we have termed in this chapter the bifurcating of the actualizing tendency. With her conscious mind choosing one way to behave, and her organism endeavoring to meet its consciously unacceptable desires, she is clearly experiencing this conflict.

23. When the experienced feelings and the concept of self-in-relationship match or are congruent, then there is this feeling of unity and wholeness. It cannot be stressed enough, however, that these theoretical thoughts are *not* what is in the therapist's mind at the moment. He is living in the immediacy of the relationship. Only afterward does he see how the theoretical constructs apply.

24. "Utopia" is a good word to describe the momentary feeling of being a whole person. The client also is recognizing that the basis of evaluations must be within her, ". . . when I do follow a feeling and I feel this good feeling inside of me, that's sort of utopia." She responds to the therapist's deep empathic understanding, tears coming to her eyes as he says,

"I expect none of us get it as often as we'd like (the utopia feeling), but I really do understand it."

25. She has moved at her own pace to being in contact—intimate and trusting—with the therapist. She is relating to him as a person and moving close to her own inner experiencing—being in her experiencing as it emerges. "I mean I'd like you for my father. I don't even know why that came to me." This is a much higher stage of process than the early portion of the interview. The therapist, in turn, is being in his experiencing, expressing his positive feelings, "You look like a pretty nice daughter." To write this whole exchange off by intellectualizing it as transference or countertransference ignores the very human and personal aspects of the I-Thou relationship.

*   *   *

Client: Yes. I couldn't be open, but I want to blame it on him. I think I am more open than he'd allow me. He would never listen to me talk like you are and not disapprove, not lower me down. I thought of this the other day. Why do I always have to be so perfect? I know why. He always wanted me to be perfect. I always had to be better and . . . yes, I miss that.

    Therapist: You were trying like hell to be the girl he wanted you to be.

    Client: Yet at the same time, rebelling.

    Therapist: That's right.

    Client: Like I almost gloated writing him a letter the other day and telling him I am a waitress, which I expect him to disapprove of. I go out at nights and I almost gloated hitting him back—like, "Now how do you like me?" And yet, I really want acceptance and love from him. I mean, I know he loves me.

    Therapist: So you slap at him and say, "This is what I am, now see."

    Client: Yes. "You raised me, how do you like it?" But do you know what I want him to say? "I knew this was you all along, honey, and I really love you."

    Therapist: You really feel badly that you think there is very little chance he will say that.

    Client: No. He won't. He doesn't hear. (Her voice sad and resigned.) I went back home to him about two years ago, really wanting to let him know I loved him although I have been afraid of him. And he doesn't hear me. He just keeps saying things like, "Honey, you know I love you. You know I have always loved you." He doesn't hear. (Her eyes moisten.)

    Therapist: He has never really known you and loved you and this, somehow, is what brings the tears inside.

Client: I don't know what it is. You know, when I talk about it, it feels more flip. If I just sit still a minute, it feels like a great big hurt down there. (*See Comment 26.*) Instead, I feel cheated.

Therapist: It is much easier to be a little flip because then you don't feel that big lump of hurt inside.

Client: And again, that's a hopeless situation. I tried working on it, and I feel it's something I have to accept. My father just isn't the type of man I'd dearly like. I'd like somebody more understanding and caring. He cares, but not in the way that we can cooperate—or communicate.

Therapist: You feel that, "I am permanently cheated."

Client: That is why I like substitutes. Like I like talking to you and I like men that I can respect. Doctors, and I keep sort of underneath a feeling like we are real close, you know, sort of like a substitute father.

Therapist: I don't feel that's pretending.

Client: Well, you are not really my father.

Therapist: No, I meant about the real close business.

Client: Well, see, I sort of feel that's pretending too because I can't expect you to feel very close to me. You don't know me that well.

Therapist: All I can know is what I am feeling, and that is I feel close to you in this moment. (*See Comment 27.*)

The film ran out at this point, and the interview ended a moment or two later.

*　　　*　　　*

26. The client has continued close to her experiencing, "If I just sit still a minute, it feels like a great big hurt down there." Her feelings are flowing into awareness and she expresses them as they occur without censorship.

27. The therapist is immediately present and accessible in the moment-to-moment relationship. He is being in his experiencing and expressing his real feelings—of affection and immediate closeness fully in the moment, "All I know is what I am feeling and that is I feel close to you in this moment."

An interesting footnote, indicating that the interview was more than words, is that Gloria has kept in occasional contact with Carl, through correspondence, for eight years, asking at one point if he objected to her thinking of him as her fantasied father. She has become increasingly open and effective in her own interpersonal relationships.

The therapist, from the beginning of the interview, established an effective therapeutic climate. He communicated a nonpossessive caring, a genuineness, and a sensitive empathy which moved forward her self-exploration, and these attitudes were perceived by the client. He demonstrated a continual belief and trust in her responsibility and capacity for self-direction. He trusted in his own experiencing, using it as a guide, and expressing his moment-to-moment feelings in the relationship.

The client, in turn, moved from the early stages of the interview where she was not owning her feelings completely, seeing her problems outside herself, somewhat remote from her immediate experiencing, guided by fairly black and white constructs, and avoiding personal encounter with the therapist to an awareness of her incongruence (where the bifurcation of the actualizing tendency can be seen), to recognizing that her basis for evaluation must be within her, being in her immediate experiencing, owning and expressing her feelings of the moment, and entering into a person-to-person relationship.

BRIEF HISTORY OF CLIENT-CENTERED THERAPY

Client-centered psychotherapy was conceived of primarily by Carl Rogers, and developed in the period from 1938 through 1950, undergoing its initial phase at Ohio State University in the years from 1940 through 1945. During the following five-year period, from 1945 through 1950, it was further elaborated at the Counseling Center at the University of Chicago. At both Ohio State and Chicago, his colleagues were drawn mostly from the graduate students who had worked with him. A number of these have become leaders in their own right. During the whole period from 1940 to the present they have greatly enriched the conceptual base, have carried out the bulk of the research, and have decidedly broadened the application of client-centered therapy.

Rogers' early approach was thought of first as a mode of counseling and psychotherapy (Rogers 1942) and was termed "nondirective." The excitement of using recorded interviews for research and training and the discovery that differing responses to the client brought about sharply differing degrees of therapeutic movement led to a heavy emphasis on technique. During this period "reflection of feelings," and "nondirective techniques" were its main identifying features. The term "client" rather than "patient" was adopted to indicate that this was not a manipulative or medically prescriptive model. The individual coming for help was perceived and valued as a self-responsible client, not as an object for treatment. Psychotherapy sessions were the client's hour and he was regarded as capable of making his own discoveries and decisions in the facilitative climate provided by the therapist.

Carl had acquired this respect for the client's capabilities out of hard-earned experience. Perhaps the first client-centered counseling session took place when he was "counseling" the mother of a boy who was in therapy at the child guidance clinic. He had done everything he could to help her to the "insight" that her child's problem was clearly her early rejection of the boy. After many interviews of trying unsuccessfully to help her recognize the pattern, he finally gave up, saying they had both tried but failed. The woman agreed. They shook hands and she walked to the door to leave. Then she turned around and asked, "Do you ever take adults for counseling here?" Carl said yes and she replied, "Well then, I would like some help." She returned to the chair she had just left and began to pour out her despair about her troubled relationship with her husband, her sense of failure, her confusion, all very different from the sterile "case history" she had given. This incident was one of a number that helped him to realize that it is the client who knows what hurts, what directions to go, what problems are crucial.

As experience, theory-building, and research broadened, the term "client-centered therapy" (Rogers 1951) underscored the focus on the internal phenomenological world of the client, not on technique. The fifties was a period of burgeoning research, and a rigorous theory of therapy and personality was developed (Rogers 1959). Client-centered therapy became recognized as not simply a mode of therapy, but an approach to all human relationships. *On Becoming a Person* (Rogers 1961), for example, a book intended primarily for professionals, was enthusiastically received by laymen in many countries.

During the sixties the approach broadened still further. Chronic schizophrenics were offered therapy, as part of a large research program (Rogers, et al. 1967). Intensive groups were held for professional workers, business executives, educators, and those who simply wished to enhance their personal growth. Perhaps nowhere was its influence more strongly felt than in education (Rogers 1969), where it sparked many innovative efforts and much research on changes in attitudes and behavior.

The client-centered point of view has become one of the stronger emphases in the trend toward the small intensive group as a source of personal growth (Rogers 1970). Client-centered therapy has also reached out to influence the philosophy of science (Rogers 1964; Coulson & Rogers 1968).

Carl never had one mentor, but instead was influenced by many significant figures of widely differing viewpoints. Consequently he was tied to no dogma,

nor to any preciously held theory, a quality which has prevented the formation of any school of client-centered therapy per se.

The client-centered view—though fed by various streams of thought—
developed primarily out of the continuing examination and re-examination,
by Carl and his colleagues, of their changing, broadening experience with
their clients. It was the client in process who constituted the basic data for
the evolving of client-centered thought.

As to more distant parallels—for they are parallels rather than roots—one
can cite the phenomenological line of thought in Europe, the existential philosophy of Kierkegaard and Buber, and perhaps the development of gestalt
psychology, particularly as expressed by Kurt Lewin.

There is a distinctly oriental flavor to the deepening philosophy of the
client-centered movement. Carl has reported in recent years how congenial
he has found certain aspects of Zen thinking, particularly their stress on
personal experience as the main avenue of learning. He has also quoted
some of the sayings of Lao-Tse, especially those which decry manipulation
and meddling, and recognize that "If I keep from imposing on people, they
become themselves" (Rogers 1973).

REFERENCES: PRINTED, FILMED, AND TAPED

Books and Articles

BARRETT-LENNARD, G. T. Dimensions of perceived therapist response related to
therapeutic change. Unpublished Ph.D. dissertation, University of Chicago,
1959.

DITTES, J. E. Galvanic skin response as a measure of patient's reaction to
therapist's permissiveness. *J. Abnorm. Soc. Psychol.*, 55, 295-303, 1957.

GENDLIN, E. T. Experiencing: A variable in the process of therapeutic change.
Amer. J. Psychol., 15, 233-245, 1961.

GENDLIN, E. T. *Experiencing and the Creation of Meaning.* New York: The
Free Press of Glencoe, 1962.

GENDLIN, E. T. Experiencing and the nature of concepts. *The Christian
Scholar*, 46, 245-255, 1963.

GENDLIN, E. T. A short summary and some long predictions. In J. T. Hart &
T. M. Tomlinson (Eds.), *New Directions in Client-Centered Therapy.*
Boston: Houghton Mifflin Co., 1970.

HALKIDES, G. An experimental study of four conditions necessary for therapeutic change. Unpublished Ph.D. dissertation, University of Chicago,
1958.

HART, J. T. The development of client-centered therapy. In J. T. Hart & T. M.
Tomlinson (Eds.), *New Directions in Client-Centered Therapy.* Boston:
Houghton Mifflin Co., 1970.

HART, J. T. & TOMLINSON, T. M. (Eds.). *New Directions in Client-Centered
Therapy.* Boston: Houghton Mifflin Co., 1970.

RIOCH, M., ET AL. NIMH Pilot Project in Training Mental Health Counselors: Summary of first year's work 1960-1961. Mimeographed report. Bethesda, Maryland: National Institute of Mental Health Adult Psychiatry Branch, undated.

ROGERS, C. R. *Counseling and Psychotherapy.* Boston: Houghton Mifflin Co., 1942.

ROGERS, C. R. *Client-Centered Therapy.* Boston: Houghton Mifflin Co., 1951.

ROGERS, C. R. Persons or science: A philosophical question. *Amer. Psychologist,* 10, 267, 1955.

ROGERS, C. R. The necessary and sufficient conditions of therapeutic personality change. *J. Consult. Psychol.,* 21, 95, 1957.

ROGERS, C. R. A theory of therapy, personality and interpersonal relationships as developed in the client-centered framework. In S. Koch (Ed.), *Psychology: A Study of Science, Vol. III, Formulations of the Person and the Social Context.* New York: McGraw Hill, 1959, p. 184.

ROGERS, C. R. *On Becoming a Person.* Boston: Houghton Mifflin Co., 1961.

ROGERS, C. R. The process equation of psychotherapy. *Amer. J. Psychotherapy,* 15, 27, 1961.

ROGERS, C. R. The concept of the fully functioning person. *Psychotherapy: Theory, Research, and Practice,* 1, 17, 1963.

ROGERS, C. R. Toward a science of the person. In T. W. Wann (Ed.), *Behaviorism and Phenomenology: Contrasting Bases for Modern Psychology.* Chicago: University of Chicago Press, 1964.

ROGERS, C. R. *Freedom to Learn: A View of What Education Might Become.* Columbus, Ohio: Charles E. Merrill Publishing Co., 1969.

ROGERS, C. R. *Carl Rogers on Encounter Groups.* New York: Harper & Row, 1970.

ROGERS, C. R. My philosophy of interpersonal relationships and how it grew. *J. of Humanistic Psychol.,* 1973.

ROGERS, C. R. & COULSON, W. R. (Eds.). *Man and the Science of Man.* Columbus, Ohio: Charles Merrill Publishing Co., 1968.

ROGERS, C. R. & DYMOND, R. F. (Eds.). *Psychotherapy and Personality Change.* Chicago: University of Chicago Press, 1954.

ROGERS, C. R., GENDLIN, E. T., KIESLER, D. J., & TRUAX, C. B. *The Therapeutic Relationship and Its Impact: A Study of Psychotherapy with Schizophrenics.* Madison: University of Wisconsin Press, 1967.

SEEMAN, J. A study of the process of nondirective therapy. *J. Consult. Psychol.,* 13, 157-168, 1949.

SEEMAN, J. Counselor judgments of therapeutic process and outcome. In C. R. Rogers & R. F. Dymond (Eds.), *Psychotherapy and Personality Change.* Chicago: University of Chicago Press, 1954.

SHAH, I. *Caravan of Dreams.* Baltimore: Penguin Books, 1968.

SNYDER, W. C. An investigation of the nature of nondirective psychotherapy. *J. Genet. Psychol.,* 33, 193-223, 1945.

TRUAX, C. B. & MITCHELL, K. M. Research on certain therapist interpersonal skills in relation to process and outcome. In A. E. Bergin & S. L. Garfield (Eds.), *Handbook of Psychotherapy and Behavior Changes.* New York: John Wiley & Sons, 1971, p. 299.

VAN DER VEEN, F. Client perception of therapist conditions as a factor in psychotherapy. In J. T. Hart & T. M. Tomlinson (Eds.), *New Directions in Client-Centered Therapy.* Boston: Houghton Mifflin Co., 1970, p. 214.

Films and Tape Recordings

Journey Into Self. Produced by W. McGaw. Sound film, 47 minutes. Encounter group of diverse strangers. 1968. Western Behavioral Sciences Institute, La Jolla, California.

Client-Centered Therapy. Film No. 1 in E. Shostrom, ed., *Three Approaches to Psychotherapy.* 1965. Sound film, in color, 50 minutes. A therapeutic interview with Gloria with explanatory comments. Psychological Films, 189 N. Wheeler St., Orange, California.

Because That's My Way. Produced by Station WQED, Pittsburgh. Sound film in color, 60 minutes. An encounter group of drug users, non-users, and a narcotics agent. 1971. Great Plains Instructional Television Library, U. of Nebraska, Lincoln, Nebraska.

Tape No. 3. Mr. Vac. 46 minute tape recording. Script available. Two interviews with a hospitalized schizophrenic. 1968. AAP Tape Library, 1040 Woodcock Road, Orlando, Florida.

Tape No. 5. Miss Mun. 47 minute tape recording. Script available. A seventeenth interview with a young woman client. 1955. AAP Tape Library, 1040 Woodcock Road, Orlando, Florida.

Tape No. 7. Mike. 40 minutes. Script available. Interview with a seventeen-year-old boy before a group of counselors. Undated. AAP Tape Library, 1040 Woodcock Road, Orlando, Florida.

Wilhelm Reich *Alexander Lowen*

8

The Body in Personality Theory:
Wilhelm Reich and Alexander Lowen

by ALEXANDER LOWEN

Today there is an increasing acceptance of the role of the body in personality theory. This, however, is a relatively late development. For a long time, personality theory and the practice of psychoanalysis and psychotherapy ignored the body. Both approaches to personality problems focused exclusively upon the psyche as the names clearly indicate. Aside from the attempt to correlate some physical disorders with psychic conflicts under the rubric of psychosomatics, the body and its physical processes were the exclusive domain of the nonpsychiatric physician. The split in the way we look at man, that is, as having a mind and a body, which influence each other but are really two separate entities, is still deeply rooted in psychology and medicine.

The man who was primarily responsible for introducing a unitary concept of mind and body, and a unitary therapeutic modality was Wilhelm Reich. Reich was a psychoanalyst and a member of the Psychoanalytic Institute in Vienna. A man of tremendous energy and great creative ability, he soon became the leader of the technical seminar in psychoanalysis in Vienna, and the assistant director of the Psychoanalytic Clinic under Gustav Hartmann. As a psychoanalyst, Reich is noted for his contributions to analytic theory. His study of resistance in the form of character defense, published under the title *Charakter-Analyse* in 1933, was and is still considered one of the most important contributions to analytic theory and practice. His investigations into sexual functioning, which was originally published in German under the title *Die Funktion Des Orgasmus*, 1927, opened the way to an understanding of the libido as a physical force instead of a purely psychic force as psychoanalysts viewed it. Yet it was these investigations into sexuality, leading to the conclusion that orgastic potency must be distinguished from erective potency and performance, that were partly responsible for the break between Reich and the psychoanalytic movement.

Let me stay with the question of orgastic potency for a minute since it is the cornerstone upon which was built the concept of the functional identity and antithesis of psychic and somatic functions. According to Reich, orgastic potency represented the ability to discharge the excess excitation in an organism. It occurred as a total body response of a convulsive nature with intense pleasure and satisfaction. This response should be distinguished from one in which only the genital area is involved and thus only genital excitation is discharged. Reich found that patients who in the course of analysis achieved orgastic potency remained free from neurosis. The difference between the sexual responses of healthy and neurotic individuals was both quantitative and qualitative. First, all excess excitation was discharged—not just the limited genital excitation—and second, the total body was involved.

The quantitative factor implies the existence of a physical force. If all excitation isn't discharged, the energy that remains will be experienced as anxiety unless it is bound by neurotic mechanisms. This undischarged sexual excitation or energy is the force that supports and maintains the neurotic mechanisms. When orgastic potency is established, the excess of energy is drained away from the neurotic mechanisms which must then collapse. In my clinical experience this does happen, and Reich's position is a fully valid one. Orgastic potency is, therefore, a goal of bioenergetic therapy. One difference between Reichian therapy and bioenergetics is that we shift the focus from orgastic potency to defenses and neurotic behavior patterns, and we work them through thoroughly to achieve orgastic potency. This approach avoids making health totally dependent on sexual functioning, which may have been Reich's difficulty. Sexuality is made to depend on the establishment of a relatively high degree of emotional health.

From 1933 to 1939 Reich, who had left Germany when Hitler had come to power, worked in Denmark, Sweden, and Norway. During this period he investigated the libido as a measurable physical energy, which he first called bioelectrical energy and later changed to orgone energy. It was also during this period that he made the connection between character attitudes expressed psychically and the muscular tensions which accompanied those attitudes in the body. I will quote from Reich's description in the English and revised edition of *The Function of the Orgasm.* "In Copenhagen in 1933, I treated a man who put up especially strong resistance against the uncovering of his passive-homosexual fantasies. This resistance was manifested in an extreme attitude of stiffness of the neck ('stiff-necked'). After an energetic attack upon his resistance he suddenly gave in, but in a rather alarming manner. For three days he presented severe manifestations of vegetative shock. The color of his face kept changing rapidly from white to blue or yellow; the skin was mottled and of various tints; he had severe pains in the neck and the occiput; the heart beat was rapid; he had diarrhea, felt worn out, and seemed to have lost hold. . . . *Affects had broken through somatically after the patient had yielded in a psychic defense attitude.* The stiff neck, expressing an attitude of tense masculinity, apparently had bound negative energies which now broke loose in an uncontrolled and disordered fashion" (p. 240).

Reich realized that tense muscles bound not only sexual energy but also anger and anxiety. "I found that whenever I dissolved a muscular inhibition or tension, one of the three basic biological excitations made its appearance: *anxiety, anger or sexual excitation*" (p. 241). Working now directly with tension in the body as well as analytically, Reich reached the conclusion that the character armor (resistances) was functionally identical with the muscular armor (tensions).

The years 1933 to 1939 were very productive ones for Reich. He worked on the energy concept which he identified with the libido. He investigated transitional forms of life which he called bions. He did considerable research into the cancer problem and added greatly to our understanding of it. And he expanded and deepened his knowledge of the body-mind relationship, and sharpened his skill in working with chronic muscular tension states.

I met Reich in 1940 at the New School for Social Research where he was lecturing on "Character Analysis." The description of the course stated that the relation of mind to body and of psychic character and muscular attitude would be the basic theme. I had been intensely interested in this subject for some years and so I eagerly registered for the course. Reich was a great teacher, with unusually exciting ideas for me. Despite my initial skepticism, I became convinced during the course of the validity of his view. I continued my association with him after the course.

My association with Reich deepened when in 1942 I entered into therapy with him. At that time he called his mode of therapy "Character Analytic Vegetotherapy." The primary emphasis was upon breathing in a spontaneous and relaxed way. In the course of his clinical observations, Reich noted that resistance to the expression of feeling was always accompanied by an inhibition of respiration. Deepening the patient's breathing resulted in an opening up of feelings. How effective this could be was shown by what happened to me in my first session. Reich had asked me to lie on the bed (I was wearing only swim trunks so that Reich could observe my body) and breathe. I lay there for a while breathing with nothing special happening. Then Reich pointed out that my chest was immobile and asked me to let it participate in the respiratory movements. I did so. My position on the bed was on my back with my head back and my knees bent. Then Reich asked me to open my eyes wide. As I did so I began to scream, or rather, a scream erupted out of me. The expression I assumed was one of fear, but I didn't feel frightened. I just screamed! We repeated the procedure and again I screamed. Some nine months later I was able to see the image that had produced the scream and to feel the fear, anger, and sadness associated with it.

Another part of character analytic vegetotherapy was direct work on the muscular tensions, on my tight jaw, for example. The aim of this therapy was to "give in" to the body and allow its spontaneous and involuntary life to take over. At the same time that one felt or got in touch with his body he learned to understand the way in which he held and moved his body. Many exciting things hapened to me in the course of my therapy with Reich. At the conclusion, after some 2½ years, I was able to "give in" and experience the pleasurable and spontaneous movement of my pelvis joined with my breathing which Reich called the orgasm reflex.

In 1945, I began to see patients as a character-analytic vegetotherapist. In my work, too, the emphasis was upon breathing and "giving-in," that is, allowing the respiratory movements to flow through the body freely and fully. Some character analytic work was done in terms of the expression of the body. At that time neither Reich nor I were doing a thorough analytic working-through of the personality.

In 1952, Dr. John Pierrakos and I dissociated ourselves from the Reichian group. We did this to gain a greater freedom to explore all the nuances of body expression and to devise as well a more sophisticated approach to the body. We also felt that there had to be a greater stress on analytic work than Reich gave it. In 1954, we organized The Institute for Bioenergetic Analysis which today has training centers in several cities.

The question—what is the difference between bioenergetics and Reichian therapy—is often asked me. In both, the basis is the body and its energetic processes. Both approaches depend on reading the personality from the body. Bioenergetics, I believe, is a more sophisticated development, more fully grounded in analytic thinking, with a greater emphasis upon working through the personality problems analytically. It also uses a greater variety of body techniques. And, as I mentioned earlier, it focuses upon personality rather than sexuality per se.

Reich, himself, had never fully worked through his character concepts systematically. In 1958 my first book, *The Physical Dynamics of Character Structure,* was published, which is now available in paperback under the title *The Language of the Body.* In it there is the first systematic presentation of character types seen both physically and psychologically. The basic energy concepts that we use in our work and which are extensions of Reich's thinking are explained there fully. Since then I have written four other books plus many articles and monographs. A list of these is given at the end of the chapter.

Many other people have worked or are working with the body in personality theory. The uniqueness of bioenergetics and Reichian therapy is that it involves the body on three levels simultaneously: analytically, expressively, and energetically. How this is done is briefly outlined in the next section of this chapter, together with a case history that illustrates this approach.

BIOENERGETICS

Bioenergetics is the study of personality in terms of the body. It is based upon two fundamental propositions. One is that each person is his body. No person exists apart from the living body in which he has his existence and through which he expresses himself and relates to the world about him. The second proposition is that the body is an energetic system. Bioenergetics is a term which is also used in biochemistry to refer to the energetic processes which take place in living tissues on the molecular level.

As students of human personality and human behavior, we study the same processes on the organismic level. How much energy an individual has and how he uses his energy are relevant questions in the study of personality and behavior.

If you are your body, and your body is you, then it expresses who you are. It is your way of being in the world. The more alive your body is the more you are in the world. When your body loses some of its aliveness as when you are exhausted, for example, you become somewhat withdrawn. Illness has the same effect, it creates a state of withdrawal. When one is very tired or very ill, the world is sensed as being distant or seen through a slight haze. On the other hand there are days when you feel vibrantly alive and the world about you appears brighter, closer, more real.

Since your body expresses who you are it impresses us with how much you are in the world. Our speech uses such terms as "a nobody" to denote a person who fails to impress us with his being or "a somebody" to indicate an individual who makes a strong impression on us. This is simple body language. We generally tend to ignore the fact that most people are aware of our state of being in or withdrawing from the world. It is not a secret. We are naturally sensitive to other peoples' bodies and their expressions. We can sense their fatigue and their illness, their excitement, their joy, and their good health. Tiredness, for example, is expressed in a number of visual and auditory signs. It is manifested in a droop of the shoulders together with a collapse of the posture, a sag in the skin of the face, a lack of lustre in the eyes, a slowness of movement, and a flatness or lack of resonance in the voice. Even the effort to hide this condition betrays itself for one can sense the strain of the forced attempt.

The word "personality" describes the impression an individual makes upon others. Thus we may speak of an individual as having a radiant or vibrant personality, a strong personality, or by contrast, a flat or weak personality. We also use such adjectives as bright or dull, quick or slow, light or heavy, etc. Terms such as these reveal how closely personality is tied to energetic factors. The more energy a person has the stronger will be his impression upon us. It is impossible to be vibrant, strong, bright, and quick when one's energy level is low and one's energy metabolism is depressed.

Turning to emotional states, we know that we can tell what a person feels from the expression of his body. Emotions are bodily events; they are, literally, motions or movements within the body that normally result in some outward action. Anger produces a tension and charge in the upper half of the body where the main organs of attack are located, the teeth and arms. One can easily recognize an angry person by his flushed face, his clenched fists, and snarling mouth. In some animals the raising of the hair along the neck and back is another sign of this emotion. The animal has his back up. The unconscious effort to suppress this emotion is revealed in the spasticity and chronic tension of the muscles that are normally used to express this feeling. Affection or love produces a softening of all the features plus a suffusion of warmth into the skin and eyes. In sadness the body looks as if it could melt into tears and break down into sobs. Here, too, the suppression of feeling results in chronic muscular tensions that are discernible and palpable. Unconscious sexual inhibitions are also revealed by chronic tensions that impede the motility of the pelvis.

We can go one step further in reading the language of body expression. A person's attitude to life or his personal life-style is reflected in the way he holds himself and the way in which he moves. The individual with a so-called noble bearing or regal carriage can be distinguished from the individual whose bent back, rounded shoulders, and slightly bowed head indicate an attitude of submission or of carrying burdens that weigh heavily upon his body.

The way a person holds himself, which is related to the way he moves, defines that person's character structure. We classify character attitudes into five basic holding patterns. These are:

1. *Holding together* out of fear of falling apart or fragmentation which is characteristic of the schizoid personality.

2. *Holding on* out of fear of falling behind or rejection (being left alone) which is characteristic of oral personalities.

3. *Holding up* out of fear of falling down which means failure, submission, and dominance by others. This pattern characterizes what we call the psychopathic personality since this individual uses his psychic powers to control and manipulate others as a defense against his own fears.

4. *Holding in* out of fear that the bottom will fall out if one lets go. The holding in is a defense against the explosive release of feeling and is the typical masochistic character attitude.

5. *Holding back* out of fear of falling forward which for this personality type is a fear of being swept along or away by strong feelings of love and surrender. This characterizes the rigid character.

Few individuals show only one pattern. We classify the problem by which one of the holding patterns is dominant, noting at the same time the presence and strength of the other patterns.

These patterns can be read directly from the form and motility of the body.* They correspond to the behavior patterns since the individual is a

---

* See *The Language of the Body* for a fuller discussion.

unity and his psychic and somatic functioning are simply different aspects of his unitary being.

It is the basic aim of almost all forms of therapy to get a patient to let go of the inhibitions, blocks, and tensions that prevent him from being fully himself. We therapists start from the assumption that the people who come to us for help are not free, that they are hung-up on illusions and are bound by irrational fears. Our intervention is not called for when a person is grounded in reality and his fears or anxieties are realistic and rational. No one consults a psychiatrist because he feels threatened by inflation or worried by the serious physical illness of a close relative. On the other hand, it is generally recognized that the person suffering from emotional problems feels that his anxieties are real. There is the further complication that many people are not aware of how their fears limit their self-expression and self-realization.

The foregoing mandates the general procedure of psychotherapy: first, to help an individual become aware of conflicts and fears that lie below the surface of his consciousness but which control and limit his responsiveness; second, to help him realize that these fears and the conflicts from which they stem are no longer valid in the present. This is generally accomplished by tracing the fear and conflict back to the past, to that period of life when the person was helpless and, therefore, trapped in a situation which allowed no other course of action than to block one's natural impulse, suppress the associated feeling, and repress the memory of the incident. The neurotic holding patterns I have described above must be viewed as survival mechanisms. No organism limits its being or restricts its freedom except in the interest of survival. If such limitation is undertaken voluntarily for a reward in the future, it can be suspended voluntarily. This is not the case with neurotic holding patterns.

These two steps aim at helping a patient gain insight into his problems. Theoretically, insight should lead to cure or at least a significant amelioration of the personality disturbance. Unfortunately, this does not often happen. The main reason for the failure of this insight therapy is that the insights which the patient gains are not deep enough nor strong enough. They are not strong enough because too often they are only ideas which lack a strong enough emotional charge to make them effective agents of change.

These difficulties can be overcome by using a bioenergetic approach. In bioenergetics a patient's awareness is extended by having him get in touch with all parts of his body. He is brought into awareness of his restriction of breathing, his limitation of motility, his incapability to fully express emotion. The various body exercises used in bioenergetics help him sense

The crying enabled Joan to confront the tragedy of her life and to muster some of the anger that lay buried within her. At the end of each session I could see the life returning to Joan's body. Her eyes brightened, her skin color improved, her voice developed more resonance, and her body moved more freely.

As we got into her past, Joan related that she had been a dreamer in childhood. Her fantasies centered on romantic love and she worshipped boys from afar. She related that during adolescence her sexual conflicts were so intense that she was close to agony. She didn't masturbate, which would have given her some relief, partly because it was taboo and partly because she was looking for someone to rescue her. She sought a hero, a prince on a white horse, who would break through the frozen rigidity and bring to life the dreaming princess. Joan was called "the princess" by her family.

During the course of therapy Joan recalled a significant dream. In the dream Joan was walking down a beautiful marble hall at the end of which she saw her mother standing like a statue on a platform. As she approached her mother she was horrified to see the statue's arms fall off and crash to the floor. It was obvious that Joan identified with her mother, whom she described as a lonely suffering woman whose pain was visible. Joan, however, went to great lengths to see that no one would see her own suffering. As a princess she was above it, as a statue she was mute to it. But Joan is also the statue in the dream. The dream is subject to the interpretation that Joan (like her mother) is impotent to reach out towards a love object.

It is impossible in this chapter to present the full account of Joan's therapy. I shall, therefore, summarize a few of the important developments in the case. Her relationship to her father had to be worked out for Joan had transferred to him her longing for warmth and support which she did not obtain from her mother. In this relationship, too, she was kept at a distance and admired but not loved in a warm, intimate way. We could establish analytically that Joan felt she was seduced by her father into becoming a statuesque person in order to gain his approval and his love. When the latter was not forthcoming Joan felt betrayed, which aroused deep, murderous feelings of rage towards her father. Since this rage was directed at the very person from whom she expected salvation, it had to be suppressed.

The bodily rigidity and associated muscular tensions that transformed Joan's body into the appearance of a statue was the mechanism by which the rage was suppressed. The same mechanism also served to suppress Joan's sexual feelings for her father, which, because of his inability to tolerate closeness and intimacy, were not acceptable. These feelings were projected into all her relationships to men and undermined the possibility of any real fulfillment. They were also transferred to me and were worked through in this connection. Opening up and cleaning out Joan's hostility to men, which at first she strongly denied, anchored the improvement in her personality.

One other aspect of bioenergetic therapy should be mentioned at this point. The exercises which the patient goes through in the therapy situation are also done at home and in special exercise classes. The release of muscular tensions cannot be accomplished through analysis alone and requires consistent body work. Their value and effect is shown in the following comment by Joan. "There are times when I feel what must be the whole armature giving way. My shoulders seem looser, as do the muscles about the pelvis, in my back, and even in my calves. My body seems to be in the throes of a conflict like the one between Lucifer and Gabriel. I groan with the terror and sweetness of it. I have felt obscurely, the currents—and even more obscurely, fear."

One other incident revealed an important physical mechanism of Joan's illness. She had related that she had a tendency to black out at dinner parties. Now, she reported:

> The same thing began to happen to me at a cocktail party—a party I found exceptionally nice. For an hour I was relaxed. The following two hours I was, I realize now, stiffening up. That well known feeling of suffocating fatigue struck me. I could hardly speak. I managed to leave and stumbled out into the air which revived me somewhat and I found a taxi. At home feeling completely drunk, though I had during three and a half hours one unfinished vermouth and later a whiskey and soda, I got out of my clothes, and leaving them on the floor, fell into bed, where I did black out. At two-thirty in the morning I wakened in a black depression and groaned that I had to live through this again. I drank a glass of milk and took a hot bath, trying to think how it came about. I relived the evening. Suddenly I realized that I was holding my breath. Every part of the breath-holding mechanism was in operation. Suddenly I knew that my drunkenness was oxygen starvation and my fatigue the result of absolutely minimum energy intake.
>
> This morning, in the light of all you taught me, I understand better the mechanism by which I have been trying to kill myself. The question is, naturally: Why do I do this? Why this extreme of unconscious terror? I recalled that I had a similar experience of terror and breath-holding when I was five or six. I see now that I do not wish to breathe.

The inhibition of breathing is the key to all personality problems. It varies in degree with the severity of the problem and in kind with the nature of the problem. Thus, in the schizoid character, which I described earlier, the respiratory movements are largely confined to the thorax. This has the effect of limiting sexual feelings in the abdomen. In Joan's case, for example, these sexual feelings, though not her genital feelings, were greatly reduced. In the rigid character structure, the respiratory movements are mainly confined to the diaphragm and upper abdomen. In this personality type heart feelings are generally locked up in a rigid thorax.

The critical task in the treatment of depression is grounding the patient in reality. The basic realities of life are the ground one stands on, one's body, and one's sexuality. The sexual aspect is the most difficult because it is strongly suppressed and associated as well with severe anxiety arising from the oedipal situation. If this aspect of the problem is not resolved, the sense of security provided by a firm "footing" or "standing" cannot be established. When excitation and feeling flow into the legs, they also flow into the pelvis and genitals.

The work with the lower part of the body involves special exercises to restore the natural mobility to the pelvis. When the vibrating movements in the legs reach the pelvis it too starts to vibrate. This is the beginning. Then as pelvic tensions are released, the pelvis will go into a swinging movement in harmony with the respiration, backward on inspiration and forward on expiration. Reich called this involuntary movement the orgasm reflex because it also occurs involuntarily at the acme of the sexual act if the individual has a full orgasm. The orgasm reflex is not an orgasm since the level of excitation is not high and the focus is not upon the genital apparatus. The presence of the orgasm reflex, however, denotes that the respiratory waves pass freely through the body and into the legs and feet. It is an indication that grounding has occurred.

Direct work with the body aimed at opening and deepening breathing and motility and self-expression had a number of important results for Joan. Her rigidity decreased markedly and pleasurable sensations began to stream through her body. She began to experience the pleasure of being alive in her body. As this increased she gained self-love since love is associated with pleasure. She felt loving and at times lovely and was able to give love rather than need it. Finally she moved out of New York City which she disliked and built a home in the country in surroundings similar to those she knew as a child.

PRINCIPLES OF BIOENERGETICS

Joan's case illustrates some of the dynamic principles that underlie the work with the body as an expression, or, I should say, as the carrier, of the personality. This approach does not ignore the role nor the importance of the ego in personality functions. The ego is part of the body for, as Freud said, it "is first and foremost a body ego." This means that the strength of the ego derives from the body processes that support it. We can show the different personality functions in their relationship to one another by means of a triangle the base of which consists of the energetic processes that provide the energy for movement, feeling, thinking, and, finally, control and direction. Like every hierarchical structure the focus of control and direction is at the top of the hierarchy. That hierarchy is pictured in Figure 2.

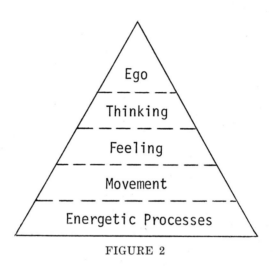

FIGURE 2

Working with the energetic processes, which are the foundation of the personality, necessarily affects all other personality functions. It is, of course, true that one can influence these functions from above. I believe that it is important to work both ways, from below and from above. Bioenergetics is characterized by this dual approach.

Seen from above, that is, from the point of view of the ego, which is the position of the conscious mind, the mind and its processes loom large and dominant. From this view the pyramid would be inverted. This is shown in Figure 3.

Since both of these views are valid, it is necessary to integrate them into a unity. This can be accomplished, diagrammatically, by superimposing one triangle upon another. We get Figure 4, which can be related to the human body.

children as confidants. Here a mother, frustrated by her husband's coldness, would share with her adolescent daughter her erotic fantasies and decry her husband's (the girl's father's) clumsiness in sexual matters. Inevitably, she would thus overtax the girl and erode the latter's trust in, and loyalty for, her father. In relating to a son, this inappropriate conspiratorial intimacy would also have incestuous undertones. The same would be true for a father's relationship with his daughter.

The "Undifferentiated Family Ego Mass"

Lack of gender and generation boundaries in families often went hand in hand with another differentiation disturbance—one that concerned each member's ability or willingness to differentiate and articulate his feelings, needs, and wishes. Only by differentiating and articulating our feelings and motivations can we understand them, assert them, and take responsibility for them, and can we individuate, separate, and grow. But just such crucial differentiation and articulation of needs and motives was found lacking in many homeostatically deadlocked families. Therefore, M. Bowen (12) spoke of an "undifferentiated ego mass," S. Minuchin (13) of "enmeshed families," and I. Boszormenyi-Nagy (14) of an "intersubjective fusion." Such defective cognitive and emotional differentiation in families is often elusive. Nonetheless, it tends to deeply disturb empathic observers and therapists. For after a while, the latter get the feeling—gradually hardening into a conviction—that they are treading on quicksand, that they can never sort out anything in these families, that all and nothing goes, that everything seems in knots, and that no point, meaning, or closure can ever be established. Schaffer et al. (15) have well described how observers experience an increasing sense of futility, if not despair, while they watch cognitively undifferentiated, and homeostatically enmeshed, families.

The Dynamics of Mystification

When I spoke of homeostasis and defective differentiation in families, I described certain family conditions (or states) rather than those actions (or contributions) of members which result in these conditions. I want now to turn to these actions (or contributions). In so doing, I widen once more the focus of our inquiry: it now introduces us to an interpersonal dialectic. I have described such dialectic elsewhere (16, 17, 18). Here it must suffice to say that this dialectic is *transitive* and *reciprocal*. It is *transitive* in the sense that a "stronger" partner often imposes on the weaker—i.e., more malleable and more dependent—partner a definition and structure of his (the weaker person's) inner or outer reality which the latter willy-nilly must accept. It is *reciprocal* in the sense that in homeostatic systems there is always a two-way exchange.

In this section I want to deal with a transitive aspect of this dialectic— i.e., with the ways in which one (or several) member's (or members')— usually the parents'—contributions may fatefully affect a weaker member's (usually the child's) view of himself. The concept of mystification, above others, conveys this transitive dimension.

R. D. Laing (19) introduced this concept into family theory. He borrowed it from Karl Marx who employed it in a socioeconomic context. Capitalist exploiters, according to Marx, would mystify their exploited workers with the help of religion, as when they made these workers believe that suffering and lowly work were tickets to a blessed after-life. Similarly, parents were seen to mystify their children about what these children really needed, wanted, or believed. Three major dynamics, according to Laing, are to be found in mystification. The first of these is *attribution*. Parents may, as Laing noted, attribute to their children such traits as insecurity, stubbornness, sickness, meanness, recklessness, etc., which, in one way or the other, implant a negative self-image. Such negative attributions can be classified either as "attributions of weakness," or as "attributions of badness" (20). As a rule, attributions of weakness damage a child more severely than attributions of badness because the latter, when internalized, often leave room for a separation via a "negative identity," whereas attributions of weakness keep the child captive to parental "protectors."

Invalidation, another term of Laing, denotes a coercive disqualification of a dependent person's statements, as when parents "in-validate" those views of children which threaten their (the parents') authority and positive self-image. Laing refers here to the first schizophrenic patient in the psychiatric literature whose major "feature" was his hate of his father. The psychiatrist, Dr. Morrel, serving as the father's agent (and becoming the inventor of the term "dementia praecox," which preceded schizophrenia), managed to invalidate this hate by declaring it to be a symptom of mental illness.

The term *induction,* also used by R. D. Laing, refers to the active molding and recruitment of another person. While the mystifier attributes badness or weakness and invalidates the other's meanings, he also tries to enlist the other's cooperation. Thus, he induces his victim to embrace his mystification, as it were, i.e., induces him to become his colluding partner. Attribution, invalidation, and induction, according to Laing, are "transpersonal defenses, whereby self attempts to regulate the inner life of the other in order to preserve his own" (21). Such transpersonal defenses interweave with, but also differ from, the intrapsychic defenses of classical psychoanalysis.

Mystification, as here defined, is common in human relations and family life. Families with schizophrenic offspring, above all others, give us an object lesson of how it works. Here the contributions of L. Wynne and M. Singer (22) stand out. These researchers illuminated the many ways in which family members may confuse, unsettle, leave stranded, etc.—in brief, mystify —other members. They do this by failing to structure and share with each other a common focus of attention, as when they frame as a question a seeming assertion, or insidiously shift the topic under discussion, or leave the partner in doubt as to whether closure has been achieved. By an innovative use of Rorschach tests, these authors identified approximately forty "communication deviances" which occurred massively, yet not exclusively, in families with schizophrenic offspring. We can therefore say that Wynne and Singer developed a phenomenology of mystification which, at one and the same time, is rich, detailed, clinically relevant, and subject to verification and scoring.

Homeostasis

As more and more families were observed, limits of the homeostasis concept emerged. Homeostasis now appeared as one important, but specific, form of family pathology. It became evident that many families—particularly broken ones—were disturbed not because they were locked into a squelching pseudo-mutuality or pseudo-hostility, but because their members had lost their anchorage in family solidarity and mutual concern. Rather than being centripetally (or homeostatically) deadlocked, these families appeared centrifugally adrift. Clearly, a model of family interaction was needed that could encompass the range of overcohesive *and* undercohesive, as well as in-between, families. While heading the Family Studies Section of the Adult Psychiatry Branch, National Institute of Mental Health, during the last several years, I attempted to develop such a model. Within this model, I conceptualize family disturbances as *transactional mode disturbances*. Here I can present this model only in briefest outline at the risk of massive oversimplification and distortion, modifying it only slightly from how I formulated it elsewhere (23).

TRANSACTIONAL MODE DISTURBANCES

Transactional modes try to grasp and reflect the interplay and/or relative dominance of pushes and pulls into and out of families throughout all stages of the individuation and separation process. In this interplay, the transactional modes operate as the covert organizing background to the more overt and specific child-parent interactions (24). When age-appropriate transactional modes are too intense, out of phase, or inappropriately blended with other modes, the negotiation of a mutual individuation and separation between parent and child will be impeded. We may therefore speak of *transactional mode disturbances*.

Transactional modes bring into view salient contributions of parents and children to the ongoing interpersonal process, but also reveal systemic properties of the evolving relationship. Therefore, we can call them transitive and reciprocal in the earlier-mentioned sense. They are transitive in that they denote the parents' active molding of a child who is still immature, dependent, and hence remains captive to their influence. The modes thus reflect the fact that parents, from the beginning, impress on their children their "stronger reality" (25). They do this often unconsciously by using covert and subtle signals and sanctions. To this "stronger reality" the child must adapt lest he perish. But also, these modes are reciprocal in the sense that there is always a two-way exchange. In this exchange, the children mold and influence their parents as much as the latter mold and influence them.

In other writings, already cited, I have delineated and illustrated the three major modes of binding, delegating, and expelling, which brings into view the transactional fates of binder-bindee, delegator-delegate, expeller-expellee. A brief summary of these modes follows.

The Binding Mode

Where the binding mode operates, we find homeostatic family disturbances, as earlier described. Here the parents interact with their offspring in ways that seem designed to keep the latter tied to the parental orbit and locked in the "family ghetto." Such binding, or homeostasis, can operate on three major levels.

First, it can operate primarily on a *dependency level* where primitive drives and affects are strong. The child appears bound by the exploitation of his dependency needs, as he is offered undue regressive gratification. I am inclined to speak in this context of "id-binding."

Second, binding can operate on a more *cognitive level*. Drives and affects contribute to this level also, but chiefly as forces that fuel and shape cognitive processes. It is this level where mystification, as described above, becomes important. Here the binding parent interferes with his child's differentiated self-awareness and self-determination by mystifying the child about what he feels, needs, and wants. He "misdefines the child to himself," as it were. In addition to R. D. Laing (26), L. Wynne and M. Singer (27), T. Lidz et al. (28), also G. Bateson (29), H. Bruch (30), H. Searles (31), and J. Haley (32) have contributed to our understanding of cognitive binding. We can call cognitive binding "ego-binding," as the binder forces the bindee to rely on the binder's distorted and distorting ego instead of developing his own discriminating ego.

The binding mode can, finally, operate on a third level where an intense archaic *loyalty and guilt* come into play. Loyalty needs, like those for dependency and cognitive guidance, can be seen as legitimate needs of children. And, as happened in id- and ego-level binding, such legitimate needs are now, at one and the same time, fostered, thwarted, and exploited. Children who are chiefly bound on this level are thus likely to experience any thought, not to mention attempt, of separation as the number one crime for which only the harshest punishment will do. These children, whom we may call "superego-bound," are prone to suffer maximal primitive "breakaway guilt" that operates often unconsciously and gives rise to either acts of massive self-destruction or of heroic atonement. I. Boszormenyi-Nagy (33), above others, has explored and described the binding force of invisible loyalties. Children who are severely bound on all three above levels appear destined to become schizophrenic.

The Expelling Mode

Where the mode of expelling prevails, we find the opposite of a homeostatic disturbance, namely an enduring neglect or rejection of children who tend to be considered nuisances and hindrances by their parents. A strong centrifugal force pushes many of these children into premature separations. These children appear not so much exploited, as they appear neglected and abandoned. Often they are diagnosed as wayward and delinquent. We find them commonly in broken and disorganized ghetto families, but increasingly also in families of the American middle-class.

The Delegating Mode

Where, finally, the delegating mode predominates, homeostatic (binding) and expelling elements blend. The child is here allowed and encouraged to move out of the parental orbit, but only to a point! He is held on a leash, as it were. Such qualified "sending out" is implied in the original Latin word "de-legare," which means, first, to send out and, second, to entrust with a mission. The latter meaning implies that the delegate, although sent out, remains beholden to the sender. Also here the loyalty to the parents must be strong, but unlike the more primitive and archaic loyalty mentioned in the binding mode proper, this loyalty must allow for selectivity and differentiation. Otherwise, the delegate could not fulfill his missions. Such missions may include his becoming a famous artist or scientist in an attempt to fulfill the parents' unrealized ego-ideals, or it may be the mission of enacting the parents' disowned delinquent impulses. Whatever the mission, the delegate is encouraged to differentiate and to separate to the extent that his specific missions require this. I have elsewhere (34) given an overview of various types of missions which here come into play. Some delegates are diagnosed as—usually remitting—schizophrenics, others as neurotics, still others as delinquents. These delinquents differ in their dynamics from those found under the expelling mode.

The above transactional modes of binding, delegating, and expelling imply a long-term view of the process of individuation-separation. Such long-range view makes it evident that parents who bind, delegate, and/or expel their children do not necessarily act in a pathogenic manner. These modes become exploitative and damaging to the child (as well as to the parents) only when they are inappropriately timed or mixed, or are excessively intense.

PSYCHOLOGICAL EXPLOITATION AND GUILT

The above family model raises ethical issues. It implies that parents who bind, delegate, or expel their child jeopardize the child's growth and chances for happiness. The damage done to the child differs under the three modes. We may say that under the binding and delegating modes the child becomes overimportant to his parents and remains an extension of themselves; under the expelling mode, he becomes under- or unimportant, as he is considered a nuisance or surplus. It is difficult to say which is the more disastrous fate.

Where children are chiefly bound or delegated, we may properly speak of their psychological exploitation by their parents. Again, it is parents of schizophrenic children who cast into clearest relief such psychological exploitation. In delegating or binding their child, they try to spare themselves painful self-assessment, self-change, and inner conflict. As a result, they subject him to conflicts and tasks which overtax his nuclear ego and make him misperceive his inner and outer worlds. While he adapts to his "stronger" (binding or delegating) parents' reality, he becomes "cognitively violated" and stirred up, and must turn himself into a "specialist in symbiotic survival." During the most formative stages of his development he must specialize his talents and skills for detoxifying, and yet retain as much as he can, the dangerous, overdemanding, and intrusive—i.e., binding and/or delegating—parent, chiefly the mother. In so doing, he must sacrifice, or leave underdeveloped, other skills and capacities needed for his progressive individuation and separation. He cannot avoid an uneven psychic, and possibly physiologic, differentiation and integration, i.e., cannot help jeopardizing his "all 'round" growth.

For the above reasons, we can expect the bound or delegated child to deeply hate his parental exploiters and victimizers. Experienced psychotherapists of schizophrenic patients, such as H. Searles, give us, indeed, an inkling of these patients' murderous hate of their parents and—in the transference—of their therapists. Yet, side by side with such (chiefly unconscious) hatred, we frequently find in them love of equal depth, revealed, above all, in their ability and willingness for sacrifice. For these patients, by their very sickness, often ensure their parents' psychological survival and, at the same time, reveal a paradoxical and therapeutic strength. For, as I. Boszormenyi-Nagy has shown, their deficiency—i.e., "sickness," "craziness," etc. —frequently turns into an asset once the whole family's therapeutic needs are considered. For while in one sense the bound or delegated schizophrenic is the weakest—i.e., most openly disturbed—member, in another sense he is strongest and therapeutically most effective—he "owns" the disturbance which the others must disown, and through such "owning" may serve as the catalyst who initiates as well as promotes the whole family's treatment and growth.

With the above perspective added, the term family homeostasis therefore encompasses a dimension of "interpersonal justice." For the above processes of "owning" and "disowning," of pain and conflict, of victimization and sacrifice, of exploitation and counter-exploitation, make all family members partners to a system of "invisible accounts," a system which I. Boszormenyi-Nagy (35 and, with G. Spark, 36) has deeply and originally explored.

The Multi-Generational Perspective

We have now been alerted to a family drama wherein massive guilt, an immense, though thwarted, need for repair work, as well as for revenge, a deeply felt sense of justice or injustice committed, and of loyalty confirmed or betrayed, all operating largely out of awareness, often become formidable dynamic forces which influence every member's move. We may speak therefore of a "morality play" which is played for the highest stakes. Yet, to do justice to this play, even a two-generational perspective is not enough, as I. Boszormenyi-Nagy and G. Spark have convincingly shown.

For, in order to be fair to, and empathic with, parents who survive while crippling their children, and children who, in being crippled, gain the power to devastate their parents by inflicting deepest guilt—we must also look at how these children's parents are crippled and exploited by *their* parents. But even recourse to three generations might not be enough, as when we—to do justice to our black fellow-Americans—may have to take into account what several generations of white slave traders and plantation owners did to these blacks' forebears.

TREATMENT IMPLICATIONS

Two forces, above others, shape a therapist's treatment approach: his theoretical model and, more elusively, his therapeutic (or nontherapeutic) style or personality. Here, in line with this chapter's intent, I focus mainly on his theoretical model.

Under this model, we found family therapy to represent a new paradigm insofar as no longer an individual patient, but the supra-individual system, became the locus for therapeutic intervention. Yet from its inception, modern family therapy was hard pressed to reconcile a systems approach with one that would do justice to individual members. There were, and still are, family therapists who decry those others—some of them psychoanalysts —who "merely treat individuals in a family context," rather than being strictly systems-oriented. But, in the actual practice of family therapy, it was difficult, if not impossible, to disregard individual members who had their own wishes and needs, who had benefited or suffered from the actions of other members, who blamed or absorbed blame, who felt guilty or made others feel guilty, and whose interests clashed or agreed.

The family model, as here presented, introduces a systems perspective, but also takes account of (past and present) individual actions, obligations, rights, and needs. Therefore, it demands from the therapist an attitude of, in the words of I. Boszormenyi-Nagy, "*multidirectional partiality*" (37) or, as I would like to call it, "involved impartiality" (38). Both terms denote that the family therapist must be involved with the family system, while he must, at the same time, remain fair and attentive to all members. All my following considerations on treatment reflect this dual orientation.

Therapy as Un-binding

The family model, as here presented, suggests differing therapeutic approaches depending on whether we deal primarily with binding, delegating, or expelling families. For brevity's sake, I shall here distinguish between, on the one side, binding and delegating and, on the other, expelling ones. Only the former types of families, we saw, fit (more or less) a homeostasis model.

So far, most treatment efforts were geared to these latter families because, in general, it is easier to recruit, treat, and study families which are homeostatically enmeshed than those which are broken or loosely adrift. In line with our greater experience with homeostatic families I shall, in the following, chiefly consider their treatment, and shall only touch on the treatment of undercohesive and fragmented families.

Essentially, in treating homeostatic families, we aim at un-binding them—i.e., we try to promote each member's (and thereby the whole family's) individuation, differentiation, and relative autonomy. At the same time, we try to explore each member's rights and obligations, as well as his "ledger of merits" (39) in the family system.

Un-binding, in the meaning here intended, implies *de-mystification, belated mourning, balancing of accounts,* and *reconciliation across generations.* Let us consider each of these aspects, one after the other.

De-mystification

Mystification, we saw, involves attribution (of negative traits which denote either "weakness" or "badness"), invalidation, and induction. De-mystification, accordingly, implies that the therapist must counter such attributions, invalidations, and inductions. To counter damaging attributions —i.e., attributions that such and such a person is weak or sick—the therapist must make sure that each member learns to speak for his own feelings, needs, and interests. For example, a mother who constantly says, "Louise (her adolescent daughter) is always so depressed," "Louise is afraid of boy friends," "Louise hates her teachers," etc., must learn that Louise can be spokesman for her own feelings, experiences, and interests. At the same time, this mother must learn to be a spokesman for herself and hence must learn to communicate: "I feel depressed," "I need to be alone," "I am annoyed when Louise wears dirty blue jeans," or even, "I need Louise as a buffer between me and my husband." V. Satir (40), above others, has described such de-mystification.

To counter invalidations, the therapist often has to validate—i.e., explore and possibly support and declare legitimate—statements of a child or patient which a parent or doctor (the possessor of the "stronger reality") invalidated. To return to the first schizophrenic patient of Dr. Morrel, he would have to validate this patient's hate for his father instead of labeling it outright a sign of mental illness.

To counter inductions, the therapist has to explore the inductee's compliance with the stronger person's definition of his—the inductee's—psychological reality. Here the therapist must focus on how the "willing victim" actively contributes to mystification and homeostasis. To this end the therapist must understand the power the victim derives from his "weakness, badness, or suffering." I. Boszormenyi-Nagy has well described this situation. In letting himself be mystified, and in living up to his parent's negative attributions, the victim delivers himself as the living proof for his parents' badness and failure as parents—even though he wrecks his life in the process. Thus, he is strategically placed to operate the guilt lever. If his parents, for a change, make demands that could promote his autonomy but also cause him anxiety (e.g., ask him to move out of the house), he can make "inoperative" these parental expectations by presenting himself as too sick, i.e., as too inept, anxious, nervous, etc., to comply with them. Many schizophrenic patients are adept at this ploy, thereby reinforcing the homeostasis. To counter this, the therapist must emphasize with the victimized (binding or delegating) victimizers no less than with the bound or delegated victim, and must interpret how this victim uses his "sickness" to devastate his parents.

Belated Mourning

De-mystification alone does usually not suffice to un-bind a tight family homeostasis. Un-binding, then, must include a belated mourning process. Since Freud's seminal paper on "Mourning and Melancholia" (41), we know that losses of all kinds—e.g., losses of beloved persons, of ambitions, of ideals, of skills and physical assets—need to be mourned in order that growth and psychological separation (from the lost person or object) can ensue. Yet a person can deny the loss and thwart the mourning process by, for example, becoming overly busy, by developing somatic symptoms, or by getting stuck in a pathological depression. Then we speak of aborted or pathological mourning. A family homeostasis reflects, as well as sustains, such aborted or pathological mourning, as all family members, glued to each other in "intersubjective fusion," prevent here those separating moves which would cause them to truly experience—and grieve—their losses. Hence, the therapist's task to facilitate belated mourning in families. N. Paul (42), above others, has spelled out this task. He spoke here of "operant mourning" whose effectiveness he demonstrated with the help of audio and video tapes. These tapes show families gripped by painful but liberating grief after years of collusive denial. After such grief experience we find that family members relate to each other more warmly and affectionately, but also more forcefully than seemed possible before. Mourning, clearly, allowed the members to differentiate themselves from each other, to become more autonomous, and hence to loosen the homeostasis.

However, such mourning often becomes difficult in actual family practice due to certain features of the binding and delegating modes. For parents who bind and delegate their children ordinarily manage to avoid the very mourning process which they, the parents, should have experienced while they related to, and tried to separate from, *their* parents. For example, one father, a lowly and frustrated government employee, had delegated his son to become the successful scientist he himself had failed to become. The son, though, overtaxed and despairing, had floundered as such delegate and dropped out of school. Yet even in his failure—or because of it—he allowed his father to abort and delay overdue mourning processes. For while this father remained preoccupied with his good-for-nothing dropout son, he continued to hold an idealized, unblemished image of his own father as a humanitarian and educator. Never throughout his life had he doubted this idealized image, which began to collapse only during family therapy. When this happened, his seemingly superachieving father turned out to have been, among other things, a cheating and, on the whole, mediocre student. This loss of his idealized father image caused the father deep grief, making him look pained and haggard. Yet, while this happened, he also began to relate differently—i.e., more warmly and empathically—to his son and realized how he had exploited the latter in order to remain faithful to his good—i.e., idealized—father. Only after he had thus accepted and worked through this loss, could he begin to understand his son in his own right. And the son, less needed as his father's delegate, yet more appreciated as a person with his own needs and interests, could now, on his part, empathize more freely with this father and his plight. Thus, "un-binding" of the homeostasis triggered, as well as reflected, a "positive—i.e., liberating—mutuality" that involved the parent and child generations.

Balancing of Accounts

Mourning, in the above example, could become an un-binding force only after some "accounts were set straight." Initially, the father here took his son to account for what *his* father had, or had not done to him—i.e., he took him to account for the latter's failure to serve as a father and model whom he, now a parent himself, could respect and love without distortive idealization. In order to redress such displaced and hence exploitative accounting, we must explore what I. Boszormenyi-Nagy (43) has called the "balance of accounts," or "ledger of merits" in families. Such "ledger of merits," according to this author, is regularly, though often invisibly, kept. Each member of a family, this means, keeps book as to what the others have—or have not—done to him, and vice versa. For example, a daughter might never forget that her mother betrayed her at a crucial juncture in her life when she (the mother), in the presence of the father, disavowed her complicity in this daughter's clandestine affair that led to a pregnancy. The daughter might never mention this fact and might even repress it; it will nonetheless become a potent motivational force throughout her life.

However, invisible loyalties may also mess up the very bookkeeping process which, on another level, they foster. A grown-up child who remains loyalty-bound to his parents may therefore take his spouse to account for his parents' unfair and neglectful treatment of him; and while he avoided and avoids blaming his idealized parents, he castigates his spouse relentlessly and hypercritically. Thus, he lets his accounting become skewed, as it were. A parent may also—in a similarly skewed manner—take his child to account for what *his* parents did—or did not do—to him, as the earlier example showed. In trying to set such accounts straight, a family therapist must therefore adopt a cross-generational perspective.

Reconciliation

To set the account straight, we saw, requires at least three generations. This, then, raises the question whether these three generations could or should participate in joint family therapy, as this was originally proposed by Mendell and Fisher (44). My answer is "yes"—if this is at all feasible. Naturally, many living parents of parents cannot attend such family meetings. They may be too feeble, live too far away, or appear too set in their ways to stomach a charged encounter with their children and grandchildren. However, thanks mainly to my contacts with I. Boszormenyi-Nagy, I have come to increasingly practice and advocate a three-generational approach. For, contrary to what common sense or compassion with the elderly may tell us, many of these parents' parents, frequently feeling burdened, alienated from their children, and approaching death, welcome the opportunity to set the account straight.

Often, though, one's parents' parents are no longer alive or are realistically unavailable for joint meetings. In these cases, such parents' parents must come alive through the memories of the living—not as targets for blame and hate, but as persons who, whatever their shortcomings or destructive actions, need to be understood and, hopefully, forgiven. What this involves has been well described by I. Boszormenyi-Nagy and G. Spark (45).

Binding Those Who Are Without Bonds

So far, I have talked about the un-binding of (more or less) homeostatically deadlocked families. These, however, we found to be not the only families who have serious difficulties. There are also those numerous other families where the expelling mode prevails, i.e., where children, rather than being excessively bound and/or delegated, are neglected, abandoned, and pushed into premature autonomy. And these children, as well as their parents, appear no less in need of help than those subjected primarily to the binding or delegating modes. Elsewhere (46) I have described these children as "wayward" which, according to Webster's Dictionary, derives from the word "awayward," which means "turned away," and suggests expulsion as well as escape. The turned away person is, again according to Webster's, self-willed, wanton, and prone to follow his or her own caprices. Along with that, he or she appears to follow no clear principle or law and tends therefore to do the opposite of what is desired or expected. Many such wayward persons are labeled as sociopaths. Unburdened by loyalties, and seemingly immune to shame and guilt, they appear able to manipulate, cheat, rob, and maybe even kill without qualms. Recently, the anthropologist Colin Turnbul described a society of seemingly wayward people, called the Ik (47). Several years ago the Iks roamed the borders of Uganda, Kenya, and the Sudan as nomadic hunters, yet when a large game preserve was created, they were resettled and forced to give up their hunting and nomadic ways. Uprooted, their social organization shattered, their skills made useless, and threatened by starvation, they turned, to all outward appearances, wayward: *Homo* became *homini lupus*. Family bonds seemed to dissolve, and only the expelling mode appeared to prevail. Turnbul compares the Iks to the inhabitants of modern shanty towns and ghettos who lost their family and social cohesion. But, if my experience and books such as U. Bronfenbrenner's *Two Worlds of Childhood* (48) are any guide, wayward youths emerge increasingly also from the wastelands of America's middle-class suburbia.

How should we treat these wayward children and their parents? Clearly, before we can un-bind them, we must bind them, i.e., must instill in them that sense of belonging and of being loved which should be every child's birthright. Yet such primary binding—the implanting of love and concern where none existed before—seems even more difficult a therapeutic task than the un-binding I tried to describe.

APPLICATION OF THEORY

To illuminate the above theoretical model, I shall now describe a family whom I shall call the Suttons. The Suttons were a homeostatically enmeshed family in which the binding and delegating modes were strong. Hence, the family therapy had to aim at un-binding the Suttons. Rather than trying to be comprehensive, I shall focus selectively on a few of those aspects in the Suttons' family relations which cast into relief the earlier mentioned concepts.

The Suttons consisted of Mr. and Mrs. Sutton, both in their 40's, and their sons Dennis and Walter, aged 24 and 20, respectively.

My contact with this family began when Mrs. Sutton called me one evening to tell me she had been referred to me by another psychiatrist. This psychiatrist, I learned, had treated her oldest son, Dennis, for approximately one year in a nearby psychiatric hospital. Now Dennis was about te be discharged. His psychiatrist had recommended couple or family therapy. She asked therefore whether I could see her together with her husband, and I arranged for a joint interview a few days later.

Mrs. Sutton turned out to be a dark-haired beauty, lively, expressive, and wearing a sweater at least one size too small. Her husband, a vice-president of a small local bank, was personable, yet apprehensive and depressed. When I asked them to tell me about their problems and family situation, they immediately began to argue and shout. As the fight got underway, I realized I witnessed a scene which, with minor variations, must have gone on innumerable times. Mr. Sutton accused his wife of spoiling Dennis. Just over the last weekend, he explained, when Dennis visited from the hospital, she had given him an expensive stereo set. And, he went on to complain, while she showered Dennis with presents, she neglected and deprived him, her husband. That was her typical pattern. Mrs. Sutton, in turn, called her husband a demanding, dependent, and never-satisfied child. She said that he had no friends, only business associates, and that all his emotional supplies had to come from her. She added that her husband, in his clinging petulance, was poisoning her relationship with Dennis and that she could not stand this any longer.

The above interchange, here massively condensed, suggested that Mr. and Mrs. Sutton were deadlocked in a homeostatic configuration of pseudo-hostility. While intensely bound-up with one another, they seemed only capable of expressing angry, hostile, and sadistic feelings. I learned later that despite repeated efforts, they had never been able to break the homeostatic deadlock. For example, a number of years ago—so I was told—Mr. Sutton had suddenly exploded in frustration, packed his bags, and taken off to a midwestern metropolis. He had then told his wife that this was the end of their relationship, that he would make a new professional start, and that he would search for and find more rewarding female company than hers. However, after ten days of dismal loneliness—spent in bars and movie theaters, sans professional initiative and sans female company—he was back home and back in the old pseudo-hostile rut.

To a large extent, the Sutton's marital arguments centered around Dennis and, to understand better their and the whole family's plight, we must now briefly turn to him.

Dennis, a lanky, handsome youth, had always been shy. As an adolescent, he had preferred to ensconce himself in his room with his piano and records, rather than "become one of the crowd." By the crowd, he meant his peers who found him increasingly difficult to deal with—i.e., too sensitive, too easily hurt, too aloof, and perhaps too grandiose in his ambitions. Yet while he had managed to maintain at least marginal contacts with male friends, he had shunned girls almost totally. He used to admire them from a distance as exotic and exciting, but also dangerous creatures who wielded enormous power over men, particularly men who made inept sexual advances. Not surprisingly, he fell in love with only one or two movie heroines, whose celluloid images haunted him while he, secretively and ashamed, masturbated in his bed.

Yet while his world of real peers and girl friends had become ephemeral, his relationship to his mother had remained intense. Throughout his childhood and adolescence his mother had hovered over him. When he, as an early adolescent, played the piano, she would sneak in some orange juice and cookies, just to let him know she was there and listened and, in the evenings, while holding his hands, she would tell him she saw him developing into a famous concert pianist, with the world at his feet, and she, his mother, sitting in the front row.

Subsequent events, though, made such maternal dreams seem hollow. For as he grew into late adolescence, Dennis neglected his piano practice and appeared torn by conflicting emotions and wishes. He would suddenly shout at his mother, slam the door, smash a present she had given him, and then embrace her frantically. Such outbursts became more and more frequent until he finally—i.e., approximately a year before my contact with the Suttons—attempted suicide and was hospitalized.

The above background information, albeit limited, reveals a lack of differentiation (and hence violation of boundaries) between Mrs. Sutton and Dennis. In important respects, Mrs. Sutton related to Dennis as if he were her adult confidant and partner. The intimacy between mother and son, charged with erotic undercurrents, contrasted with Dennis's and Mrs. Sutton's otherwise barren sex lives. (Intercourse between the spouses had come to a stop during the last five years—except in rare situations where, exhausted from fights and loosened up by one or two drinks, they engaged in sex "like animals.")

If we look now at the workings of transactional modes, we notice that Dennis was bound up with his mother on all three major, above-mentioned levels. He was "id-bound" in the sense that his mother subjected him to constant regressive gratification, of which cookies, orange juice, and expensive gifts formed only a small part. He was "ego-bound" in the sense that he was mystified by her. For she attributed to him an extreme sensitivity and nervous fragility and weakness which caused him to develop the—largely negative—self-image of a precariously vulnerable artist-patient. At the same time, she invalidated Dennis's angry outbursts by labeling them signs of nervous imbalance and, finally, in collusion with a psychiatrist, as evidence of mental illness. And she induced Dennis into becoming a willing, self-sacrificing victim, but one—as we shall see shortly—who gained the power to inflict on her severest guilt and pain. This, then, implied, lastly, massive binding on the loyalty level. Dennis sensed here that his mother could not psychologically survive without him, which burdened him with deepest breakaway guilt.

Dennis was thus bound, yet he was also delegated. As her delegate, he was to become a world renowned pianist and thereby realize her own unfulfilled ego-ideal. Yet while she delegated him, she interfered also with the implementation of his mission—which would have required him to move out of the maternal orbit, train with good teachers, compete with other pianists, struggle in the world—i.e., do the very things which her binding strategems prevented him from doing.

In sum, mother and son, no less than father and mother, were caught in a homeostatic deadlock. Whatever Mrs. Sutton and Dennis tried in order to get away from each other, they seemed to end up more bound-up than before. For example, when Dennis moved tentatively to meet a girl, his anxiety level rose; but so did that of his mother. He feared rebuff and humiliation from the girl; she, abandonment from Dennis. Thus, centripetal forces between them quickly won out over centrifugal ones, and Dennis, once more, returned to his mother's orbit. Yet, while in her orbit he could not help torturing her in overt and covert ways—he cut her down, was rude, or annoyed her by just sitting there and doing nothing. Thus, he delivered himself as the living proof of her failure and badness as a parent, increasing *her* despair and guilt. She, in turn, to relieve such despair and guilt, would further blame him, pressure him, intrude on him; in brief, would further victimize him by acting as his binder and delegator. And so the negative homeostatic mutuality worsened.

Liberating Moves

As the Suttons' therapist, my task was to counter mystification and victimization in the family. However, merely telling Mrs. Sutton to stop mystifying and victimizing Dennis would not have been enough. In fact, at this juncture it would probably have been counterproductive. Consumed by guilt and self-doubt, she perceived me then as trial judge and accuser and whatever I could have said most likely would have increased her guilt. Accustomed to discharge such guilt via projection, she would then have turned into an even fiercer—albeit perhaps more underhanded—victimizer of Dennis. Therefore, I focused on Dennis. I suggested to him that he, in being stubbornly passive or crazy, had the power to make his mother anxious and guilty, for he could thereby deliver himself as the living proof of her failure or badness as a parent. This might have looked as if I was further accusing and victimizing Dennis, already a victimized patient; in reality, I believed I reassured him—I let him know I was aware of his potential destructiveness and thereby lessened *his* anxiety and guilt over it. For a sense of destructiveness could mushroom in his imagination as long as it remained unacknowledged, uninvestigated, and hence unchecked. (From my individual therapy with schizophrenic patients, I have come to view the handling of a patient's real and imagined aggression and destructiveness as the most difficult, yet also most important, therapeutic task.) At the same time, I allowed him to see and possibly accept a share of the responsibility for the family's plight. Yet also, while focusing on his masochistic power ploys, I lessened his mother's guilt: I avoided singling her out for an attention which she, under the circumstances, would have perceived as blame. This, in turn, lessened her need to compulsively blame and victimize Dennis. As a result, she could then begin to reflect on the nature and sources of her own behavior vis-à-vis the boy and could thus begin to "own" some of the pain and conflicts she had so far disowned by binding and/or delegating Dennis. Such "owning" became central to this whole family's "un-binding." It implied a family-wide de-mystification and made Mr. and Mrs. Sutton into more assertive and effective parents. In order to trace important moves here, we return once more to Mrs. Sutton.

Mrs. Sutton: Overt Giver and Covert Demander

The subsequent therapy sessions showed that Mrs. Sutton's binding and delegating of Dennis fitted into a basic role which permeated her dealings with all family members and even outsiders. That was the role of the overt giver and covert demander.

Her overt role as generous giver was visible to all, and shaped her conscious image of herself. In accordance with it, she showered—or tried to shower—people, but most of all Dennis, with gifts, unending attention, and interest. Also, it was consonant with this role that her husband viewed and courted her as an inexhaustible source of nurturant warmth, emotional support, and sexual gratification. And in appearing able—though possibly unwilling—to give all these things, she appeared strong. She therefore seemed destined to keep the rocky family boat afloat while everybody else faltered, i.e., became sick, agitated, or clingingly dependent.

However, as the therapy progressed, her role as the strong giver showed flaws. For it became evident that she, in giving, shunned reciprocity. She simply could not tolerate being given to; if others were giving her gifts, or doing her favors, she always had to outgive or outdo them. Similarly, she could be strong only by keeping others dependent and weak. Thus, she helped to cement a homeostasis of rigidly fixed, but complementing family roles, as earlier described.

Yet, in being the strong and seemingly inexhaustible giver, she also acted as covert demander. And Dennis, the target of her most lavish and devoted giving, inevitably became also that of her strongest (though covert) demands. For example, she demanded from him that he fill the emotional—and even erotic—void left by her husband; she demanded that he, as her loyal delegate, realize her unrealized ego-ideal and become a renowned pianist; she demanded from him that he embody—and thus keep at a safe working distance from her ego—the frailty and helpless dependence she had to disown; and she demanded that he (contrary to what even the above mission would have required) jeopardize his growth and separation and remain forever captive to, and bound up with, her. In living up to these demands, Dennis turned victim, but in this very process, we saw, gained also the leverage to devastate his mother.

Mrs. Sutton's Belated Mourning and Repair Work

How had Mrs. Sutton developed into overt giver and covert demander? The answer to this question—which puzzled me, as it did also increasingly Mrs. Sutton—pointed to Mrs. Sutton's mother. This mother, Dennis's grandmother, was still alive when the family therapy began. As the therapy progressed, her name came up more frequently, and I began to ponder how she might possibly join our meetings. However, unforeseen events brought such plans to naught—one evening Mrs. Sutton's mother was attacked on the street and thrown to the ground. (She lived in an area with a rather high crime rate and had steadfastly rejected all proposals to move into a safer part of the city.) She suffered multiple fractures which required hospital treatment in an intensive care unit, and finally, after several agonizing weeks, led to her death. But although her injury and death precluded a three-generational therapy with her being present, they proved pivotal in reorienting the lives of Mrs. Sutton and the family as a whole.

To grasp what was here involved, we have to realize that Mrs. Sutton's mother, up to the time of the assault and injury, had always seemed undaunted. Also, she had never been ill enough to elicit or warrant active nursing care from the others, particularly her children. Therefore, like Mrs. Sutton, she was cast into the role of a powerfully independent lady, and, like Mrs. Sutton, she was seen as a generous giver. Almost from the first family session on I heard tales of how she, "this extraordinarily strong and loving person," would never forget to send a birthday gift, and how she, out of her deep concern for her children's welfare, solicited their (the children's) daily telephone reports, dutifully executed by the latter throughout their adult lives. But, also here, as in the case of Mrs. Sutton, overt strength and generous giving hid covert dependence and demandingness. Through her giving and constant show of strength, she made her daughter (Mrs. Sutton) indebted to her, and never gave her a chance to pay back her debts. Accordingly, Mrs. Sutton's mother could no less help binding and delegating her daughter than the latter could help binding and delegating Dennis. There existed an intergenerational chain of binding and delegative involvements.

It was the above dramatic and tragic events which, more than anything else, cracked this chain. For these events caused the grandmother to become bed-ridden and helplessly dependent, and thereby provided Mrs. Sutton with a final chance for repaying her debts. And she eagerly embraced this chance when, from early morning until night, she tried to make her mother's last weeks as comfortable as possible. When her mother finally died, she was desolate over not having been a more effective comforter and nurse, the more so as her mother's mostly comatose and unresponsive condition left her in doubt as to how much she had really helped. Still, for the first time in her life, she had been the giver and her mother the recipient.

Therefore, with her mother's death, she mourned not only the loss of her as a person, but also the loss of further opportunities for paying off her excessive debts—debts, she now began to realize, she had *faute de mieux* tried to pay off to Dennis. For, in having been prevented from giving to her mother, she "gave" inordinately and lavishly to Dennis—only to bind him tragically, just as her own mother had bound her.

As the family therapy went on, it aimed at more unbinding across generations. Thus, it fostered, among other things, a shift in Mrs. Sutton's major relational focus—*away* from Dennis and *to* her mother. While she mourned the latter and revived and reappraised her relationship with her, Dennis, almost to his surprise, found himself (relatively) neglected, i.e., less bound and hence more apt to go his own way. But this, Dennis now realized, was not an unmixed blessing. For just as his mother, in psychologically separating from her own parent, had now to "own," i.e., accept and work through, *her* so far disowned dependency and her avoidance of age-appropriate challenges, so had he. He now had to face the fact that he often, too easily and readily, would retreat into his mother's protective orbit rather than face peer competition, and uncertainties of the job market, and the hazards of heterosexual relationships. As it turned out, to un-bind, and keep unbound, mother and son was no easy task. Whenever Dennis felt lonely or discouraged about his progress with peers, girl friends, or difficult academic subjects, he would tend to alarm his mother with his floundering or seeming re-emerging craziness, thereby unleashing—or hoping to unleash—the binding maternal juggernaut. And she, in turn, would anxiously scan Dennis for just such signals whenever she felt overtaxed by the task of "owning" her so far disowned feelings, needs, and problems. The family therapy, no less than an individual therapy or analysis, again and again had to re-plow familiar ground in order to break up entrenched homeostatic patterns.

Balancing of Accounts

We learned from the above how Mrs. Sutton, in binding and delegating Dennis, took the boy to account for what her parents, and particularly her mother, had done to her. In order that accounts could now be balanced, it was necessary that Mrs. Sutton's mother—in one way or the other—become an active factor in the system of treatment. As it turned out, this came about in a tragic, unexpected turn of events which, nonetheless helped to unbind this family. For these events, while triggering appropriate and belated mourning in Mrs. Sutton, cast into relief some of the skewed accounting this family had practiced and suffered. And to the extent that accounts were thus reappraised—and, hopefully, balanced—Mrs. Sutton, along with her experience of guilt, could begin to experience some of the hate and frustration she had felt, yet disowned, vis-à-vis *her* exploitative mother, just as Dennis, on his part, could now more openly experience and "own" such hate vis-à-vis his mother, rather than channel it into mostly masochistic power ploys.

Reconcilation

But to feel and express hate and frustration *vis-a-vis* one's binding and delegating parents is not enough. Such feelings are but elements in the process of un-binding. Reconciliation is finally needed. And this requires, most of all, that bound and delegated children (and also grown-ups remain here children to *their* parents) try to understand and, out of such understanding, try to forgive their parents. Thus, Mrs. Sutton had to understand her mother's exploitative binding of herself in the light of her mother's experience with her own parents (here omitted), just as Dennis had to understand—and could, hopefully, forgive—his mother's exploitation of himself in the light of Mrs. Sutton's experiences with *her* mother. Thus, reconciliation implied, in the words of I. Boszormenyi-Nagy (49), "a reconstructive dialogue across the generations."

Concluding Note

Because of space limitations, I had to omit many other aspects of this family's treatment. Thus, I had to omit a description of how the father's relationship with his wife and with Dennis, as well as with his other son, formed part of the binding and delegating modes that accounted for this family's plight. Also, I could not describe how the father's relationship to his own parents, and particularly to his mother, contributed to the prevailing homeostasis. However, I would like at least to mention that this mother entered treatment, thereby making it, after all, a three-generational venture.

SUMMARY

Family theory represents a new paradigm in which the unit of treatment is no longer the person, but a set of relationships. Many family disturbances suggest a homeostatic deadlock marked by restrictive, impoverished, stereotyped, and nearly unbreakable family ties. Pseudo-mutuality and pseudo-hostility are two varieties of such deadlock. Disturbed families lack also essential differentiations as when boundaries between the generations and genders are insufficiently drawn and members fail to articulate their needs, wishes, and roles *vis-à-vis* each other. Mystification reflects and causes such lacking differentiation. The mystifying person (mostly a parent) attributes to another (mostly a child) negative feelings or qualities, invalidates this other's view of himself, and induces him to comply with the mystifier.

We can define family disturbances as transactional mode disturbances. Transactional modes operate as the covert organizing background to the

more overt and specific child-parent interactions. When age-appropriate transactional modes are too intense, out of phase, or inappropriately blended with
other modes, the negotiation of a mutual individuation and separation
between parent and child is impeded. We can distinguish between the modes
of binding, delegating, and expelling. Where the binding mode operates,
families are homeostatically deadlocked. This can occur on a dependency
level, a cognitive level, or an archaic loyalty level. Where the delegating
mode predominates, binding and expelling elements blend. Held on the
long leash of loyalty, the delegate carries out parental missions, as when
he fulfills his parents' unrealized ego-ideal or enacts their disowned delinquent impulses. Psychological exploitation and guilt are further dynamic
forces in families. To deal with them therapeutically, a multi-generational
perspective is needed. The process of "unbinding" homeostatically deadlocked families includes de-mystification, belated mourning, balancing of
accounts, and reconcilation across generations. A case description illustrates
these therapeutic principles.

REFERENCES

1. KUHN, T. *The Structure of Scientific Revolutions*. Chicago: University of
   Chicago Press, 1962.
2. HALEY, J. & HOFFMAN, L. *Techniques of Family Therapy*. New York:
   Basic Books, 1967, p. 1.
3. I heard this from Otto A. Will while serving on the staff of Chestnut
   Lodge.
4. JACKSON, D. D. Family interaction, family homeostasis, and some implications of conjoint family psychotherapy. In J. H. Masserman (Ed.),
   Science and Psychoanalysis. Vol. 2. *Individual and Familial Dynamics*.
   New York: Grune & Stratton, 1959.
5. JACKSON, D. D. & WEAKLAND, J. H. Conjoint family therapy: Some considerations on theory, technique and results. *Psychiatry*, 24, 30-45, 1961.
6. ACKERMAN, N. W. *The Psychodynamics of Family Life*. New York: Basic
   Books, 1958; especially see Chapter V.
7. WYNNE, L. C. Selection of the problems to be investigated in family
   interaction research. In J. L. Framo (Ed.), *Family Interaction. A
   Dialogue between Family Researchers and Family Therapists*. New
   York: Springer, 1972, pp. 86-92, but especially p. 89.
8. WYNNE, L. C., RYCKOFF, I. M., DAY, J., & HIRSCH, S. I. Pseudo-mutuality
   in the family relations of schizophrenics. *Psychiatry*, 21, 205-220, 1958.
9. SINGER, M. T. & WYNNE, L. C. Thought disorder and family relations of
   schizophrenics. III: Methodology using projective techniques. *Arch.
   Gen. Psychiat.*, 12, 187-200, 1965.
10. STIERLIN, H. *Conflict and Reconciliation*. New York: Doubleday-Anchor,
    1969; Science House, 1969.
11. LIDZ, T., FLECK, S., & CORNELISON, A. R. *Schizophrenia and the Family*.
    New York: International Universities Press, 1965.

12. BOWEN, M. Family psychotherapy with schizophrenia in the hospital and in private practice. In I. Boszormenyi-Nagy and J. L. Framo (Eds.), *Intensive Family Therapy*. New York: Harper & Row, 1965, pp. 213-243.

13. MINUCHIN, S. Structural family therapy. In S. Arieti (Ed.), *American Handbook of Psychiatry*. Vol. III. New York: Basic Books, in press.

14. BOSZORMENYI-NAGY, I. A theory of relationships: Experience and transaction. In I. Boszormenyi-Nagy and J. L. Framo (Eds.), *Intensive Family Therapy*. New York: Harper & Row, 1965, pp. 33-86.

15. SCHAFFER, L., WYNNE, L. C., DAY, J., RYCKOFF, I. M., & HALPERIN, A. On the nature and sources of the psychiatrist's experience with the family of the schizophrenic. *Psychiatry*, 25, 32-45, 1962.

16. STIERLIN, H. Family dynamics and separation patterns of potential schizophrenics. In Y. Alanen (Ed.), *Proceedings of the IVth International Symposium on Psychotherapy of Schizophrenia*. Amsterdam: Excerpta Medica, 1972, pp. 169-179.

17. STIERLIN, H. & RAVENSCROFT, K., JR. Varieties of adolescent "separation conflicts." *Brit. J. Med. Psychol.*, 45, 299-313, 1972.

18. STIERLIN, H. Interpersonal aspects of internalizations. *Int. J. Psycho-Anal.*, 54, 203-213, 1973.

19. LAING, R. D. Mystification, confusion, and conflict. In I. Boszormenyi-Nagy and J. L. Framo (Eds.), *Intensive Family Therapy*. New York: Harper & Row, 1965, pp. 343-364.

20. STIERLIN, H., LEVI, L. D., & SAVARD, R. J. Parental perceptions of separating children. *Family Process*, 10, 411-427, 1971.

21. LAING, R. D. *The Politics of the Family*. Toronto: CBC Publications, 1969.

22. WYNNE, L. C. & SINGER, M. T. Thought disorder and family relations of schizophrenics: I. A research strategy. *Arch. Gen. Psychiat.*, 9, 191-198, 1963. II. A classification of forms of thinking. *Arch. Gen. Psychiat.*, 9, 199-206, 1963. Also *op. cit.*, ref. 9.

23. *Op. cit.*, 16, 17, 18.

24. I am indebted to Dr. Kent Ravenscroft, Jr., for this formulation.

25. STIERLIN, H. The adaptation to the "stronger" person's reality. *Psychiatry*, 22, 143-152, 1959.

26. *Op. cit.*, 19, 21.

27. *Op. cit.*, 9, 22.

28. LIDZ, T., FLECK, S., & CORNELISON, A. R. The transmission of irrationality. In T. Lidz, S. Fleck, and A. R. Cornelison (Eds.), *Schizophrenia and the Family*. New York: Int. Univ. Press, 1965.

29. BATESON, G. Double Bind, 1969. Paper presented at the Symposium on the Double Bind, Annual Meeting of the American Psychological Association, September 2, 1969; also, with his co-workers: G. Bateson, D. Jackson, J. Haley, and J. Weakland. Toward a theory of schizophrenia. *Behav. Sci.*, 1, 251-264, 1956; and G. Bateson, D. Jackson, J. Haley, and J. Weakland. A note on the double bind. *Family Process*, 2, 154-161, 1963.

30. BRUCH, H. Falsification of bodily needs and body concepts in schizophrenia. *Arch. Gen. Psychiat.*, 6, 18-24, 1962.

31. SEARLES, H. The effort to drive the other person crazy—an element in the etiology and psychotherapy of schizophrenia. In H. Searles, *Collected Papers on Schizophrenia and Related Subjects*. New York: Int. Univ. Press, 1959.

32. HALEY, J. The family of the schizophrenic. A model system. *J. Nerv. Ment. Dis.*, 129, 357-374, 1959.

33. BOSZORMENYI-NAGY, I. Loyalty implications of the transference model in psychotherapy. *Arch. Gen. Psychiat.*, 27, 374-380, 1972.
34. *Op. cit.*, 17.
35. *Op. cit.*, 33.
36. BOSZORMENYI-NAGY, I. & SPARK, G. *Invisible Loyalties.* New York: Hoeber & Harper, 1973.
37. *Op. cit.*, 33.
38. STIERLIN, H. Countertransference in the family therapy with adolescents. In M. Sugar (Ed.), *The Adolescent in Group and Family Therapy.* In press.
39. *Op. cit.*, 33, 36.
40. SATIR, V. *Conjoint Family Therapy. A Guide to Theory and Technique.* Palo Alto: Science and Behavior Books, 1964.
41. FREUD, S. (1917). Mourning and melancholia. *Standard Edition*, 14, 237-258. London: Hogarth Press, 1957.
42. PAUL, N. & GROSSER, G. Operational mourning and its role in conjoint family therapy. *Comm. Ment. Health J.*, 1, 339-345, 1965.
43. *Op. cit.*, 33, 36.
44. MENDELL, D. & FISHER, S. An approach to neurotic behavior in terms of a three generation family model. *J. Nerv. Ment. Dis.*, 123, 171-180, 1956. Also, D. Mendell and S. Fisher. A multi-generation approach to treatment of psychopathology. *J. Nerv. Ment. Dis.*, 126, 523-529, 1958.
45. *Op. cit.*, 36.
46. STIERLIN, H. *Separating Parents and Adolescents.* New York: Quadrangle, 1974.
47. TURNBUL, C. *The Mountain People.* New York: Simon & Schuster, 1972.
48. BRONFENBRENNER, U. *Two Worlds of Childhood: U.S. and U.S.S.R.* New York: Russell Sage Foundation, 1970.
49. *Op. cit.*, 33.

BIBLIOGRAPHY

ACKERMAN, N. W. *Treating the Troubled Family.* New York: Basic Books, 1966.

BOSZORMENYI-NAGY, I. & FRAMO, J. L. (Eds.). *Intensive Family Therapy: Theoretical and Practical Aspects.* New York: Harper & Row, 1965.

BOWEN, M. Family psychotherapy. *Amer. J. Orthopsychiat.*, 31, 40-60, 1961.

BRODEY, W. M. The family as the unit of study and treatment: Image, object and narcissistic relationships. *Amer. J. Orthopsychiat.*, 31, 69-73, 1961.

ENGELS, F. *The Origin of the Family, Private Property and the State.* New York: International Publishers Co., 1971.

FRIEDMAN, A. S. ET AL. *Psychotherapy for the Whole Family.* New York: Springer Publishing Co., 1965.

GAP Report: Treatment of Families in Conflict. The Clinical Study of Family Process. (Formulated by) The Committee on the Family Group for the Advancement of Psychiatry. New York: Science House, 1970.

HALEY, J. *Changing Families. A Family Therapy Reader.* New York: Grune & Stratton, 1971.

HALEY, J. & HOFFMAN, L. *Techniques of Family Therapy.* New York: Basic Books, 1967.

JACKSON, D. D. & WEAKLAND, J. H. Conjoint family therapy: Some considerations on theory, technique and results. *Psychiatry*, 24, 30-45, 1961.

As I said, in this respect, to one of my most self-denigrating woman clients, "You say that you lack self-confidence. That is ironic! For if you told me that you lack confidence in your ability to, say, paint well, there might be nothing that you could do about it. To be confident—to know, that is, with a high degree of probability—that you can paint adequately, you would first have to learn and practice painting, often for quite a period of time, and then you would have to prove, to yourself and others, that you really *do* paint quite well. And, of course, you might never persist at this learning and practice, and, even if you did, you might just have no talent at painting, and might never prove you are good at it. But *self*-confidence you can always have—and for the mere choosing! For to have *self*-acceptance, at what we call point C in RET, after you have continued to try painting, at point A, you merely have to decide, to strongly convince yourself, at point B, 'I will *always* accept myself and utterly refuse to down myself *whether or not* I do well at painting (or anything else). No matter how bad (or good) I may be at painting, I am *me,* I shall never be anything else but *me,* and I shall pigheadedly continue to accept *me, myself,* my *essence,* my *being* whatever my painting (or other) performances may amount to.' So obtaining self-acceptance or self-confidence is as simple as A-B-C—if you use the A-B-C's of rational-emotive therapy intelligently!" In this particular case, after seeing the client for only seven sessions, and having little more than a distinctly didactic relationship with her, she was able to accept herself with many flaws and failings, and to throw herself into a painting career even though her family and her close personal friends thought she was foolish for doing so.

6. Although RET is a cognitive theory that stresses insight or understanding, it opposes the psychoanalytic view of insight as being highly superficial and strives for a much deeper view. The usual psychodynamic therapies help people to see that their current emotional difficulties have "causative" antecedents—especially in the experiences of their childhood. RET holds that giving clients "insight" into their past experiences is largely misleading. For it is not the Activating Events or Experiences (A) of their previous lives that "cause" their disturbed emotional Consequences (C). Much more importantly, it is their inborn *and* acquired tendency to interpret these events and experiences unrealistically—to have irrational Beliefs (iB's) about them.

The *real* (or more direct) cause of peoples' emotional upsets, consequently, is *not* what happens to them but what they *think, interpret,* and *tell themselves* about these happenings. Their experiences themselves inevitably have a strong cognitive component, or conceptual bias, while they are occurring and after they have taken place. And their remembrances of and the meanings they give to these experiences are notably cognitive. RET, therefore, tries to help them gain three types of insight:

Insight No. 1 is the realization by clients that their self-defeating behavior is related to antecedent conditions—e.g., they hate women today partly because their mothers abused them during their childhood—and the acknowledgement that they *also* interpreted and gave special meaning to these original conditions. Thus, instead of convincing themselves rationally, when their mothers first abused them, "Isn't that unfortunate! I wish I had a more loving mother, but alas I don't! Too bad!" they irrationally convince themselves (at point iB), "How horrible that my mother is treating me like this! I can't stand it! She *must* not treat me this way, and is a total louse for doing what she must not do!" Their original hostility or "trauma," therefore, was *not* truly caused by their mother's negative behavior but by their irrational *reaction* to this behavior.

Insight No. 2 is the realization by the clients that even when they became disturbed (or, more accurately, *made themselves* disturbed) in the past, they are *now* suffering because they *continue* to indoctrinate themselves with the same kind of irrational, magical Beliefs (at point B) that they first chose. Moreover, they do not "automatically" keep holding these Beliefs because they were once "conditioned" by their parents or other external forces to hold them. On the contrary, they are still *actively reindoctrinating themselves,* and thereby reinforcing the Beliefs. It is this active self-propagandization, and hardly anything else, that keeps the irrational ideologies alive. Clients, therefore, would damned well better acknowledge their *own* responsibility and culpability for holding irrational Beliefs and retraumatizing themselves by them today. Else it is highly unlikely that they will work at vigorously uprooting these Beliefs and changing their personality structure.

Insight No. 3 is the realization by the clients that because their irrational Beliefs are longstanding, because they are exceptionally powerful, because they are both biologically and socially rooted, and because they are still being actively reinforced by the disturbed individuals themselves, it normally requires a tremendous amount of *continuous and energetic hard work and practice* to uproot and annihilate them. Merely *understanding* that these irrational Beliefs exist and that they are irrational and self-sabotaging is far from enough—just as understanding that one is superstitious rarely suffices to extinguish the superstitiousness. To effect elegant and enduring personality change, clients would better be exceptionally vigilant and counterattacking. Anything less than their concerted, prolonged, and forceful attacking of their own basic irrationalities is unlikely to work too well.

When I first clearly propounded the A-B-C theory of emotional reaction almost twenty years ago, there was very little experimental evidence to support it. Since that time, cognitive psychology has come into its own and there have been literally hundreds of experiments demonstrating that emotion and behavior are highly dependent on mediating processes and that if an experimenter induces subjects to change their thinking they will concomitantly change their emotional responses. Some notable experimental work in this area has been reported by Carlson, Travers, and Schwab (1969), Hekmat and Vanian (1971), Lazarus (1966), Marcia, Rubin and Efran (1969), Mischel (1973), Nisbett and Schacter (1966), Schacter and Singer (1962), Valins and Ray (1967), Velten (1968), Wine (1971), and others. More specific studies of RET, showing its effectiveness in controlled clinical experiments, have also been widely reported in the psychological literature, including studies by Davies (1970), Ellis (1957), Goldfried and Merbaum (1973), Maes and Heimann (1970), Maultsby (1971a), Meichenbaum (1971), Meichenbaum and Goodman (1971), O'Connell (1970), Sharma (1970), and Trexler and Karst (1972).

Confronting and Attacking Irrational Beliefs and Values

RET holds that since an individual's irrational beliefs and values are so important in the creation of his disturbed behaviors, probably the most efficient and elegant way of helping him to make a basic personality change is directly to confront him with his philosophies, explain how these make him disturbed, attack them on logico-empirical grounds, and teach him how to change or eliminate them. It hypothesizes how teaching, training, modeling, and persuasion are central to effective therapy.

Persuasion and teaching are perhaps the oldest models of psychotherapy, but have unfortunately been sidetracked by the great emphasis placed on psychological exhumation and on client-therapist relationships by post-Freudian writers. Before RET came along, the last great book on persuasive therapy was written by a Belgian psychiatrist, Paul Dubois, and published, in its English edition, in 1907. Alfred Adler (1927) favored the educational model of therapy, but even he waylaid himself by placing undue emphasis on early childhood memories, dreams, sibling rivalry, analysis of organ inferiority, and other techniques that he partly took over from Freud. Jerome Frank beat the drum for persuasive methods (including RET) in 1961, but his message, again, largely fell on deaf ears.

RET confronts clients with their irrational Beliefs and persuasively attacks, challenges, questions, and disputes these Beliefs because of its basic theory, and not merely because this methodology works. After its A-B-C's comes D:

Disputing. D follows from the theory that if clients truly keep disturbing themselves by believing in ideas that are magical, dogmatic, intolerant, absolutistic, and logically contradictory, there is probably some effective method of inducing them to surrender these ideas, and that this is what we usually call the scientific or logico-empirical method. Since the logico-empirical methodology is teachable and since it can be used to dispute and destroy almost any hypothesis that does not conform to reality and that merely stems from unverifiable, bombastic premises, there is every reason to believe that effective therapists had better vigorously employ this method, so that they can help their clients give up their self-destructive ideologies.

Another way of saying this is to posit the RET hypothesis that emotional health is largely synonymous with the individual's consistent use of hard-headed empirically-based thinking and that personality disturbance is little more than another name for devout religiosity, absolutism, magical thinking, and antiscientism. When, for example, John Jones becomes exceptionally anxious about a college test that he is to take a few days hence, he starts with the realistic assumption that it would be advantageous for him to pass this test and disadvantageous or unpleasant for him to fail. This is an empirically verifiable assumption, because if he does fail the test, it is highly probable that (1) he will have to take the course over; (2) he may never get his bachelor's degree; (3) his friends may think him stupid; (4) his parents will give him a hard time; and (5) various other things that are inimical to his basic values—that is, remaining alive and happy—will occur. Consequently, John's internal statement at B, "I hope I don't fail this test, because it would be unfortunate if I did," is a highly sensible statement or rational Belief (rB).

If John stayed rigorously with this rational Belief, he would (according to RET theory) feel appropriately concerned and distinctly motivated to study for and pass the test, but he would not be overconcerned or anxious. His anxiety, especially when it is overweening and destructive, follows from a set of highly irrational Beliefs (iB's) that he *also* entertains. These absolutistic, magical, anti-empirical Beliefs are along these lines: "It would be utterly horrible if I fail this test! I just couldn't bear failing! I'd be a complete turd if I did!" Why are these Beliefs unverifiable and magical? Because:

1. By calling his potential failure "horrible," John really means, in addition to the empirically valid notion that certain disadvantages or misfortunes would accrue if he failed the test, three unprovable assumptions: (a) That his failure would really be *more than* one hundred percent unfortunate; (b) that there could not possibly be *any* advantage to his failing and that the

results would have to be *all* bad; (c) that because failure is so bad—or *more than* bad!—he *should, ought,* and *must* not fail; and conditions in the universe have got to be so arranged that he *cannot* fail. John may not fully realize that by describing his potential failure as "horrible" rather than as "distinctly unfortunate" he is dreaming up these three untenable assumptions. But he is!

2. By contending that he can't bear failing, John is spouting pure nonsense. He may never, of course, *like* failure, but he certainly, until he is dead, can *bear* or *tolerate* it. If he *thinks* he can't bear failing the test, he may indeed—quite foolishly—kill himself if he finds he has done poorly in it. But that still is no evidence that he *could* not bear failure—but merely evidence that he *chose* not to bear it. Empirical evidence for any human "cannot" is unobtainable, since the term really means "under no conceivable conditions can this thing be accomplished." And how is such a proposition ever to be verified?

3. John's feeling like a complete turd, or a worthless individual, in case he fails the test results from an arrant, magical overgeneralization. That his *act* of failing is inept, incompetent, stupid, or turdy is indeed provable—because, as noted above, it most probably will bring him disadvantageous, frustrating results. But that *he* is a louse because one of his *behaviors* is lousy is a conclusion that is illogical and unprovable. In fact, that he is *not* a rotten *person* no matter how rotten any of his *deeds* may be is almost certain, since the term *rotten person* clearly means—when you stop to *think* about it!—an individual who (1) consistently does bad acts; (2) can *only* and *always* perform badly; and (3) deserves, by some theological law of the universe, to be eternally damned and roasted in hell for acting badly. Although the first of these propositions is empirically verifiable, the last three clearly are not.

RET, then, hypothesizes that virtually all deepseated, intense feelings of anxiety, depression, guilt, and hostility (and the concomitant dysfunctional behaviors or psychosomatic ailments that often accompany such feelings) stem from the human tendency to "awfulize," "terribilize," "horribilize," and "catastrophize"—that is, to go beyond empirical data and to assume that unpleasant, unfortunate or disadvantageous experiences absolutely *should, ought,* and *must* not exist. And it teaches clients (and nonclients, such as school and college students), how to use the logico-empirical method of science to dispute and annihilate their unrealistic thinking and thereby to change their emotions and personality.

RET, again, shows people that their emotional upsets almost invariably stem from their insistences on deifying and glorifying or on devilifying and damning themselves and others (Ellis 1958a, 1962, 1970a, 1971a, 1973a, 1973g). It reveals to them how they demand, command, and dictate that (1) they do outstandingly well and be incredibly popular; (2) others treat them kindly, considerately, and nobly; and (3) the world be invariably easy and rewarding. It teaches them how to dispute and attack these utterly unrealistic and unattainable expectations and demands, how to accept themselves and others unconditionally, and how to put up with inevitable annoyances when they cannot be changed. Although it is possible for someone to be religious, in the sense of having a strong system of beliefs, practices, and ethical values, or in the sense of conscientiously pursuing some cause, and for this person still to be rational, it is highly dubious whether anyone who is deeply afflicted with religiosity, dogmatism, or magical thinking can truly be a rational person.

In rational-emotive therapy, it is hypothesized that there are only a limited number of major irrational ideas that people devoutly believe and that when they do rigidly adhere to these or similar ideas, they become disturbed. The three ideas listed in the previous paragraph are typical of the irrationalities that are clinically found in individuals with severe disturbance. I first hypothesized these ideas and their crippling emotional and behavioral correlates in talks given in 1955 and 1956 (Ellis 1957a, 1957b, 1958b). Since that time, a large number of experimental studies have been done that confirm the fact that disturbed individuals do tend to hold irrational, illogical, unrealistic, and overgeneralized ideas significantly more often than do less disturbed people. These include studies by Argabrite and Nidorf (1968), Beck (1967), De Wolfe (1971), Hoxter (1967), Kemp (1970), Jones (1968), Lidz, Cornelison, Terry, and Pleca (1958), MacDonald and Games (1972), Overall and Gorham (1961), Payne and Hirst (1957), and Platt and Spivack (1972).

Because it espouses teaching the individual to use the logico-empirical method of science in checking and modifying his personal values and philosophies about himself and others, RET is one of the few systems of psychotherapy that largely eschews the medical, the warmly relating, and the psychodynamic models and that utilizes the educational model. Even when it is used in one-to-one sessions, between one therapist and his or her client, it is, perhaps more than anything else, a didactic process. To be sure (as noted above), it employs emotive and behavioral methods, too. But many of the emotive-dramatic techniques it employs—such as role-playing, the giving of the client unconditional acceptance, and forceful confrontation of the client by the therapist—include a good deal of modeling and behavioral rehearsal. Hence, they are quite in keeping with educative procedures. As for RET's use of behavioral methods—such as homework assignments, assertion training, and modification of irrational ideas by operant conditioning procedures—these, too, tend to be employed in an active-directive manner that has the therapist playing the role of a teacher more than that of an intensely relating partner.

RET has pioneered, moreover, in the application of its principles to work with small and large groups and to other kinds of procedures that are closer to education than they are to conventional therapist-client dyads. At the Institute for Advanced Study in Rational Psychotherapy, in New York City, many kinds of public education are regularly scheduled, including talks, workshops, film and recorded presentations, and classes. A great deal of bibliotherapy is promoted through the distribution of books, pamphlets, and recordings on the principles of rational living. A dozen or so once-a-week therapy groups are conducted at the Institute, and several different kinds of educational materials, such as homework assignment forms and tape recordings of actual therapy sessions, are utilized with the individual and group therapy clients at the Institute's psychological clinic and with other members of the public who wish to use these materials in their own self-help programs. Finally, as noted previously in this chapter, the Institute operates a private school for normal children, at which pupils are given regular academic training and are also given, in the course of their general curriculum, continual emotional education in the theory and practice of rational-emotive psychology. Not only, therefore, does RET uphold the hypothesis that basic personality change is better enhanced through various forms of direct teaching rather than through more conventional forms of psychotherapy, but RET practitioners in various parts of the world tend to practice this preachment and to emphasize rational-emotive education, both preventively and curatively, through a number of different audio-visual modalities. I personally believe that the future of psychotherapy is likely to be applied mainly within the school system and am happy to keep discovering that RET procedures are notably effective on the elementary, high school, and collegiate levels.

A good many general and research papers have begun to appear in recent years supporting the position on emotional education that is taken by RET. Among the psychologists and educators who have written significant papers in this area are Bersoff and Grieger (1972), Breen (1970), Daly (1971), Ellis (1969a, 1971b, 1972c, 1973e), Grieger (1972), Gustav (1968), Hartman (1968), Hoxter (1967), Knaus (1974), McGrory (1967), Maultsby (1968), Parrino (1971), Sydel (1972), Tobie (1972), and Wolfe (1970).

Homework Assignments

When I first started to employ activity homework assignments and incorporated them as an integral part of RET (which was in the beginning of 1955), this kind of procedure was almost unheard of in the field of psychotherapy. Only a few therapists, such as Alexander Hertzberg (1945), had ever spoken up in their favor at that time. But even before I was a psychologist and had ever heard of Hertzberg, I had independently invented such assignments for my own use, and had used them very satisfactorily in the course of overcoming some of my own hangups about speaking in public and striking up acquaintanceships with women in whom I was interested (Ellis 1972g). I therefore *knew* that they could work, and I enthusiastically employed them with almost all my clients, especially with those who were inhibited, shy, or withdrawn. Although I had never heard of Joseph Wolpe either, in 1955, I had independently figured out that if *in vivo* desensitization is to be used with clients—and that is what RET homework assignments frequently consist of—the desensitization process usually has to be done gradually, with a hierarchy of graded assignments which slowly increase in difficulty for, otherwise, the person one is helping to desensitize finds the going too rough, and will not continue with the process.

RET gives activity homework assignment to clients on theoretical grounds and not merely pragmatically. For, as noted above, it not only holds that cognitions usually precede action but also that, at least at certain times, actions importantly precede and influence cognition. Thus, if a woman is terribly afraid and guilty in regard to having intercourse and she forces herself to have it over and over again with an attractive partner, it will usually not take her too long to lose both her anxiety and her guilt.

RET, in addition to giving clients activity homework assignments that are designed to help them desensitize themselves to some anxiety, also specializes in cognitive homework. A man who unreasonably loathes his mother-in-law, for example, will be given the doubleheaded assignment of (1) deliberately keeping in much closer contact with her than he normally would, while (2) actively and vigorously disputing (at point D) his irrational Belief (iB), "My mother-in-law is a rotten bitch whom I absolutely cannot stand!" The cognitive part of this assignment might be for him to spend at least ten minutes a day asking himself such questions as: (1) "What am I telling myself when I feel so hostile to my mother-in-law?" (2) "Is my self-statement true?" (3) "Where is the evidence that it is true?" (4) "How can my mother-in-law be a total bitch even if it can be factually shown that she consistently acts bitchily?" (5) "Even if I could prove that my mother-in-law were a bitch and that she deserves to be condemned for eternity, why can't I stand her behaving the way she indubitably behaves?"

Another common form of RET homework consists of rational-emotive imagery (REI) assignments (Maultsby, 1971b). In REI, a woman who is terrified about public speaking may be asked to imagine vividly, to fantasize as clearly as she can, her getting up before a group to speak, and her hardly being able to get a word out of her mouth. She is asked to see, in her imagination, her failing miserably at giving this talk, and to note that her audience is snickering and obviously thinking that she is one of the worst speakers they have ever heard.

She is then asked her gut-level feeling as she imagines herself in this predicament. One woman replied, "Utter panic! I feel like I'm rooted to the floor, that I would like to flee precipitately, but that I'm so scared that I can't even do that, and I just stand foolishly there, with my mouth open but nothing coming out of it!"

"Fine!" I said. "You're doing this exercise very nicely. Now, see if you can't *change* your feeling, in your gut. Keep the same picture in your head— imagine that you are still facing this group and unable to say practically anything. But change your feeling in your gut to a feeling of *only* disappoint- ment and frustration. Not panic, mind you; not anxiety; not depression or despair—only disappointment and frustration. Can you, if just temporarily, change your feeling to that?"

"It's hard! I still feel panicked."

"I know it's hard; but I'm sure, at least temporarily, that you can do it. Try!"

"All right. I've got it, I think. I'm only, right now, feeling disappointment and frustration."

"Good. Now, what did you do in your head, to *make yourself* feel this way and to get rid of the panic?"

"I—uh, I managed to say to myself, 'It's just a talk. It isn't your whole life. It only shows that you're pretty bad in this area. But even though they all, the audience all thinks you're a rotten speaker that doesn't make you a bad person!'"

"That's fine," I said. "That's exactly what you might tell yourself, in this kind of situation. Now, what I want you to do is take five or ten minutes every day, put the time aside, and practice just this kind of rational- emotive imagery during this time. Vividly imagine, just as you have just done, speaking very badly in public. Let yourself, first, feel utterly panicked. Let yourself really experience that feeling. Then, just as you did now, change that feeling to one of disappointment and frustration, using the same kind of thinking you just used. Do that, for five or ten minutes every day, for the next few weeks or so. Then we'll see how your anxiety about public speaking is affected!"

As I predicted, this woman's anxiety about public speaking decreased appreciably as she continued to do this rational-emotive imagery homework assignment. A few weeks later, when she was scheduled to give a talk to a fairly large group of her business associates, she was only moderately anxious and acquitted herself well in the talk.

The theory behind RET homework assignments is that humans, consciously or unconsciously, *practice* telling themselves all kinds of irrational ideas (or negative internalized sentences) that create their feelings of anxiety, depression, guilt, and hostility. Instead of being externally conditioned—as we commonly condition rats in a laboratory experiment in psychology—they are mainly *self*-conditioned by their own thinking and imagining processes. Even though their negative self-verbalizations are not reinforced or rewarded in the usual Skinnerian sense—since they frequently achieve painful rather than pleasurable results from following them—they are reinforced in some *other* important ways. First, they get the certainty and satisfaction of having their catastrophizing prophecies fulfilled. Thus, my client with the intense fear of public speaking commonly predicted, to herself, that she would fail at speaking, and, normally, she *did* fail. By this kind of negative self-fulfilling prophecy she was able to create a good deal of order and certainty in her world, which was one of the main satisfactions—or "reinforcements" —that she craved.

Secondly, almost all exceptionally anxious people (like this client) are short-range hedonists with high degrees of low frustration tolerance. They would much rather avoid almost any momentary discomforts, especially the discomfort of anxiety, even at the expense of foregoing all kinds of long-range satisfactions. Consequently, when they tolerate even a little anxiety— which they really had better do, in order to work through it and eliminate it —they make it feel so intolerable (mainly by telling themselves, "I can't stand it!) that they are practically forced to run away from the Activating Experience that they (wrongly) view as its "cause"—e.g., in my client's case, the experience of speaking in public. This avoidance of the Activating Experience leads them to such immediate satisfaction (short-range relief of their anxiety) that they feel immensely reinforced by it, and hence continue to keep avoiding such experiences for the rest of their lives—even though this very avoidance really prolongs and intensifies their anxiety.

Because people unwittingly reinforce their disturbed feelings and behaviors in these ways, RET homework assignments usually are ways of encouraging them to become longer-range hedonists: to stick with their present pains—that is, their anxieties, depressions, guilts, and hostilities—and even temporarily exacerbate them in order ultimately to diminish or eradicate these self-defeating behaviors. Just as these clients have *practiced* telling themselves irrational ideas and *practiced* feeling needless disturbances consequent to these ideas, RET homework is a method of helping them *practice* counterconditioning rational ideas and appropriate feelings.

Experimental evidence favoring the efficacy of RET homework assignments or *in vivo* desensitization has now been published by many investigators, including Barlow et al. (1969), Cooke (1966), Davison (1965), Dua (1970, 1972), Leitenberg et al. (1970, 1971), Litvak (1969a, 1969b), Marks (1971), Maultsby (1971), Mitchell and Mitchell (1971), Perlman (1972), Rimm and Madeiros (1970), Ritter (1968), and Rutner and Bugle (1969).

The Theory of Human Worth

RET has a somewhat unique theory of human worth, which may not yet be duplicated in any other school of psychotherapy, though it overlaps somewhat with some of the ego-less philosophies of the Orient (Suzuki 1956; Watts 1959). Originally, I went along with the philosophy of human worth or value espoused by Hartman (1967), Maslow (1954), Tillich (1953) and other existentialist thinkers. In our popular book, *A Guide to Rational Living,* Dr. Robert A. Harper and I (1961a) consequently concluded that to base an individual's value on his traits, deeds, and performances is foolish—since these may easily change, and are not exactly the essence of *him* or *her.* Human value or worth, consequently, would much more safely and wisely be based on the person's aliveness. For you are quite safe, and can never feel yourself rotten or worthless, if you stick to the proposition: "I am worthwhile because I am alive—merely because I have existence."

I became increasingly skeptical of the validity of this assumption, and in 1962, in *Reason and Emotion in Psychotherapy,* wondered whether there really is such a thing as "intrinsic worth" or the "intrinsic value of a human being" (Hartman, 1967). I not only wonder today; I have become increasingly convinced that there is not. I give the reasons for this new conviction in my paper, "Psychotherapy and the Value of a Human Being" (Ellis 1972e). Some of the main reasons include: (1) Intrinsic worth or value is a Kantian thing-in-itself which may possibly exist but is unobservable and unvalidatable. (2) Intrinsic value of a human being seems to be definitional or tautological: you are intrinsically valuable to yourself because you say or think you are and not because of any other reason. (3) Intrinsic value cannot very well be measured or rated, like other kinds of value can be. It either exists or does not exist—by choice or fiat—and doesn't seem to have any referent. (4) The "self" that you value, when you say "I value myself," is a higher-order abstraction, or overgeneralization, that is not very definable and that seems to be in much the same category as your "soul" or "spirit." (5) To value your "self" is to create a redundant hypothesis. You can prove that you have such traits as aliveness, existence, or enjoyability, but you cannot very well prove that you have a "self," and you get into difficulties when you try to prove this or when you assume it. (6) If you rate your "self" or your "ego," you invent a kind of heaven or hell, for you can have a "good self" (heavenliness, holiness, or holier-than-thouness) and a "bad self" (hell, damnation, or intrinsic shithood). The real purpose of ego-rating is to prove that you are better than other humans—that you are superhuman. And when you have that purpose, since you are not really superior to others as people (although you may have some superior traits to theirs), and since you are invariably fallible, you will end up by feeling inferior and somewhat devilifiable. (7) Believing in your intrinsic value and globally rating your "self" will almost always lead to various other evils: your becoming self-centered and self-evaluative rather than problem-centered and joy-seeking; your becoming self-conscious and narrow in your range of interests and involvements with others; your tending to damn and down yourself and others; your becoming intolerant, bigoted, and fascistic; your tending to become overmanipulative; your giving up desires, preferences, and choices in favor of absolute needs, demands, and compulsions; and your sabotaging your and others' basic goals and values in various other important ways that I list in my paper on psychotherapy and the value of a human being.

The RET theory of human worth has several important corollaries, which are important for the therapy process itself—including the relationship between the therapist and the client—and for the goals for which this process is presumably designed. In terms of the therapy experience, most schools of thought now go along with the Rogerian hypothesis that the therapist had better have unconditional positive regard for the client and that this kind of regard is in itself an extremely important part of psychological treatment. These schools, however, tend to give no psychological or philosophic rationale for their espousal of the therapist's fully accepting the client. They largely do it because it seems to work.

RET provides the rationale for this kind of pragmatism. For if, according to its percepts, humans as a whole—that is, their personality, "self," or being

—are not legitimately rateable, but only their deeds, acts, and performances are to be measured and evaluated (in order to enable them to enjoy themselves rather than to get into some kind of mythical heaven), then it easily behooves a therapist to fully accept (that is, refuse to judge) his or her *clients* while still constructively pointing out their erroneous, self-defeating, and socially reprehensible *behaviors*. Or, in other words, the therapist, using the RET theory of human worth, can legitimately say to his clients (as I fairly frequently say to mine), "Although you, like Adolf Hitler and Charles Manson, cannot be accurately judged as a louse or stinker—since *no* human is ever truly nonhuman or subhuman—you'd better honestly face the fact that several of your deeds or performances consistently seem to be malodorous, and that unless you work hard to change them, you will continue to foolishly defeat yourself and get along less enjoyably with others. Not that you *have* to change in these respects, nor, again, that you will be a rotten person if you don't. But for your own good—and not, incidentally, for *mine*—you'd better modify your performances. Or suffer what *you* will consider most unfortunate consequences!"

A second important corollary of RET's theory and practice of teaching clients (and members of the general public) to stop damning themselves no matter how execrable are some of their behaviors is that it is one of the few modern therapeutic systems that tries to consistently uproot and extirpate feelings of anger, hostility, resentment, fury, violence, and war-mongering, whereas some of the other systems try to merely induce people to suppress, repress, ventilate, or "cope with" these antisocial feelings (Ellis 1973c). RET hypothesizes that virtually every time you make yourself truly angry or hostile toward others you are not merely (if you are honest with yourself) negatively assessing and condemning their acts or traits, you are really judging and damning *them*.

RET theorizes, in other words, that when you feel, in your gut, anger or hostility, you are first healthfully and appropriately telling yourself something like, "I don't like So-and-so's improper and unjust behavior, and I am determined to try to get him to change it!" If you rigorously stayed with these rational Beliefs (rB's), you would feel strongly displeased with So-and-so's acts but would not feel furious and vindictive against him and his entire existence. In anger, however, you go far beyond this to an unhealthy and inappropriate judgment: "You are a rotten louse and I totally loathe *you* for committing this displeasing behavior! You absolutely *must* not do what I don't like you to do! And since you have had the consummate gall to displease me, I am going to vindictively damn and punish *you,* if it's the last thing I do!"

The rational-emotive therapist or teacher, if you go to him or her with this problem of anger, tries to show you that however legitimate your displeasure about being treated unfairly by another may be, your intense hostility to this other does *not* result from this displeasure but from your Jehovian demand or command that he or she must not act displeasingly. The therapist or teacher, therefore, tries to help you give up this whining commandingness, to accept the individual who has acted displeasingly as a fallible, essentially unjudgeable, always forgivable *person*—and then, perhaps, to continue your efforts to get him or her to act more pleasingly and fairly in the future. In this way, RET is a most humanistic form of teaching that fully accepts all people *as* human—and never in any way as (on the one hand) subhuman or nonhuman nor (on the other hand) superhuman or metahuman.

Hereditary and Environmental Influences

Although most modern theories of personality stress hereditary tendencies as well as environmental influences on human functioning, RET is more definite—perhaps more honest?—in this respect than Freudian, Adlerian, neo-psychoanalytic, and behavioristic theories, all of which heavily emphasize early conditioning and the influence of the past on present disturbances. I think this is because so many therapists would rather dramatically "explain" dysfunctional behavior than eradicate it, and because many of them, with ironic insistency, also mistakenly believe that if a human tendency is inborn it is virtually impossible to change it. The psychoanalysts, in particular, although Freud himself was rather biologically oriented, have an overweening faith in "insight," and often are hung up on the notion that if you clearly see how your psychological problems originated and developed, you will somewhat magically extirpate them.

Actually, there is an enormous amount of evidence that shows that the tendency of an individual to be severely emotionally disturbed is at least in part biological (Bender 1963; Chess, Thomas, and Birch 1965; Jellinek 1973; Kallmann 1960; Mahler 1968; Meehl 1962; Rimland 1964; Rosenthal 1970; Rosenthal and Kety 1968; Slater and Cowie 1971; Willner and Struve 1970). This demonstrated biological influence on disturbance could also easily be figured out on logical grounds—if only therapists and personality theorists stopped to do a little thinking. Because even if the psychoanalytic and behavioristic theories are correct, and early environment is an important influence on personality development (as is almost certainly true), it seems obvious that human conditionability or suggestibility must be innate *for* conditioning to occur, and it is most unlikely that all of us are born equally conditionable.

Anyway, RET has posited, from its beginnings, that people are born with strong tendencies toward "healthy" functioning—that is, toward surviving, seeking for happiness or self-actualization, living cooperatively with others, and intimately relating to or loving several other humans during their life-time—and that they are also born with strong tendencies toward "unhealthy" or self-defeating functioning—that is, toward being oversuggestible, over-cautious, grandiose, burdened with wishful thinking, short-rangedly hedonis-tic, and prone to overgeneralization and magical thinking (Ellis 1962, 1971a, 1973a). Facing this, RET practitioners frequently choose to explain to their clients, in biological as well as sociological terms, how they could have *very easily* become emotionally disturbed and how it is in all probability going to be *extremely difficult* for them to change their inborn *and* acquired tendencies to think crookedly and to consistently fulfill their other bio-social tendencies to think rationally and sanely. Instead of being either pollyannish or unduly pessimistic in this respect, rational-emotive therapists try to stick with a highly realistic, and therefore ultimately more beneficial, position in this respect.

There is an immense amount of evidence, from historical, anthropological, religious, psychological, and biological sources that virtually all humans, individually and in groups, at all times and places have been exceptionally irrational and self-defeating in much of their behaviors and that, in all probability, they have inborn as well as environmentally acquired tendencies to behave this way. Some of the evidence in this respect has been summarized by Bain (1946), Barber (1961), Ellis (1942), Frazer (1959), Hoffer (1951), Hogden (1938), Jahoda (1969), Kaufmann (1973), Levi-Strauss (1962), Parsons (1969), Pitkin (1932), Shumaker (1966), and Tabori (1959, 1961).

APPLICATION OF THEORY

An attempt has been made in this chapter to outline the most important theoretical bases of rational-emotive therapy and to indicate that there already exists a considerable amount of evidence—not merely of a clinical nature but in the form of controlled experimental studies—supporting each of its major theses. A detailed clinical example will now be given to indicate how its theories are actually put into practice in order to help a troubled individual to understand and change some of his or her main disordered thoughts, feelings, and actions. I mentioned Gladys P.'s rational-emotive reeducation briefly in an article on RET in *Psychology Today* (Ellis 1973d), and will now give more details.

She was amazingly troubled, in spite of her attractiveness, proven competence in several important areas, and what she considered to be a highly successful three-year, three-times-a-week experience with psychoanalysis. Looked at from a conventional standpoint, she presumably should not have been in my, or any other psychotherapist's, office at all. For she had just been offered an exceptionally good job, far better than any she had previously held, she was popular with several eligible males, now that she had been widowed, and her eighteen-year-old daughter was making a fine social and academic adjustment at an out-of-town college.

But she was in an extreme state of panic, slept little and fitfully each night, and vacillated enormously about accepting the new job offer. These were recent, and she thought surface, manifestations of her anxiety. More important, she felt, was her constant fear of failing on *any* job (though she never had). She also knew in her heart that her husband had lost interest in her before his death (though he had given no outward signs of unlovingness). And she felt exceptionally inadequate about never achieving an orgasm during intercourse (although all her sex partners, throughout her life, had thought her to be "terrific" in bed and had bemoaned their own inadequacies rather than hers).

Surprisingly—considering her serious symptoms—she said that she knew what the basic sources of her psychological problems were. Her analyst, a woman well-trained in Freudian and Sullivanian methods, was "a lovely person," whom she really liked and still occasionally saw. She had "helped immensely" with her former problems of shyness and guilt about sex. She had shown her that the main origins of her disturbance were connected with her attitudes toward men. First, Gladys had vainly sought her father's love when she was a child, but had never succeeded in weaning him away from his obsessive interest in her older brother. Second, she had consequently always (according to the analyst) unconsciously hated herself. Third, she had falsely resolved this problem by forcing herself to compulsively compete with men and to win out over them in the business world. Finally, she had found it too dangerous to compete with men sexually, since they were invariably better at having orgasms than she, so she had given up on coitus and resorted almost exclusively to extravaginal stimulation, especially oral-genital relations, in her heterosexual contacts.

All this she knew, and was comforted in knowing. But in the last six months her analysis had been "getting nowhere." It had "bogged down to an almost complete halt." And instead of feeling better, especially in the face of her recent business and social successes, she was becoming more anxious and depressed. In desperation, after a friend told her of the outstanding results he had after three months of rational-emotive therapy, she had come to see me.

In the course of our first few sessions, I gently but firmly explained to Gladys that the psychoanalytic interpretations of her basic disturbability may have sounded very "true" and "deep," but that they were probably not deep or philosophic enough. Assuming, for example, that she really had vainly sought her father's love when she was a child but had never succeeded in weaning him away from his obsessive interest in her older brother, why had she *made* those sorry facts of life *all-important* and why had she insisted on *affecting herself* about them up to the present day?

After all, many females have older brothers who are extremely favored by their fathers—but do they all, like her, unconsciously hate men forever, and compulsively compete with them to win out over them in business deals? Obviously, I pointed out, they don't. What, therefore, was her fundamental belief system or philosophy of life that she *derived from,* and then *re-brought* to, her unsuccessful attempts to win her father's love? What, as both a child and adult, did she *conclude* about being rejected by her father? And what important feelings stemmed from her original and present conclusions?

I began to teach Gladys, in other words, the A-B-C's of rational-emotive therapy and to show her how psychoanalysis had helped her acquire a misleading or superficial "explanation" of her disturbance; also, to show her why, after three years with a liked and respected analyst, her therapy had bogged down and was not showing her how to stave off or conquer her present state of panic.

"Let's assume," I said, during our second session, "that your analyst was quite correct: that your father did reject you in favor of your brother; that you took that rejection very badly; and that you therefore still have problems with men, in business as well as in your sex-love life, because you took it so badly. The question still remains: *Why* and *how* did you, even as a child, take your father's rejection so badly?" Our dialogue continued as follows:

Client: But wouldn't *any* child, practically, take it the bad way that I did?

Therapist: Yes, *most* would. But not *all!* A few would have consciously hated their fathers (not unconsciously, as you presumably did) and would have overtly despised him rather than themselves. A few would have said to themselves something like, "Tough! Why do I need *my father's* approval? If he's so hung up on my brother, I'd better try for someone else's love, instead!" A few would have given up on men entirely, perhaps become lesbians—as you didn't. The main point is that you *did* take the loss of your father's love very seriously. Now, what do you think you told yourself, convinced yourself, in order to react—that is, *make yourself react*—in that manner?

Client: I don't think I told myself anything. I just felt the way I did. Why shouldn't I?

Therapist: Because humans, as far as I can see, don't *just* feel anything. That's the psychoanalytic theory—something happens to you, early in your childhood, such as the loss of your father's love, and you *just* react to that happening by feeling anxious or hostile. Then you *just,* consciously or unconsciously, carry on that anxious or hostile feeling forever. Bullshit!

Client: Why is that bullshit? Why isn't it so?

Therapist: Because that's not the way human beings behave. Maybe lower animals, such as rats or guinea pigs, behave that way—become automatically conditioned against obnoxious stimuli that impinge on them from without, and thereby become anxious or upset. But humans are not rats and guinea pigs. They have a much larger cerebral cortex, and the thinking and evaluation that originates from this cortex importantly *mediates* between Activating Events or Activating Experiences that impinge on them, at what I call point A, and the emotional Consequences that follow these events, at what I call point C.

Client: Are you trying to tell me that, even when I was a young child, if my father didn't love me, at what you call point A, and I felt anxious and depressed, at what you call point C, my C responses were *not* caused by my father's rejection but by my own mediation processes, what I *thought* about this rejection?

Therapist: That's exactly what I'm trying to show you!—that A virtually never causes C, when C is a disturbed emotional response. Instead, C is caused by or a consequence of B.

Client: And what is B?

Therapist: In RET, we call it your Belief System—that is, your assumptions, values, ideals, or philosophies.

Client: But how could I, at the age of three or four, have any definite values or philosophies?

Therapist: How could you not? If you didn't, how would you have any reaction at all to what happened to you? If you didn't *value* your father's love—that is, firmly *believe* it to be good and beneficial for you—you would not have had *any* emotional response, not even mild displeasure, when he rejected you and favored your brother. And if you did value his approval, but merely thought it was *somewhat* rather than *all*-important that you receive it, you would have felt keenly regretful or annoyed by his refusal to give it to you, but you would hardly have felt terribly insecure, self-hating, and defensively hostile, as apparently (if your analyst is correct) you did feel.

Client: You are trying to show me, then, that my deep emotional response to the lack of my father's love only occurred because I *made* it occur? Because I *chose* to value his approval highly, when I could have made other choices?

Therapist: Exactly! That's why psychoanalysis is so wrong in its theory and practice and why it often helps so little when people have troubles. Because it falsely assumes that the Activating Experiences, A, of your early life made you the way you then were and still are—gave you emotional Consequences of insecurity and hatred, at point C. Actually, *you* gave yourself those Consequences, by *choosing* to make certain value assumptions, or Beliefs, at B. What is more, once you chose these Beliefs during childhood, you then continued to choose to hang on to them, and you are still doing so today. That is why you are *now* insecure, defensive, and hating, even though you have succeeded admirably in life. You are *still* childishly demanding—hell, commanding!—that your father (and virtually all other males) be completely devoted to you. And you will not be free of anxiety and hatred till you give up that three-year-old demandingness.

Gladys was not easily convinced. Although she was able to see, on theoretical grounds, that Activating Experiences or Events do not cause emotional Consequences in humans unless their Beliefs *about* these experiences or events are strongly positive or negative (that is, *assess* or *evaluate* the experiences as being "good" or "bad" for the person experiencing them), she did not *feel*—that is, *powerfully believe*—that this was so. Her strong conviction that emotions *just* or *naturally* arise out of her experiences, helped block her accepting this RET hypothesis. And her ardent allegiance to her previous analyst and to the analytic theory that present feelings are determined by past history (which many people *want* to believe, so that they can cop out at *working* to change themselves) helped increase this blocking.

Her unblocking started to occur during the fifth session, when her eyes suddenly filled with tears as she was telling me about her father's death a year ago, and the unveiling that was to take place at his grave the following Sunday. Our dialogue at this point proceeded:

Therapist: What are you crying about right now?

Client: Nothing. I guess I just thought it was sad that he died so young —only fifty-five. What a waste—!

Therapist: Was it really that? After all, from the picture you've given of him so far, it seems that he was enormously self-centered. He didn't care for you too much—didn't even care for your brother, except insofar as he could get reflected glory from his exploits. And he certainly didn't treat your mother, or virtually anyone else, very well. Why is his death such a "waste?" Do you really think that?

Client (hesitatingly): No, I guess I don't. I don't hate him any longer, as I once did, but I'm not terribly sorry about his being gone. I don't even want to attend the unveiling. I'm only going because my mother wants me to go. To tell the truth, I was thinking, just before the tears came to my eyes, "The unveiling of his headstone makes it utterly final. Now he'll *never* be able to care for me!"

Therapist: No, I said. You thought *more* than that. That thought alone couldn't produce those tears—and the feeling of self-downing which, as far as I can see, went with them. Never!

Client: What do you mean? Why wouldn't I cry as I said to myself, "Now he'll *never* be able to care for me!"?

Therapist: Because that's merely a description of what's happening to you at A: "My father is irrevocably dead. So he'll surely not be able to care for me (or anyone else) any more." How could that mere *description* of what's going on in the world make you feel *anything*—sad, depressed, self-loathing, or anything else?

Client: Oh. You, uh, you mean that according to, uh, your theories I also have to have an *evaluation* of what is going on, an evaluation of the non-existence of my father."

Therapist: Don't you?

Client: No, I can't see that I—. Oh. Oh, yes! Of course! "And it's very bad that my father will never be able to care for me!" That's what I was thinking, too—that I still value his love highly, and it's most unfortunate that I'll never in any way be able to get it now.

Therapist: Right! That's *partly* it. But there's even more than that. Look for it; look into your own head. You'll see I'm right.

Client: How do you *know* there's more than that? Why can't I merely be thinking and telling myself *that,* in order to produce my emotion of sadness? Merely *that?*

Therapist: Because I don't think that it's *only* sadness, sorrow, or regret that you're feeling. As I said before, I think you're also feeling self-downed or depressed. Aren't you?

Client: Hmmm. You're, uh, probably correct. Yes, to be honest, when I was crying there, I was also feeling depressed. And I guess I still am, whenever I fully face the fact that he's gone, gone forever, and that I'll *never* get from him the love I always craved.

Therapist: So you see, there *is* something more, something additional that you're telling yourself. What do you think it is?

Client: I feel you're right. There probably is something else. But I, I'm completely lost in finding it. You seem to know what it is, so you tell me.

Therapist: No, let's have you find it for yourself. You're just not bothering to look. Now let me put the whole thing in A-B-C form, and I think it will become clear to you what's going on in your head to create your feelings of depression whenever you face the fact of your father's irreparable death. First, at point A, we have the usual kind of Activating Experience. What is that, again?

Client: Well, uh, I—. I guess, the fact that I acknowledge the final loss of my father and the fact that he will not, cannot ever love me now.

Therapist: Yes, that's A. Now, what is C, the emotional Consequence that we're now interested in?

Client: My feeling depressed.

Therapist: Right. Now B, your Belief System, has two main parts. First, a quite sane, rational Belief—or what I call rB. What is that?

Client: What I said before, I guess: that I still value my father's love and it's therefore very unfortunate that I'll never be able to get it now.

Therapist: Yes. And if you stuck with that rational Belief—which is a provable empirically validatable Belief, since it *is* unfortunate if you want your father's approval and now cannot in any way get it—you would feel sorrowful, sad, regretful, or frustrated—but that is *all* you would feel. You would not, not in a million years, feel worthless or depressed.

Client: I wouldn't?

Therapist: Well, *would* you? If you *only* believed that it is unfortunate, or even *very* unfortunate, for you not to have, ever have, your father's love?

Client: No, I guess I would just feel sad. But I *do* feel more than that. So I must be telling myself—?

Therapist: What?

Client: Oh, I can see you're determined to let me figure this out for myself! No matter how hard it is!

Therapist: Yes, because if I tell you, you'll know it, all right. But it won't be as much an integral part of your knowing, as if you think it through, figure it out for yourself. For then, when I'm *not* around to help you in any way, you'll still have it—and still be able to apply it to any *other* kind of situation about which you depress yourself. So, to return to this one, about your father, you are probably telling yourself—*what?*

Client: "It's *awful* that he's not ever going to love me! I *must* be able to win his acceptance! And now I can't!"

Therapist: Yes, that's probably it. And that makes you—?

Client: A rotten person! A no-good, lowdown rotten person, whose own father never could, and now never will, love her!

Therapist: Ah! Do you see, now, what really made you cry? Do you see what truly caused your feelings of depression and self-deprecation?

Client: I see!

That turned the therapeutic tide. From that time onward, Gladys P. stopped copping out on what caused her emotional disturbances (as well as her nondisturbed feelings), and fully acknowledged what *she* did to create them.

I then began a highly active-directive, confrontational, philosophic, and behavioral *attack* on Gladys's irrational Belief System. I helped her clearly differentiate her *wants* and *preferences* from her presumed *needs* and *necessities.* She had several of the major irrational ideas, or false needs, that I have listed in my writings on RET, and I showed her what these ideas were and why they were foolish. Among other things, she had these unreasonable, demanding ideas: (1) "I *must* do exceptionally well at work, to prove that my father was wrong about favoring my brother over me, and to show that I am truly a worthwhile person." (2) "In order to show, again, that I am a valuable individual who can accept myself, I must have a hundred per cent love from any man with whom I am intimately related. And since my late husband did not love me completely, he really didn't love me at all, and that proves what a shit I really am!" (3) "If I don't regularly get terrific orgasms during intercourse, I am really not a woman, and that means that I am essentially unlovable and am a no-goodnik!"

In addition, Gladys had two second-order irrational Beliefs, which followed from her main demands that she be utterly competent and completely loved, and with which she afflicted herself after noting her own anxiety and depression. These were: (1) "I must not be panicked, depressed, and indecisive, and since I am, I'm no damned good!" (2) "Now that I have admitted my problems and gone for psychotherapy and even benefited from my psychoanalysis, I must be utterly rid of my symptoms for all time. Since they have returned, maybe I really *am* hopeless and worthless and will *never* be able to get better!"

As is usual in RET, I showed Gladys that she held these ideas, proved to her how foolish they were, and strongly tried to induce her to attack them herself. I showed her that her irrational Beliefs (iB's) about *needing* competency and love (not to mention absence of panic!) were magical, unprovable, and unrealizable.

In many ways in different sessions I continued to teach Gladys anti-awfulizing approaches to life. Essentially, I showed her how to accept reality, give up all magical assumptions, and to rigorously apply the logico-empirical, or scientific, method to her everyday life. This does not mean that I taught her to be unemotional—but merely nondisturbed. Rational, in RET, *doesn't* mean unemotional. In fact, the more rational Ms. P. became—meaning, determined to be fully self-accepting, long-rangedly hedonistic, and self-actualizing by *working* with her head and other faculties—the more emotional (especially, loving) and the more in touch with her feelings she tended to become.

In addition to anti-awfulizing philosophies, I used several other cognitive-oriented methods with this client. I gave her salient information about sex, including the knowledge that a large percentage of women rarely or never receive an orgasm during intercourse and yet there is nothing wrong or "inferior" about their sexuality (Ellis 1972f). I taught her imaging techniques—including, first, sexual imaging that helped her achieve greater arousal and more intense climaxes, and, second, rational-emotive imagery (REI) that helped her fantasize failing situations and practice feeling sorry and frustrated, rather than destroyed and depressed, as she imagined herself failing (Ellis 1973f). I used bibliotherapy with her, especially some of the RET pamphlets distributed by the Institute for Advanced Study in Rational Psychotherapy in New York City and some books (including *A Guide to Rational Living, Growth Through Reason*, and *Executive Leadership: A Rational Approach*).

Emotively, I used several evocative-confrontational procedures to help Gladys combat her basic irrational thinking and inappropriate emoting. She joined one of my regular therapy groups, where she was given various kinds of risk-taking exercises, including speaking up about her own and others' problems, even when she was reluctant to do so. She was directly confronted, during some group sessions, with her hostility to men, after she kept denying that she was any longer hostile to them. She was given empathy training, particularly through role-playing, and was asked to put herself in the "skin" of a man who was trying to relate to her and to satisfy her sexually. She was given what Rogers (1961) calls unconditional positive regard and what RET calls undamning acceptance, by both me and the members of her group, even when she at times behaved inconsiderately or angrily toward us. She was helped to acknowledge and reveal some of her positive and negative emotions—especially by telling some of the male members of the group that she liked them when she was hesitant to do so. She was given shame-attacking homework assignments, including going without a bra all week, because she was ashamed of people noticing her ample breasts.

On the behavioral side, several more active-directive techniques were used in the course of Gladys's RET individual and group therapy sessions. She was helped, through assertion training (role-playing and modeling with other members of her group), to be more forward in asking her lover to engage in sex acts that she liked but had been afraid to discuss with him. She was shown how to desensitize herself, by rational-emotive imagery, in regard to her extreme fear of making public speeches. She was given homework assignments of accepting a new job offer and working through her panic about making a wrong move in accepting it, and of letting herself become emotionally involved with her lover, even though she was afraid that he would later reject her.

After eight months of RET, mostly in group therapy, Gladys appeared to be remarkably improved. Her state of panic had long since vanished, and she only occasionally became seriously anxious. She worked satisfactorily on her new job; and, in fact, did so well that she was presented with still another job offer and was able to accept it without any vacillation and with little help from her therapy group. She was looking forward to starting the new job, knew that she might well fail (or not succeed perfectly well) at it, but felt that if she did fail, that would be "really too bad, and in fact *very* sad, but hardly *awful* or *terrible,* now that I rarely think in those terms any more." She still achieved orgasm only through direct manipulation of her clitoral region, and never during intercourse. But she was not bothered by this "deficiency" and viewed herself, indeed, as a "very good" sex partner to her lover. Even though she never came coitally, she enjoyed intercourse considerably and engaged in it, in addition to noncoital relations, most of the time she had sex.

Most important of all, perhaps, Gladys fully accepted herself with her symptoms. When she was anxious, indecisive, compulsively competitive, or inorgasmic, she deplored her *behavior* but not *herself.* She vigorously believed, at those times, "It's bad!" instead of "I'm bad!" She therefore was able to use her time and energies to work at changing her unfortunate performances instead of at flagellating and damning herself *for* these performances. As she said during one of the closing sessions of therapy, "I am determined, now, to accept my existence, my being, my me-ness, no matter how bad some of my traits and manifestations may be. I try, as you have taught me to try, to rate my *acts* and not my *totality.* That certainly works much better!"

This is one of the main essences of rational-emotive therapy. Its theory of personality and personality change is highly complex, has many nuances and ramifications, and constitutes a truly comprehensive system of psychotherapy. As shown in this chapter, it is substantiated by many controlled clinical and experimental studies that support the validity of the A-B-C of emotional disturbance and change and by many other studies that show that its main methods—especially RET teaching and behavioral homework assignments—are effective. Basically and simply, however, rational-emotive therapy is a multifaceted mode of tolerance training: a scientific procedure derived from and aiming at maximum humanization, or the more efficient and happiness-producing relating of the individual to himself or herself, to other humans, and to the world.

BIBLIOGRAPHY

ADLER, A. *Understanding Human Nature.* New York: Greenberg, 1929.

ARGABRITE, A. H. & NIDORF, L. J. Fifteen questions for rating reason. *Rational Living,* 3(1), 9-11, 1968.

BAIN, R. Man, the myth maker. *Sci. Mo.,* 65, 61-69, 1946.

BARBER, B. Resistance by scientists to scientific discovery. *Science,* 134, 596-601, 1961.

BARLOW, D. H., LEITENBERG, H., & AGRAS, W. S. Experimental control of sexual deviation through manipulation of the noxious scene in covert desensitization. *J. Abnorm. Psychol.,* 74, 596-601, 1969.

BECK, A. T. *Depression.* New York: Harper-Hoeber, 1967.

BENDER, L. Mental illness in childhood and heredity. *Eug. Quart.,* 10, 1-11, 1963.

BERSOFF, D. N. & GRIEGER, R. M. An interview model for the psychosituational assessment of children's behavior. *Rational Living,* 7(1), 14-22, 1972.

BREEN, G. J. Active-directive counseling in an adult education setting. *J. Coll. Stud. Personnel,* July, 1970, 279-283.

BURTON, A. (Ed.). *Encounter: The Theory and Practice of Encounter Groups.* San Francisco: Jossey-Bass, 1969.

BURTON, A. *Interpersonal Psychotherapy.* Englewood Cliffs, N. J.: Prentice-Hall, 1972.

CARLSON, W. A., TRAVERS, R. M. W., & SCHWAB, E. A., JR. A laboratory approach to the cognitive control of anxiety. Paper presented at American Personnel and Guidance Association Meetings, Las Vegas, March 31, 1969.

CHESS, S., THOMAS, A., & BIRCH, H. G. *Your Child Is a Person.* New York: Viking, 1965.

COOKE, G. The efficacy of two desensitization prccedures: An analogue study. *Behavior Res. & Ther.,* 4, 17-24, 1966.

DALY, S. Using reason with deprived pre-school children. *Rational Living,* 5(2), 12-19, 1971.

DAVIES, R. L. *Relationship of Irrational Ideas to Emotional Disturbance.* Masters Degree thesis. Department of Educational Psychology, University of Alberta, Spring, 1970.

DAVISON, G. C. Relative contributions of differential relaxation and graded eposure to *in vivo* desensitization of a neurotic fear. *Proc. 72nd Annual Convention Amer. Psychol. Assn.*, 209-210, 1965.

DAVISON, G. C. Anxiety under total curarization: Implications for the role of muscular relaxation in the desensitization of neurotic fears. *J. Nerv. Ment. Dis.*, 143, 443-448, 1967.

DEWOLFE, A. S. Cognitive structure and pathology in associations of process and reactive schizophrenics. *J. Abnorm. Psychol.*, 78, 148-153, 1971.

DUA, P. S. Comparison of the effects of behaviorally oriented action and psychotherapy reeducation on introversion-extroversion, emotionality, and internal-external control. *J. Counsel. Psychol.*, 17, 567-572, 1970.

DUA, P. S. Group desensitization of a phobia with three massing procedures. *J. Counsel. Psychol.*, 19, 125-129, 1972.

DUBOIS, P. *The Psychic Treatment of Nervous Disorders.* New York: Funk & Wagnalls, 1907.

ELLIS, A. *A History of the Dark Ages: The Twentieth Century.* Manuscript, 1942.

ELLIS, A. *How to Live with a Neurotic.* New York: Crown Publishers, 1957. (a) New York: Award Books, 1969.

ELLIS, A. Outcome of employing three techniques of psychotherapy. *J. Clin. Psychol.*, 13, 334-350, 1957. (b)

ELLIS, A. *Sex Without Guilt.* New York: Lyle Stuart, 1958. (a) New York: Lancer Books, 1969.

ELLIS, A. Rational psychotherapy. *J. Gen. Psychol.*, 59, 35-49, 1958. (b)

ELLIS, A. *Reason and Emotion in Psychotherapy.* New York: Lyle Stuart, 1962.

ELLIS, A. What *really* causes therapeutic change? *Voices*, 4(2), 90-97, 1968. (a)

ELLIS, A. *Is Objectivism a Religion?* New York: Lyle Stuart, 1968. (b)

ELLIS, A. Teaching emotional education in the classroom. *School Health Rev.*, 10-13, November. 1969. (a)

ELLIS, A. A cognitive approach to behavior therapy. *Int. J. Psychiat.*, 8, 896-900, 1969. (b)

ELLIS, A. A weekend of rational encounter. In A. Burton (Ed.), *Encounter: The Theory and Practice of Encounter Groups.* San Francisco: Jossey-Bass, 1969. (c)

ELLIS, A. The case against religion. *Mensa Bull.*, No. 138, 5-6, September, 1970. (a)

ELLIS, A. The emerging counselor. *Canadian Counselor*, 4(2), 99-105, 1970. (b)

ELLIS, A. *Growth Through Reason.* Palo Alto: Science and Behavior Books, 1971. (a) Hollywood: Wilshire Books, 1974.

ELLIS, A. An experiment in emotional education. *Educational Technology*, 11(7), 61-63, 1971. (b)

ELLIS, A. *Executive Leadership: A Rational Approach.* New York: Citadel Press, 1972. (a)

ELLIS, A. *How to Master Your Fear of Flying.* New York: Curtis Books, 1972. (b)

ELLIS, A. Emotional education in the classroom: The Living School. *J. Clin. Child Psychol.*, 1(3), 19-22, 1972. (c)

ELLIS, A. Helping people get better rather than merely feel better. *Rational Living*, 7(2), 2-9, 1972. (d)

ELLIS, A. Psychotherapy and the value of a human being. In J. W. Davis (Ed.), *Value and Valuation: Essays in Honor of Robert Hartman.* Knoxville: University of Tennessee Press, 1972. Reprinted: New York: Institute of Rational Living, 1972. (e)

ELLIS, A. *The Sensuous Person: Critique and Corrections.* New York: Lyle Stuart, 1972. (f) New York: New American Library, 1974.

ELLIS, A. Psychotherapy without tears. In A. Burton (Ed.), *Twelve Therapists.* San Francisco: Jossey-Bass, 1972. (g)

ELLIS, A. *Humanistic Psychotherapy: The Rational-Emotive Approach.* New York: Julian Press, 1973. (a)

ELLIS, A. Rational-emotive therapy. In R. Corsini (Ed.), *Current Psychotherapies.* Itasca, Illinois: Peacock, 1973. (b)

ELLIS, A. Healthy and unhealthy aggression. Paper presented at the American Psychological Association Convention, Montreal, August 27, 1973. (c)

ELLIS, A. The no cop-out therapy. *Psychol. Tcday,* 7(2), 56-62, 1973. (d)

ELLIS, A. Emotional education at The Living School. In M. M. Ohlsen (Ed.), *Counseling Children in Groups.* New York: Holt, Rinehart and Winston, 1973. (e)

ELLIS, A. Are rational-emotive and cognitive-behavior therapy synonymous? Paper presented at the Annual Meeting of the New York State Psychological Association, New York City, April 14, 1973. (f) *Rational Living,* 8(2), 1973.

ELLIS, A. What does transpersonal psychology have to offer to the art and science of psychotherapy. *Voices,* 8(3), 10-20, 1972. Revised version: *Rational Living,* 8(1), 20-28, 1973. (g)

ELLIS, A. Empirical confirmation of rational-emotive therapy. *Counseling Psychologist,* 1974. In press.

ELLIS, A. & BUDD, K. Bibliography of articles and books on rational-emotive therapy. New York: Institute for Rational Living, 1975.

ELLIS, A. & HARPER, R. A. *A Guide to Rational Living.* Englewood Cliffs, New Jersey: Prentice-Hall, 1961. Hollywood: Wilshire Books, 1972. (a)

ELLIS, A. & HARPER, R. A. *Creative Marriage.* New York: Lyle Stuart, 1961. Under the title: *A Guide to Successful Marriage.* Hollywood: Wilshire Books, 1972. (b)

EPICTETUS. *Enchiridion.* Chicago: Henry Regnery, 1967.

FRANK, J. D. *Persuasion and Healing.* Baltimore: Johns Hopkins University Press, 1961. Rev. ed., 1973.

FRAZER, J. G. *The New Golden Bough.* New York: Criterion Books, 1959.

GOLDFRIED, M. R. & MERBAUM, M. (Eds.), *Behavior Change Through Self-Control.* New York: Holt, Rinehart and Winston, 1973.

GOODMAN, D. & MAULTSBY, M. D., JR. *Emotional Well-Being Through Rational Behavior Training.* Springfield, Illinois: Charles C. Thomas, 1973.

GRIEGER, R. M. Teacher attitudes as a variable in behavior modification. *Rational Living,* 7(2), 14-19, 1972.

GUSTAV, A. "Success is—" Locating composite sanity. *Rational Living,* 3(1), 1-6, 1968.

HARTMAN, B. J. Sixty revealing questions for twenty minutes. *Rational Living,* 3(1), 7-8, 1968.

HARTMAN, R. S. *The Measurement of Value.* Carbondale: Southern Illinois University Press, 1967.

HAUCK, P. A. *Reason in Pastoral Counseling.* Philadelphia: Westminster Press, 1972.

HAUCK, P. A. *Overcoming Depression.* Philadelphia: Westminster Press, 1973. (a)

HAUCK, P. A. *The Rational Management of Children.* Revised ed. New York: Libra Press, 1973. (b)

HEKMAT, H. & VANIAN, D. Behavior modification through covert semantic desensitization. *J. Consult. Clin. Psychol.,* 36, 248-251, 1971.

HERTZBERG, A. *Active Psychotherapy.* New York: Grune & Stratton, 1945.

HOFFER, E. *The True Believer.* New York: Harper, 1951.

HOGDEN, L. T. *Retreat from Reason.* New York: Random House, 1938.

HOXTER, A. L. *Irrational Beliefs and Self-Concept in Two Kinds of Behaviour.* Doctoral dissertation, University of Alberta, 1967.

JAHODA, G. *The Psychology of Superstition.* London: Penguin, 1969.

JELLINEK, R. Mythology as a science. *N. Y. Times,* May 12, 1973, 31.

JONES, R. G. *A Factored Measure of Ellis' Irrational Belief System, with Personality and Maladjustment Correlates.* Ph.D. thesis, Texas Technological College, August 1968.

KALLMANN, F. J. Heredity and eugenics. *Amer. J. Psychiat.,* 116, 577-581, 1960.

KAUFMANN, W. *Without Guilt and Justice.* New York: Peter Wyden, 1973.

KEMP, C. G. Influence of dogmatism on counseling. *Personnel Guid. J.,* 39, 662-665, 1970.

KNAUS, W. *Rational-Emotive Education: A Manual for Elementary School Teachers.* New York: Institute for Rational Living, 1974.

LAZARUS, A. A. *Behavior Therapy and Beyond.* New York: McGraw-Hill, 1971.

LAZARUS, R. S. *Psychological Stress and the Coping Process.* New York: McGraw-Hill, 1966.

LEITENBERG, H., AGRAS, S., EDWARDS, J. A., THOMSON, L. E., & WINCZE, J. P. Practice as a psychotherapeutic variable: An experimental analysis within single cases. *J. Psychiat. Res.,* 7, 215-225, 1970.

LEITENBERG, H., AGRAS, S., BUTZ, R., & WINCZE, J. Relationship between heart rate and behavioral change during the treatment of phobias, *J. Abnorm. Psychol.,* 78, 59-68, 1971.

LEVI-STRAUSS, C. *La Pensée Sauvage.* Paris: Plon, 1962.

LIDZ, T., CORNELISON, M. S. S., TERRY, C., & PLECA, S. Infrafamilial environment of the schizophrenic patient. II. The transmission of irrationality. *Arch. Neurol. & Psychiat.,* 79, 305-316, 1958.

LITVAK, S. B. A comparison of two brief group behavior therapy techniques on the reduction of avoidance behavior. *Psychol. Rec.,* 19, 329-334, 1969. (a)

LITVAK, S. B. Attitude change by stimulus exposure. *Psychol. Rep.,* 25, 391-396, 1969. (b)

MACDONALD, A. P. & GAMES, R. G. Ellis' irrational values. *Rational Living,* 7(2), 25-28, 1972.

MAES, W. R. & HEIMANN, R. A. *The Comparison of Three Approaches to the Reduction of Test Anxiety in High School Students.* Washington: Office of Education, U.S. Department of Health, Education and Welfare, 1970.

MAHLER, M. S. *On Human Symbiosis and the Vicissitudes of Individuation.* New York: International Universities Press, 1968.

MARCIA, J. E., RUBIN, B. M., & EFRAN, J. S. Systematic desensitization: Expectancy change or counterconditioning? *J. Abnorm. Psychol.,* 74, 382-387, 1969.

MARCUS AURELIUS. *Meditations.* Chicago: Gateway, 1967.

MARKS, I. M. Recent advances in the treatment of phobic obsessive-compulsive and sexual disorders. Paper presented at 2nd Annual Conference on Behavior Modification, Los Angeles, Oct. 9, 1971.

MASLOW, A. H. *Motivation and Personality*. New York: Harper, 1954.

MAULTSBY, M. C., JR. The pamphlet as a therapeutic aid. *Rational Living*, 3(2), 31-35, 1968.

MAULTSBY, M. C., JR. Systematic written homework in psychotherapy. *Psychotherapy*, 8(3), 195-198, 1971. (a)

MAULTSBY, M. C., JR. Rational-emotive imagery. *Rational Living*, 6(1), 24-27, 1971. (b)

McGRORY, J. E. Teaching introspection in the classroom. *Rational Living*, 2(2), 23-24, 1967.

MEEHL, P. Schizotaxia, schizotype, and schizophrenia. *Amer. Psychologist*, 17, 827-838, 1962.

MEICHENBAUM, D. H. *Cognitive Factors in Behavior Modification: Modifying What Clients Say to Themselves*. Waterloo: University of Waterloo, 1971.

MEICHENBAUM, D. H. & GOODMAN, J. Training impulsive children to talk to themselves: A means of developing self-control. *J. Abnorm. Psychol.*, 77, 115-126, 1969.

MISCHEL, W. Toward a cognitive social learning reconceptualization of personality. *Psychol. Rev.*, 80, 252-285, 1973.

MITCHELL, K. R. & MITCHELL, D. M. Behavior therapy in the treatment of migraine. *J. Psychosom. Res.*, 15, 137-157, 1971.

NISBETT, R. E. & SCHACTER, S. Cognitive manipulation of pain. *J. Exp. Soc. Psychol.*, 2, 227-236, 1966.

O'CONNELL, W. E. & HANSON, P. G. Patient's cognitive changes in human relations training. *J. Indl. Psychol.*, 26, 57-63, 1970.

OVERALL, J. E. & GORHAM, D. Basic dimensions of change in the symptomatology of chronic schizophrenics. *J. Abnorm. Soc. Psychol.*, 63, 597-602, 1961.

PARRINO, J. Effect of pretherapy information on learning in psychotherapy. *J. Abnorm. Psychol.*, 77, 17-24, 1971.

PARSONS, A. *Belief, Magic and Anomie*. New York: Free Press, 1969.

PAYNE, R. W. & HIRST, H. L. Overinclusive thinking in a depressive and a control group. *J. Consult. Psychol.*, 21, 186-188, 1957.

PERLMAN, G. Change in self and ideal self-concept congruence of beginning psychotherapists. *J. Clin. Psychol.*, 28, 404-408, 1972.

PITKIN, W. B. *A Short Introduction to the History of Human Stupidity*. New York: Simon and Schuster, 1932.

PLATT, J. J. & SPIVACK, G. Problem-solving thinking of psychiatric patients. *J. Consult. Clin. Psychol.*, 39, 148-151, 1972.

RIMLAND, B. *Infantile Autism*. New York: Appleton-Century-Crofts, 1964.

RIMM, D. C. & MADEIROS, D. C. The role of muscle relaxation in participant modeling. *Behavior Res. & Ther.*, 8, 127-132, 1970.

RITTER, B. The group desensitization of children's snake phobias using vicarious and contact desensitization procedures. *Behavior Res. & Ther.*, 6, 1-6, 1968.

ROGERS, C. R. *On Becoming a Person*. Boston: Houghton-Mifflin, 1961.

ROSENTHAL, D. *Genetic Theory and Abnormal Behavior*. New York: McGraw-Hill, 1970.

ROSENTHAL, D. & KETY, S. S. (Eds.). *The Transmission of Schizophrenia*. Elmsford, New York: Pergamon Press, 1968.

RUTNER, I. & BUGLE, C. An experimental procedure for the modification of psychotic behavior. *J. Consult. Clin. Psychol.*, 33, 651-653, 1969.

SCHACTER, S. & SINGER. J. E. Cognitive, social and physiologocal determinants of emotional state. *Psychol. Rev.*, 69, 379-399, 1962.

SHARMA, K. L. *A Rational Group Therapy Approach to Counseling Anxious Underachievers.* Thesis, University of Alberta, 1970.

SHUMAKER, W. *Literature and the Irrational.* New York: Washington Square Press, 1966.

SLATER, E. & COWIE, V. *Psychiatry and Genetics.* London: Oxford University Press, 1971.

SUZUKI, D. T. *Zen Buddhism.* New York: Doubleday Anchor Books, 1956.

SYDEL, A. *A Study to Determine the Effects of Emotional Education on Fifth Grade Children.* M.A. Thesis, Queens College, New York City, 1972.

TABORI, P. *The Natural Science of Stupidity.* Philadelphia: Chilton, 1959.

TABORI, P. *The Art of Folly.* Philadelphia: Chilton, 1961.

TILLICH, P. *The Courage to Be.* New Haven: Yale University Press, 1953.

TOBIE, W. C. Self-help in psychotherapy. *ART in Daily Living*, 2(6), 12-13, 1972.

TREXLER, L. D. & KARST, T. O. Rational-emotive therapy, placebo, and no-treatment effects on public speaking anxiety. *J. Abnorm. Psychol.*, 79, 60-67, 1972.

VALINS, S. & RAY, A. A. Effect of cognitive desensitization on avoidance behavior. *J. Pers. & Soc. Psychol.*, 7, 345-350, 1967.

VELTEN, E. C. A laboratory task for induction of mood states. *Behavior Res. & Ther.*, 6, 473-482, 1968.

WATTS, A. W. *The Way to Zen.* New York: New American Library, 1959.

WILLNER, A. E. & STRUVE, F. A. An analogy test that predicts EEG abnormality. *Arch. Gen. Psychiat.*, 23, 993-999, 1970.

WINE, J. Test anxiety and direction of attention. *Psychol. Bull.*, 76, 92-104, 1971.

WOLFE, J. L. Emotional education in the classroom: the living school. *Rational Living*, 4(2), 23-25, 1970.

B. F. Skinner

11

Behavior Modification Theory: B. F. Skinner and Others

by JOHN N. MARQUIS*

It is formally difficult to place the views of the behavior therapist next to those of other schools in a book about personality because most of us feel that personality theory has failed us and that there are more fruitful approaches to understanding and helping people.

It is interesting to speculate about peoples' personalities and study individual differences, but the ultimate economic and practical justification of a theory is that it provides a basis for action. Personality theory is valuable if it enables us to predict the behavior of real, individual people in specific situations. Only then does it cease to be a toy.

* I want to acknowledge with thanks the kind assistance of Nathan Brody, Brian Danaher, Arnold Lazarus, Patricia Marquis, and John Silk in the preparation of this chapter.

Validity

Except for ability measures, which closely approach behavioral samples, assessment variables have seldom enabled us to predict the score of an individual on any other measure at a practically useful level. Correlation coefficients in the .30's, the usual level of personality measures not obtained from the same data source, are of scientific interest, but account for less than 16% of the variance in the criterion measure, which is obtained by squaring the correlation coefficient.

Therefore it is my position that until better personality theories are developed all that they can do is lead the therapist away from the respectful consideration of the data which his client presents to him.

Mischel (personal communication) has been studying the effects of organizing information describing individuals in terms of personality traits vs. concrete behavior He has found that when the information is used to infer personality traits, the subject stereotypes the individual and then imputes characteristics to him which are at variance with the information he has been given. Interestingly, if the subject is asked to remember the information, he construes it behaviorally but if he is asked to predict to a new situation, he uses it to infer personality traits. Since ordinarily the best personality traits can be used to predict less than 16% of the variance in some criterion behavior this seems unfortunate.

Reliability

Lewinsohn et al. (1963) had psychologists describe patients using data from their hospital charts and psychological test results. Their descriptions were divided into traits that were rather close to the data (for example, saying that a person is likely to become angry when threatened), or more genotypical (as stating that he has unconscious hostility towards his mother). Sines (1966) analyzed the data of Lewinsohn et al. and found that the agreement between clinicians was .17 for the genotypical traits and .51 for the ones which were more closely related to the data. In this case if a clinician used a genotypical trait that was perfectly correlated with a behavior to be predicted he could predict only 3% ($.17^2$) of the variance because the trait is so unreliable.

Method Variance

In personality research it has long been known that the correlations tend to be higher between different variables measured in the same way or rated by the same person than between the same variables measured in different ways or rated by different persons. Thus, in the case of ratings of children's aggressive behavior by their parents, their teachers, and their classmates, it will be found that teachers' ratings of various aggressive behaviors will correlate more highly with each other than the rating of a particular behavior by the teachers will correlate with the rating of that behavior by classmates. This makes it possible to get results that look very good if measures are from the same source of data. If the experimenter asks adolescents about the methods their parents used to rear them and correlates this information with their ratings of their own current behavior he will likely get highly significant results. If he asks the parents how they raised the adolescents and correlates these measures with the adolescents' self reports, the results are never good enough for valid individual prediction.

One reason is that personality ratings tap the stereotypes of the raters about what variables they think are correlated within the subject. It has been shown that personality factors can be extracted which are very much like those found in usual personality research when one uses, instead of subjects, hypothetical persons, such as a college football player, an army general, a used car salesman, a cocktail waitress, etc. Indeed I suspect it would be possible to ask the residents of some communes to rate the personality characteristics of their fellows and extract personality factors which upon examination would prove to be the signs of the zodiac. In any event the data on personality theory can best be summarized by saying that any prediction from a personality variable to the behavior of an individual stands an extremely good chance of being what my delinquent clients would refer to as a "bum beef."

THE BEHAVIOR THERAPIST'S VIEW OF MAN

Behaviorism is a scientific view, not an ethical system. Its basic position includes the philosophical belief that behavior is orderly and that honest, carefully controlled experiments will reveal the laws that control behavior. The position that it is most fruitful to stick close to the data and keep theoretical inference at a minimum is probably a point of philosophical faith with most behaviorists, but has a great deal of empirical evidence to back it up. If these basic principles are satisfied, few modern behavior therapists would quibble about the terms that are used. Davison and Taffel express it very well. "We would define the field simply as applied experimental psychology, with the usual concern for careful measurement, operationalization of terms and dispassionate examination of ideas which can be experimentally tested" (Davison and Taffel 1972, p. 2).

Thus, behavior therapy is like engineering in applying any relevant scientific information to finding technical solutions to human problems. Behavioral science takes its place next to other practical scientific knowledge and is applied to human problems as science is applied in medicine or engineering.

When one has at his disposal the effective means of changing behavior, individual differences can become minor technical problems. If a client has less experience in an area or is less intelligent than another person, it may take him longer to learn something. However, operationally this becomes the simple matter of giving more trials in order to produce the same results. While behavior therapists and behavioral educators are usually interested in measuring the base line level of behaviors they are about to change, it is often possible to change behaviors in less time than it takes to diagnose them.

For example, the problem of dyslexia is doubtless effected by genetic and constitutional factors. In the usual classroom approximately 10% of children are unable to read at the end of the first grade. Heroic measures advocated by the two main schools of thought offering therapeutic remediation derived from theories have no sound evidence that their methods provide any better results than a little extra attention by the teacher. In contrast, the best behaviorally based programmed instruction methods for teaching children to read turn out approximately 1% of children who are unable to read at the end of the first grade.

When therapeutic techniques are effective in changing the behavior of a client, as he becomes more relaxed and competent, his remaining anxieties and behavioral deficits stand out with increasing clarity and uniqueness and can then be dealt with one at a time. This is similar to mowing a lawn where it is easy to see the places which have been missed and mow them, trimming up around the edges. Thus, in each individual case, the behavior therapist validates and refines his techniques.

Behaviorists Study Basic Processes of Learning

Psychological experiments are designed in such a way as to emphasize the sources of variation in which the experimenter is interested. If you tell a batter "strike two," his behavior can usually be predicted from the situation. If he is told "strike three," there is much more room for individual variation in his behavior. Brody (1972, p. 23) gives a neat illustration of these two approaches. The personnel psychologist, in order to do an efficient job of employee selection and placement, calls upon the traditions and methods of the study of individual differences. He measures aptitudes and interests and compiles data about past education and job performance in order to maximize his predictions of which prospect or employee will do best in which job. Those characteristics which people have in common are seen as error variance. In contrast, the human engineer tries to design a man-machine system in which every one will function with maximal efficiency. To him individual differences are seen as a nuisance and a source of error in performing his job.

The approach of the behaviorist is generally more like that of the human engineer. Most behaviorists feel that people's behavior in specific situations is as variable as the experiences to which they have been exposed. Therefore it is not as fruitful to study *what* pople have learned to make general statements about it, as it is to study *how* people learn and what general control situations have over people's behavior. The process of learning stays still across content, whereas what people learn depends on their individual and cultural learning histories.

A Third Approach

In addition to the approach of the experimental psychologist as exemplified above by the human engineer and the assessment approach exemplified by the personnel psychologist there is a third major approach to studying the nature of man. It consists of clinical botanizing and forms the basis for most of the theories set forth in other chapters of this book. It grows primarily from the work of psychiatrists who have gotten to know a few patients well through their psychotherapeutic contacts with them and try to generalize and summarize their experiences with their patients.

The Psychoanalyst Has a Limited Sample

Let us take the case of a hypothetical psychoanalyst writing about his personal experience with patients at the height of his career at the age of fifty. Let us assume that he completed his own training at age 30 and has been practicing psychoanalysis for 20 years, that he spends 20 hours a week doing psychoanalysis and that, being a famous professor, half of his analysands are professional people in training without severe psychiatric problems. This leaves him 10 hours a week to spend with real patients. In order to perform a complete analysis he spends 5 hours a week for two years so he can completely analyze one real client a year or 20 between the time he is 30 and the time he is 50. Thus, the broad generalizations that he makes about particular problems or diagnostic categories are likely to be based on the complete analysis of a single patient in many cases, even though they represent the results of many years of experience. The implicit assumption is that all persons with the same diagnosis or problem are the same. This limited number of patients probably accounts for the unusual generalizations and frequent lack of agreement among psychoanalysts.

In contrast, the behavior therapist practicing 20 hours a week, seeing all real clients for an average of 25 hours each, sees 40 patients a year with $\frac{3}{4}$ rather than $\frac{1}{2}$ of them showing largely successful conclusions. This provides him with a much broader, though admittedly not deeper, sample. The result is to generate a profound respect for the variety of ways in which individuals can develop similar problems and the folly of generalizing from one behavior or personality characteristic to another. (A few such follies of mine will be found elsewhere in this chapter.) We listen respectfully to our clients rather than make theoretical assumptions which generate certain beliefs about the client. Such assumptions, if not confirmed by his verbal reports, lead the therapist with a personality theory to believe that the client is defending, unconsciously distorting, or lacking insight into himself.

Rather, we search for the stimulus conditions which are supporting the clients' maladaptive behaviors, ask him what he finds reinforcing, and explore his unique stimuli for anxiety and behavioral deficits. Nevertheless, while the individual is completely free to vary in what he has learned and been conditioned to do, the hard data of the principles of learning and conditioning remain constant in their applicability to all clients.

Behavior therapy, although drawing heavily on learning principles, is not limited to the application of learning theory to human problems, but could include the use of information from other branches of psychology, from physiology, pharmacology, or sociology. For example, I frequently counsel my clients to drink less coffee when excessive consumption of that stimulant is making them anxious. I try to get them started on exercise programs because regular exercise will decrease their anxieties, improve their social stimulus value, and enhance self-reinforcement. I am also interested in the fact that it improves their health. Sociological data are useful because when a person moves from one society to another his origins can provide clues to look for behavioral deficits in his learning and conditioning vis-à-vis his new environment.

Mischel (1968) goes over a great deal of evidence that most people behave quite differently in different situations and that their behavior is more predictable from the stimulus situation in which they find themselves than from their personality characteristics.

PLAN OF THE CHAPTER

In this chapter I shall attempt to give a brief history of the development of the behavioral point of view with some attention to other historical traditions for the purpose of contrast. I shall try to outline some of the basic concepts of learning theory, operational science, and the methods of behavior therapy with some attention to how these relate to a behavioral view of man. Both Mischel (1968) and Brody (1972) have given brilliant and capable reviews of the literature of personality from a behavioral point of view and I shall make no attempt to be complete.

HISTORICAL BACKGROUND OF BEHAVIOR THERAPY

Watson

In the second decade of this century John B. Watson (1925) gave birth to Behaviorism as the culmination of psychology's struggle to free itself from its roots in religious philosophy. His approach was objective and parsimonious, defining variables in terms of rigorous laboratory operations and theorizing close to the data. He redefined the subject matter of psychology in peripheral terms and provided a model of experimental objectivity that dominated American psychology during the first half of the century.

A Classical Example of Counter-Conditioning

A student of Watson's, Mary Cover Jones performed an experiment in fear reduction with a little boy who had developed a severe phobia of small, furry animals which was generalized to similar things such as cotton, furry objects, feathers, and wool. He was placed at a table down a long hall from a large caged rabbit. Each day the rabbit was brought closer while he ate his lunch until eventually he could eat while he held the rabbit in his lap and played with it. After treatment, the counterconditioning of his fears was found to have generalized to all of the other objects involved. In this paper (Jones 1924), a number of other ways of treating anxieties by behavioral means were discussed, but this seminal work slumbered on for 25 years, the sleeping beauty of behavior therapy.

Pavlov

Ivan P. Pavlov (1849 to 1936) was professor of physiology at the Military Academy of St. Petersburg during the period of his greatest work around the turn of the century and continuing until his retirement in 1924. He received the Nobel Prize for his pioneering work on digestive secretions, in the course of which he produced a method of collecting saliva externally. He noticed that the dogs began to salivate externally in the anticipation of food and dropped his work on digestion in order to pursue the study of this phenomenon. His theory leaves something to be desired, but his work was done so carefully that his model of conditioning survives as a living classic and his data are as good as ever.

The Classical Conditioning Model

In the naïve animal an unconditioned stimulus (food) is capable of arousing the unconditioned response or UCR (salivation). Conditioning takes place by presenting a neutral stimulus to the dog such as a sound or light (known as the conditioned stimulus or CS) prior to or concurrent with the introduction of the UCS. Through repetition the CS takes on the power to evoke some elements of the UCR which then constitute the conditioned response or CR. This process has later been referred to as stimulus substitution or SS contiguity learning, and it has been demonstrated that it can take place in the absence of the reward. The CS will share its ability to arouse the CR with similar stimuli through a process of primary stimulus generalization.

Eysenck

Hans Jurgen Eysenck is the only person who is identified with behavior therapy who has developed an elaborate theory of personality. The obvious reason for this is that he was a personality theorist before there was any such thing as a school of behavior therapy. He developed a theory of genetically influenced personality dimensions (very capably reviewed by Brody [1972]) which would be on a par with intelligence. To date, like other personality theories, it has not proved its worth in the clinics and is not really germane to Eysenck's support of behavior therapy.

Brody (1972) reviews the literature on the inheritance of individual differences and concludes that the contribution of heredity is much greater than most social learning theorists imply. He points out that there is good evidence that personality variables of identical twins are more similar if they are reared apart than if they are reared together. It is possible that future research with more fortunate choice among the infinite number of ways to cut the nomethetic pie and more careful measurement will identify other important genetically based dimensions of individual difference similar to intelligence. If so, scientifically honest behaviorists would welcome the information. Certainly there would be nothing in such a theory to conflict with the work of Skinner since he has assiduously avoided dealing with physiology and the genetics of behavior in developing his psychology.

B. F. Skinner

B. F. Skinner was born in Susquehanna, Pennsylvania, the son of a small town lawyer. As a member of a warm, stable, and high-status family he was a confident and very active child. He was constantly inventing and building toys and vehicles and contraptions. His success in these ventures reinforced a pattern of finding better ways of doing things and an interest in mechanical devices which later enhanced his contributions to behavioral science.

As an undergraduate at Hamilton College he majored in English literature and then attempted a career as a creative writer. He was unable to get his literary career off the ground and entered graduate school at Harvard, majoring in psychology. A very independent thinker, he was probably influenced more by his readings in the psychology of science and the behaviorist literature than he was by any of his professors.

Watson had taken the bold step of throwing out consciousness from psychology but had to some extent replaced it by using physiological constructs to explain his behavioral data. Skinner went one step further in the direction of parsimony. His doctoral dissertation in 1931 defended the thesis that the only thing necessary to account for behavior was the correlation between stimulus and response. In this position he followed Percy Bridgeman, a Harvard physicist, who formulated the position of operationalism. In reality, concepts in science are defined by the laboratory operations which measure them, and the addition of surplus meaning only leads to the creation of pseudo-problems and the loss of predictive power. It should be made clear that Skinner did not advocate the abandonment of physiological investigation but simply meant to say that behavioral data could stand on its own legitimately and fruitfully without recourse to explanatory constructs. This ushered in what has been called the era of the empty organism. Having already lost its soul and its mind, psychology now lost its body. Nevertheless, the science that developed from this position has proved to be extremely fruitful and, in spite of its narrow elegance, Skinner has never been afraid to discuss its implications for broad social phenomena.

The development of Skinner's approach. After finishing his Ph.D., Skinner worked for five years in the laboratory at Harvard. *A Case History in Scientific Method* (Skinner 1956) gives a fascinating account of how his theory and technology developed. He looked for lawfulness in the behavior of the intact organism, taking his clue from Pavlov, "Control your conditions and you will see order."

Skinner describes how his freedom in the laboratory allowed him to drop everything and study an interesting new phenomenon when he came upon one. He was clever in designing and building contraptions to make his work easy and took advantage of the fact that his gadgets broke down to make important discoveries. In this way he developed the "Skinner box," a basic tool of much of his research. The animal presses a bar which feeds information into automatic programming equipment that delivers food pellets according to a schedule, and the rate of bar pressing is automatically recorded.

Skinner is against using large groups of subjects in order to obtain statistical significance with weak relationships between variables. If experimental conditions are carefully controlled, results are orderly and data reflect the fine texture of the behavior. Usually working with a single organism he was able to get learning curves similar in fine detail for the pigeon, the rat, and the monkey under each different schedule of reinforcement.

During World War II Skinner (Skinner 1960) trained pigeons to guide drone planes to their targets with unerring accuracy. His practical program was turned down irrationally by a group of congressional and military leaders and he left in utter frustration to spend the summer writing a utopian novel, *Walden Two* (Skinner 1948), which proposed the design for a better society.

Skinner's Basic Concepts. Skinner divides behavior into *operant* and *respondent* responses. *Respondents* are those reflexes in which the stimulus inexorably drives the response. They are thought of as involuntary and under the control of classical or Pavlovian conditioning. *Operant* behavior is spontaneously emitted at a rate determined by genetics and past conditioning. The rate can be increased or decreased by reinforcing consequences as set forth in Table 1.

TABLE 1

	ADDITION	SUBTRACTION
Positive reinforcer (Positive valence)	Positive reinforcement	Response cost
Negative reinforcer (Negative valence)	Negative	Punishment reinforcement

If an operant response is cued by a stimulus it becomes a *discriminated operant*. The stimulus sets the occasion for the response, but does not drive it. If you are standing on the corner talking to a friend and the light turns green you do not have to walk across the street. Skinner has always maintained that punishment is a very dangerous and ineffective means of controlling behavior and therefore much of his work has been devoted to positive reinforcement.

Shaping. Bar pressing in rats and disc pecking in pigeons usually has an operant level of zero. Therefore Skinner *shapes* the desired response by rewarding the animal for any response that leads in the right direction. This saves a great deal of frustration for the experimenter, teacher, or therapist and enables him to deal with the subject, student, or client in a more loving way.

Schedules of Reinforcement. Several different schedules of reinforcement have been studied. Intermittent reinforcement leads to a higher rate of response and a greater resistance to extinction than 100% reinforcement. A fixed interval schedule, where the animal is reinforced after the passage of a certain amount of time, gives a very low rate of response. This is like an hourly wage. In the fixed ratio schedule the animal is reinforced after every so many responses, which resembles piece work and gives a much higher rate of responding. A variable interval, where the animal is reinforced on the average every so many minutes, gives an intermediate rate of response and greater resistance to extinction. A variable ratio, which would correspond to the schedule of a salesman or a prospector gives the highest rate of all, and the most resistance to extinction.

The laws and learning curves describing the behavior of animals in response to various schedules of reinforcement are set forth in Skinner's *The Behavior of Organisms,* first published in 1938 (Skinner 1961). The findings are not theoretical or inferential but constitute the actual data that the subject draws for the experimenter. Therefore Skinner need have no concern for his findings holding up. They are Humian correlations and nothing intervenes between the stimulus and the response to cause the behavior.

APPLICATIONS OF OPERANT CONDITIONING

As Skinner has so eloquently pointed out in his latest book, *Beyond Freedom and Dignity* (1971), people cling tenaciously to their sacred cows of sin and virtue and must laud and blame each other even though as Salter (1949) puts it, "People do not do what they ought to do, they do what they have learned to do." Therefore the effective control of behavior through the application of learning principles is seen as a moral outrage. As a result of this, most of the early applications of operant conditioning have involved modifying the behavior of mental defectives and psychotics, or at best, children. The whole area of programmed learning, of course, grows out of the work of Skinner and his students, and an interesting exception to my last statement is the increasing use of programmed texts to alter the behavior of normal adults (parents and teachers) by teaching them to use operant procedures in training children. This promises a more radical solution to social and individual psychological problems by prevention and early solution. Not only can the children be taught adaptive behaviors, but learning problems in school have a great effect on the social adaptation of children and, as Skinner suggests, more benign pedagogical methods may some day lead to the day when a school building can be left unattended without having the windows broken out.

The First Token Economy

One fall day in Cambridge an undergraduate student from the previous year appeared in Skinner's office (Skinner, personal communication). He had worked as a counselor at a camp the previous summer and had been apprehensive about his first experience in handling children. He decided to put into practice the principles that he had learned in Skinner's class and had gone to the dime store and bought $10 worth of things that boys like such as toys, tricks, jack knives, comic books, etc. The first day at camp he showed them to his campers, who asked "How do you get them?" "You buy them with this," he answered, showing them a handful of play money he had run off on a ditto machine. "How do we get that?" they asked, and he said "Wait and see." The following morning he took a handful of the money and passed it out to the campers who were making their beds, sweeping the floor, and dressing themselves neatly. In short order he had the best behaved group of campers that any of the old time staff members had ever seen, and the children loved it.

Ogden Lindsley

Shortly after this and about the same time his colleagues at Harvard were developing the first teaching machine, Lindsley (1956) performed the first systematic experiments using operant conditioning procedures with psychiatric patients. He designed a set-up completely analogous to a Skinner box and studied the effects of various SD's, reinforcement schedules, and reinforcers which included not only cigarettes and candy, but also nude pictures, and the delivery of milk to a hungry kitten. It was a scientific experiment rather than an attempt at therapy but paved the way for later work with psychotic patients. As an example of a Skinnerian personality theory, Lindsley describes one patient who made incessant manneristic movements with one hand. By arranging the apparatus so that the patient had to use his manneristic hand to pull the lever he said he was "able to make the psychosis go over into the other hand."

Today Lindsley is one of the country's top behavioral engineers. An outstanding folk singer and captivating speaker, he has designed a system which allows for the pyramiding of operant technology from a behavioral engineer through school psychologists to counselors and from there to teachers. It uses a simple technology for modifying both classroom behaviors and learning problems. Unbelievably efficient methods of data handling allow the teachers to track the behavior of the children with ultimate economy. The results of therapeutic interventions are fed into a computer which feeds back information on the most successful intervention for any given problem (Lindsley 1971).

Teodoro Ayllon

Ayllon and Michael (1959) describe the first therapeutic work applying operant techniques to practical therapeutic problems in a mental hospital. Using nurses as the actual behavior modifiers, they extinguished towel hoarding behavior of a schizophrenic lady by giving her all the towels she requested until her room was full of towels up to the ceiling and she finally quit taking them. Another woman, who entered the nursing station 16 times a day, had this behavior extinguished by having the nurses pay no attention to her, since their scolding and leading her away was reinforcing. (A number of studies have shown that staff members, parents, and teachers are often reinforcing the behavior of their charges inadvertently as in the case of self-destructive behaviors in mental defectives. As Ken Swift says, the problem is not the abnormal behavior of the patients, it is the normal behavior of the staff.) Another schizophrenic lady who would not put her own food and utensils on her plate in the chow line was conditioned to do so by the use of shaping procedures using candy as a positive reinforcer.

Encouraged by these results, Ayllon went to Anna State Hospital in Illinois where he collaborated with Nathan Azrin (Ayllon and Azrin 1968) to establish the first professional token economy. Patients are rewarded with tokens for desirable behaviors and the tokens can then be spent for reinforcers, but what is reinforcing to a chronic psychotic on the back ward of a mental hospital? Dynamic therapists have known that the big problem in dealing with such persons is that they are unmotivated. Premack (1965) provides the answer. Any response that has a higher probability of occurrence will reinforce a preceding one that occurs less frequently. Therefore, all that was necessary was to watch what the patient did frequently and charge them tokens for it. By this principle one of the most powerful reinforcers turned out to be doing nothing. Patients proved to be willing to work to buy the privilege of sitting on the ward, although of course, many more predictable things were used as reinforcers. The results in this and later token economies have been most impressive.

An Early Experiment with Children

A fascinating study by Wahler et al. (1965) provides a laboratory model for the training of parents to modify the deviant behavior of their children. Subjects were preschool children who exhibited a variety of severe deviant behaviors. These were carefully defined in an interview with the mother. Then she was placed in a play room and asked to play with her child as she did at home. The experimenters observed the child through a one-way mirror and tallied the frequency of the deviant behavior and also of an incompatible constructive behavior which they had agreed upon. After reaching acceptable levels of reliability and establishing a base line rate for the two behaviors, they attached a red light to the switch which recorded the deviant behavior and a green light to the switch which recorded the constructive behavior. The mother was then told to play with the child when the green light was on and to read a magazine and pretend to be deaf, making no response to the child, when the red light was on. The originally frequent deviant behavior decreased almost to zero within a half hour and the rare prosocial behavior rose to a high level of frequency. Then the wires on the two lights were switched and the experiment was repeated. The frequency of the constructive behavior plummeted and the antisocial behavior rose to its previous level. Thus in less than half an hour they were able to demonstrate to the mother the means of eliminating the child's deviant behavior and building any constructive behaviors she wanted.

I cannot help but contrast this with the situation in many psychoanalytically oriented child guidance clinics. There, the staff may spend as much as 20 hours in doing a diagnostic workup on the child, whereupon he is placed on a waiting list which may be several months long, before he is called in for psychoanalytic play therapy. The therapy usually continues for several months and often for years with an unimpressive percept of good therapeutic outcomes.

SELF-MANAGEMENT TECHNIQUES

When Skinnerians began to apply the results of their animal experiments to humans, a concern arose about the permanence of results. It is easy to see how desensitization brings about permanent improvement, and since relaxation is self-reinforcing, most people tend to continue practicing it (I have an aunt whom Dr. Jacobson taught to relax before World War I who is still practicing her skills). When behavior rehearsal teaches appropriate social behaviors that are reinforced in the environment, this also leads to permanent change, but what of the classroom where external reinforcement improves the behavior of the student? To be sure, academic skills are learned which are reinforced and persist but if the teacher stops reinforcing desirable classroom behaviors and reverts to attending to disruptive behaviors things rapidly revert to their previous state of affairs. Ferster (1958) pointed out that an individual can control his own behavior by using the same methods that he would use to control the behavior of someone else. He was thinking primarily of programming schedules of external reinforcement of a fairly tangible sort but Lloyd Homme discusses the use of coverants, "the operants of the mind," in his classic paper (Homme 1965). Just as praise and criticism from others is effective in changing and maintaining behavior, so a person can reward and punish himself by his praise or criticism. Thus, if it is possible to build in techniques of self-reinforcement, behavior can be permanently changed.

The technology of self-management has proved to be very useful in dealing with elimination of undesirable habits such as smoking and excessive eating or drinking. It is also a very efficient means of improving work habits and study habits. Fox (1966) took six consecutive students coming to the counseling center with neurotic complaints and taught them to improve their study habits using self-management techniques. The following semester the worst one had improved one complete grade point while the best one had gone from a straight D to a straight B average. One of them studied Saturday mornings, but the rest kept weekends free for reinforcers. None of them studied in the evenings. At the end of the experiment none of them had neurotic complaints although no attention was given to the personality problems.

Unhappy and perfectionistic people often show a severe deficit in self-reinforcement, and tend to have severe work problems. It is essential that people praise themselves for real improvement in their behavior or their self-praise lacks credibility. The crucial thing is to learn to self-reinforce for improvement rather than perfection and as the process gathers steam, the work problems straighten out. A two percent improvement every week adds up to 100% in a year. An excellent account of developments in this rapidly growing and very promising field is to be found in Thoresen and Mahoney (in press).

Bandura's Social Learning Theory

Bandura and Walters' *Social Learning and Personality Development* (1963) is firmly based on the data from their creative and rigorous laboratory experiments with children. Their theory of personality development is anti-psychoanalytic and devotes much attention to the social learning of stylistic habits through modeling. It is a behavioral learning theory, accepting and integrating much of Skinnerian technology. However, they espouse the concept of internal verbal and symbolic behaviors as important determinants of overt behavior. These phenomena can be studied by controlling internal events by instruction and by asking the subject about internal behaviors.

Bandura and his associates have delivered in the area of modeling and imitation what Miller and Dollard (1941) only promised to do. Most of their experiments involve having the subjects observe a model performing some act, and then measure the effects of this upon the behavior of the observers. They have studied a wide variety of learning phenomena in this context, studying vicarious reinforcement, vicarious extinction, etc. For example, they have demonstrated that children are more likely to copy the behaviors of models who are reinforced or who control reinforcers.

They are interested in the disinhibiting effects of models on sexual and aggressive behavior and have shown that viewing a film of an aggressive model can enhance the aggressive behavior of children for months after. In spite of his personal aversion to censorship, Bandura is prominent among social scientists concerned about the effects of television on the aggressive behavior of children.

In other interesting studies children have been taught different standards of self-reinforcement and delay of gratification in return for greater ultimate rewards, both by means of modeling techniques.

Bandura's *Principles of Behavior Modification* (1969) is an outstanding integration of all areas of behavior therapy and behavior modifications which has earned for him the current presidency of the American Psychological Association.

M. B. Shapiro

In his position as head of clinical teaching at the Institute of Psychiatry of London, Shapiro developed through the 1950's a relatively independent school of behavior therapy. This fact is often overlooked because Eysenck was his department head and is often given credit for his highly original and important contribution by ignorant Americans, and even ignorant South Africans. Yates (1970) describes his contribution in detail. Briefly, he did laboratory-type experiments on individual patients which were designed to change their maladaptive behaviors. Most involved great rigor in measuring and modifying a single, well-defined behavior. He and several of his students have made major contributions to behavior therapy.

Joseph Wolpe

Coming from a psychoanalytic tradition, Wolpe worked with Leo Reyna, an American psychologist in South Africa, reading widely and conducting animal experiments to find better ways of ameliorating neurotic problems. The results are set forth in his *Psychotherapy by Reciprocal Inhibition* (1958). He kept to the psychoanalytic view that anxiety and the inhibition of sexual and aggressive behavior were central in most neurotic problems, a position which was compatible with the Hullian view that drive is basic to motivation and drive reduction to learning, which Reyna subscribed to. Wolpe saw neurotic behavior as the result of learning and conditioning but took great pains to spell out the biological basis of these phenomena.

There were many instances in the first half of the century of the application of learning and conditioning techniques to psychiatric problems, which were isolated and have been left out for the sake of brevity. Because their methods were derived from animal experiments they dealt simply and specifically with monosymptomatic problems. Wolpe's unique contribution was in recognizing the client as a human being capable of communicating verbally and conjuring up verbal and visual images which could be used as stimuli in modifying his behavior. He also brought together or invented a wide variety of techniques so that for the first time a behaviorist could deal with most of the presenting problems of a suffering human being who came to his office.

Systematic Desensitization

The experimental model for systematic desensitization is set forth in an early experiment. Wolpe administered a high level of electric shock to cats and found that when they were introduced into the same experimental room and cage where they had been shocked they showed severe fear behavior. He then established a hierarchy of rooms of increasing similarity to the one in which the animal had been shocked. Using the method of Jones

(1924), he gradually fed the animals in one room after another and eventually found that they could stay in the cage in which they had been shocked in the room in which they had shocked, without exhibiting fear behaviors.

His search for a powerful physiological response which was incompatible with anxiety and could be substituted for feeding in the above experiment lead him to the work of Jacobson (1938) who has been teaching people to relax since before World War I.

Systematic desensitization begins with a careful behavioral analysis of the stimuli which elicit anxiety responses in a particular unitary area, such as criticism, rejection, and disapproval. A list of situations is then drawn up usually consisting of 10 to 20 items. These are designed to constitute a comprehensive sample of the situations which bother the client and are arranged in order from the worst situation that the person can imagine down through ones which arouse a moderate amount of anxiety to one which bothers the client not at all. Items might include things the client has experienced and felt anxious about, things that he is afraid might happen, and in particular things that he would like to do but is afraid to. Details are specified so that the client is not searching for them while he pictures the items and so that anxiety level of each item can be carefully specified.

By this time the client has been taught to relax using a modification of Jacobson's method and relaxes deeply. In this state most clients can picture things with almost hallucinatory clarity. He is then asked to picture the lowest item on the list until he can accomplish this two or three times without experiencing any increase in his level of arousal. This process is repeated until the most anxiety-arousing item can be pictured without anxiety. At this point the client can usually experience situations high on the list with a minimum of anxiety although there is often a little slippage between the imagined and the real situations.

This basic process has been elaborated and adapted to a wide variety of methods and individual problems (see Marquis, Morgan & Piaget 1971). For example, the process can be conducted using real stimuli (*in vivo* desensitization), if the subject has difficulty in imagining things or if the stimulus situation is easily controlled as it can be with a phobia of high places, snakes, loud noises, or elevators. Besides relaxation and eating responses, a number of other responses have been used to decondition anxiety including assertive responses, drug induced states, sexual responses, and positive, pleasant imagery. Bandura and his students have also shown remarkably good results with vicarious desensitization.

The experimental literature evaluating desensitization is somewhat misleading. In order to control experimental conditions most of the work has been done with simple, monosymptomatic phobias, such as test anxiety or the fear of small animals. However, in actual clinical practice more time is spent with complex and unique social anxieties and existential fears. Among the most common are fears of criticism, rejection, disapproval and failure, shyness and self-consciousness. Desensitization of these areas will ameliorate problems traditionally viewed as feelings of inferiority and inadequacy. This in turn often paves the way for the learning of new social skills which had been prevented by anxiety and facilitates the teaching of assertiveness, expression of feelings, and habits of self-reinforcement. It is not that therapists using desensitization deal only with clients suffering from phobias but rather that a wide variety of problems can be viewed as conditioned anxiety responses and the stimuli which control them can be identified, and developed into anxiety hierarchies.

At this point the effectiveness of systematic desensitization in reducing or eliminating a wide variety of anxieties is clearly established. It is certainly one of the most useful and effective techniques available to therapists.

Relaxation Techniques

Jacobson's (1938) original techniques for teaching relaxation are extremely effective but very ponderous and time consuming. Wolpe (1958) streamlined them considerably with very little loss of effectiveness. At first the primary use of relaxation by behavior therapists was for systematic desensitization but increasing numbers of therapists have taught clients how to generalize relaxation skills in order to go about most of their daily activities in a relaxed manner.

Initially clients are trained to be aware of sensations of tension and relaxation in their various muscles by having them tense the muscles, study the sensations, relax them and then once more direct their attention to the feelings that take place while the muscles relax further and further. Through this process the client learns to identify tension, and to relax completely with the help of instructions from the therapist, either in person or by means of a recording. The depth of relaxation is tested carefully by observing the client visually and by shaking and moving extremities to determine that the tension is gone.

Relaxation is practiced initially in conditions of reduced stimulation on an easy chair or bed in a quiet place. After learning to relax deeply with verbal instructions, the client practices relaxing without verbal instructions daily for a week or so. He is encouraged at all times to program his relaxation by kinesthetic cues rather than by using verbal or visual programming to direct his behavior. Kinesthetic cues allow more efficient increase in the speed of relaxing and facilitate development of an automatic, unconscious motor skill.

When the client can relax efficiently, without verbal instructions, he works on relaxing more and more quickly. When he can relax in a few seconds he then works on staying relaxed with his eyes open, walking around, and performing simple tasks. He then works on staying relaxed during increasingly difficult and complex activities and, eventually, in situations which originally aroused considerable anxiety. Often, some stimulus control is set up to remind him to relax, such as relaxing every time there is a commercial on the radio or television, any time the phone rings, or every time he starts to smoke a cigarette.

Subvocal Speech

In the context of relaxation training let us examine for a moment the clinical use of Watson's concept of thought as consisting of tiny movements in the vocal apparatus. Jacobson (1938) and others have done physiological research on this phenomenon, which can be picked up electronically and studied. In the process of socialization, the child's verbal behavior rapidly comes under the control of social reinforcement. If he says something unintelligible, people say "huh?" or ask him to repeat. An appropriate verbal response can produce a reinforcer for him and later there are many complex patterns of reward and punishment for verbal behavior. As a result the child learns to speak clearly and produce different verbal patterns for different people, through differential reinforcement. Thus, most people come to see speech as a voluntary action. In contrast, the person's thoughts are not brought under the discipline of social control, and therefore tend to be seen as a spontaneously occurring phenomenon rather than an action. From a behavioral point of view, thought can be controlled as easily as speech, by the actual use of the same voluntary muscles.

Many obsessive people keep up a constant flow of verbal thoughts. If these are stimuli which arouse and maintain tension in other muscles, the activity is called worrying. If not, an obsessional chattering to oneself can interfere with the perception of other enjoyable or useful stimuli by preempting the person's attention. The client can learn to stop a pattern of worry by relaxing his vocal apparatus and thus turning off the stimuli which are maintaining his anxiety. Then he relaxes the rest of his muscles and finds himself starting from a very different position when he resumes his activity.

For many people, being able to control obsessional thoughts opens up a whole new world. By turning off the head trip they are able to enjoy smelling the flowers, seeing the trees, and listening to the music that surrounds us. Often they can really listen to people for the first time without rehearsing an answer before the other person is done speaking, and therefore coming out with some irrelevant comment. They are able to be aware of the good feelings within their own bodies and can try out the views of other people which they read in books without having them contaminated with their own thoughts.

Fear Survey Schedule

Behavior therapists have generated many scales and inventories to help them in their work, including behavior rating scales, inventories of what people find reinforcing, and surveys of assertive skills or sexual behaviors. One of the most useful of these is the Fear Survey Schedule, the first of which was published by Wolpe and Lang (1964). The design is very simple. The client is given a list of items that often serve as anxiety stimuli and asked to indicate how much each of them bothers him. For example, being a passenger in a car, failing a test, rats and mice, life after death, being criticized, meeting someone for the first time, blood, swimming alone, people in authority, cemeteries, speaking before a group, and being with a member of the opposite sex. The therapist then goes over the results with the client, one item at a time, and the items are sorted into categories, which are unique to each individual and represent his areas of anxiety. It is surprising to most therapists who have worked with traditional therapy to find how frank most clients are in admitting their anxieties when presented with this kind of task. Some of the most frequent themes that are identified include criticism, rejection, and disapproval; center of attention; self-consciousness; pity, suffering, death; violence and expressions of anger; anxieties about specific people; shyness about courtship and sex; work anxieties; jealousy; and being away from help. The results of this process can then be discussed in terms of setting priorities and deciding which areas are most important and which are not worth bothering with.

Behavior Therapy Techniques

In addition to techniques which are directed toward the reduction of anxiety, behavior therapists spend a lot of time teaching people social behaviors. A pioneer in this area was Andrew Salter (1949), who started from a Pavlovian theory of inhibition and excitation, equating inhibition with all kinds of neurotic problems and excitation with assertive behavior. Wolpe early picked up Salter's work and began teaching people assertive behaviors by means of modeling, rehearsal, and coaching. Bandura and his students have done many experiments with modeling. However, a recent paper (McFall and Twentyman 1973) suggests that rehearsal and coaching may be sufficient without modeling.

In a typical problem a client may be having difficulty in dealing with a vituperative neighbor in an assertive fashion. First the client plays the role of the neighbor, modeling it for the therapist while the therapist models the way he thinks the client could handle him. Then they switch roles with the client trying his new behavior and the therapist playing the role of the neighbor. They break character and the client coaches the therapist on how to play the neighbor more realistically and the therapist coaches the client on how to be more appropriately assertive with him. Often a shaping is required where the desired behavior is reached by approximations and a certain amount of deconditioning of anxiety takes place as the new behavior is polished. For example, an amazing number of people are unable to speak above a conversational tone of voice. They are asked to say something louder and louder, and reinforced each time they are able to add a few decibels until they can sound convincingly angry. Assertion from Salter's point of view also involves the expression of positive feelings and enthusiasm and such responses are often rehearsed and shaped. Behavior rehearsal is often used with couples in practicing better ways of communicating with each other and at this point behavior therapy interfaces with a systems approach to family therapy (Piaget 1972).

SOME ETHICAL AND PHILOSOPHICAL CONSIDERATIONS

Humanistic Psychology

Humanistic beliefs in the ability and perfectibility of mankind, with their values of liberty and esthetics, have been a civilizing force in the world. Indeed, most behavior therapists, like most psychoanalysts, social workers, and experimental psychologists, are personally humanists who believe in personal freedom, civil liberties, and the amelioration of social problems. However, there is an anti-intellectual flavor in the hostility of a few advocates of the new humanism towards the canons of evidence and the discipline of coherent and consistent conceptualization. It is a short step from there to the assumption that being a good human being who is sympathetic, warm, expressive, and understanding is sufficient qualification for a therapist. It is entirely reasonable to argue that these are essential characteristics of a good therapist, but being a good human being is no more sufficient qualification for being an effective therapist than for being an architect.

The Problem of Behavioral Control vs. Free Will

Krasner (1966) discusses the ethical concerns that have arisen as in response to the increasingly obvious effectiveness of behavior modification. Krasner points out that behavioral control is nothing new, and that parents, teachers, clergymen, policemen, and judges have exercised powerful controls over human behavior since the dawn of time. Judicial and penal systems can be used for political control and people can be paid for working at jobs they detest. Behavioral technology, like other means of controlling human behavior, can be used either for good or for ill. If it is more effective, it can be used more effectively to improve the quality of human life. If the technology of behavior modification is free from values, society or the individual client is more free to choose whatever goals are most valued.

Behaviorists believe in psychological determinism. If we had a perfect psychology and complete data on an individual's physiological makeup and history of learning and conditioning, together with complete information about the situation in which he finds himself, we would be able to predict a person's behavior perfectly. While this is incompatible with the concept of free will, it raises an interesting paradox. The choice of a free moral agent, whether benign or hostile or maladaptive, is viewed as an independent phenomenon, which occurs autonomously and mysteriously and cannot stand the light of further analysis. In contrast, a behavioral technology can place in the client's hands the means of achieving benign and adaptive goals. If he can reduce his anxieties, learn better ways of doing things, solve problems, relax, work effectively, and influence the behavior of others effectively and benignly without coercion then we have given him the means to achieve freedom and dignity. If indeed his behavior is under the control of his conditioning and patterns of reinforcement, he can never be free by any other means than understanding and controlling the learning and conditioning variables that determine his behavior.

A number of interesting and practical considerations arise when one considers the problem of voluntary treatment vs. a coercive assignment to treatment. Population control specialists report that when men in India are paid to have vasectomies (thus decreasing the voluntary nature of this decision), they frequently report bad consequences such as impotence, headaches, insomnia, and depression. If on the other hand they are charged a small fee for their vasectomy, they usually report no ill effects, and indeed are likely to become missionaries to their friends in advocating the operation. Most of us have been conditioned to experience unpleasant emotions in response to stimuli associated with coercion and respond better when we feel that we have chosen something freely.

However voluntarily one makes a commitment to a situation, if the situation is not to his liking he can come to feel coerced, as when a college course, a marriage, or an enlistment in the service does not turn out as well as anticipated. An interesting example is the outstanding drunk driving course in Phoenix. The students were assigned to the course by court order and came in very resistant to the idea, joking or complaining. In the course, they were presented with interesting and effective materials which convinced them of the seriousness of the problem of drunk driving and the risks that they had taken of ruining their lives by killing or injuring themselves or others. They were actively involved in planning how they would make sure that these risks were never taken again. By the end of the course they were so enthusiastic that they had, in effect, become volunteers.

AN EXPEDIENT MODEL FOR BEHAVIOR THERAPY

Let us examine a simple model for organizing behavioral treatment which arose from discussions with Wesley G. Morgan of the University of Tennessee. It is described in more detail elsewhere (Marquis 1970). It embodies a number of the principles of the behavioral approach discussed above and can facilitate benign and effective behavior change. First, a careful analysis is made of the present state of the behaviors a client wishes to change. Then a clear understanding is reached of the terminal behaviors which are to be sought with the client's full participation in every part of the process of setting goals. These may involve his being able to perform some new behavior or being able to perform comfortably and effectively something which now involves considerable anxiety and loss of effectiveness. On the other hand the client may need to learn how to be comfortable without doing something that he does but would rather not do. The second step is to consider with the client alternative paths that may be taken from his present condition to the terminal behaviors. Often this involves considering several possible paths of therapeutic intervention in order to produce the desired results. The third step is to construct a program, usually based on small incremental steps, leading from the starting point to the goal. Treatment planning would also include orchestration of the several programs with proper timing. When difficulty arises in putting a program into effect the usual reason is that the steps have been made too big, but the important thing is to remain constructive and goal oriented when difficulties arise, rather than to become frustrated and blame the client for being unable to accomplish the task which we have set for him. It is necessary to remember that everything the client does is what he must do, given the situation he is in and his history of learning and conditioning.

Relationships

The application of a benign educational model leads to quite a different client-therapist relationship than a medical model which views the patient as a sick person who is qualitatively different from the therapist. While the therapist's respect for the client is similar to that of the client-centered therapist, the relationship is more genuine and straightforward since the therapist is free to give advice and shares responsibility with the client for the conduct of therapy. The result is similar to the personal and complex relationship involved in the architect's using his technical skills to design and build for the client a house which matches his needs and life-style.

APPLICATION OF THEORY

The case of Charles will illustrate the planning and behavioral treatment of a person who was chosen after three hours of treatment. The outcome will be unknown, since at this writing he is still in treatment. Of course, identifying data have been changed to protect him.

Charles is a 28-year-old, slightly built young man who has been arrested 19 times for indecent exposure, the first time when he was 13 or 14. He was awaiting sentencing on a new charge when his probation officer referred him to me because he had complained of a lack of progress with his psychoanalytic therapist.

He works in a two-man office with the president of a small business, filling the roles of secretary, bookkeeper, errand boy, and general flunky. He described himself as not being assertive, and being self-conscious about not being athletic, about his size, and about body odors in social situations. His favorite pastime was driving fast and riding around in his car.

At times he has been able to go up to six months without exposing himself, but says, "If I get very depressed, I'll do it all day, like if some chick shot me down." He preferred to expose himself to girls 6 to 12 years of age because he thought they were less likely to turn him in. He particularly liked having a little girl take a second or third look, but was often quite fearful that they would tell their mothers, who would call the police. He often exposed himself in the window of his own house to little girls who were passing by, but would sometimes go out in the yard or expose himself on the street.

Charles' father is a banker whom he describes as a very severe, harsh, punitive, unloving, and authoritarian person who was disappointed that his son was not athletic. His mother he describes as a "weak version of Dad." His only sibling is a brother 10 years younger "who wasn't much help." The father frequently became enraged and beat him severely. He succeeded in reducing Charles to almost complete conformity and subservience and severely undermining his confidence. Charles was a good student and played in the high school band. He was terribly shy with girls and remained only slightly improved at the time treatment began.

He was interested only in beautiful girls because of fantasies of compensating for his own feelings of inferiority by showing them off. He succeeded in getting a date with a beautiful but very shy girl for the final dance of his junior high school class. He danced two dances with her, stepped on her feet, and she finished the evening with other partners. He didn't have another date until he was a senior in high school.

At about that time he was standing naked in his bedroom and saw the 8-year-old girl next door observing him from a tree. He demonstrated his penis to her and she smiled and lifted her skirt in return. On the austere background of his treatment by parents and peers (as Ken Swift says, "a low rate of reinforcement is the devil's playground"), this was about the nicest thing that had ever happened to him, implying acceptance and reciprocity. He has been looking for such a response ever since.

He continued to expose himself to her on and off until he left home for the Army, as a rule masturbating in order to keep her attention. By that time the pattern was highly sexualized although triggered by rejection and serving an anxiety-reducing function as well.

He was given a Fear Survey Schedule which we sorted into three severe areas of anxiety and one less severe. He was very shy and self-conscious in a variety of situations. These feelings centered around concern about his slight build, lack of *savoir-faire* with women, and lack of athletic ability. He was also terrified at having his cool facade detected as false by showing his fear or anger and was therefore very self-conscious about any expression of feeling. His parents' ridicule, criticism, and lack of appreciation of his efforts also left him extremely anxious about criticism, rejection, and disapproval, again, especially by women. His assertive responses are further undermined by a terror of anything with the possibility of inflicting pain, which was conditioned by his father's beatings. A related but less severe area includes fear of robbery or attacks by drunks, toughs, or strangers in a crowd.

TABLE 2

Improvement to date	Problem	Treatment	Incremental Step	Terminal Behavior
B	Exhibitionism	Orgasmic (1) reconditioning	Decreased sexual responses to fantasies of exhibiting himself.	Exhibitionism does not turn on.
		Aversive conditioning	Increased anxiety about exposing himself.	Cessation of desire to expose himself.
		Cost Analysis	Increasing awareness of consequences of exposing self.	
A	General tension, insomnia	Relaxation	More relaxed in wider range of stimulus conditions.	Relaxed in most circumstances, no more insomnia.
B,D	Hypersensitive to criticism, rejection and disapproval	Systematic (2) desensitization	Increased intensity of stimulus with no anxiety.	Able to tolerate criticism and rejection.
B,D	Self-conscious, shy	Systematic desensitization	Increased intensity of stimulus with no anxiety.	Able to be relaxed under scrutiny, naked. Able to approach women. Able to express feelings.
A	Premature ejaculation	Semans (3) technique	Able to go longer without ejaculation.	Able to have intercourse for 15 minutes without ejaculating.
C,D	Excessive fear of pain and violence	Implosion (4)	Decreasing anxiety to same intensity of average stimuli.	Only afraid when in danger. Able to tolerate high places, crowds, bees, drunks, etc.
B,D		Behavior rehearsal	Increased social and assertive skills. Increased comfort on expressing feelings.	Able to avoid being dominated. Able to express feelings.

A. Currently no problem.
B. Improved.
C. Unimproved.
D. Treatment continuing.

(1) Marquis (1970)
(2) Marquis, Morgan & Piaget (1973)
(3) Semans (1956)
(4) Stampfl & Levis (1967)

At the beginning of therapy his sexual experience had been limited to a two-month relationship with a girl while he was in the Army, his two brief marriages, and one girl whom he dated only twice. He attended junior college before and after enlistment in the Army, which was terminated by an undesirable discharge following court martial for indecent exposure. He has served a total of 21 months in jail and two years at a state hospital for the criminally insane. He has worked at a number of white collar jobs as clerk and bookkeeper. He worked as an orderly for a while and is currently rooming with his old charge nurse whom he loves as a mother.

He seemed to be eager to change his behavior and willing to work hard to cooperate in solving his problems. He responds well to positive reinforcement and is a fairly well organized and disciplined person. We discussed the problems represented in his complaints and the Fear Survey Schedule and set forth the treatment plan outlined in Table 2. The plan was to start immediately with a relaxation program to reduce his general level of anxiety and to give first priority to an attempt to get his exhibitionism under control. He was able to masturbate using fantasies of normal heterosexual behavior and was asked never to imagine a girl looking at his penis when he masturbated in order to extinguish the sexual responses to these fantasies. The next priority was to set up a list of stimuli associated with exposing himself and pair these with electric shock to the fingers in order to create an aversion which would suppress the behavior and be incompatible with sexual response These situations were as follows:

Exposure Stimuli

1. Senior year in high school, you are in your room. Pat is in the tree outside. You expose yourself to her and she throws her dress up.
2. There are three little girls playing outside your current house and you open the blind and expose yourself to them.
3. You are walking down the street by a school with your long coat on. There are two or three little girls in front of you. You let your coat fall open casually and look off at the sky. The girls whisper and giggle.
4. Pat next door is peeking over the hedge at you and giggling while you expose yourself.
5. One girl has walked by the house and you have exposed yourself to her. Now she has brought back three little friends, one of whom is strutting and acting like Mae West.
6. You walk down the street with your long coat on and an older girl comes toward you, you expose yourself and she takes off in total fear.

7. The episode when you were in the Army in the trailer, where two girls on bicycles came by, stared at you for two minutes and then came back with 8 other girls.

8. You're at your apartment. Two little girls walk by. You slam the lid on the mail box, stand inside the door nude and one girl nudges the other.

9. You have just found out that Dinah was using you to make her boyfriend jealous and you go home and expose yourself.

10. You are watering the lawn when an attractive girl of 13 or 14 in hot pants walks by. She has a dark tan, is a wholesome looking blonde and you think of exposing yourself to her.

11. You get out of your car at home and find yourself about 4¼ feet from an attractive high school girl and think of exposing yourself to her.

The items on this list were chosen to include the most enjoyable and frequent experiences that Charles had had, as well as stimuli that would tempt him to expose himself.

The above description, history and plans for Charles were presented to his attorney and his probation officer essentially as presented here. I stated that I felt that he would respond well to treatment and that incarcerating him would serve no useful purpose, because he does time very graciously. This was after seeing him for three hours.

The judge was encouraged by this letter to postpone sentencing for a month and see how he responded. By that time I was able to write to his probation officer as follows:

Dear Mr. Probation Officer:

I am writing to provide information to supplement my letter of April 9, in the hopes that your plans for Charles and those of Judge ———— can take these developments into consideration.

At this writing I have seen Charles for 8 hours and am very much gratified with his attitude of cooperation and hard work and with the progress he has already shown. He has been listening to a tape which teaches muscular relaxation and practicing it between times so that he feels his anxieties already much relieved. He reports that several people who do not know what he is up to have told him how much more calm and relaxed he seems.

After nine lonely months he has formed a very close relationship with a new girl friend whom he describes as an "ego builder." He reports that he has not used fantasies of girls looking at him either when masturbating or when making love to his girl. He has been working with the Semans technique to solve a problem of premature ejaculation. Masters and Johnson report almost 100% success with cooperative clients using this method. He is very much excited about the progress he has already made.

Charles worked with great speed in helping me prepare a list of stimulus conditions which have aroused an impulse to expose himself in the past. We have already had him picture each of the 9* things 7 times for aversion conditioning for a total of 63 shock trials. He has recently experienced a couple of situations in which he formerly would have felt a strong urge to expose himself. He experienced the thought that the situation presented an opportunity to do so but without any feeling of urge or desire to expose himself. He experienced great relief on both occasions at the change in his motivation.

Another thing we have done is a cost analysis of his exposing himself. Past experiences provide an estimate of the probability of getting caught each time he exposes himself. This is multiplied by the amount he would charge to do the amount of time of his next sentence as best he can guess it. This gives a figure in the neighborhood of $2,000 for each exposure. He seems impressed with this.

We have an anxiety hierarchy for desensitization of his sensitivity to criticism, rejection and disapproval. Again, he is very organized and rapid in writing items which augurs well for rapid progress with this method.

I feel that the possibility of Charles reoffending grows more remote every day as he progresses and at this time is already highly improbable. While he could continue to see me if on work furlough a great deal would be lost in not having available the rest of his life to deal with, especially the opportunity of learning more about relating to women, which is of central importance in solving his problems and not available if he is locked up. The State of California has had four years of his life without benefit to him or his victims. I respectfully suggest that he be given a chance to continue working with me.

Yours sincerely,

He had met his new girl friend at a friend's house. The friend later called him and said that she was dying to go out with him. He was particularly impressed with two things—her telling him "You turn me on more than any guy I've ever met" and that "She rubs me as if I weren't skinny."

The Semans technique involves stimulation of the penis until the approach, but not the inevitability, of ejaculation is felt. At that point the blood is

---

* Two more were added later.

squeezed from the head of the penis and 20 or 30 seconds is allowed to pass without further stimulation. The process is continued under various conditions of stimulation usually until the man can go 15 minutes without squeezing and without ejaculating. Conditions of stimulation might include masturbating, masturbating with the use of lubricant, being stimulated by the partner, penile containment, and, eventually, movement. Charles started with the masturbation program and the following session reported with delight the previous time he had made love to his girl he had held out for only four to six pumps but that he must have gone 15 or 20.

He came in for his ninth session after the court hearing in a state of great euphoria. He had been able to stay relaxed enough to speak fluently in his own defense and had received 5 months suspended sentence and 2 years probation with no fine and no time in jail. He reported that he was able to go more than 5 minutes without ejaculating and that he was sleeping 8 hours a night. At this point after 17 hours he has had one week when he got careless about staying relaxed and had a return of his insomnia, but this quickly cleared up as he paid more attention to staying relaxed. He eventually found the courage to ask his girl-friend's help in the Semans program and is now able to go 20 minutes without ejaculating at times.

The following anxiety hierarchy was set up for desensitization of criticism, rejection, and disapproval:

1. Sandra (client's ex-wife) is telling you about going over to Chuck's house seeking comfort and sympathy and ending up in bed with him.
2. You call Virginia for a date and her little brother says she is out with Freddie. It dawns on you that she is only going out with you to make Freddie jealous.
3. You are driving down First Street, check out a chick in the car next to you at a stop light, look at her and smile, she sneers and tosses her head.
4. You lose your temper with Bill and say "You'll get your grass back when I get my $10 back."
5. Boss says, "Charlie, you're fucking up too much, kid. It appears you don't give a shit. You don't belong here so get out."
6. Your father yells at you that you don't come home from church. "You don't do as you're told, you are too independent. Where were you?" Charles: "In church." Father: "You're a liar."
7. You are all alone at home watching TV with nothing else to do and no one to call.
8. Your boss has lost a phone message and says, "Where in hell is that

phone number? How come I don't have it?" Charles: "It is probably right where you left it."

9. Girl-friend's roommate says, "You're a fucking fag."

10. You're having lunch with your boss and a bunch of his business associates and they are talking shop on a technical level that is over your head.

11. You are checking out a pretty woman in a car, she turns to her husband and speaks to him and they laugh.

12. You are going to sleep at your girl-friend's house and the thought occurs to you that her roommate will disapprove when she finds you there in the morning.

13. You are playing the role of a new patient in the skit at the state hospital.

14. You are walking around the house nude with your girl friend and she is looking at you.

15. The interior of your car is cluttered and messy. A client follows you out to your car and looks in.

16. You have been driving in the wind and your hair is blown out of shape and a nice blonde pulls up next to you at a stop light.

17. You are chairing a ward meeting at the state hospital.

18. A friend says "Your feet smell." You answer "Your nose smells, my feet stink."

19. Sitting around at girl-friend's house with button off your shirt.

20. Your landlady is hanging on as you corner hard on a freeway.

21. Your girl's roommate looks askance at you while you are cutting up.

At this point in four desensitization sessions we have progressed up to item number 6. Charles reports having become much less sensitive to the kinds of situations represented on the list and says that he has become much more assertive with all of his friends and especially his boss as a result. At this point he has an anxiety hierarchy in the area of self-consciousness at home, so that he can write items between sessions. We will polish it up in the next session and begin desensitizing him.

We are just beginning to organize stimulus material to use for implosive therapy to decondition his anxieties about violence and painful stimuli. This method, which was developed by Thomas Stampfl (Stampfl and Levis 1967), starts with imagining an everyday situation with an ongoing thematic story line. The client is reminded of the things that he would experience in this situation in all sensory modalities in order to increase the vividness of his imagery. For example, "I want you to picture yourself sitting at the kitchen table on a hot summer day when you are about 10, eating a peanut butter sandwich. Feel the contact of your body with the hard kitchen chair and you will find that the table is a little bit too high for you. You pick up your sandwich and feel the spongy smoothness of the bread and smell of peanut butter, feel the weight of your arms as you raise the sandwich to your mouth and feel your teeth sinking into the sandwich. Now you are chewing, feel the peanut butter sticking to the roof of your mouth and feel your teeth meet each time they go through the sandwich. Reach for your glass of milk and feel the cold of the glass in your fingers as you raise it to your lips. Then lean back and be aware of the heat of the summer day, feel the heat on your skin and perhaps you are sweating a little and hear the chair creak as you lean back. You can see your mother standing at the sink, doing dishes, wearing a plaid cotton dress, with her hair up, wiping the sweat from her brow. . . ."

After some practice with this the theme leads smoothly into some anxiety arousing situation, perhaps with his mother scolding him and eventually slapping his face. Imagery is continued at each level until the client shows some sign of anxiety reduction and then the level is escalated, eventually including things far beyond anything that he has experienced, with mosquitoes, spiders, ants, and wasps swarming over him, being brutally beaten and lynched, and being mauled and severely injured in a football game. We will probably have him picture falling from a cliff, striking rocks at the bottom, lying there, broken and bleeding and dying. At the same time that the client is exhorted to imagine the stimuli for anxiety with maximal vividness and intensity he is asked to focus on the specific sensations of the anxiety response in his muscles and internal organs, so that both are vividly present at the same time.

He will be vilified, persecuted, and beaten until he feels completely helpless, downtrodden and destroyed. This is then kept at maximum intensity as long as possible and the client is watched for physical signs of growing anger. He is then encouraged to build and elaborate and augment this response until he rises from the floor and vents his wrath on his persecutor; striking, cursing, and eventually disemboweling and pulverizing his father. Then as this is maintained at maximum intensity for as long as possible, he once more begins to feel guilty and the process is reversed as his persecutor rises to torment him once more. He is asked to rehearse these scenes at home for 15 or 20 minutes a day until the conditioned anger and anxiety no longer occur and the scene often seems ludicrous.

While this method seems brutal, the client usually finishes an implosion session with a great feeling of relief and mastery as long-standing and much feared conditioned emotional responses are vented and deconditioned rapidly.

Stampfl is an outstanding theorist and can give 16 distinct theoretical formulations as possible reasons why implosion is effective. Perhaps most simply it can be thought of as an extinction process since the pain which provides the primary reinforcement for anger or anxiety is absent in imagining the situation.

After 17 hours, Charles is approximately halfway through our original estimate of 40 hours of treatment. Almost every hour he is visibly more confident and hopeful, and often comes in with some illustration of this. For example, in his 11th hour he reported seeing two little girls going by his office and thinking that was like "the old days." He coughed and they looked up and stood there looking at him for some time. He wondered if they were old victims of his and he experienced a great feeling of superiority that he now had control over his behavior and they were in the dark. He laughed.

In his 16th hour he described a particularly satisfying session of making love with his girl friend when he lasted for 20 minutes and she had three orgasms for the first time. He remarked on how much better a way this was of showing that he's a man than exposing himself. "It does a lot more for the old ego." As his confidence increases he is beginning to talk about getting a better job where he will make more money and not have to work so hard, but his criminal record will make this difficult.

I wonder how much of his progress is due to his fine relationship with his new girl friend and am fearful about how he will respond if she leaves him, but every week's progress with the various treatment plans makes the "old days" more remote.

Follow-up Note as of January 1, 1974. Charles has now been seen 13 more times for a total of 31 sessions (vs 40 projected) over a period of 8 months. He exposed himself once while I was on vacation to his landlady's 2½-year-old daughter and on one other occasion over three months ago. He reports no impulses to do so since with four booster sessions of aversion conditioning. Five implosion sessions went much as planned and dramatically cleared his anxieties about pain and violence. He has gained 20 lbs. and appears healthy, confident and assertive. He is now starting a new career in sales. He is living with the same girl friend but has related well to other girls and knows he could meet new girls if the need arose. His relationship with his parents has improved dramatically. All complaints are gone. He will return at increasing intervals for chats and booster sessions of aversion conditioning.

BIBLIOGRAPHY

AYLLON, T. & MICHAEL, J. The psychiatric nurse as a behavioral engineer. *Journal of the Experimental Analysis of Behavior*, 2, 323-334, 1959.

BANDURA, A. & WALTERS, R. H. *Social Learning and Personality Development.* New York: Holt, Rinehart, & Winston, 1963.

DAVISON, G. C. & TAFFEL, S. J. *Effects of Behavior Therapy.* Paper presented at the convention of the American Psychological Association, Honolulu, 1972.

FERSTER, C. B. Reinforcement and punishment in the control of human behavior by social agencies. *Psychiatric Research Reports*, 10, 101-118, 1958.

HOMME, L. E. Perspectives in psychology XXIV. Control of coverants, the operants of the mind. *Psychological Record*, 15, 501-511, 1965.

JACOBSON, E. *Progressive Relaxation.* Chicago: University of Chicago Press, 1938.

JONES, M. C. Elimination of children's fears. *Journal of Experimental Psychology*, 7, 382-390, 1924.

KRASNER, L. Behavior control. In R. Ubrich, T. Stachnic, & J. Mabry (Eds.), *Control of Human Behavior.* New York: Scott, Foresman, 1966.

LEWINSOHN, P. M., NICHOLS, R. C., PULOS, L., LAMONT, J. F., NICKEL, H. J., & SISKIND, G. The reliability and validity of quantified judgments from psychological tests. *Journal of Clinical Psychology*, 19, 64-73, 1963.

LINDSLEY, O. R. The beautiful future of school psychology: Advising teachers. In M. C. Reynolds (Ed.), *Proceedings of the Conference on Psychology and the Process of Schooling.* Minneapolis: University of Minnesota, Audio Visual Extension, 116-130, 1971.

LINDSLEY, O. R. Operant conditioning methods applied to research in chronic schizophrenia. *Psychiatric Research Reports*, 5, 118-139, 1956.

MAHONEY, M. J. The self-management of covert behavior: A case study. *Behavior Therapy*, 2, 575-578, 1971.

MARQUIS, J. N. Orgasmic reconditioning: Changing sexual object choice through controlling masturbation fantasies. *Journal of Behavior Therapy and Experimental Psychiatry*, 1, 263-271, 1970.

MARQUIS, J. N., MORGAN, W. G., & PIAGET, G. W. *A Guidebook for Systematic Desensitization.* Veterans workshop, Veterans Administration Hospital, Palo Alto, 1973.

McFALL, R. M. & TWENTYMAN, C. T. Four experiments on the relative contributions of rehearsal, modeling, and coaching to assertion training. *Journal of Abnormal Psychology*, 81, 3, 199-217, 1973.

MILLER, N. E. & DOLLARD, J. *Social Learning and Imitation.* New Haven: Yale University Press, 1941.

PIAGET, G. W. Training patients to communicate. In A. A. Lazarus (Ed.), *Clinical Behavior Therapy.* New York: Brunner/Mazel, 1972.

PREMACK, D. Reinforcement theory. In D. Levine (Ed.), *Nebraska Symposium on Motivation.* Lincoln: University of Nebraska Press, 1965, 123-180.

SEMANS, J. H. Premature ejaculation: A new approach. *Southern Medical Journal*, 4a, 353-357, 1956.

SINES, J. O. Actuarial methods of personality assessment. In B. Maher (Ed.), *Progress in Experimental Personality Research*, Vol. 3. New York: Academic Press, 1966.

WOLPE, J. & LANG, P. J. A fear survey schedule for use in behavior therapy. *Behaviour Research and Therapy*, 2, 27-30, 1964.

SELECTED READINGS

AYLLON, T. & AZRIN, N. H. *The Token Economy*. New York: Appleton-Century-Crofts, 1968.

BANDURA, A. *Principles of Behavior Modification*. New York: Holt, Rinehart, & Winston, 1969.

BRODY, N. *Personality: Research and Theory*. New York: Academic Press, 1972.

FOX, L. Effecting the Use of Efficient Study Habits. In R. Ulrich, T. Stachnick, & J. Mabry (Eds.), *Control of Human Behavior*. Chicago: Scott, Foresman, 1966.

MARQUIS, J. N. An expedient model for behavior therapy. In A. A. Lazarus (Ed.), *Clinical Behavior Therapy*. New York: Brunner/Mazel, 1972.

SALTER, A. *Conditioned Reflex Therapy*. New York: Farrar, Straus, 1949; Capricorn Books-Putnam's Sons, 1961.

SKINNER, B. F. *Walden II*. New York: Macmillan, 1948.

SKINNER, B. F. A case history in scientific method. *American Psychologist*, 11, 221-233, 1956.

SKINNER, B. F. Pigeons in a Pelican. *American Psychologist*, 15, 28-37, 1960.

SKINNER, B. F. *The Behavior of Organisms*. New York: Appleton-Century-Crofts, 1961.

SKINNER, B. F. *Beyond Freedom and Dignity*. New York: Knopf, 1971.

STAMPFL, T. G. & LEVIS, D. J. Essentials of implosive therapy: A learning theory based psychodynamic behavioral therapy. *J. Abnorm. Psychol.*, 72, 496-503, 1967.

WAHLER, R. G., WINKEL, G. H., PETERSON, R. F., & MORRISON, D. C. Mothers as behavior therapists for their own children. *Behaviour Research and Therapy*, 3, 113-124, 1965.

WATSON, J. B. *Behaviorism*. New York: Norton, 1926.

WOLPE, J. *Psychotherapy by Reciprocal Inhibition*. Stanford: Stanford University Press, 1958.

YATES, A. J. *Behavior Therapy*. New York: Wiley, 1970.

Gordon Allport

12

Eclectic and Integrated Theory: Gordon Allport and Others

by DONALD T. LUNDE

Eclecticism is a point of view that has existed as long as philosophy itself. Diogenes Laertius, the 3rd century biographer of eminent philosophers, referred to an eclectic school that flourished in Alexandria in the 2nd century A.D. In the 19th century, eclecticism, as espoused by Victor Cousin, was the dominant philosophy of post-Revolutionary France. It is a viewpoint that has gone in and out of favor as attitudes in philosophy have changed. Eclecticism in psychology, specifically in personality theory, was recently advocated by Gordon Allport (1), although he was well aware of the disfavor with which eclecticism has been viewed by many people in the field.

* The author gratefully acknowledges the assistance of Karen Train in the preparation of this paper.

Because this approach has been wrongly maligned in the past, it is worthwhile defining the term by discussing what it is and what it is not.

Eclecticism Defined

The word "eclecticism" comes from a Greek word meaning to select. To be an eclectic in any age has meant to select parts from a variety of theories or a set of facts. The term has not been confined to philosophy, but has been applied to anyone in any field who takes his personal point of view from a variety of sources. Some early eclectics were thought to hold the belief that all truth had already been discovered and that it need only be separated from the falsehood with which it was mixed. This assumption is obviously not valid nor is it an accurate statement of a modern eclectic point of view. A more appropriate formulation would be that there is some truth to many theories which have seriously been proposed and that there are many questions which remain unresolved. A true eclectic tries to maintain an open mind in order to perceive the element of truth in any theory, whether old or new, and also to maintain a proper amount of skepticism in matters that are not yet resolved.

It has also been claimed of eclectics that they are at sea among the various more definite theories and have no system or principles to guide them. This piecemeal approach should be distinguished from that of systematic eclecticism. It is essential to have some basic guidelines in view of all the various conflicting theories of personality that one encounters. This is entirely consistent with and, in fact, basic to the eclectic point of view. One purpose of this chapter will be to outline some of those guidelines.

Another criticism that has been leveled against eclecticism is that, in an attempt to unify the elements of truth from various theories, it ends up equating opposites and erroneously glossing over irreconcilable differences. Certainly eclectics and non-eclectics alike would welcome a unified, and unifying, theory of personality. Whether this ideal can ever be reached is debatable, but the attempt is certainly justifiable and understandable. It must be recognized that in a science as young as psychology no theory now known can be complete. When compared with the physical sciences, which have been systematically investigated for centuries, psychology's seventy-five year history seems brief. It is too soon to be calling any theory "final" or "all-encompassing." The balance to be achieved by a proper eclecticism is one between the contradictions that may arise from too accepting an approach and the closed-mindedness that can result from espousing a single theory too exclusively. The process of unification is going on from various well-defined centers, with little more than a far-off hope of ultimate and complete unification. This, however, if viewed philosophically, is the Eclectic state of mind in its highest form, which is not ". . . an uncritical and unmethodical assemblage of unreconciled truths; but rather an orderly coordination of definite scientific aspects which, though preliminary, do not in their preliminary character militate against a closer approximation and an ultimate harmony" (2).

Philosophical Issues

A final objection to eclecticism is that it is a nebulous way of thinking that does not recognize the larger issues of philosophy and psychology. It is a gross misconception, however, to equate the rigorous approach to these problems that eclecticism can be with mere indecisiveness and shabby thinking. A systematic eclecticism draws upon the various personality theories and upon philosophy to define the major questions of human nature. Some of these basic questions are: the mind-body problem, the nature vs. nurture controversy, free will vs. determinism, the concepts of time, consciousness, and self; and the subject-object dilemma. For instance, implied in some of the theories put forth in this book is a denial of free choice or the possibility of any true voluntary behavior, be it creative or destructive. Dostoevsky foresaw this scientific determinism over 100 years ago and wrote (3):

> It is, of course, quite true that if one day they really discover some formula of all our desires and whims, that is to say, if they discover what they all depend on, by what laws they are governed, how they are disseminated, what they are aiming at in one case and another, and so on, that is, a real mathematical formula, man may perhaps at once stop feeling any desire and, I suppose, most certainly will. For who would want to desire according to a mathematical formula? And that is not all. He will at once be transformed from a man into an organ-stop, or something of the sort. . . . For when one day desire comes completely to terms with reason we shall of course reason and not desire, for it is obviously quite impossible to desire nonsense while retaining our reason and in that way knowingly go against our reason and wish to harm ourselves. And when all desires and reasons can be actually calculated (for one day the laws of our so called free will are bound to be discovered) something in the nature of a mathematical table may in good earnest be compiled so that all our desires will in effect rise in accordance with this table. . . . But I repeat for the hundredth time that here is one case, one case only, when man can deliberately and consciously desire something that is injurious, stupid, even outrageously stupid, just because he wants to have the right to desire for himself even what is very stupid and not to be bound by an obligation to desire only what is sensi-

ble . . . and in particular it may be more valuable than any good even when it is quite obviously bad for us and contradicts the soundest conclusions of our reason about what is to our advantage . . . it preserves what is most precious and most important to us, namely our personality and our individuality.

In a time when Skinner is putting forth a view of strict determinism, advocating social engineering, and criticizing the humanists for "excessive aggrandizement of the individual" (4), we cannot afford to neglect the message of the novelist.

In addition to a discussion related to the philosophy of science, I shall put forth eclecticism in an historical context. In the course of the latter discussion I hope to convey a sense of the importance not only of the flow of past, present, and future in understanding the theories, but also its importance in understanding personality. History is not limited to a fixed chronicle of the past, but is intimately bound to our concept of the present and our aspirations for the future, whether individually or collectively viewed. Any one of the three segments of time will be incompletely comprehended to the extent that it is separated from the other two, and this is a major facet of the eclectic point of view.

THE PRINCIPLE OF RELATIVITY

To move on to the metatheoretical considerations in evaluating personality theories, an analogy from the field of physics illustrates a common misconception about theories that is encountered among psychotherapists, i.e., the idea that there is only one right theory or that a newer or more general theory must supersede an older or more limited one.

A theory in any field, whether psychology or physics, is a tool, a human creation designed to bridge the gap between what we know about a subject and what we would like to know or predict about it. Newtonian mechanics, for example, organizes a vast number of observations about the physical world. It makes what was once only accessible as empirical observation, rational and quantitative. It enables us to explain and predict a myriad of data with a few fairly simple concepts.

But if Newton's theory is so economical and so useful, why do we need Einstein's more recent theory of relativity? Einstein recognized that for objects traveling at slow speeds, Newton's laws are easier to use and accurate enough. But they are grossly in error when used to predict the behavior of objects at very high speeds (approaching the speed of light). The theory of relativity, which describes the interconvertibility of matter and energy, can explain observations and predict outcomes in a much broader realm than that known to Newton. The theory of relativity is therefore a more general theory than Newton's, but it is not necessarily more useful than Newton's in every case. In the realm of everyday objects to which Newton's theory applies, it gives as much predictive power as Einstein's theory with much simpler calculations. When one is applying a theory, the question is not simply which theory is the more encompassing, but which theory is the most useful for the situation at hand. Usefulness is a balance between the accuracy of predictions and the ease of application of theory. Einstein's theory of relativity may be the more correct portrayal of nature in its entirety, but Newtonian mechanics continues to be useful.

This pragmatic aspect in the eclectic approach cannot be denied and is particularly important to the clinician. There is a close analogy between this example and the situation in personality psychology today. Some theorists, especially the academic psychologists, deal primarily with the relationship between a theory and the data it is meant to explain. They are interested in checking the observations and verifying the conclusions upon which a given theory is based. Working in another direction they may formulate specific hypotheses based on a particular theory in order to test them in a controlled situation. Much of this kind of investigation is aimed at articulating the correlation of the theory with the data. This is an important undertaking from both the philosophical and scientific points of view, but it does not directly help the psychotherapist who wants to use the theory in a more subjective, clinical setting. Much as a clinician may value an effort to refine a theory scientifically, the accuracy and verifiability of a theory are not his primary concerns. The psychotherapist may use a theory that he does not know to be wholly accurate or provable in an objective sense. He judges the value of a theory in part by its usefulness in explaining and predicting what he observes in the clinic. He does not limit himself to consideration of the client as an object of study, but views the client as a subject as well. There are, of course, variations here. The orthodox analyst tends to view the patient more as an object and himself as an observer. More humanistic therapists tend to view the client as a subject and the therapist as a participant (subjective mode of being) as well as an observer (objective mode of being). The rigorous controls of the academic, striving for total objectivity, are difficult to apply and often counterproductive in the clinic; the questions of interest to the clinician are difficult to recreate in the laboratory. To the extent that these problems can be circumvented, the interests of the clinic and the laboratory may be reconciled. Certainly Freud pioneered in this effort, and current theorists such as Rogers have continued to demonstrate that theories should and can be tested in practice. Too much time has been spent, however, in debates that pit the theories of experimental psychology against those based on clinical practice. This seems a futile and unnecessary undertaking at this time, because each has its own uses. Some apply more directly to the clinical situation; others lend themselves better to the rigors of scientific investigation. Rychlak has made the following observation on this subject (5):

> When an individual selects the various constructs from different theoretical orientations in the hope of making sense out of some group of facts or series of phenomena, we speak of this as an eclectic theoretical orientation. Most practicing clinical psychologists find it essential to combine and patch together constructs from many personality theories in order to understand their clients. The danger here, of course, is inconsistency, and the fact that in patching together various orientations the psychologist may do violence to the construct in question. Eclecticism has gotten a bad name in psychology, primarily because of the inadequate form of integration which often results. . . . But it is equally important to grasp the fact that all theories are in one sense eclectic. As Rotter phrased it: "All systematic thinking involves the synthesis of pre-existing points of view. It is not a question of whether or not to be eclectic but of whether or not to be consistent and systematic." (Rotter, J. B. *Social Learning and Clinical Psychology*. Englewood Cliffs, New Jersey: Prentice-Hall, 1954, p. 14).

Cultural Factors

In addition to appreciating the necessity for sometimes being the participant, sometimes, the observer, and sometimes both, the eclectic recognizes the relativism imposed by history and culture both in theory and in practice. To no small degree, to translate Freud's psychoanalytic theory out of the German language and the 19th century middle-class European culture in which it was formulated is to lose some of its original significance. Similarly, to understand behavioral modification in its full sense necessitates some knowledge of the experimental psychology and the American culture from which it arose. J. B. Watson is the historical founder of this school and reacted in the extreme to prior personality theories based on introspection. He was obsessed with the notion that there are inherent inaccuracies in the self-reported phenomena of patients or therapists. He sought to explain personality in terms of tangibles—objective observations which by definition could not include intrapsychic phenomena. Of course, the paradox here is that "objective" observations are still made through subjective filters—the observer's perceptions of what he has seen, heard, or touched. Watson and the behaviorists who have followed him, such as B. F. Skinner, have also rejected the nature side of nature vs. nurture, or heredity vs. environment, in discussing human development. Given a free hand in controlling the environment of a normal infant, Watson claimed he could raise the child to become anything he chose—doctor, lawyer, artist, merchant, chief, and even beggar or thief—regardless of his inherited characteristics. This extreme view is better understood in light of the avowed egalitarianism of American democracy which espouses the notion that any man, no matter how humble his origins, could become President of the United States. Since Watson's time, our knowledge of genetics and related fields has increased tremendously and it has become increasingly apparent that all men and women simply are not created equal.

The social and historical relativity of theories cannot and need not be stripped away. Even those therapists who claim to be adherents of a particular school of personality theory modify that theory to suit their own personalities and ideologies. Those who do not become advocates of one particular theory tend to be open to ideas from other theories and, indeed, often use therapy techniques derived from several different sources. Whether acknowledged or not, the vast majority of practicing therapists is eclectic. Some, like Maslow, have attempted to formulate an all-encompassing, holistic personality theory, but such efforts are premature. The time may come when such a synthesis can be achieved, but it is a long way off. In fact, in the field of personality there will probably never be an "ultimate" theory. Uncertainty is inherent not only in the observer but also in the object of his study. The eclectic therapist must be able to tolerate a certain amount of uncertainty and must be able to move from one theory or technique to another depending on the particular patient or sometimes, as in the following example, depending on the stage of therapy with a given patient.

Application of Theory (I)

Mr. W., a thirty-nine-year-old divorced businessman, was first seen in a hospital emergency room. He had agreed to see the therapist at the urging of a business associate who was alarmed by his behavior and felt he needed psychiatric care. He had been losing a considerable amount of money and injuring his reputation by his involvement in grandiose business schemes and his recent practice of calling people at all hours of the night with his exciting new proposals. He could literally go for days without sleeping and had lost considerable weight, but saw nothing unusual in this. He finally agreed to be seen in order to reassure his friend that he was "normal." He agreed to be seen only by me because of a previous association and our limited but apparently meaningful relationship. On examination, it was obvious that he was manic.* He finally agreed to hospitalization on grounds that he needed a "rest." At this point lithium carbonate therapy was started.** Routine measurements of lithium in the blood were taken until a therapeutic level was reached and maintained. Recovery was gradual but striking. Within two months the patient was back at work handling a complicated demanding business.

Individual Factors

There are other determinants of a theory's appeal and appropriateness to an individual besides his or her perception of its usefulness. These factors from an eclectic point of view are important determinants in the therapist's choice of patients as well as choice of theory and techniques for treatment. All other factors being equal, there may be valid grounds for selecting patients and techniques based on consideration of the therapist's own *personality, age,* and *sex.* Mention has already been made of the historical and cultural relativity of the personality theories. These same factors apply to the match among the therapist, the theory, and the patient. Obviously someone trained in Europe in the 1930's is apt to have a different viewpoint from someone trained in the United States in the 1970's. There have also been some changes in the kinds of problems patients present and what treatments they expect will work. The differences may be too complex or too subtle to explain but they can be sensed.

Beyond the time and place of the therapist's *training* are the differences imparted by the type of training that is received. A person trained in medicine is far more likely to entertain the possibility that a mental disorder has a physical or genetic etiology than someone who is less familiar with biology. He may also be better equipped to make use of the case study method of investigation. Conversely, a person trained in research psychology is apt to have a greater facility with the statistical research methods of his field. Someone trained in psychiatric social work may have a far more sociological point of view than either the physician or the psychologist. The clergy has yet another outlook on the human condition. From the eclectic viewpoint, it would be extremely valuable if all members of these various fields made more use of each other's expertise. The broader the training of

---

* At this point the therapist was acting in very much of a participant, subjective mode as one acquaintance to another.

** Here the therapist moved to an observer mode and the patient was, in operational terms, being treated "objectively." Note here also that therapy in this respect was directed to the "body" although concurrent psychotherapy (treatment of the "mind" in dualist terms) was also taking place.

casualties. It was clear that there were not enough psychoanalysts to treat so many patients, nor was there time for the extended analyses that had become standard treatment for many disorders. Newer, faster methods were needed to make more efficient use of the therapist's time. For the eclectic a wider variety of therapies became available.

The war and other factors had led to the development of new techniques and an increased interest in other techniques that had been only minor aspects of psychotherapy until then. Short-term psychotherapy and crisis intervention were among these. Rather than daily sessions for several years, weekly sessions for several weeks or months were found to be sufficient, at least for relief of symptoms, which in many cases was all the patient wanted. To some extent the "brief therapies" evolved out of necessity. It was found in World War II, the Korean War, and in Vietnam, that soldiers who were needed on the battlefield could be treated at a base hospital not far from the front lines and could return to duty in a fairly short period of time. Patients treated in this manner showed higher and faster recovery rates than those who were sent home to hospitals to be treated more extensively. In part, the expectations of the situation seemed to play an important role in determining the length of treatment.

Although this represented a change in technique from analysis in terms of intensity and length of treatment, the same past-oriented theory was still in vogue. The emphasis was on rapid restoration of prior functioning, but the past was still explored, at least the recent past. However, new theories began to appear along with the new techniques of psychotherapy. Notable among these new theorists was Carl Rogers, who derived a theory from his clinical practice in which he incorporated the client's present and future along with the past. While some new developments brought about changes in individual psychotherapy, others replaced the one-to-one model entirely with a new phenomenon—"The Group." Group psychotherapy, among other things, is a way of making more efficient use of a therapist's time. It also is more economical for the patient-consumer and hence more available to a greater segment of the population. This mode of treatment allows the eclectic a greater choice of patients, as well as a new theory and technique.

Encounter Groups

Group therapy had its origins in the morale building, supportive groups conducted by Joseph Pratt for tuberculosis patients some seventy years ago in Boston. In the 1920's a similar approach was used with schizophrenic patients. Some analysts experimented with psychoanalytically oriented groups and Freud himself wrote an article on the subject. By 1945, group therapy was accepted and used by various analytic and non-analytically trained therapists.

In recent years, group therapy and encounter groups have come to be almost indistinguishable in the hands of some practitioners, but the two methods were quite distinct in their origins, theories, and purposes. The beginnings of the encounter group movement can be traced to a workshop for community leaders on interracial tension that was conducted by Kurt Lewin in 1946. What began as an educational technique to help normal people learn about a specific social issue grew into a general method for helping groups of psychologically healthy people become more sensitive to other people and to their own feelings. From its beginnings as a workshop in Connecticut, encounter groups and T-groups have come to be ubiquitous. They are conducted in schools from the grade school level through college, in businesses, in adult educational programs, in "Awareness Centers," and so forth. Hardly an aspect of life exists that has not been explored by an encounter group somewhere.

There are many proponents of the group methods including the National Training Laboratory and the Esalen Institute, Synanon, Alcoholics Anonymous, Fritz Perls, Eric Berne, William Schultz, George Bach, and others. With time the group psychotherapy and the encounter group movements grew together. If the members of the group are considered to be psychiatric patients, the group is a therapy group; if they are not patients, it is an encounter group. Needless to say, it is nearly impossible to distinguish between the two populations in all cases; there is considerable overlap. Given the orientation that anyone can profit from increased self-awareness, there has been a tendency to use the more neutral term "client" rather than the designation "patient."

The most striking characteristic of encounter groups is the strong emphasis on the here-and-now. What happened to the members before the group began becomes irrelevant. Sometimes even present events outside the group are banned from discussion. Attention is focused on events occurring within the groups, especially on feelings generated within and between members. "Encounter groups are brief, intensive experiences; they are truly encounters that rely on the immediate present. A group of strangers assemble, interact intensely, and then become strangers again" (11). Not only is the emphasis on the present but on a strictly circumscribed, somewhat "artificial" present.

There is also a strong anti-intellectual bias to the encounter movement as evidenced by the stress given to such qualities as spontaneity, emotional intensity, and total honesty, sometimes to the point of brutality. "In general, regardless of other differences among the groups, participants expected a 'feelingful' analysis of here-and-now behavior, giving and receiving feedback in the process" (12). The encounter movement stands in sharp contrast to the psychoanalytic tradition. While one method makes a slow, methodical, relatively intellectual investigation of an individual's past, the other scraps all that to work with what he is now. Where psychoanalysis tries to bring about personal change in months or years, encounter groups sometimes try to accomplish this in a weekend. Where one is in the tradition of medicine, seeking to help the disabled, the other arises from no particular professional tradition, having sprung from quite diverse sources. The goals are personal growth and "expansion of awareness."

Although some regard encounter group theory and technique as an improvement over the more time-consuming and expensive individual psychotherapies, first indications from systematic investigation of this new medium for instant change show it can be less successful and may produce more casualties than the more traditional techniques. The casualties are not just coincidental or the result of an incompetent leader, but are an intrinsic risk produced by the ground rules of encounter. It is sometimes assumed that if some people have benefitted from encountering, everyone can; that if a little emotional honesty is good, more is better. The indiscriminate application of these principles can lead to destructive behavior as this case indicates:

Application of Theory (II)

Janice R., a twenty-four-year-old mother of an eighteen-month-old child, had been involved in "encounter therapy." She was depressed and had been encouraged to express anger in order to feel better. More specifically, she was encouraged to express and act out angry feelings toward her child who was viewed as the source of her present frustration and depression. She was made to physically beat and strangle a pillow in the therapy sessions, all the while imagining it was her child she was beating. Over the weekend following such a session, she became panicky, experienced impulses to act out on her child, and was frightened. She called the therapist who told her to discuss her fears at the next session. The day before the session, she killed her child by strangulation and beating.*

---

* The point here is not just the irresponsibility of the therapist, for which a case can be made. The selection of treatment for the patient was inappropriate in the first place. The patient was released from custody and placed on probation at which time she entered therapy in a much more supportive setting and has responded very well.

The eclectic views both the theory and practice of "new methods" such as encountering within the philosophical framework previously described. To the extent that encounter groups focus on a particular aspect of being, namely the here-and-now, they may be of value to the patient whose problems are existential in nature, e.g., the patient undergoing a specific crisis of identity. To the extent that the techniques involved focus on interpersonal relationships and provide the opportunity for patients whose difficulties lie in the area of interaction to participate, observe, and be observed relating to others, encounter groups may be particularly valuable. Yet such theory and techniques will not meet the needs of each client and should be prescribed with the same care that one takes in prescribing medication, including consideration of the "side effects."

Behavior Therapy

Another post-war development in therapeutic techniques has come from a quarter that until recently has contributed more to theory of personality than to treatment of the disturbed. That quarter is experimental psychology. New methods based on the learning theory of the experimental psychologists have come to be known as behavior modification. The theory came out of the tradition of experimental psychology that began in the latter half of the nineteenth century when psychology separated itself from philosophy. Because rigorous scientific standards were applied to its development, most of the data supporting behavioral learning theory comes by necessity from animal studies involving pigeons and rats. These origins are quite different from Freud's much more qualitative, subjective investigation of neurotic humans. As we have noted earlier, the behaviorists adhere to the belief that eventually human as well as animal behavior will be explained in mathematical and "scientific" terms. These fundamental principles have led in the case of behavior modification to a much more mechanistic view of human behavior, whether normal or abnormal. Nonetheless, a significant resemblance exists between the Freudian and behavioristic theories about the development of personality. Both rely totally on the individual's past history to explain present behavior. Behavior modifiers explain fetishes and phobias as instances of faulty conditioning in the person's past experiences. That is, a specific sequence of reinforcements led to a present behavior that disrupts the functioning of the organism. The treatment applied is a reconditioning through use of both positive and negative reinforcement in an organized sequence designed to extinguish the undesirable behavior. The explanation of the difficulty is rooted in the past, but the therapy is totally present-oriented.

The unwanted behavior is taken as a starting point, a given; its specific etiology is not sought in treating it.

The quality of givenness that is attributed to what a person is now is the same as that seen in the encounter group movement. Both behavior therapy and encounter group therapy are *present-oriented,* both also promise very quick results, and both are immensely popular at the moment. In the hands of some practitioners, both appear in extreme forms and have become quite faddish. Some of their popularity is probably the result of the novelty phenomenon. New therapies often seem more powerful than they turn out to be later on.

Popularity and novelty notwithstanding, however, one major limitation common in both group therapy and encounter movements is their overriding concern with the client's present as the only aspect of him to which they need attend. A theory or method that focuses on a person's past, present, or future to the exclusion of the other two aspects of his life is inherently limited. There is also potential harm in emphasizing the expression of affect, particularly anger and hostility, in the absence of any provision for controlling or channeling that anger, as the previous case example shows.

In discovering that the exploration of the past is not the best or the only way to understand our clients and bring about change, we may have gone too far in our faith in the significance of the present, thus committing the same error again. It would seem more fruitful for patient and therapist to examine both past and present to understand and treat disturbances.

Therapies of the Future

Eclectic theory encompasses the patient's future as well as his present and past. There have been theorists since the time of Freud who have differed from him on the importance of the past versus the importance of the future. Carl Jung, for one, believed that one's aspirations were as instrumental in shaping his life as were the drives and instincts arising from his individual and collective past. The contributions of motivational theorists (13) have been of tremendous value, although the area is in need of further development. Eclecticism recognizes that the future pulls us forward as much as the past pushes us from behind. An individual can evidence psychopathology in the manner in which he thinks about an act relative to the future.

Application of Theory (III)

Mrs. F. is a thirty-nine-year-old working mother of three children. Her husband of twelve years suffered from a chronic form of schizophrenia which led to his frequent hospitalization. When home he was at times reasonable and gentle, particularly when taking tranquilizers. At other times, off his medication and drinking, he became abusive, belligerent, and threatening. He had assaulted various individuals, and Mrs. F. knew he kept guns in the house. There had been indications that her husband could become violent, but she had failed to take precautions, such as getting rid of the guns or arranging with neighbors to respond or to call the police in time of emergency. One day he threatened to kill her after beating her and the children. He went to the garage to get a gun. She located another gun in the house and shot him when he returned. Subsequently, in the course of therapy, it became apparent that she had "blocked out" the possibility of this eventuality even though it was highly predictable. Neither her previous therapist nor her husband's therapists had ever encouraged her to think about this future possibility and to develop contingency plans.

This case demonstrates the notion that a feared future event can become repressed and can adversely affect present functioning in a manner analogous to a traumatic past experience as described by Freud. This woman's dread of the violence that her husband might do paralyzed her ability to plan rationally. She was unable to consider various alternatives that might have averted the tragic outcome she so feared. Just as some patients experience relief of present symptoms by investigation of childhood experiences, it seems apparent that other patients can be helped, particularly in a *preventive* sense, by exploring their fears about the future and by educating them to better methods of coping with the possibilities that confront them. It is to be remembered, of course, that no matter what time span in the patient's life is most problematical to him, it is in the present that he manifests his difficulties, and it is in the present that the therapy is applied. Eclectic treatment should reorganize the present so that the past and future can be brought to consciousness rather than haunting the person with unthinkable thoughts.

Orientations in Time

Jung and Adler took issue with Freud and his preoccupation with the past. In addition to the influence of the individual's past, Jung, unlike Freud, postulated a collective unconscious that extended back for thousands of years. He did not reject religion as a real and powerful element in human existence, and considered the person's hopes and plans for the future to be of equal importance with his past. Adler acknowledged the importance of conscious and unconscious forward-looking motives with his concept of striving for superiority and the notion of the creative self. Behavior was recognized by Adler as being goal-directed, not simply overdetermined by past experience.

Allport's concept of functional autonomy also de-emphasized the role of the past in motivating a person's behavior. One may be led to undertake activity because of some unfulfilled need from the past, but sometimes one continues that activity in the present, not because of the original drive, but simply because of the immediate pleasures of the act. Allport recognized that not all present behavior need be traced to its most distant antecedents and that a person's ambitions for the future are also strong determinants of the present actions he will take.

Along with Jung, Adler, and Allport, the group of theorists that make up the humanist and existential movements have put new emphasis on the present and future aspects of life and, therefore, have also helped to balance the previous obsession with the past. Among such theorists are Carl Rogers, Rollo May, Abraham Maslow, Frederick Perls, Victor Frankl, Ronald Laing, Ludwig Binswanger, and Eugene Minkowski. To Freud's instinct theory of sexual and aggressive drives, the existentialists have added the realization of man's mortality and his quest for meaning.

In practice, some therapists have used existentialism to justify their present-oriented approach, but this is an over-simplification of the contribution of the existentialists to the understanding of the complex, interrelated concepts of time and being as experienced by man. Existentialism does emphasize the present, but not to the exclusion of the past or the future. "The term existential therapists use for the distinctive character of human existence is *Dasein*. Binswanger, Kuhn, and others designate their school as *Daseinanalyse*. Composed of *sein* (being) plus *da* (there), *Dasein* indicates that man is the being who *is there* and implies also that he *has* a 'there' in the sense that he can know he is there and can take a stand with reference to that fact. The 'there' is moreover not just any place, but the particular 'there' that is mine, the particular point *in time* as well as space of my existence at this given moment. . . . The significant tense for human being is thus the *future*—that is to say, the critical question is what I am pointing toward, becoming, what I will be in the immediate future" (14).

Recently, there have been signs of the development of some new therapies that address themselves more specifically to the manner in which the individual copes with his future. Some examples of this new type of therapy are: *future-oriented* therapy (FOR) as described by Fred Melges; the efforts of people like Elisabeth Kübler-Ross to help dying patients to face and accept their imminent deaths; and the time management consultation techniques of Alan Lakein, a management consultant who works with normal, often very successful, people to help them recognize their goals more clearly and use their time more effectively.

Future-oriented therapy involves using part or all of the therapeutic hour with both patient and therapist pretending that the coming week is actually past. The discussion centers around what the problems of the week "were" and how the patient handled them. A "future autobiography" is constructed. The rationale is that this will help the patient learn new means of coping with his life and will reduce his anxiety thereby. It also helps the patient realize his ego-ideal. Since much of neurotic anxiety comes from the excessive fears and worries of the future of such patients, future-oriented therapy is aimed at making the diffuse, insurmountable problems that lie ahead more concrete and, therefore, more manageable. It gives the individual a means of making conscious his fears about his immediate future and gives him practice in preparing solutions to the potential events that may be upsetting to him (15).

Another technique that forces people to think about the future in more concrete, manageable ways is Lakein's method for helping a wide variety of people to use their own time more wisely in terms of their own personal goals. Alan Lakein is a management consultant, so he does not necessarily see his work as psychotherapy, but his methods might be constructively adapted by eclectic therapists. His clients are asked a series of questions about what they would like to do and have happen in their futures. They are asked to make lists of these goals in three sets: short-, medium-, and long-range. Then they are asked to go over these lists and mark the goals that are most important to them in numerical order. Any conflicts between the various lists need to be reconciled in some way. The question should be asked whether these various goals are mutually exclusive by their very nature—for instance, to have a lot of leisure time and to become a neurosurgeon. Once the individual's primary goals are stated, the client and the consultant try to formulate specific actions that can be taken today, tomorrow, next week, and in the ensuing months or years to achieve these goals. Finally, they work up a specific allocation of time for the person so that he will have a better chance of realizing his most important goals without sacrificing time for contemplation and relaxation. In the course of this investigation the reality of the goals has to be assessed. It is here that the boundary between psychotherapy and management consultation becomes blurred. One might speculate that the client's maturity is closely related to how realistic he is about his future, how appropriate his level of anxiety is to his prospects, and how well he can plan in a specific way to make his wishes come true, without obsessively ruminating about them.

Religion and Death

Until this century, religion was paramount in its influence on man's thinking about his future (and in its reminders to consider the future seriously!). The one event that is certain to be in the future of all men is death, and it was one role of the church to help people cope with that eventuality. This is still one of the main duties of the clergy for those people who remain within the church, but many people now turn to other sources for help in facing death. One of these alternate sources is psychotherapy. Freud viewed religion as a universal neurosis, a sickness to be overcome. His view was doubtless influential in the twentieth-century exodus from organized religion which has been well documented. However the situation arose, many people now turn to non-religious counselors, to psychiatrists, and to psychologists to aid them in the areas that were once religion's domain. Jung in Freud's time and Maslow and Allport since then have disagreed with Freud's view of religion. Far from viewing religiosity as a weakness or a superficial aspect of mankind which can be removed at will, these men saw religious experience as an intrinsic part of human nature.

In recent years there have been signs of waning in the alienation that has existed between psychotherapy and religion. More therapists are recognizing the value of religion in the individual's life and are no longer trying "to cure" their patients of their religious convictions or practices. On the other hand, the clergy, who have long been counselors to the troubled, have adopted many of the techniques of therapy, and in a sense are doing psychotherapy. More clergy today than ever before refer churchgoers to professional therapists and seek psychotherapy for themselves as well. Much is to be gained by both fields from the continued sharing of experiences and expertise.

In the past five to ten years, several significant books have been published on the subject of death. One example is Elisabeth Kübler-Ross's book, *On Death and Dying,* in which she elaborates five stages in coping with impending death observed in terminally ill patients. These stages of coping are denial and isolation, anger, bargaining, depression, and acceptance. She has found that the patients whom she has seen are often able, with help, to work their way through the denial and depression they and their families may feel to a genuine acceptance of their ultimate death.

The eclectic sees an application of these findings to other patients, who do not necessarily have a terminal disease, for life is fatal and all men are mortal. The attitudes of denying or accepting this certainty may be apparent at any stage of personality development. Among other things, this approach exemplifies the eclectic view that *significant others may be as important to* *the therapeutic process as the identified patient* and often must be involved as part of the therapeutic process.*

Along with the recent emphasis on man's future, the existential therapists have also helped to turn attention to man's awareness of his own end as a subject of study in itself. Rollo May has noted a crucial fact that differentiates man from the animals: "Man . . . is the particular being who has to be aware of himself, be responsible for himself, if he is to become himself. He is also that particular being who knows that at some future moment he will not be; he is the being who is always in a dialectical relation with the non-being, death" (16).

This concern with helping people face life's last crisis may also reflect a theme introduced by Erik Erikson, the human life cycle. Erikson has emphasized the fact that the major developmental conflicts that people face do not end with childhood but continue through adolescence and adulthood—even unto death. Erikson has helped broaden our view of development and has helped provide a framework for the eclectic therapist whose concern with crisis or personal growth extends to patients of all ages, including the very old. We are made aware of the preventive aspects of therapeutic intervention, say in middle age, which may help determine whether old age is filled with despair or a sense of fulfillment. Therapy, if it is appropriate to the individual's stage of life and state of existence, can be helpful at any age, as Kübler-Ross has shown.

CONCLUSION

The practitioner must select his approach to a patient from a wide variety of theories and techniques currently available. None encompasses all, but most have value relative to particular cases. To be eclectic requires adherence to the principle of consistency. The eclectic therapist must be able to incorporate new data as it appears. And finally, the therapist must ultimately judge for himself what is useful and what is of value among the many established as well as popular theories, realizing in advance that there is no simple answer nor is there a single answer.

---

* In the case of Mrs. F., for instance, there was a notable failure on the part of her husband's therapist to involve her sufficiently and to communicate with her regarding his progress (or lack of it). Fortunately, there is now an increasing tendency to inform spouses and children of a patient's progress and prognosis, as well as to involve them in the therapeutic process. This is exemplified by Don Jackson's theory of schizophrenia and the family therapy that arose from his early work in this field.

REFERENCES

1. ALLPORT, G. "The fruits of eclecticism: Bitter or sweet? In *The Person in Psychology: Selected Essays*. Boston: Beacon Press, 1968.
2. MERZ, JOHN T. *History of European Thought in the 19th Century*. Edinburgh and London: William Blackwood & Sons, 1907, Vol. 3, p. 190.
3. DOSTOEVSKY, FYODOR. *Notes from the Underground*. (Trans. by David Magarshaik.) New York: Modern Library, pp. 131-134. Permission to quote given by Random House.
4. SKINNER, B. F. Humanism and behaviorism. *The Humanist*, 1972.
5. RYCHLAK, J. *A Philosophy of Science for Personality Theory*. New York: Houghton Mifflin Co., 1968, pp. 68-69.
6. See, for instance, D. A. Hamburg and D. T. Lunde, Sex hormones and the development of sex differences in human behavior. In E. E. Maccoby (Ed.), *The Development of Sex Differences*. Stanford University Press, 1966, 1-24; and D. T. Lunde and D. A. Hamburg, Techniques for assessing the effects of sex hormones on affect, arousal, and aggression in humans. *Recent Progress in Hormone Research*, 28, 627-663, 1972.
7. ALLPORT, G. W. The open system in personality theory. *J. Abn. Soc. Psych.*, 61, 301-310, 1960.
8. LAZARUS, A. *Behavior Therapy and Beyond*. New York: McGraw Hill Book Company, 1971, p. 29.
9. *Ibid.*, p. 47.
10. ALLPORT, G. W. *Op. cit.*, p. 7.
11. LIEBERMAN, M., YALOM, I. & MILES, M. *Encounter Groups: First Facts*. New York: Basic Books, 1973, p. 451.
12. *Ibid.*, p. 277.
13. McCLELLAND, D. C. (Ed.). *Studies in Motivation*. New York: Appleton-Century-Crofts, Inc., 1955.
14. MAY, R., ET AL. *Existence*. New York: Basic Books, 1958, p. 41.
15. MELGES, F. T. Future-oriented psychotherapy. *Amer. J. Psychother.*, 26, 22-23, 1972.
16. MAY, R. *Op. cit.*, p. 42.

BIBLIOGRAPHY

ADLER, A. *Individual Psychology*. Paterson, New Jersey: Littlefield, Adams & Co., 1959.

ALEXANDER, F. & SELESNICK, S. *The History of Psychiatry*. New York: Harper & Row, 1966.

ALLPORT, G. W. *The Individual and His Religion*. New York: The Macmillan Co., 1950.

BOURNE, P. *Men, Stress, and Vietnam*. Boston: Little, Brown & Co., 1970.

BRIM, O., FREEMAN, H., LEVINE, S., & SCOTCH, N. *The Dying Patient*. New York: Russell Sage Foundation, 1970.

BURTON, A. *Encounter*. San Francisco: Jossey-Bass, 1969.

CARLSON, R. Where is the person in personality research? *Psych. Bull.*, 75, 203-219, 1971.

ERIKSON, E. *Identity: Youth and Crisis*. New York: W. W. Norton and Co., Inc., 1968.

FEIFEL, H. (Ed.). *The Meaning of Death*. New York: McGraw-Bill Book Co., 1959.

Ford, D. & Urban, H. *Systems of Psychotherapy*. New York: John Wiley and Sons, Inc., 1963.

Freud, S. *Moses and Monotheism* (1937). London: Hogarth Press, 1964.

Freud, S. *The Future of An Illusion* (1927). New York: Doubleday & Co., Inc., 1964.

Fromm, E. *Psychoanalysis and Religion*. New Haven: Yale University Press, 1950.

Grinker, R. *Toward a Unified Theory of Human Behavior*. New York: Basic Books, Inc., 1956.

Hamburg, D. & Adams, J. A perspective on coping behavior: Seeking and utilizing information in major transitions. *Arch. Gen. Psychiat.*, 17, 277-284, 1967.

Hamburg, D. (Ed.). *Psychiatry as a Behavioral Science*. Englewood Cliffs, New Jersey: Prentice-Hall, Inc., 1970.

Holt, R. & Luborsky, L. *Personality Patterns of Psychiatrists: A Study of Methods for Selecting Residents*. New York: Basic Books, Inc., 1958.

Jackson, D. D. (Ed.). *The Etiology of Schizophrenia*. New York: Basic Books, Inc., 1960.

James, W. *The Varieties of Religious Experience: A Study in Human Nature* (1902). New York: The New American Library, Inc., 1958.

Jung, C. *Psychology and Religion*. New Haven: Yale University Press, 1938.

Kadis, A., Krazner, J., Winick, C., & Foulkes, S. *A Practicum of Group Psychotherapy*. New York: Harper & Row, 1963.

Kastenbaum, R. & Aisenberg, R. *The Psychology of Death*. New York: Springer Publishing Co., 1972.

Kubler-Ross, E. *On Death and Dying*. New York: Macmillan Co., 1969.

Lakein, A. *How to Get Control of Your Time and Your Life*. New York: Peter H. Wyden, Inc., 1973.

Lazarus, A. In support of technical eclecticism. *Psychol. Reports*, 21, 415-416, 1967.

Maslow, A. *Motivation and Personality*. New York: Harper and Brothers, 1954.

Maslow, A. *Religions, Values, and Peak-Experiences*. Columbus: Ohio State University Press, 1964.

Melges, F. Future oriented psychotherapy. *Am. J. Psychoth.*, 26, 22-33, 1972.

Mowrer, O. *The Crisis in Psychiatry and Religion*. Princeton, New Jersey: D. Van Nostrand, Co., 1961.

Mullen, H. & Rosenbaum, M. *Group Psychotherapy: Theory and Practice*. New York: The Free Press of Glencoe, 1962.

Rogow, A. *The Psychiatrists*. New York: G. P. Putnam's Sons, 1970.

Rosenbaum, M. & Berger, M. *Group Psychotherapy and Group Function*. New York: Basic Books, Inc., 1963.

Singer, J. & D. Personality. *Ann. Rev. Psychol.*, 1968.

Torrey, F. *The Mind Game: Witchcraft and Psychiatrists*. New York: Emerson Hall Publishers, Inc., 1972.

Weisman, A. *On Dying and Denying*. New York: Behavioral Publications, Inc., 1972.

Woodworth, R. *Contemporary Schools of Psychology*. New York: The Ronald Press Co., 1948.

Yalom, I. *The Theory and Practice of Group Psychotherapy*. New York: Basic Books, Inc., 1970.

13

Concluding Postscripts

by ARTHUR BURTON

It seems beyond my capacity to synthesize the theories of personality described in this book, and to offer in turn an integrated formulation. But this book is in no sense a personality Tower of Babel. The underlives of the various theories offer a concordance of a sort. The apparent variegation is more one of linguistics, of conceptual readiness, and the values of the theorist. Not the least of the difficulty is that theories of personality become personified by their achetypal heroes, so that *being a Jungian* is at times more important than what Jung wrote . . . being a Rogerian, more important than what Rogers had in mind . . . being a Freudian . . . etc. The theoretical campaign is most often pitched at the level of the focal personality rather than of basic conceptions, and much of the internecine differences in personality theory is of this nature. On the instrumental level, the healing operations themselves, unity is much more a regular thing, but is often refused recognition.

The study of personality is at any rate not yet ready for a supertheory or a metatheory. To propound one at this point would, in my opinion, ossify a most dynamic field into a rigidity which would do neither science, the patient, nor the therapist any good. It would deny the study of personality the incubation period required for the formulation of a more useful theory. Psychotherapy exists by virtue of its openness, its humaneness, and even its floridness. To precipitate and mechanize it would be to destroy it. No personality prophet has this right.

A value-free psychotherapy would belie its name, and behavioral therapists fool themselves when they claim that conditioning contains no values. But I agree with Hillman that the question is not whether or not "personality" exists, but what exactly constitutes its nature. This book speculates on just this point, albeit imperfectly. There is disagreement over a broad spectrum, and even differences as to what it is in any therapy that induces the growth-change. Even after a century of work, we cannot be unanimous about the genesis of personality, or of neurotic trauma. We weigh infancy, childhood, adolescence, and adulthood in the personality balance, according to our predilections. Very few personality theorists are synthesizers—holists —even though they claim to be, and they tend to abstract simple observation and reify them into systems. No personality theory lives or dies by its postulates, but rather how it fits into a total concept of man, and the culture in which he resides as well.

Freud and Jung were men of a special order because they were basically scholastics who sought the alchemical secret of behavior. They would have been fully at home in Aesculapian Greece or in the Renaissance. It comes as a shock that 80% of Jung's collected works deal with the alchemical problem of the transmutation of base instinct into higher-order spiritual values. In this quest he ransacked Latin, Greek, Eastern, Babylonian, and other texts, as well as the more modern psychiatric ones. Freud was as well no stranger to antiquity, although he was less philosophical about it. Both sought the unification of personality in history—personal or collective—and phenomenology certainly suffers in that it demeans such a project.

We need a new theory of the neurosis. It simply will not do to continue amending Freud. But for this theory we must wait for the founder-designate, who will give it to us when the time is socially correct. Until then, we can only say that a neurosis is the inhibition of personality by fixation, accompanied by a deprivation of psychic energy. Each of the following situations runs counter to the establishment of neurosis, and is thus at the basis of a fully functioning personality. There are undoubtedly others, but these seem most significant to me.

Amnesia

The limitation of amnesia, and the associated openness of consciousness, bring the widest sensitivity and experiencing to the person. He does not in this state feel secretly deprived of a part of himself, of having missed experiences others have, and can more easily accept the travail of the human condition. The LSD experience revealed to many young people what was possible in this direction, and every addiction has at any rate underneath it such consciousness as a goal. Society sets limits on personal consciousness and either reveres the "conscious one" or calls him mad. Schizophrenia is, as we know, a special talent for insight, but is a madness by social definition. Whatever the theoretical model, awareness and consciousness are the desiderata of every personality.

Social Renunciation

We accept Freud's postulation that living in society calls for a renunciation of pleasure. Psychiatry mediates the pleasure needs of the patient against the needs of society. Involuntary psychiatric treatment is a capitulation to society and it certainly reduces the consciousness of the individual. Society not only demands conformance but introjected approval of the conforming behavior as well. Nudism, sexuality in groups, families without marriage, etc., are all modern manifestations of a return to the primitive of a pre-society. The commune movement of the young was an attempt to form a new society but with different organizational ground rules.

Personality flourishes in an atmosphere of freedom in which individuation can take place. Individuation involves in turn an experiential exploration of the inner and outer selves in a way more related to childhood or savagery than to a highly civilized social state. Only when the great social taboos have been tested can one individuate his personality. Psychotherapy encourages freedom from society but buttresses it by reason. It also does it with timing and historical/future perspective. The descent into the Unconscious, which is the therapy, results in a new *modus vivendi* with the demands of society. The personality then goes with society rather than counter to it, and expresses itself more fully and with less anxiety.

Pleasure

Pleasure is a necessity of the body. Neurosis is the failure to be orgastic, and a failure of pleasure aspiration as against reality. The body has become diluted by the Judeo-Christian concept of sin, and pleasure is over-symbolized and over-sublimated. Touch and olfaction are dissociated from being, and bodily response corrupted by shame and guilt. The natural and elemental responses of the body lose their sensual quality and the neurotic, in effect, loses his body.

There is nothing inherently disagreeable or sinful about pleasure—about the body and the way it speaks. No psychotherapy succeeds without the return to the body. It is to Frederick Perls' credit that after a lifetime practice of psychoanalysis, he realized and accepted this missing dimension. Wilhelm Reich had something similar in mind.

Social Fragmentation

No person can exist in fragmentation, as a collection of ununified parts. Psychic suffering is of this order and manifests itself as non-achievement, boredom, restlessness, loss of life-meaning, alienation, and the like. There is a delicate balance between distress and joy. Either extreme can submerge one in despondency and depression. For this reason society provides for relief of distress, but stops short of joy.

Neurosis is distress unrelieved by minimal joy. It is the unhappiest state known to man. Neurosis is personality at bay for it brings the entire purpose of man into question. He questions his personality! And neurotics fight desperately to keep their non-personality, to keep themselves in bondage to the past. Society is actually in greater danger from its neurotics than from its criminals. The latter are from time to time relieved of their distress by parole, by action rather than passivity, but the neurotic never has parole. By his internalizing, and his creative productions, he changes the mainstreams in the direction of pessimism, of a world of despair. But it is not such a world once he can see and feel the pleasure aspect of the equation denied him by his neurosis.

Destiny

Each person seems thrown into the world with a destiny to complete. That is, his life is a course similar to a stream with a source and a termination. Behaviorists would of course say that this smacks of vitalism and that life is merely a matter of reinforcement. But the lives of a few men stand forth with particular brilliance, and we have to inquire why they assume such numinosity. The meta goal of man seems to be how to transcend organic structure and to derive a higher order of meaning in life. The existentialists portray this personalistic quest best of all.

There is a difference in ontic thrust among men. Some begin a pursuit of a goal and surrender all pleasure to this work goal. It becomes transcending and their joy. Others seem without proper reason doomed to depression, addiction, or neurosis, which sap their creativity. In a Christian society they tolerably survive in a form of crippledom. But ontic thrust is not congenital. It probably derives from the earliest family background, backed by an endowed energy and temperament, and is a torrent which sweeps life obstacles ahead of it. Where it is diminished in the personality, or seriously blocked, existence becomes stasis, and the person may become a clinical problem.

Intentionality

Beyond the fact of a motivational thrust of the individual toward being (which I call ontic thrust) there is a cognitive-perceptual function in man which, following Husserl, I call *intentionality*. Intentionality is a cognitive readiness, an intention to-be-in-the-world, and to be a dynamic part of it. It is cognition and intellection put to the use of experience and meaning rather than raw sensation. It is an indigenous focusing of perception on living rather than a diffusion of perception. It makes of cognition less a function of adaptation, survival, and adjustment than a means of experiencing humanness on the highest cortical levels. It is also the conscious intention to love and be loved within a cognitive framework. The individual differences between people in this function are easily observable.

* * *

Now that some of the general factors which are the background of fully-functioning personalities have been outlined, it is possible to schematize the significant descriptive variables of the theories contained in this book. By eliminating the special linguistics and metastructure of each theory, the essential functional components seem to be the following.

Energy/Instinct

Most theories of personality are still based upon physical analogues. Their sources are Newton, electromagnetic phenomena, quantum theory, and applied neurophysiological models which followed physical discoveries. They posit a limited fund of psychic energy, a specific distributing system, and assumptions regarding the collection of such energy in pools. They lean heavily upon reflexive-instinctive formulations of inborn potentialities and give them primacy. They posit a variety of ways in which psychic energy is projected outward to the environment. Higher-order psychic functions are displacements or sublimations of this primitive energetic system, and homeostasis, rest, or peace, represent energy finding its own non-potential level.

This theoretical outlook is best exemplified by Freud, but is part and parcel—perhaps more implicitly—of most others. It is often assumed as the ground of *all* theory but insufficient in and of itself. Freud himself often conceded a spiritual factor but felt it could not lead to a science of behavior and thus had to wait in the background. The idea, wish, and symbol are still paramount in such systems, but they are less important for themselves than for the energy attached to them. Pleasure, the oldest and most primitive possession of mankind, is given center stage as the *deus ex machina* of the energy model.

Psychopathology, according to this model, is a matter of repression and fixation, an inability to cathect energy to objects and people. An early trauma keys the energy to its own inner processes, so that an obsessive and unrewarding social press is established. The psychotherapy then becomes the reduction of the trauma, the freeing of the bound/repressed energy, and its channeling into love and creativity. The organism becomes more efficient in the use of itself.

Sensory/Body

There are analysts like Wilhelm Reich and Alexander Lowen who believe that Freud did not go far enough in instinct theory or, instead, did not particularize it properly; they offer amendments to psychoanalysis in both theory and technique. This trend is also in the more modern tradition, as with certain members of the Esalen group, to return touch, olfaction, breathing, and total body responsiveness to the person. Old Hindu and Yoga texts have been resurrected as well for this purpose.

The body is conceived by these theorists as not only containing the essence of the psyche but the focal point of energetic calmness and joy. Energy attached to organs, and of distributed systems, becomes focused on orgastic bodily properties which are equated with a fully functioning personality. Body language, body image, and organ function assume prepotency. Sexuality, since it is expressed through the body, is overvalued, and its fantasy properties reduced. Symbols, as Jung insists they do, do not for them carry energy, or discharge it.

Psychotherapy involves the return of the body to the client, and thus to his psyche as well. An attempt is made to sensitize the body, remove its blockages, make it orgastic as well as esthetic. Lowen brings a deep analytic process to bear upon this goal, but others are satisfied with an expressive body learning process.

Power/Control

The function of social power comes through in such theories as those of Adler and Stierlin (family structure). Inferiority (the inability to take action) is a source of discomfiture and disability. One becomes in this way the victim of more powerful people or more powerful circumstances. The helplessness may be real or imagined; it makes little difference which. The inferior person finds himself at a disadvantage in love and work and in most other ways. He also falls heir to displacements of affect, none of which he likes, but for reasons yet unknown he gradually assumes. His psychic symptoms then portray his resentment and, after a certain point, they become a part of his life-style and more or less immutable. Such theories offer ego-power within the family romance as the crucial element in growth and fulfillment.

Psychotherapy involves realignment of power structures—often through several generations—and a change in the ego's conception of one's place in the world of power. The treatment calls for auxiliary egos, cognitive restructuring, taking risks, and traditional analytic work up to a point. The emphasis is upon a newer social facilitation rather than the catharsis of trauma as such. Much of this therapy appears to be relearning and reeducation rather than psychotherapy as such.

Symbol/Archetype

There are a group of theorists—C. G. Jung and M. A. Sechehaye come to mind—who place the symbol at the centerfold of personality. This is so relevant that Hillman prefers to call the Analytic Psychology of Jung by the alternate term of Archetypal Psychology. The symbol not only gathers to itself all of the individual energy of the person but the collective aspects as well. The myths, dreams, images, etc., are contiguous with his personal and primordial history, and his traumas are expressed through them. But they are releasing and transcending as well. Individuation, the final stage of evolvement, is the flowering of the self, which is the basis for a fulfilling identity. All aspects of personality lead to such completion of the self.

Symbols in Archetypal Psychology are different from those in Freudian psychology in that in the latter they serve merely as vehicles for repressed libido whereas the former represent the holistic and growth aspects of the person. Freud makes a technique of the symbol while Jung sees it as personality itself. Sechehaye invariably finds schizophrenia noted in the major symbolizations of the client. The unconscious is thus not the Pandora's box of the repressed but the source of all creation and joy with the symbol as its vehicle.

Psychotherapy becomes the process of individuation in which the person's major symbolic metaphors are held up to scrutiny, made a part of insight, and then reformed. This process is a freeing one, provides energy for expression, and draws the individual's history, present, and future closer together. Stress is given to creative artistic productions, the analysis of dreams and archetypes, and to the interpersonal relationship of client and analyst. The symbol of self, the mandala, is the final evocation of treatment.

Interpersonal/Transpersonal

There are theories of personality which maximize therapeutic humanism and make it the dynamic principle of treatment. One gets the feeling that the client is very precious and fragile. Directness, interpretation, and confrontation may damage him. Above all, the patient needs a well-meaning friend. I am speaking here of Rogers' and Sullivan's theories.

In no theory are love, transference, and countertransference so important as in these approaches. Nowhere do the healer's feelings and goodwill come in for such scrutiny as they do here. Indeed, the cure may be more a function of the personality of the healer than the personality of the client, and methodology and technique assume subsidiary positions. There is something unique—may I say, almost spiritual—that takes place in the dyadic encounter of Rogerian and Sullivanian psychotherapy. Above all, genuineness, earnest availability, and empathy are the desiderata.

The patient's phenomenal world, his capacity to change (and responsibility for it), and the beauty of the world rather than its aggression are all focal treatment matters. Sullivan would not be put off by the supposed inviolability of the walled-off schizophrenic's world, by his presumable organic condition, and by the pessimism of his psychiatric colleagues. In the encounter with the patient, he found a core of self which was not so supremely metaphoric that it could not be touched by love and reason. Rogers also found a normality and positive being shining forth in every client and elected to work from this rather than despair.

Logic/Order

Those personality theorists who stress the verbal and communicative structures in the individual in his nuclear and extended family can be described as logic and order theorists. Their belief is that personal values remain hidden under inexact or secret communication, the metamessage, and that if this were clarified the benevolent human purposes and goals underneath would reveal themselves. Most of the evidence for this approach comes from the study of families with either delinquent or schizophrenic members.

Beyond the need for clarity is the need for a kind of administrative order in the ego as well as an order between people. Emotion is logic and logic funds reason. But the logic here is a passionate reasonableness which accepts boundaries, functions, and roles. The hidden need to exploit and limit others through a logical means is decried, but is also recognized as carrying a heavy unconscious freight.

The psychotherapy which evolves from this theory is a group design where several people—none designated as patients—meet regularly to become more logical. The various family therapy approaches, illustrated in this book by Stierlin, reveal the delicate and difficult nature of such task. It begins with an identified patient who may not be a patient at all. The interpersonal forces which counter the melioration of his patienthood slowly come into focus, albeit without much initial help from the patient, and the sick role either shifts to someone else, or is given up. The family is a homeostatic device which finds its own level.

Family therapy disturbs the equilibrium, which at any rate has served its members unequally. The therapist's role is to be the monitor of logic and communication, and add his ego to one or another family member as needed in the sessions. The result is a better family energy distribution, more joy, and the release of the identified patient from patienthood.

Rational/Directive

Rosen, Thorne, M. Erickson, Ellis and others do not see much value in a symbolic theory of healing, although they do not oppugn symbols. They believe in the cognitive, in reason, and the molar action which follows such cognition. A principle of this personality outlook might be that while fear does inhibit action, the doing in the face of fear reduces such fear by firsthand experience. The danger is never as great as the imagination of it! Such theorists are actional men themselves, and in their own personal lives tend to cut through to the heart of the problem.

Desensitization has now become coupled with rationality. The reasoned approach is buttressed by techniques which reduce the anxiety which inhibited the reasoning to begin with. Reassurance, relaxation, persuasion, stimulus gradation, and similar methods used by the behavioral therapists may be employed by rational-emotive therapists as well. Indeed, these theories are eclectic in their operational aspects, for whatever works is used. The emphasis, however, is on stimulating the patient to see that he is not as helpless as he feels—that the world is not against him, that coming up short of his ideals is not the end—and on offering him hope and guided-graded experiences with the therapist as a concurrent model. Clients of such therapists are impressed by the power of their therapists, but also somewhat afraid of them. With this brushwork out of the way, a cognitive-intellectual restructuring takes place which frees the client from his false perceptions and gives him felt successes—often for the first time.

Learning/Conditioning

Personality theories which have learning modes as their focus are not new. They are currently having a resurgence in the form of behavior modification techniques applied to a wide spectrum of human events. Personality theorists of this persuasion deny that theirs is a theory of personality as such and point rather to S-R phenomena as elaborated by Pavlov, Skinner, and others. Anxiety and its conditioning and reconditioning are their tools, and they see no purpose in the psychoanalysis of wish, fantasy, or dream. The problem seems to be to remove inhibition in the quickest and most empirically approved manner possible without the metapsychological structure of Freud, Jung, etc.

More specifically, Skinner divides behavior into respondent and operant types depending upon the relationship of stimulus to response. In the latter form, the stimulus acts as a cue or sign but does not drive the response. Operant conditioning is used to interpret the facts of the neurosis, and is the active mode of change in behavioral modification therapy. Although simple in principle, it can become exceedingly complex in practice. Modeling, social learning, reciprocal inhibition, and a host of other concepts presumably explain the change which occurs with treatment.

As a form of therapy, behavioral modification uses relaxation, reassurance, token-reward, hypnosis, home assignments, and even more traditional psychotherapeutic adjuncts in its work. The idea is to extinguish patterns which produce anxiety and reinforce those which do not. Interestingly enough, it seems to have had its greatest success with a kind of primitive captive group: mental deficients, autistic children, chronically hospitalized, institutionalized delinquents, and similar cases. Success has also been reported with out-patient neurotics, but the results here are less clear. Behavioral therapy brings into focus a large number of philosophical questions as to the nature of cure or relief. But it certainly does facilitate learned behaviors.

Now that I have to some extent isolated some of the dynamic agents in the theories of personality described in this book, it is incumbent upon me to comment upon them as a conglomerate. In this regard, I must say that theories are intercurrent mythologies by which altered behavior is explained and may not be the correct or total story. As I have said earlier, we are still awaiting a super theory or a mythologized theory with a better behavioral fit. But this is not to say that there is no theory of personality, or that such theories, because non-mensurational, are not useful at the present time. Psychic therapies, in the broad sense, are a viable and important aspect of socialized living, and we can hardly do without them. Society ultimately validates that which is true . . . that which is useful to its survival and happiness. Ergo: psychotherapy has a validity beyond the verbal, and beyond even the dispute of scientists. In this sense, the theories which support the operations described here have momentary validity on the way to still greater truths.

Index